EUROPE: GRANDEUR AND DECLINE

A J P Taylor was born at Birkdale in Lancashire in 1906. He was educated at Bootham School, York, and at Oriel College, Oxford. He was a lecturer in Modern History at Manchester University from 1930 to 1938, and from then until 1976 a Fellow of Magdalen College, Oxford, of which he is now an Honorary Fellow. A Fellow of the British Academy, he was Ford's Lecturer in English History at Oxford (1955–6) and Leslie Stephen Lecturer at Cambridge (1960–61). In autumn 1976 he was Joseph Meaker Visiting Professor at Bristol University. Recently he has given the Creighton Lecture at London University and the Andrew Lang Lecture at St Andrews. He is an honorary D.C.L. of the University of New Brunswick, D.Univ. of York University and honorary D.Litt. of Bristol University, Warwick University and Manchester University.

He has given many history lectures on television and is the only lecturer to face the cameras for half an hour without notes or visual aids. He contributes regularly to the *Observer* and the *London Review of Books*.

His books include *The Course of German History, The Struggle for Mastery in Europe, 1848–1918, Bismarck, The Troublemakers, From Sarajevo to Potsdam, The Second World War: an Illustrated History, My Darling Pussy: the Correspondence of Lloyd George and Frances Stevenson, The Last of Old Europe, The Russian War 1941–1945* and *How Wars Begin*. A number of his books have been published in Penguins: *The Origins of the Second World War, The Habsburg Monarchy, The First World War: an Illustrated History, English History 1914–1945, Europe: Grandeur and Decline, Beaverbrook, The War Lords* and *Essays in English History*. He has also contributed a long introduction to the Penguin edition of *The Communist Manifesto*. His most recent book is *A Personal History*.

D0951212

EUROPE: GRANDEUR AND DECLINE

A. J. P. TAYLOR

PENGUIN BOOKS

in association with Hamish Hamilton

Penguin Books Ltd, Harmondsworth, Middlesex, England
Viking Penguin Inc., 40 West 23rd Street, New York, New York 10010, U.S.A.
Penguin Books Australia Ltd, Ringwood, Victoria, Australia
Penguin Books Canada Ltd, 2801 John Street, Markham, Ontario, Canada L3R 1B4
Penguin Books (N.Z.) Ltd, 182–190 Wairau Road, Auckland 10, New Zealand

—

First published by Hamish Hamilton in the three volumes:
From Napoleon to Stalin (1950)
Rumours of Wars (1952)
Englishmen and Others (1956)
This selection published in Pelican Books 1967
Reprinted 1969, 1971, 1974, 1977, 1979, 1981, 1983, 1985

—

—

Printed and bound in Great Britain by
Cox & Wyman Ltd, Reading

Set in Monotype Times

CONTENTS

PREFACE
to the Penguin selection

These historical essays have themselves become history. The earliest was written in 1943, the latest in 1955. Some of the references to individuals are now obscure, particularly in the essays which were once contemporary. Who on earth, for instance, was M. Vishinsky? Fortunately, it does not matter. He and his like are for ever with us.

An attentive reader may observe that most of the essays on the origins of the Second World War accept the common legends of the time. They assume that Hitler was a demon of fantastic genius who carefully and deliberately planned every step towards war. I no longer take this view, and it was while writing these essays that I began to doubt it. They therefore provide curious illustration of how a writer can change his interpretation without knowing that he is doing it.

I wrote in the Preface to *Englishmen and Others*: 'I am not a philosophic historian. I have no system, no moral interpretation'. I have never claimed to draw any lesson from history. Nevertheless a political lesson or conclusion peers at me from these essays now that I read them again. Throughout modern times Europe has been composed of independent states, some of them considerable Powers. One Power has tended to predominate or at least to be stronger than others. In the earlier part of the nineteenth century, the preponderant Power still seemed to be France. In the later part of the century and then into the twentieth century, the preponderant Power threatened to be Germany. When her ambitions were defeated, most fortunately in my view, many people supposed that Soviet Russia had taken her place, and they regretted what had happened. Some of them, particularly in the United States, even tried to undo it. I think they were wrong. Soviet Russia was a preponderant Power with a difference. Unlike France and Germany, all she asked of Europe was to be left alone. This was also Great Britain's attitude to Europe, or should be. Anyone who claims to learn from history should devote himself to promoting an Anglo-Soviet alliance, the most harmless and pacific of all possible combinations. I have done my best for this cause, and to no effect. Instead we have acquiesced in, and sometimes supported, the American attempts to upset the peaceful balance of the world. It does not seem that a knowledge of history does much good, at any rate when it is faced with the prejudice which masquerades under the name of anti-Communism.

A.J.P.T.

NOTE

Most of these pieces were originally book reviews or essays for some anniversary and carry their dates with them. The few attempts at general speculation (Nos. 49–52) were written between 1950 and 1953 at the request of American editors. The essays appeared in the *New Statesman*, the *Manchester Guardian*, the *Times Literary Supplement*, *Critique*, *History Today*, the *New York Times Magazine*, and the *Listener*. The present selection has been made from three volumes, all published by Hamish Hamilton: *From Napoleon to Stalin* (1950); *Rumours of Wars* (1952); and *Englishmen and Others* (1956).

1

NAPOLEON

(1) ON HIMSELF

A LIFE of Napoleon written by himself! The appeal seems
irresistible. Mr de Chair, the editor,[1] describes it as 'the voice
of the giant himself'. The conversation of giants, then, must be
very dull. The proclamations and bulletins of Napoleon show
him to have been a propagandist of genius; so, too, was Goebbels.
Yet the Memoirs of the one are as dreary as the Diaries of the
other. In fact, the Memoirs of Napoleon – undoubtedly a genuine
product of his mind – convinced me that the Goebbels' diaries
were genuine; if Napoleon could write as boringly as this,
Goebbels could also. Both works are, of course, full of lies; that
was to be expected. It is the drabness, the fatuity, the common-
placeness of mind, that are surprising. What, for instance, could
be more idiotic than Napoleon's explanation of polygamy in his
chapter on Egypt? It occurs, he says, in countries inhabited by
men of several colours and 'is the only means of preventing them
persecuting each other', since every man can have a black wife, a
white one, a copper-coloured one 'and one of some other colour'.
He proceeds to recommend it in the French colonies as the
solution of the colour question, so that every man can have
'one white, one black, and one Mulatto wife, at the same time'.

Napoleon knew well that he was not a brilliant author; and he
protected himself by speaking contemptuously of writers, as he
did of his other enemies. Just as he described the English as
'men who were continually at table, almost always intoxicated,
and of uncommunicative disposition', so he dismissed writers
as men of no practical sense.

He was not concerned to compete with those detestable
ideologues; he had no interest at all in creating a work of art –
his life in action had been creation enough. His reminiscences
were written, or rather dictated, for effect. They were to launch a

1. *Napoleon's Memoirs*. Edited by Somerset de Chair.

legend, the legend of Divine Caesar. Cold and aloof like a marble statue in classical robes, they are without personality; and it was a great error of judgement by Mr de Chair to substitute the first person singular for 'Napoleon', 'the Emperor', 'the general' of the original text. For Napoleon's statue is not vocal even after the fashion of the statue in *Don Giovanni*; and the essential purpose of these writings is in their remoteness from life. Napoleon the man was finished; Napoleon the institution had to be perpetuated.

It is not surprising therefore that the only section of Memoirs which Napoleon completed and finally polished is the part dealing with the campaign of Waterloo. A defeat of such finality needs a good deal of explaining away. Napoleon had an excuse in Grouchy's failure to come up with Blücher on June 18; and he repeats this excuse again and again. But he is pulled up by an uneasy sense that the real failure lay in the faulty orders which Grouchy received from his Supreme Commander; and Napoleon swings off on the other tack that Waterloo was an indecisive battle, the effect of which could have been undone by a further campaign. This line, too, has its dangers; for the failure to continue the war could be explained only by the war-weariness of the French. This was not an argument with which to appeal to posterity. The only way out is to assert that his strategy was throughout correct and that Wellington and Blücher committed 'every conceivable mistake'. Thus Napoleon persuaded himself that he had in fact won the battle of Waterloo and his Memoirs end with an expression of sympathy for the people of London 'when they learnt of the catastrophe which had befallen their army'.

The main section of the record, which runs from the siege of Toulon to the battle of Marengo, lacks the finish of the Waterloo narrative. Napoleon dictated these chapters haphazard to two amanuenses; and the two rivals kept their work separate when they published it after Napoleon's death. Mr de Chair has sorted out the two sources and pruned away the asides with which Napoleon relieved the tedium. In this story of his early success Napoleon had less to explain away; all the same he never missed a chance to heighten the emphasis on the unique character and achievement of 'the Emperor'. Thus Paoli, the Corsican patriot, 'used frequently to say of the young artillery officer [myself], "He is a man for a Plutarch's biography".' With this unlikely anecdote Napoleon blots out the story of his equivocal behaviour in Corsican affairs. Entertaining, too, in their way are the passages on naval warfare, in which Napoleon proves that it is much easier to win battles at sea than on land; Trafalgar is successfully rubbed out of existence. But for the most part the principles of Plutarch are observed all too seriously. There are accounts of Italy and Egypt which could have been taken from any gazeteer; even the military narrative lacks spirit. This served Napoleon's purpose. 'The general' remained without a rival figure; and Napoleon could conclude with an account of Marengo, which conceals that he had lost the battle and slides, almost without mention, over Desaix who had come to Bonaparte's rescue. It is a fitting end to a narrative which is unreliable from beginning to end.

Can Napoleon have supposed that this dull and lying record would really secure his fame? This puzzle is the only point of interest raised by this book. Some part of the explanation may be found in the decline of his faculties. The only exciting passages are the quotations from the proclamations which Bonaparte wrote as the young general of the Army of Italy; these still ring with life, and their author could not have written dully however hard he tried. Success corrupts; and Napoleon had achieved success without parallel in modern history. The spare, beautiful artillery officer had become fat and coarse; and his mind became coarse at the same time. Besides, Napoleon had expected everyone to sacrifice himself for the Empire; and the first sacrifice had been his own personality. The young Bonaparte had been vital, though no doubt unattractive; Napoleon had squeezed the life out of him. Flashes of personality persisted, even at St Helena. These make Napoleon interesting to history; they did not interest Napoleon himself. He was concerned only with his public performance. Stendhal found the key to Napoleon, when he described Julien Sorel, after his first night with Mme de Rênal, asking himself: 'Ai-je bien joué mon rôle?' Sorel, like Napoleon, was dominated by ambition; he lacked inner life and so fails to hold the reader's sympathy or even attention. Napoleon's was a more complicated case. He had begun as a romantic figure in the spirit of Rousseau; he ended as an abstraction from Plutarch. To use the clumsy contemporary phrase, this destruction of Napoleon by himself was the last triumph of the Classical over the Romantic. The essence of the Romantic movement was the elevation of individual sentiment and of individual character; yet Napoleon, with a more remarkable character than any, was ashamed of possessing it and returned to a Classical worship of the external world.

The explanation of this outmoded artificiality is simple; and Napoleon himself hints at it in the early pages of his Memoirs. He could have been genuine – 'romantic' – only as a Corsican patriot; once he deserted his natural cause, he could only play parts and to do this he had to crush out his individuality. Sometimes, as when he played at being a French patriot or even a French Emperor, the part came off; at others, as when he played at being a Moslem in Egypt or wished to play at being the liberator-general after Waterloo, the pretence was too blatant. But, for a man who claimed to possess a sense of reality, Napoleon's judgement was strangely unreliable from start to finish. The eighteenth of Brumaire was as wild an adventure as the Hundred Days; in neither case did Napoleon have any clear idea what he was doing – he was simply 'playing his role'. For that matter Marengo was as much a gamble as Waterloo. It implanted in Napoleon the belief that he had truly mastered the external world; this gave him the necessary self-confidence for his career, though it ultimately brought him to disaster. Traditional ideas and traditional institutions had lost their force. Losing faith in God, men sought a human saviour. The first of these human gods was Napoleon; and the condition of his fame was the confident readiness to attempt the impossible. Napoleon believed in himself; he continued to believe even when reality had shattered the basis of this belief, and he supposed that others would believe too. Hence he even believed that readers could be found for his Memoirs.

All the same, despite Napoleon, a human being is buried in these writings. Napoleon no doubt thought that he was building a monument to his future fame. Most of the time, in reality, he was fighting his battles over again simply for the pleasure of it; and this time without risk of failure. No reader can be persuaded that the catalogue of divisions and the description of obscure skirmishes serve any literary purpose. Napoleon had ceased to think of the reader. He had escaped from the unpleasant reality of St

Helena and was manoeuvring imaginary armies. There once more he could exercise the devotion to detail and the implacable demands for speed that had been the secret of his success (though also of his failure). Bending over the map of Lombardy, he could once more forget that Josephine had been unfaithful to him immediately after marriage (and he expected the reader to forget it too). In fact, if only he exerted his will strongly enough, he might again master the external world: St Helena would disappear and Lombardy, or Paris under the Consulate, become once more reality. It was this belief in the human will, at any rate his own, that made Napoleon the representative and culmination of the French Revolution.

The essence of the Revolution was belief in man. Once you believe that man is naturally good, you must believe, too, that he can do anything. Napoleon certainly held this belief about himself. And no doubt man can do anything, if he goes the right way about it. The right way, as the events of the last century and a half have shown, is the way of science: the improvement of technique. The men of the French Revolution, and Napoleon with them, supposed that they could master the world by will alone. Hence the Napoleonic armies, for example, marched faster than other armies simply by the compelling force of Napoleon's command; modern armies move faster by train or aeroplane. Napoleon killed his secretaries by over-work; with the dictaphone and the typewriter they would have survived quite easily. Napoleon was following the wrong course; the further his will carried him, the greater was bound to be his final catastrophe. He supposed that events could be made; in the end events took their revenge on him. There was no essential difference between Napoleon in victory and in defeat (hence his own bewilderment at Waterloo): he always asked the impossible, and sometimes it was granted him. This is the real basis of the Napoleonic legend (as it will be for the legend of Hitler). Napoleon is the hero of all those who resent reality, of all those who will not trouble to master 'the art of the possible'. Napoleon is the supreme example of the human being who became more than life-size; and those who admire Napoleon are really flattering the human being in themselves. Yet what did this wonderful human being end in? A querulous sick man on a sub-tropical island dictating a drab and meaningless record to

while away the time. The Memoirs of Napoleon suggest that there
is something to be said for not thinking that you are God.

(2) THE VERDICT OF HISTORY

Events are well enough in their way; what historians write about
them is much better. Who really cares about the later Roman
Emperors, about Dutch William, or even about Pericles? These
survive by grace of Gibbon, Macaulay, and Thucydides. The
greatest figure of modern times made himself such by providing
a myth which would provide endless fascination for historians.
Napoleon knew the secret of survival: *quel roman que ma vie!*
His own literary gifts were those of an amateur – characteristic of
one who carried that second-rate tear-jerker, *The Sorrows of
Werther*, in his hip-pocket; the Napoleonic legend would never
have taken hold had it depended on Napoleon's own writings.
Napoleon's great stroke was to provide raw material for works
of genius, so that French historians wrote about Napoleon inevitably, as every Greek playwright interpreted the story of the
Trojan wars. Of course there is always a certain amount to be
discovered about Napoleon, as no doubt matter of archaeological
interest can be found by grubbing in the ruins of Troy. But the
profundities of the human spirit are to be found in what men have
made of the legend, not in the archives and the rubble. The career
of Napoleon is the greatest of modern legends.

This fact, once noticed, seems obvious and inescapable; and
it is surprising that no one has had the idea long ago of discussing
what French writers have made of Napoleon. To discover the
obvious which no one else has thought of is the speciality of
Professor Geyl,[1] one of the great historical minds of our time.
It would be unfair to say that he demolishes the reputations of the
great French historians; though he exposes their flaws, there
remains, in his words 'what life and energy, what creative power,
what ingenuity, imagination and daring!' These words are a
reminder of peculiar value for the English reader. Every continental student of history, even if he be a German, knows that the
French are the greatest practitioners of the art. English historians
have never recovered from the fraud put over on us by Acton (or

1. *Napoleon: For and Against*. By Pieter Geyl.

perhaps Carlyle) and still suppose that serious history – scientific history as it is called – was perfected in Germany. But what tawdry stuff the German historians are compared to the stars of Professor Geyl's book – and how long-winded!

Professor Geyl gives a plain analysis of what French historians from the Restoration to the present day have written about Napoleon. He starts with Chateaubriand and ends with Georges Lefebvre. Each writer is summarized with the painstaking detachment with which a newspaper correspondent gives a summary of the foreign press. There are no graces of style, no novelty in the point of view; the general effect is humdrum, almost dull. It is like listening to a conversation where tones are never raised, where there is never a flicker of emphasis nor even, one supposes, of interest. As the conversation proceeds, it gradually becomes clear that Professor Geyl, far from being the club bore, declines to raise his voice simply because he is discussing the most profound topics of human experience. It is rare enough to find a work of history which is interesting, let alone exciting. This book is vastly more, an infinite consolation to the professional historian: it shows that history is a subject which can provoke thought. For my part, I would rather have written Professor Geyl's book than invented Existentialism or the new fashion in academic philosophy – what is it called? The subject, at any rate, which now spends its time debating whether it was once correct to describe itself as logical positivism. Professor Geyl's book enables the historian to look the philosopher in the face without cringing for quite a week.

His book teaches one, in the first place, a great deal about Napoleon. French historians have found in Napoleon infinite variety; and all of it was there. It is impossible to read this catalogue of their judgements without realizing that Napoleon really was a most extraordinary man, probably the most extraordinary figure that has ever appeared in the world of politics. Sorel saw him as the man who devoted his life to the defence of the natural frontiers; Bourgeois as the man who lived only for the creation of a great Empire of the Middle East; Driault as the restorer of the Roman Empire in Europe, the greatest of the Caesars; Vandal even discovered in him the pacifier of the world – no wonder he spoke of 'the ultimate justice and grandeur of his aim'. The same variety and the same vastness are revealed in the descriptions of Napoleon's work as a civilian ruler – the heir of the Revolution, the restorer of order, the architect of the Code Napoleon, the founder of the French Empire, the protector of the Catholic Church. All these things happened in Napoleon's time; yet the cumulative effect of them is not to increase admiration for Napoleon, rather to rouse doubts.

Here Professor Geyl, as it were, turns the tables on Napoleon: for his book, despite its cool tone and its scholarship, is an anti-Napoleonic tract, the most formidable ever composed. He has given the legend a good showing in order to show that it is a legend, that it over-reaches itself by its very absurdity. He quotes the rhetoric of Thiers, the brilliance of Vandal, the sophistication of Sorel; then brings them to earth with a gentle query – the murder of the Duke of Enghien? the breach of the Treaty of Amiens? the oppression and exploitation of Europe? the stifling of French Liberalism? Above all, the lies, the intrigues, the dishonesty? Professor Geyl has no doubt of his own verdict:

He was a conqueror with whom it was impossible to live; who could not help turning an ally into a vassal or at least interpreting the relationship to his own exclusive advantage; who decorated his lust of conquest with the fine-sounding phrases of progress and civilization; and who at last, in the name of the whole of Europe, which was to look to him for order and peace presumed to brand England as the universal disturber and enemy.

This is not, however, only the verdict of a dispassionate Dutch observer. The historians of the legend do not exhaust French writings on Napoleon. Indeed, all Professor Geyl's criticism of the admirers of Napoleon is based on the work of French scholars; and his analysis of the two attitudes, *for* and *against*, is a splendid contribution to the study of French ideas. The cleavage is, in the first place, political. In England admiration for Napoleon has often (perhaps usually) been found on the 'left' – a line running from Lady Holland to Hilaire Belloc and (dare I say it?) Bernard Shaw. What English admirers of Napoleon have in common is simple: they are all 'agin the government' and, since Napoleon was also against the British Government, they suppose that he was on their side. In France, however, the 'establishment' has been on the left, especially in the time of the Third Republic; and

Napoleon has been the hero of the Conservatives. They did not need to pretend that Napoleon cared for liberty: they were delighted that he had destroyed it and wished to follow his example. They echoed the phrase of Barrès: 'Napoleon, Teacher of Energy', and praised, perhaps exaggerated, those qualities which made Napoleon the precursor of Fascism. Moreover, unlike English writers, they did not conceal that Napoleon was the enemy of England, not merely of the British Government; for, since England represented the principles of liberty, of constitutional government, and of agreement between the nations, she was their enemy also. This tradition, though strong, was the school of a minority in France. French writers who cared for liberty, who opposed militarism, had no illusions about Napoleon and exposed the errors of those who had. French Liberals in the nineteenth century, and Socialists in the twentieth, stood unanimously for 'the other France' which repudiated Napoleon with his gospel of energy and violence.

The cleavage *for* and *against*, as well as being political, is also professional; this is a point of peculiar interest fully worked out by Professor Geyl. The men of letters, with the exception of Taine, have been for Napoleon, and Taine was only against Napoleon because he recognized in Napoleon himself; the men of learning have been against him. The men of letters have often been distinguished scholars, as Vandal and Sorel were; but, in the last resort, they were concerned to produce an effect, to write a work of literary genius. It is a very different Napoleon who appears in the school text-books. Indeed one is almost driven to postulate the general rule: the better written a book, the more unreliable as history. But there is more in it than that. Tocqueville said of Napoleon: 'He was as great as a man can be without morality'; and the truth is that all men of letters, that is all who care for good writing, are, in this sense, immoral. They will always subordinate reality to effects and facts to phrases. Paine's judgement on Burke will serve for every French writer on Napoleon whose works one reads for pleasure: 'He pities the plumage but forgets the dying bird.' Nothing is stranger than the delusion of our time that men of letters are, by nature, champions of political, or even of intellectual liberty. If Professor Geyl's book is not evidence enough to the contrary, consider the famous writers who made the pilgrimage to Mussolini. Of course, scientists are even worse – but then one hardly expects political sense from them. It was only when reading Professor Geyl's book that I realized that professors of history, at any rate in France, are so much better. Their record of integrity has been almost unbroken. Even in the Second Empire the committee of scholars, employed to publish the correspondence of Napoleon I, was too resolutely honest to please Napoleon III; it had to be replaced in 1864 by a committee of literary men (including Sainte-Beuve) which set out to publish only what Napoleon 'would have made available to the public if he had wished to display himself and his system to posterity'. Still, the achievement of the French professional historians cannot necessarily be counted to the general credit of the trade. What German historian stood out against the cult of Bismarck, at any rate until Bismarck had failed? And what chance is there that any German historian will stand out against the coming cult of Hitler? As for English historians, they have hardly escaped from the Anglican sycophancy which marked the universities until the beginning of this century. Chaplains of the pirate ship, they have extolled the British Empire as persistently as the French men of letters extolled the Empire of Napoleon. The French professors represented a general 'university' culture which hardly exists outside France. As Professor Geyl says: 'The scholarliness of their method ... disciplines their mental attitude. But it would be foolish to overlook the fact that these authors came to Napoleon with their own, with different, *a priori* ideas, that they measure him against standards of spiritual freedom, of culture, of humanity, of social progress, that politically they are as a rule of the left. With some of them anti-clericalism is predominant, with others liberalism, or socialism.' What a wonderful country of which these things can be said of university professors!

The last quotation is a reminder that Geyl's book, as well as being a book about Napoleon and about French historians, is about clerical values (using the word in Benda's sense). Geyl concludes his praise of the professional historian, Georges Lefebvre, in whom he finds the most convincing version of Napoleon, with criticism: 'I should like to see the eternal postulates of respect for the human personality, of the feeling for spiritual freedom, of lofty idealism, of truthfulness, taken into account when the final reckoning is made.' This is a startling evocation of the shade of Acton; and it leaves me wondering whether the virtues of a historian and those of a 'clerk' are the same after all.

2

METTERNICH

MEN live after their own deaths in the minds of others. Samuel Butler thought that this was the only form of immortality. For most men it is a wasting asset. Memories fade; causes change. Who now cares what Gladstone said in 1868? Occasionally the historian acts as a resurrection-man. He discovers that some forgotten figure was the real saviour of his country or maker of empire. Our nineteenth-century Prime Ministers, for instance, are being pushed aside; and their fame is being usurped by civil servants, hitherto obscure. There is another, and more lasting, way to survival. The historical figure is turned into a symbol. The man becomes a myth; and, though his real deeds are forgotten, he is mobilized in defence of some cause which might have surprised him. The founders of the great religions have all enjoyed this fate. Millions of men repeat their names, while knowing nothing of the details of their lives. The carpenter's son of Galilee blesses the grandeurs of the Papacy; and the tyranny of the Politburo is carried out in the name of a crabbed German scholar.

Metternich knew this success, even in his lifetime. His name was the symbol of resistance to the revolution – abused by the radicals, praised, though more rarely, by conservatives. His fall in 1848 was the decisive sign that 'the springtime of peoples' had begun. Soon he was being treated as the great opponent of German unity, his immortality turned to ridicule by Treitschke, only his interminable 'five metaphors' remembered. Every text-book of history rejoiced that 'the system of Metternich' had been overthrown; and the most humble politician assumed that any future settlement would improve on the work of the Congress of Vienna. The peace-making of Versailles began the disillusionment. Metternich crept back into favour as the exponent of a less idealistic diplomacy. The Balance of Power seemed a more sensible and a more effective principle than the League of Nations. But Metternich had to wait for his full restoration until the present cold war of creeds. He has re-emerged as 'the rock of order', and every renegade liberal in America discovers an admiration for this desiccated aristocrat. Metternich is again to fight the Jacobins, but this time with the big battalions on his side. Nationalism is frowned on; and Western Union is to replace 'the mouldering edifice' of the Habsburg monarchy, which Metternich lamented that he had spent his life in propping up.

The new saint of conservatism is a long way from the Metternich of history. He was a very silly man. This is revealed even in the flattering portrait by Lawrence. Vain and complacent, with fatuous good looks, his first thought in a crisis was to see whether his skin-tight breeches fitted perfectly and the Order of the Golden Fleece was hanging rightly. Even his love-affairs – and he had many – were calculated for their political effect. He sought influence on Napoleon through the Queen of Naples and learnt the secrets of Russia from Countess Lieven. It must have been disturbing when he whispered political gossip in bed. He never made a clever remark. His thoughts, like those of most conservatives, were banal and obvious. 'Things must get worse before they get better'; 'after war Europe needs peace'; 'everyone has his allotted place in society'. Most men could do better than this when shaving. As he grew older, he grew more sententious. His deafness gave him an irresistible hold over his visitors. Bismarck wisely slept during his discourse and so won the old man's favour. There are those whom we would recall from the dead. Metternich is not among them. Even Mr Viereck and Professor Morgenthau would blench if he appeared on their doorstep, his empty sentences already phrased.

He was good at his job, though it was not so difficult a job as is often supposed. His job was diplomacy, and in particular, to maintain the greatness of the house of Habsburg. He was spared the greatest difficulty of the diplomat, which is to convince his own employer. The Emperor Francis gave Metternich a free run so long as Austria was kept out of war; and even the Austrian generals counted on being beaten. He liked to present himself in later life as the symbol of resistance. In reality he had been the greatest of appeasers. His first stroke was 'the Austrian marriage', by which he hoped to buy off Napoleon with an Austrian arch-duchess. Far from being the enemy of Napoleon, Metternich was the most anxious of allied statesmen to compromise with him. He hesitated to enter the last coalition; strove for an agreed peace; and regretted Napoleon's downfall. He justified his policy by fear of Russia; it was pointless, he argued, to overthrow one tyrant of Europe if another took his place. The truth is that he wanted others to do the fighting for him. Besides, he supposed that a plump arch-duchess would turn Napoleon into a harmless, almost legitimate monarch and that the man who had grown great through the Revolution would now tame it. It made the delusion no less absurd that Napoleon sometimes shared it.

Metternich did not invent the Balance of Power, nor do much to develop it. The Great Powers of Europe existed without his assistance; and his only initiative at the Congress of Vienna was to project an unnecessary war over Poland – a war which others had too much sense to fight. In international affairs, too, he offered a series of platitudes. 'All I ask is a moral understanding between the five Great Powers. I ask that they take no important step, without a previous joint understanding.' Even the United Nations would work if Metternich's request were granted. But what if the Great Powers disagreed? Metternich offered only lamentations and reproaches. He abused Canning for putting British interests first; yet was ready to wreck his conservative partnership with Russia for the sake of Austrian interests in the Balkans. In the usual way of statesmen who rule over a decaying empire, he urged others to preserve the Austrian monarchy for their own good. He invented an Austrian 'mission' and assured his foreign visitors how unwillingly he had added Lombardy to the empire in 1815. It is, of course, rare for upholders of empire ever to admit that they get advantage or profit from it. And as Metternich went from one palace to another or pocketed the rewards which other sovereigns as well as his own showered upon him, the cares of office were no doubt the only thought in his mind.

He played some diplomatic problems competently, though Palmerston, his contemporary, did better with less fuss. The two shared the credit for a peaceful outcome to the eastern crisis of 1840. But ten years earlier Metternich might have muddled the Belgian alarm into a war, if it had not been for Palmerston's firm handling. Again, Metternich put years of wasted effort into attempts at intervening in the Spanish civil wars. His most original move in Austrian policy was to concentrate her strength on Italy. Though himself a German from the Rhineland, he encouraged Austria's withdrawal from Germany. He did not assert her supremacy in the German confederation nor even grudge Prussia her private score of the Zollverein. Yet he was too much a man of Western Europe to be content with the Balkans as compensation. For him Asia began at the road eastwards from Vienna. Italy alone seemed worthy to be the Habsburg prize. And Metternich taught the doctrine – quite erroneous, as it turned out – that the Habsburg monarchy could remain great only so long as it continued to dominate in Italy. All his diplomatic combinations centred on the Italian provinces. Yet he knew both that the Italians hated Austrian rule and that France would not tolerate it indefinitely.

This double threat was in itself an attraction to him. It was always his aim 'to fight the revolution on the field of international politics'. He had no faith in principles or ideas despite his theoretical posturing. Though he claimed to be a disciple of Burke, he doubted whether historical institutions would hold against radical ideas. In any case, there were no historical institutions in Central Europe except for the Hungarian parliament; and this Metternich never managed to control. The kings and emperors were almost as new as Napoleon, who had indeed created many of them. The Habsburgs had laid their hands on the historic states of Hungary and Bohemia; and Poland, the greatest historic state of all, had been eaten up by Metternich and his two conservative partners of the Holy Alliance. If tradition was useless, concession was dangerous. Metternich never wearied of explaining that moderate liberalism inevitably opened the door to extreme radicalism – a judgement repeatedly belied by events. Indeed, he argued in a perverse way that extreme radicalism, being less concealed, was somehow less alarming, even less destructive, than moderate reform.

His only answer to either liberalism or radicalism was, in fact, repression. If people were not allowed to think for themselves, they would be satisfied with material prosperity – and even this could be neglected. Since he had no genuine conservative ideas

himself, he denied that radical ideas were genuine; and solemnly
maintained that discontent everywhere was the result of 'a conspiracy'. When Confalonieri, the Italian patriot, was brought as a
political prisoner to Vienna, Metternich wrangled with him for
hours in the hope that 'the conspiracy' would at last be revealed.
His view of radicalism was exactly that of Senator McCarthy.
The good conservative must look under the bed every night. One
day he will find a radical lurking there. A conspiracy needs a
centre; and Metternich found it in Paris, as his present admirers
find it in Moscow. How much easier to forget men's political
grievances and to raise the cry of foreign war. But Metternich had
more sense than those who now tread in his footsteps. Though he
advocated a conservative crusade against France and 'the revolution', he proposed that it should be fought by others. Austria did
her duty to civilization by existing; it was for others to keep her
going. He said in old age: 'Error has never approached my spirit.'
And certainly he never made the error of getting into the front
line if he could avoid it. In this way at least he set an example to
us all.

3

1848

(1) YEAR OF REVOLUTION

'WE are making together the sublimest of poems.' Lamartine embodied the revolutions of 1848 in speech and in deed; and his grandiose phrase was echoed by every radical in the revolutionary year. Heaven on earth seemed nearer in 1848 than at any other moment in modern history. Eighteen forty-eight was the link between the centuries: it carried to the highest point the eighteenth-century belief in the perfectibility of man, yet, all unexpectedly, launched the social and national conflicts which ravage Europe a century later. Socialism and Nationalism, as mass forces, were both the product of 1848. The revolutions determined the character of every country in Europe (except Belgium) from the Pyrenees to the frontiers of the Russian and Turkish empires; and these countries have since shown common characteristics not shared by England, Russia, the Balkans, or Scandinavia. Politically speaking, a 'European' is an heir of 1848.

The moment of the revolution was determined by the financial crisis of 1846 and by bad harvests in 1846 and 1847. These caused food riots in the towns and sharpened the long-standing grievances of the peasants in Eastern Germany and in the Austrian Empire. Economic discontent gave force to revolts; only the moral upheaval turned these into a revolution. Eighteen forty-eight was the victory of the 'ideologues', as Napoleon had contemptuously named them. Respect for traditional beliefs and forms of government had broken down; as a German poet wrote, 'Monarchy is dead, though monarchs still live.' Even the rulers had lost faith in themselves. The King of Prussia received the revolutionary poet Herwegh in order to bow 'before a worthy opponent', and Metternich denounced 'the rotten edifice' which it was his duty to uphold.

The revolutions repudiated 'throne and altar'; equally they

repudiated existing State frontiers and the treaty settlement of the Congress of Vienna. After forty years of peace and stability men were bored: they wished to translate into real life the poetry of Victor Hugo and the music of Berlioz. Most of the radical leaders were between thirty-five and forty years of age; they represented the generation which had caught only the echoes of the Napoleonic Empire and which wished to hear again through Europe the thunder of the guns – though this time on the barricades. The barricades, built in every city in Europe and often erected even when there was no fighting, were the symbol of 1848. The ideologues had evoked the masses for sixty years; in 1848 the masses at last took their call.

The ideas of 1848 were the ideas of the French Revolution, applied now without doubt or reserve. The men of 1789 had been concerned with freedom from arbitrary government and equality before the law; though they used democratic phrases they restricted 'the people' to the property-owning middle class – even Robespierre only brought in the skilled artisan and petty shopkeeper. The men of 1848 had infinite faith in 'the people', whom they identified with themselves; and every little radical club spoke for 'the nation', as, say, the British Communist party speaks for the British 'working class'. The liberals, prizing the rights of 1789, saw these endangered by the intrusion of the masses and were thus driven on to the side of the counter-revolution; indeed, in most of Europe, the defeat of the revolution was achieved by liberals, to their own subsequent ruin. In the enmity between liberal and radical, too, 1848 created a political pattern peculiar to the continent of Europe.

Though the masses certainly broke on to the political stage, they did not fill the humble parts which had been allotted to them by the ideologues. The urban movements were revolts against hard conditions of life and work; caused not by the Industrial Revolution but by its absence. They were 'Luddite' in character, seeking to destroy the new machines (especially seeking to destroy the railways which were being built by British capital and labour in western Europe). With the general increase of population, towns were growing; these, as yet, lacked the cheap goods of mass production which make urban life tolerable. The less industry, the more revolution. Belgium, the only industrialized country in Europe, escaped revolution; Italy, with no modern industry, had seven.

Marx, prophesying revolution for the rest of his life, was in fact foretelling the revolution of 1848 which he had experienced as a young man; but he drew the wrong conclusion. Far from industrial development producing revolution, it was a protection against it; a century later the most advanced industrial countries are the least in danger from Communism. The urban masses of 1848 had no Socialist programme; they demanded 'the right to work', the programme of Napoleon III and, subsequently, of Hitler. Their 'social republic' was not Social Democracy; it was a longing for the days of mercantilism. Still, 'the right to work' challenged 'the rights of property', which had been the essential revolutionary condition for the middle class; it was the claim by the disinherited of the great revolution that they, too, had rights, and so announced the class struggle between capitalists and proletarians.

Social conflict broke the unity of 'the people' within the nation; national conflicts broke the unity of 'the people' throughout Europe. The French Revolution had preached nationalism; it meant by this only the right of existing nations to succeed to the inheritance of their kings. The revolution of 1848 aspired to destroy existing States and to create new ones in accordance with the national principle. This doctrine was destructive of existing monarchies; it menaced also the preponderance of France, the existing Great Power. The 'historic nations', Italy, Hungary, and Poland, announced their claims in 1848; they were overshadowed by Germany, where the revolutionary idea reached its highest point. The German movement was at once the most romantic and the most radical; and 1848 ushered in 'the German century', which has left Europe torn in pieces.

The 'historic nations' all had a past, a literature and an intellectual class; their appearance was expected. The surprise of 1848 was the appearance of the 'unhistoric nations', the submerged Slav peoples of east-central Europe. Emancipation of the peasants brought to life nations without aristocrats or burghers – their only spokesmen the educated sons of peasants – and therefore at one bound most under the leadership of ideologues. The historic nations, challenging the traditional order of Europe, were themselves challenged by the unhistoric nations. Slovenes and Croats disputed the historic claims of national Italy; Slovenes, Croats, Serbs and Rumanians (not a Slav people, but with similar social conditions) repudiated Great Hungary; the Czechs questioned German predominance in Bohemia; the Poles fought in both camps – they resisted the claims of the Germans in Posnania, yet to the east their own 'historic' claims were challenged by the Little Russians or Ukrainians. In the words of Professor Namier: 'With 1848 starts the Great European War of every nation against its neighbours.' Metternich's Europe, in spite of its dullness, lasted more than a generation; the Europe of Lamartine never came into existence.

The sovereignty of the people was the cardinal doctrine of 1848; all frontiers were to be redrawn and all political institutions remade in its name. Hence the great practical expression of 1848 was direct universal suffrage, practised for the first time: the people were not to be limited in their sovereignty, nor was the power of the people to be weakened by any intermediary. France set the example for the political events of the following hundred years. The sovereign people were offered the 'ideologues'; they chose Louis Napoleon. Proudhon, a democrat without illusions, drew the lesson: 'Universal suffrage is counter-revolution.' This lesson was applied by Bismarck and, later, by Hitler and Mussolini. Hitler, incorporating the General Will of the German people, united Nationalism and Socialism and redrew the map of Europe according to the German principles of 1848. Like the German radicals of 1848, Hitler ran against the rock of Slav resistance; and the Slav peoples were the residuary legatees of 1848.

(2) THE FRENCH REVOLUTION

24 February 1848, was the last day of great France, the last day of the France which had overshadowed the rest of Europe and had called the tune in political ideas. It was the last time when France sneezed and the rest of Europe caught a cold; henceforth France caught colds from others, as in the recent malady of Vichy. In 1848 the radicals of all Europe still looked to Paris, as the Communists now look to Moscow. Paris was the mother of

revolutions; but in 1848 her progeny got out of control. Though there had been previous outbreaks in Galicia and in Sicily the revolution in Paris gave the signal for the real storm, and the street fighting which overthrew Louis Philippe brought down, too, Metternich and the absolute monarchy in Prussia. Yet the revolutions which swept Europe did not remain under the spell of French ideas; still less did they restore French hegemony in Europe, as the French radicals had expected. Instead the French began to realize that the victory of the national principle, which they had launched, far from restoring Napoleon's domination of Europe, would destroy French security and would bring France under the threatening shadow of a Germany more powerful than herself.

Once a revolution is successful the revolutionaries become conservative in their turn. This is the key to French history in the hundred and fifty years since the Great Revolution. In 1789 the rights of man were subversive of the existing order and had to be fought for; later they became the existing order and had to be defended, until today the adherents of the rights of man are the most conservative element in European politics. The transition from one attitude to the other took place in France between February and June, 1848; on both occasions the radicals fought – but on different sides of the barricades. The revolution of 24 February had no deep-seated cause; as Proudhon said, it was made 'without an idea'. The demand for an extension of the franchise, which was its excuse, could have been met without a revolution; indeed, Louis Philippe had already granted it before his fall. But peaceful reform would have seemed a drab outcome, unworthy of the traditions of revolutionary France. The revolution was, in fact, its own object; the emotional experience provided the satisfaction of a religious conversion. A radical journalist expressed this: 'My hopes are in an act of providence, in a religious transformation to regenerate society.' The revolutionaries repeated the attitudes of 1789, as in 1939 the French tried, in vain, to recapture the inspiration of 1914. Tocqueville, sitting in the Chamber when it was invaded by the mob, was puzzled that he felt no fear; suddenly he realized that he was watching men striking postures which they had seen in an old print, not a spontaneous revolution – it is difficult to be frightened of a musket which was loaded sixty years before and has become a theatrical prop.

The radicals established a Provisional Government; this was hard put to it to find a programme. Lamartine describes the members of the Provisional Government sitting round and racking their heads in vain for some great symbolical act which should make the revolution worth while. He solved the problem by proposing the abolition of the death penalty; within four months it was restored for political offences and applied wholesale to those who had won the battle of February for the Provisional Government. Though the radicals proclaimed the sovereignty of the people, they feared it in practice. They had no agrarian programme with which to win the allegiance of the peasants, who made up the majority of the population. The revolution of 1789 gave the peasants their land, free of feudal duties; the revolution of 1848 compelled the peasants to pay their debts and increased the taxation on land. For the radicals of 1848 tried to combine revolution and a stable currency; not surprisingly, the peasants preferred Louis Napoleon, distinguished by his debts as well as by his great name. The radicals knew that universal suffrage would go against them; yet they insisted on perishing from their own principles. Lamartine declared: 'The people must be left free to make mistakes.' This mistake was the Second Empire.

Before 1848 the radicals had thought little of internal affairs. Their greatest grievance had been against the humiliation of the Congress of Vienna, and they expected to escape from their problems by renewing the glories of revolutionary war. Lamartine reserved his highest rhetoric for the circular dispatch in which he declared that France no longer recognized the treaties of 1815. Still, though France wished to see these treaties disappear, she would not herself make the effort to destroy them. Besides, on reflection it was not in the interests of France to replace the weak States across the Alps and the Rhine by a united Italy and a united Germany; and – in spite of past lip-service to the idea – even radical Frenchmen saw the defeat of Italian and German nationalism with some relief. The army originally prepared to go to the assistance of revolutionary Italy went off in 1849 to restore the Pope. There could be no such practical arguments against aiding Poland, and war for Poland was the slogan with which the extreme radicals, Blanqui and Barbès, attempted to overthrow the Provisional Government on 15 May. In 1848, as in 1939, France could aid Poland only by resuming the mastery of Europe which Napoleon had won and then lost; the task was already beyond her. Hence the defeat of Blanqui and his associates marked the turning-point in France's position in the world, as well as being the crisis of the revolution.

Still, behind the revolutionary echoes a true revolution existed. This was the movement of the town working classes, especially in Paris. The Great Revolution had found no place for them; rather it had established an alliance of peasants and *bourgeoisie* against them. Now to the traditional rights of man they claimed to add 'the right to work'. This demand sprang from handicraft workers, threatened by the machine, not from factory workers, enslaved to it. In England at the same time the workers, more mature, were demanding the right to work less. 'The right to work' was a demand for recognition rather than an economic programme; it was rejected by all those who had profited by the Great Revolution. The result was the June Days, the most formidable slave-war of modern times. The workers of Paris fought without leaders and without hope against a united front of nobles, middle class, and peasants. Reactionaries and radicals, estranged since the execution of Louis XVI, were reconciled over the bodies of the Parisian workers. The June Days showed that radicalism would not satisfy the working class; they became, and remained, an alien body in the French Republic. The radicals of 1848 had tried to be a 'third force'; instead the June Days drove France into the arms of Napoleon. A hundred years later, the shadow of the June Days, and of its sequel, still lies across French political life.

(3) VIENNA AND BERLIN

On 13 March 1848, revolution reached Vienna: Metternich was driven from power after thirty-nine years of office. The Vienna revolution was the central event of 1848, as significant as the fall of the Bastille in 1789. The Bastille was an antiquated fortress, virtually without a garrison; Metternich a feeble old man without supporters. Yet both symbolized the old order and brought it down with them. Monarchical authority over 'subjects' lost its divine sanction on 14 July 1789; dynastic right over peoples lost its hold on 13 March 1848. The Rights of Man triumphed in the streets of Paris; the rights of nations in the streets of Vienna. It was the end of government based on tradition. Henceforth peoples could be ruled only by consent – or by force. European history of the following hundred years recounts the oscillations between these two methods.

Though the Habsburg dynasty maintained a precarious existence in 1848 (and indeed for another seventy years) the fall of Metternich ended its independent position. Previously it had stood above the peoples; thereafter it manoeuvred between them. The Vienna revolution was the cardinal date in the history of both national Hungary and national Italy; it was a victory for Kossuth and Mazzini. National Italy sought only separation from Central Europe (a separation never fully achieved from the days of the Triple Alliance to the Axis or the present). National Hungary hoped to remain a great State without the Habsburgs, or rather to substitute the Magyar landowners for the dynasty as the ruling authority in Central Europe. This aim was subsequently realized, though in association with the dynasty, in the period of Dualism (1867–1918); in the end it brought 'thousand-year-old' Hungary to ruin.

Once the dynasty lost its traditional appeal, Central Europe needed some other principle of association. The Slav peoples (who were in the majority) would not accept German and Magyar hegemony which was offered them as an alternative. Against this they raised the demand for their own national freedom and thus prepared the way for the national States of 1918. Still, they wished also for association; and the few far-sighted Habsburg ministers, after Metternich's fall, saw that the empire could be saved only by invoking the peasant masses against the disruptive Liberalism and Nationalism of the middle classes. This was the significance of the emancipation of the peasants on 7 September 1848, the enduring achievement of the Austrian revolution. Aristocrats and liberals alike accused the Habsburg ministers of 'Communism'. A century later the same programme is being operated, though by the heirs of the Romanovs, not of the Habsburgs.

Still, the Vienna revolution found its greatest immediate impact

in Germany. National Germany, too, was born in the streets of
Vienna. If Hungary and Italy were to shake off the Habsburgs
the remaining Austrian dominions could also follow the national
principle: the way seemed open for Greater Germany. This faced
the Hohenzollerns, the only other real power in Germany, with
a problem of existence. If they resisted German nationalism they
would be swept aside; if they went with it they would be submerged. Frederick William IV, astute though neurotic, avoided
the dilemma and, with unconscious genius, stumbled on the
programme of Little Germany. The revolution of 18 March 1848,
in Berlin, though a victory for liberalism, did not break Hohenzollern power; the Army remained confident and intact. Frederick William IV granted a Constitution with a semblance of
goodwill; this was his bid for German leadership. He announced:
'Prussia merges into Germany.' The phrase was fraudulent.
Prussia continued to exist with an independent strength; the
German liberals were invited to accept Berlin as the capital of
Germany, solely in virtue of Frederick William's word. The revolutions in Vienna and Berlin offered to Germany alternative
solutions. The Vienna revolution aspired to a Greater Germany,
based on radical violence, which would embrace all Germans and
extend German supremacy throughout south-eastern Europe.
The Berlin revolution was the first announcement of a more
limited Germany, based on an alliance of moderate liberalism and
Prussian military strength, and which would repudiate the German inheritance in the south-east. Berlin anticipated Bismarck,
and Vienna Hitler.

In 1848 neither programme won unreserved acceptance.
National Germany rejected both Vienna and Berlin, the two
seats of power; it looked to Frankfurt, symbol of unification by
consent. The greatest event in the history of German liberalism
was the meeting of the National Assembly at Frankfurt on 18
May 1848. The Frankfurt Parliament hoped to give Germany
freedom and unity; but above these it rated power (Macht).
When German claims were challenged in Bohemia and in Posen,
German liberals forgot the Rights of Man and invoked the
right of the stronger; they expected the Austrian and Prussian
armies to provide the strength which they themselves did not
possess. They applauded the Habsburg victory in Prague over the

Czechs and sought to use Prussian power against the Poles. In November the Frankfurt liberals even welcomed the victory of Frederick William IV over the Prussian Parliament, which they regarded as an impudent rival.

These victories did not help liberal Germany; it became the next victim of the power which it worshipped. In April 1849, delegates from Frankfurt went humbly to Berlin to offer the Imperial Crown to Frederick William IV: liberal Germany was willing to merge into Prussia. The offer was rejected by Frederick William IV, and the Frankfurt Parliament was soon after dispersed by Prussian soldiers. Nevertheless Bismarck took up the offer, on terms still more favourable to Prussia, twenty years later.

Two great negatives were the legacy of the German revolutions of 1848. Dynastic power could not survive unless it took on a national colouring; on the other hand the Germans could not maintain the hegemony over Poles and Czechs on which the liberals most of all insisted unless they compromised with the possessors of power. This compromise is still sought by the Germans a century later; equally the foreign Powers who have replaced the dynasties compete for the favour of German nationalism.

13 March will not be celebrated this year in Germany; it is the symbol of Greater Germany and so of Hitler's vanished Empire. The Russians have decreed 18 March as Germany's 'day of freedom': like Frederick William IV they hope to pass off a spurious revolution as the real thing and, succeeding the Hohenzollerns as rulers in Berlin, announce that Prussia merges into Germany. As in the days of Bismarck, Little Germany is the best outcome for the Russians – a protection at once against Greater German power and against the West. The Western Powers follow in the footsteps of the liberals of 1848 to Frankfurt; they, too, will find themselves embarrassed by frontier disputes with Poland and by the agitation of Germans from Bohemia. Disappointment awaits those who seek national Germany at Frankfurt; as in 1848, Frankfurt is the symbol of the Germany of the idea, peaceful, liberal, contented – and non-existent.

(4) THE SLAV CONGRESS

The Slav Congress which met in Prague on 2 June 1848, was the least expected event in the year of revolutions. The Slav peoples of Central Europe had not been allowed for in radical calculations. Engels wrote of the Czechs and Croats (he was unaware even of the existence of the Slovaks): 'The natural and inevitable fate of these dying nations was to allow the process of dissolution and absorption by their stronger neighbours [Germany and Hungary] to complete itself.' Exception was made only for the Poles, as a historic nation, not as Slavs; the German radicals proposed to push Poland against Russia and then to jettison her later (the reverse of Russia's Polish policy a century later). Since Bohemia had been included in the Holy Roman Empire, it was assumed that it would become part of the new national Germany, and distinguished Bohemians were invited to join the preliminary meetings at Frankfurt. Palacky, the first historian of Bohemia and the recreator of Czech national consciousness, refused the invitation; he repudiated allegiance to Germany – 'I am a Bohemian of Slav race' – and looked instead to the Habsburg dynasty as the protector of the Slav peoples from German tyranny. 'If the Austrian Empire did not exist, it would have to be created in the interest of Europe and of humanity.' This famous sentence launched the programme of Austroslavism, the idea of maintaining a modest national existence under the wing of the most clerical and traditional dynasty in Europe.

In 1848 the dynasty seemed too shaken to act as the sole bond of union between different peoples, and those who feared incorporation in Greater Germany sought some more popular alternative. They thought to have found it in their Slav race. This was more than crude racialism: it assumed that all peoples with a Slav language had a common cultural background. In reality most Slav peoples outside Russia had been submerged by the culture of their conquerors, German, Hungarian, or even Turkish; hence the importance of ethnography in the Slav movement – the evidence for a common Slav 'folk' had to be found in the designs on peasant costume or pottery. The Slav Congress was intended as a gesture against the German National Assembly

at Frankfurt. This threatened directly only the Czechs and the
Slovenes – another reason for draping Slav 'folkdom' round the
practical political issue. The Slavs of Hungary (Croats, Serbs, and
Slovaks) were indifferent to the German menace; the Czechs
wished to avoid a conflict with Hungary, yet would not repudiate
the Slovaks, who alone could swell their numbers.

The real stumbling-block for a common Slav policy came from
the Poles. The Poles of Galicia were indisputably Slavs and
indisputably Habsburg subjects; yet Russia was their only
enemy, and they welcomed both Greater Germany and Great
Hungary. The Poles, who were threatened by the Germans, were
under Prussian rule in Posnania. To exclude them would weaken
the struggle against Frankfurt decisively; to include them would
trespass beyond the frontiers of the Habsburg monarchy and so
make nonsense of Austroslavism. In fact, the Slav Congress had
stumbled on the Polish problem. The Poles of the Austrian
Empire would not work with the Czechs or against the Germans;
the Poles of Posnania would work against the Germans, but
equally emphatically would not work with Russia. The Czechs
inssited that Poles from outside the Austrian Empire should
attend the Congress only as guests; the Poles would not recognize
the frontiers of the Polish partitions, and when the Polish section
of the Congress met it made the Poles from Posnania full members, one of them, indeed, becoming its chairman.

This intrusion of non-Austrian Slavs had a further embarrassing consequence. No one minded the presence of Serbs from
Turkey: the solidarity of the 'master nations' did not yet extend
to the Turks. But if the Slav Congress was to include all Slavs it
was impossible to exclude the greatest branch of the Slav race,
and the revolutionary Bakunin imposed himself upon the Congress as the solitary, self-appointed representative of the Russian
people. Bakunin had no patience with the cautious Austroslavism of Palacky; he demanded both the destruction of the
Habsburg Empire and revolution in Russia. His goal was a
federation of free peoples, based on the natural democracy of the
Slav peasants. Like later versions of Pan-Slavism, Bakunin's
vision rested on the dogma of virtues innate in Slav peoples which
would save them from the failings of others.

Pan-Slavism evoked no response from the Slav Congress;

indeed, Pan-Slavism had sense only as a translation into racial mysticism of the Byzantine and Orthodox heritage shared by some Slav peoples, and almost all those present at Prague were Western and Roman Catholic. The Slav Congress produced two contradictory programmes. The Poles drafted a manifesto to the Peoples of Europe which recognized the existence only of the 'historic nations'—Poland, Germany, Hungary, and Turkey—and politely invited these to treat their minorities better. The Czechs drafted an address to the Austrian Emperor which asked for the remodelling of the Austrian Empire into a federation based on national units. Perhaps the most concrete effect of the Congress was its division into three sections – Polish-Ukrainian, Czechoslovak and South Slav – for these anticipated the 'national amalgamations' which served as the basis for pseudo-national States (Poland, Czechoslovakia, and Yugoslavia) in 1918.

All these programmes received only preliminary statement. The Congress met for the last time on 12 June. Then fighting broke out between the Prague radicals, both Czech and German, and the Imperial forces; and on the suppression of the rebellion the Congress was dissolved. In its ten days of activity it had stated all the solutions for the problem of Central Europe which have been attempted from then until now. The Czechs followed Austroslavism for half a century after 1848; its essential condition, a federation of free nationalities, was granted by the Habsburg Emperor only on 16 October 1918, when the Empire was already in ruins. The last echo of Austroslavism was heard in the Slovakia of Tiso and the Croatia of Pavelic. The Poles tried to act as the partners of Greater Germany and Great Hungary in the days of Colonel Beck, and thought that they had reached their aim when they established a common frontier with Hungary in March 1939 – six months before their destruction. Bakunin's first demand was fulfilled with the dissolution of the Habsburg monarchy in 1918; failing the establishment of democracy in Russia, the Slavs had to look for support to the Western democracies and suffered ineffaceable disappointment at the time of Munich. Now fear of Germany makes them pretend that Bakunin's second condition has been fulfilled, and the 'democracies of the new type' rest on the double pretence of Russian democracy and Slav solidarity.

4

DE TOCQUEVILLE IN 1848

REVOLUTION is for society what a passionate love is for the individual; those who experience it are marked for ever, separated from their own past and from the rest of mankind. Some writers have captured the ecstasy of love; hardly any have rekindled the soul-purging fires of revolution. The writer of genius lives, for the most part, in a private world; it is not surprising that he deals usually with private passions. There have been some good observers of revolution – the best of them, I would guess, John Reed. Still, they observe from outside; it is like reading about the love-affair of the man next door. Two writers of the highest eminence, Lamartine and Trotsky, played the leading part in a revolution and created works of surpassing literary merit, but though their books tell us much about Lamartine and Trotsky, they do not tell us what revolution is like. The more brilliantly they write, the more the truth eludes them. For revolution calls in question the foundations of social life; it can be grasped only by one who has experienced it and yet possesses the detachment of a political psychologist.

Alexis de Tocqueville was this unique man; and his *Recollections of 1848* is the best book about a revolution ever written by a contemporary. Yet even Tocqueville was overwhelmed by his experience. This book is not a finished work, a complete work of art like his two masterpieces, *Democracy in America* and *The 'Ancien Régime' and the Revolution*. He wrote to instruct himself, not to persuade the public. Usually he reined in his brilliance; here, writing only for himself, he was not ashamed to be clever. The *Recollections* were only published thirty years after his death and then only with many omissions, where his pen still seemed too sharp or – more occasionally – where his political judgement ran counter to the illusions of the Third Republic.

Alexis de Tocqueville was a liberal aristocrat: he understood both the world that was dying and the world that was coming. As a historian in politics, he both observed events and tried to shape them. Liberty was his passion; and his life was dominated by the question – how can liberty survive the fall of traditional institutions and of traditional morality? Louis Philippe and the men of the *bourgeois* monarchy thought that society could exist without belief: they pinned their faith to legality and supposed that nothing could happen so long as they observed the terms of the Charter. 'They resembled the man who refused to believe that his house was on fire, because he had the key to it in his pocket.' The Opposition were in no better case; they evoked the spectre of revolution without ever fearing that it would become a reality. Their sole motive was 'a taste for holding office and a desire to live on the public money'. Tocqueville describes this as 'the secret malady which has undermined all former [French] governments and which will undermine all governments to come'. Tocqueville was alone in his doubts. A few weeks before the revolution he asked – how can you expect men to respect private property when all other beliefs and privileges have lost their force? The French revolution of 1848 posed 'the social question'; it is still without an answer.

Earlier revolutions had been the work of the middle classes; the masses had been merely cannon-fodder. In 1848 the masses acted independently, without leaders and without a programme. This was symbolized on the morning of 24 February, when Tocqueville passed along the deserted boulevard:

There was hardly a soul to be seen, although it was nearly nine o'clock; but ... the great trees along the curb came tumbling down into the roadway as though of their own accord. These acts of destruction were the work of isolated individuals, who went about their business silently, regularly and hurriedly, preparing in this way the materials for the barricades which others were to erect.

The political events of 24 February had no connexion with this elemental force; they merely echoed the sentiments of previous revolutions – the love-affair expressed the nostalgic regrets of a middle-aged man.

Men were fruitlessly endeavouring to warm themselves at the fire of our fathers' passions, imitating their gestures and attitudes as they had seen them represented on the stage, but unable to imitate their enthusiasm or to be inflamed with their fury.... Although I clearly saw that the catastrophe of the piece would be a terrible one, I was never able to take the actors very seriously, and the whole seemed to me like a bad tragedy performed by provincial actors.

The leaders did not know what to do with the revolution for which they had become responsible: 'in a rebellion, as in a novel, the most difficult part to invent is the end'. The only novelty was universal suffrage; this 'shook the country from top to bottom without bringing to light a single new man worthy of coming to the front'.

Universal suffrage revealed an aspect of the social question which had never occurred to the revolutionaries. 'In establishing universal suffrage they thought they were summoning the people to the assistance of the Revolution; they were only giving them arms against it.' Alexis de Tocqueville was almost the first to realize that once the peasants acquired their land free of land-lords and feudal dues they would become the most conservative of all classes. This was not grasped by Marx or by later Marxists, who went on treating 'workers and peasants' as a revolutionary combination until the events of 1932 in the Ukraine and the present political situation in eastern Europe revealed that the conflict between town workers and peasants is the most ghastly as it is the most fierce of all civil wars. In 1848 the revolutionaries, faced with a conservative National Assembly, were at a loss how to proceed. They did not attempt to conquer the countryside, or even to seduce it; they supposed that it would be enough to stage a new revolution in Paris. The last of the romantic revolutions occurred on 15 May; its only programme was war for the liberation of Poland. It was then that Tocqueville set eyes on the most persistent of revolutionaries:

He had wan, emaciated cheeks, white lips, a sickly, wicked and repulsive expression, a dirty pallor, the appearance of a mouldy corpse; he wore no visible linen; an old black frock-coat tightly covered his lean, withered limbs; he seemed to have passed his life in a sewer and to have just left it. I was told it was Blanqui.

15 May brought all the known revolutionaries to prison; and their absence completed the terrible impact of the June Days:

the most extensive and the most singular insurrection that has occurred in our history and perhaps in any other.... The insurgents fought without a war-cry, without leaders, without flags and yet with a marvellous harmony and an amount of military experience that astonished the oldest officers. ... It was not a political struggle, but a struggle of class against class, a sort of Servile War ... the revolt of one whole section of the population against another.

The proletariat had appeared on the stage of history; even Marx drew all his teachings of the proletarian revolution from the June Days. Yet Marx saw less deeply than Tocqueville. The revolution of the masses was a revolution of destruction. Marx regarded the proletariat merely as a slave of the lamp, which would carry him to supreme power; Tocqueville recognized that the masses had repudiated all leadership, the leadership of Blanqui and of Barbès as much as the leadership of Lamartine and of Ledru-Rollin. The contrast explains much that happened in his day and more in ours. The Communist revolutions, far from fulfilling the wish of the masses, establish a dictatorship over the masses; they are the last device by which intellectuals bar the way against anarchy. When traditions and beliefs have perished, only force remains; this cannot be concealed by synthetic beliefs and simulated devotions. Yet force cannot provide a lasting answer. One day the masses will knock again at the door – and they will knock more fiercely at the Communist door than at any other.

Tocqueville's revolutionary memories end abruptly with the days of June. The revolution was over. There follows a strange epilogue, out of tone with the rest of the book, yet essential to it – memoirs of the few months when Tocqueville attempted to lead a life of action. Of course he had acted during the revolution. He had been elected a member of the National Assembly, he had kept his courage on 15 May and during the June Days, he had served – though without much effect – on the committee which drafted the Constitution. Still, this was not action of the first order. Twelve months later, in June 1849, Tocqueville suddenly appeared as Foreign Minister in a cabinet formed 'to save the Republic'. The great political philosopher proved a signal failure as a practical politician. The lover of liberty became the minister of Louis Napoleon, looking for support to a clericalist majority in the Assembly; and this government of 'pure' Republicans first suppressed a radical rising in the streets of Paris and then restored Papal rule in Rome. Had Tocqueville remained longer in power, he would have anticipated the foreign policy of Vichy; for, arguing that France was in decline, he proposed to build up a united Germany as a barrier against Russia. There is some danger in public life from stupid politicians; there is even more from politicians who are too clever. Political understanding of the highest order led Tocqueville into being the associate of Louis Napoleon and of the clericals; it would have been better if he had understood less. He wished to show that Republicans could be conservative in home and foreign policy. This served to suppress the radicals and to destroy the Roman republic; it did not save the republic in France.

Tocqueville knew that somewhere he had gone wrong. When he left office, after some four months, he withdrew for ever from public life; and his apology in this last chapter is laboured, unconvincing even to himself. He had fallen victim to the doctrine of 'the lesser evil' – better Louis Napoleon than anarchy, better Falloux and his clerical associates than a new radical revolution. So nowadays we say: better Wall Street than the Kremlin, better de Gaulle than the Communists. Yet Tocqueville himself, in the conclusion of *Democracy in America*, had seen the falsity of this argument; liberty cannot be saved by resistance. He could not apply this teaching when it came to his own country. The social peril threw him off his balance. Hence the malignancy of his picture of Blanqui, who, despite his madness and his pallor (acquired from a lifetime of imprisonment) was also a soldier of liberty – and one who paid a far higher price for it than Tocqueville did. No doubt the masses threatened all sorts of 'civilized' values; the answer to this danger was to bring the masses within the pale of civilization, not to shoot them down in the June Days. After all, anarchy is a form of liberty, which is more than can be said for dictatorship or clericalism. The greatest invention of 1848, which Tocqueville disowned, was Social Democracy; this was the only way in which civilization could be saved.

Thus Tocqueville's recollections provide an object-lesson as well as a social analysis of the first order. They are a warning against being too clever in politics; in fact, the intellectual more than others should have simple principles and should stick to them. Liberty has to be defended against all comers; all the same, the constant enemies of liberty are on the right, and the lover of liberty must never be shaken from his position on the left. Above all, he who loves liberty must have faith in the people. Otherwise he will, like Tocqueville, withdraw from public life and despair of the future.

5

1848: OPENING OF AN ERA

ROBERT OWEN, on a visit to Paris, described his economic system as 'the railway which will take mankind to universal happiness'. His phrase crystallized the spirit of the year of revolutions. Movement, and a conviction that Utopia could be reached, were the essence of 1848: underlying these was a faith in the limitless goodness of human nature. The revolutionary cry, 'All change!' sounded across Europe. Hope lit the dawn of a new Europe; and mankind clambered into the trains of political and social upheaval, all of which claimed to be directed to the same terminus – the Kingdom of Heaven on Earth. New faiths, new nations, new classes announced their arrival; each was the confident possessor of an exclusive truth. Before 1848 the rights of individuals and of States were a matter of history and of settled law; the revolutions substituted the rule of abstract principle. Louis Phillipe said bitterly of the revolution of 1830 which brought him to the throne: 'What perished in France in 1830 was not respect for a dynasty, but respect for anything.' This was demonstrated anew in France in 1848 and, for the first time, was demonstrated throughout Europe as well. Reason took the place of respect; and self-interest the place of tradition.

Movement was both the cause of the revolutions and their outcome: the revolutions threw down established landmarks that were already ruinous. In the preceding fifty years tumultuous development had taken the place of imperceptible change. There was an unprecedented growth of population, an unprecedented advance in the methods of industry and of transport, and an unprecedented novelty in the world of ideas; the three together composed the background to the revolutions. The old order had assumed stable populations; these ensured stability between classes and stability between States. For half a century before 1848 the increase of population had been gathering strength, and this contributed more than anything else to the illusion of progress. The increase was less in France than elsewhere in Europe; and the wise student of population figures might already guess that France, hitherto the greatest European Power and the most revolutionary nation, would soon become the most conservative and the least great of the Powers. The universal growth of population had profound consequences. Where the peasant was already free, as in western Germany, the surplus was being pushed into the towns. In the Austrian Empire the peasants could no longer tolerate the burden of feudal dues and of feudal subordination; moreover, with the increasing demand for food, the great landowners could no longer operate their estates by the traditional methods. Both lords and peasants turned against the old order of settled obligations; both demanded freedom of movement and the rule of the market. Almost the first act of the liberal parliament in Hungary was to abolish the old agrarian social order; and the Austrian Constituent Assembly followed suit (its only effective act) on 7 September. The destinies of fifty million people were affected. The more prosperous peasants got the chance of survival; the poorer peasants lost their last traditional protection and were the victims both of the richer peasants and of the capitalistic great estates. The way was clear for the emigration to the towns and overseas which characterized the second half of the century. It was no accident that England and Russia, the only countries of Europe to escape the revolutions, had already found the way of emigration before 1848: the road to Siberia had been open since the beginning of the century, and the emigrant-steamers took the life out of Chartism when they began to sail from Liverpool in 1844. The rest of Europe had lacked the technical and social conditions for mass emigration: peasant emancipation came in 1848, and railways followed. These provided a safety valve which postponed further European explosions until the twentieth century. Modern industrial America, as well as modern industrial Europe, would have been impossible without the revolutions of 1848.

The ideas of 1848 spread later to Russia; and the Russian revolutions of the twentieth century were in the true spirit of 1848. In fact, Russia, missing the disillusionment which followed the failure of 1848, alone retained faith in the revolutionary course. America was already democratic, and therefore for her, though there was no need for revolution, there was no need for disillusion-ment either. For a generation after 1848, and even longer, America offered to the peoples of Europe the economic and political prizes which failure had denied them in Europe. Still, 1848 left no tradition in either Russia or America. Eighteen forty-nine has some meaning in the history of both countries. For Russia it brought a victorious repression of revolution in Hungary; for America it marked the discovery of gold in California. To the present day, the one Great Power offers Europe repression, the other material wealth. Neither can offer the liberty of spirit which was the true aim of 1848.

The staggering growth of towns throughout Europe was a consequence of the revolutions. Still, even before 1848, the swelling towns amazed and alarmed contemporaries; and their isolation – urban islands in a rural continent – emphasized their revolutionary character. The conscious revolutions of 1848 were all exclusively urban. 'The German revolution' is a misleading generalization for the Berlin revolution and the Vienna revo-lution; 'the Italian revolution' still more misleading as a title for the revolutions in Venice, Milan, Florence, Rome, Naples and many more. The contrast was sharpest in France. The Great Revolution of 1789 had been the movement of a people, the revolution of 1848 was a movement of Paris against the rest of the nation. Isolated in place, the revolutions were equally insular in idea: they had no agrarian programme and offered the peasants – troglodytes, in Marx's phrase – nothing but extinction. For the first time news of a revolution passed from one town to another by telegraph; it no longer needed to filter through, and so to affect, the countryside. The revolutionaries travelled by train from one revolution to the next; they had neither eyes nor thoughts for the country through which they passed. The revolutionaries equated revolutions with street-fighting. Their occasional forays into the countryside – from Hecker's raid on Baden in April 1848 to Garibaldi's march across Italy in July 1849 – were the organ-ized hikes of town dwellers.

Even the largest towns lacked industrial development. Labour had arrived before capital was ready for it. Only Belgium had experienced an industrial revolution; and therefore, despite its urban character, enjoyed an unique freedom from revolutionary danger. The revolutions elsewhere were not revolts against the machine; they were demands to be employed by it. The slogan of 'the right to work' was a symbol of immaturity; an industrial proletariat would have demanded the right to work less – as indeed the English working-class had already done with success in 1847. 'The right to work' was a protest as much against social inequality as against harsh living conditions. Nevertheless, by formulating this protest in economic terms, it launched the idea that liberty and political equality were negligible, or indeed valueless, in comparison with food and clothing. This idea was not intended by the social revolutionaries of 1848, who took up economic grievances principally in order to add greater force to their political demands. All the same the damage had been done. Continental Socialism, which had its origins in 1848, wrote off political democracy as *bourgeois* and accepted the doctrine that violence and intolerance were a small price to pay for social change. Class war took the place of the struggle for political liberty, and the Rights of Man were a casualty of 'the right to work'.

The announcement of an economic programme was certainly the startling novelty of 1848; nevertheless the revolutions were not simply the product of economic circumstances. These determined the moment of revolution, not that it should occur. The economic upheaval and the upheaval in men's minds were two aspects of the same process. Certainly the age of coal and iron enforced daring political schemes and made them possible; but equally it needed a daring mind to think of the railway and the blast furnace. The great towns of modern Europe could not have been maintained without railways, steam power and a revolution in agriculture; but the movement to the towns depended just as much on the spread of new ideas which prised men away from their traditional beliefs and traditional surroundings. The railways found people ready to move; otherwise they would have run empty. Reason was the great dissolvent force. This made men dissatisfied with their traditional homes and with their traditional place in society just as much as with the traditional methods of production. The radicals of 1848 were the heirs of eighteenth-century enlightenment: sublimely confident in human nature (except that of their fellow revolutionaries), they believed that their only task was to shake off the hold of established beliefs and established institutions. Their common programme was 'to strangle the last king with the bowels of the last priest'. The natural goodness of man would do the rest.

The old order, thus dramatically threatened, claimed to depend on habit, on history and on established rights. No historical conflict is, in fact, fought on these easy terms. The old order was itself more rational and artificial – just as the revolutionaries were more traditional – than either side liked to admit. Revolutionary ideas had affected the upper classes before they spread to the masses; and the impact of the great French Revolution had long shaken the foundations of the European system. Men were argued into conservatism as they were argued into revolution. The kings who were threatened by the movements of 1848 had less than a century of possession behind them, and many more were the creations of Napoleon. Even the house of Habsburg, the only genuine historic dynasty, had acquired a new title and new territories a generation previously and had knocked all life out of historic institutions everywhere in its dominions except in Hungary – and there from lack of strength, not of will. The 'old aristocracy' was a creation of the eighteenth, or occasionally of the seventeenth century. Most of all the territorial settlement of the Congress of Vienna was as artificial as the Empire of Napoleon which it replaced. The peace which followed the Napoleonic wars sprang from exhaustion, not from belief or from content; and the society which perished in 1848 had no moral justification other than the desire of the possessing classes to enjoy their privileges.

The kings, aristocrats and states of the Vienna system had not even given themselves the trouble of being born; they had been conjured up ready-made by conservative theorists. Thus Metternich, to give historic character to the Austrian Empire (which had acquired legal existence only in 1804), proposed to invent for the Emperor a traditional ceremony of coronation. Metternich, symbol and chief exponent of Conservatism, claimed to be building a dam against revolution. In reality, his effort to set up a universal 'system 'of political ideas and institutions was typical

of an eighteenth-century doctrinaire. He approached politics in
the spirit of Robespierre: the only difference was in his employer.
The dissolvent of reason could have been resisted only by communities with a living history; few such existed on the continent
of Europe, and these few (Switzerland, Hungary and perhaps the
Low Countries) did not accord with Metternich's conservatism.
As a result, the system of Metternich was not overthrown in 1848;
it collapsed. This collapse astonished contemporaries, other than
Metternich himself: he had always appreciated the artificiality of
his own system and had never felt the faith which he demanded
in others.

In 1848 Europe broke consciously with its past. This was the
indelible achievement of the year of revolutions. Yet more than
destruction was intended. Bakunin, most extreme representative
of the spirit of revolution, once declared that if his plans succeeded he would at once begin to pull down again everything he
had ever made; this did not take the zest from a lifetime of
planning. The radicals of all schools were as convinced as
Metternich of the need for belief; and, unlike Metternich, themselves believed in the systems which they expounded. Their
systems, too, were universal and dogmatic. All assumed that
reason was adequate as the sole guide in human affairs; and they
assumed also that there was no limit to what reason could do.
The revolutionaries differed as to the means by which the human
race might be made perfect; none disputed that the goal would be
attained. The radical systems provided new Absolutes for old and
gave final answers in politics, in society and in international
affairs. The sovereignty of the people overthrew the sovereignty
of kings; nations took the place of states; and intellect ousted
heredity as the source of authority.

Though the sovereignty of the people had already served as
inspiration to the French Revolution of 1789, its operation had
been restricted. The distinguishing mark of 1789 had been the
confidence that universal principles could be limited in their
application and a revolution arrested in its course. This expectation was not proved false until 1848. When all hereditary rights
were repudiated, the right of private property had remained
inviolate and was indeed reinforced; and the dogma of the
sovereignty of the people was used to justify the franchise of the

property-owning middle class. In 1848 the term of this compromise expired; and the *bourgeoisie*, once the leaders of revolution, became the symbol of conservatism. Almost the first act of the victorious revolution in France was to abolish the property qualification and to proclaim universal suffrage. This became everywhere the most concrete expression of the revolutionary programme. Only Hungary, which combined – or perhaps stifled – revolutionary principle with historic institutions, held out against universal suffrage until the twentieth century. The events of 1848 challenged also the economic privilege of the owners of property. The June Days in Paris gave dramatic announcement of the arrival of a new revolutionary class, 'the proletariat'. The June rising was not fought to promote any practical economic change; it was a social war, a slave revolt, and its repudiation of the moral superiority of the *bourgeoisie* could not be wiped out by all the executions and deportations which followed defeat. Before the June Days private property had been regarded as essential for liberty; after the June Days it became the symbol of oppression, and the capitalist took the place of priest and noble as the object of democratic hostility. Henceforth the *bourgeoisie* was morally on the defensive, ashamed and anxious. This was true not only of the French *bourgeoisie*, who had genuinely experienced the 'social peril'. The alarm of the June Days spread across Europe; indeed, apprehension increased as the reality of danger became more remote. The middle classes outside France abandoned the revolutionary cause almost before they had taken it up and sought for allies against a proletariat which was still imaginary. Thus, the October Revolution in Vienna, though it had a programme with no social implications, sent the German-Austrian middle classes over to the side of absolutism; and within a few years of 1848 German liberalism came to regard universal suffrage as its mortal enemy. The French *bourgeoisie* had pride enough to remain radical though they ceased to be revolutionary and adhered to the sovereignty of the people in the sense that they took into partnership the French peasants who had saved them in the June Days. Though universal suffrage, the work of the revolution of 1848, became everywhere a mainstay of conservatism, in France it sustained at least the Third Republic and later, in the Dreyfus case, upheld the

Rights of Man. In Germany, however, it was the instrument of Bismarck and in Austria it became in 1907 the last prop of the Empire of Francis Joseph.

In the world of nations, too, the revolutions of 1848 ended the compromise which had been the outcome of the revolution of 1789. The French revolutionaries had launched the national principle; they supposed that this would operate to the sole advantage of France and that when all else of the old order was destroyed the predominance of France would remain unchallenged. France liberated other nations as the French *bourgeoisie* liberated the French people: freed from their hereditary rulers, they were expected to welcome French leadership instead. The Empire of Napoleon expressed the French version of the national principle: German, Italian, Polish and even South Slav nationalism were evoked as auxiliary weapons for the French cause. France was the only one who knew how to wield the national appeal, and remained the greatest single power in Europe even after the fall of Napoleon; the other Great Powers of the Continent were states, not nations, and therefore without the strength of popular enthusiasm. Thus the French nation claimed the cultural and political heritage of Louis XIV, despite the guillotining of Louis XVI and the renewed expulsion of the Bourbons in July 1830. This cultural headship was recognized for the last time at the beginning of 1848, when the other nations of Europe waited for the February Revolution in Paris before starting their own. Thereafter it was no longer enough to have taken the trouble to be born French. The laws of inheritance were repudiated between nations as much as between individuals. The lesson was not lost on the French themselves; henceforth the French nation was as much imperilled as, say, the dynasty of Habsburg by European upheavals, and France – previously the promoter of change – became the principal advocate of conservatism and of the *status quo*.

In 1848 every nation followed the example set by the French in 1789. Each claimed to be perfect: each, therefore, was entitled to lay down its own limits or, if it preferred, to recognize none. Moreover, each nation asserted a purity and greatness of character which made it an example to Europe and justified its bringing other less noble people under its own rule. Thus, Poland had long announced herself as 'the Christ among the nations', and her liberation was regarded as the first object of the revolutionary cause; this liberation did not, however, extend to the Ukrainians under Polish rule. Similarly Mazzini, despite his denunciations of French arrogance, set up Italy as 'God's word in the midst of the nations'. Rome was to be the capital of a new federation of nations, all duly humble, which were to be cut and shaped to suit Italy's convenience. Kossuth, too, insisted on the unique civilization and political gifts of the Magyars. Though partly Slovak by birth, he denied the existence of a Slovak nation, and, since he could not deny the existence of the Serbs, proposed to root them out with the sword.

Magyar exclusiveness was relatively harmless, except to the subject nations of Hungary. The will to dominate was a more dangerous matter when it was taken up by the Germans, already the most numerous nationality in Europe. The revolutions of 1848 discovered 'the German mission'. This mission was simple: it was, simply, to be German. Europe was corrupt – French sophistication, English materialism, outworn institutions were all to be redeemed by the irruption of the clear-eyed, healthy German barbarian:

> *Und es soll am Deutschen Wesen*
> *Noch einmal die Welt genesen.*

A unique character was found in the German spirit (*Deutscher Geist*), and for that matter even in German rivers and trees – the one wetter and the other more arboreal than any others. Other nations based their claims on superiority of culture, as in the case of France or Italy, or at any rate on superiority of class – as Polish and Magyar nationalism sprang from their landed nobility. German nationalism was the first to depend solely on language: the future Germany was to extend wherever German was spoken. The *Volksdeutsche* were an invention of 1848. Since Germany had no 'natural frontiers' – or none that gave such an easy excuse for expansion as the Rhine to France or the Alps to Italy – national Germany used a simpler argument and claimed whatever was necessary to her existence. Thus Bohemia, despite its Czech majority, could, according to Engels, 'only exist henceforth as a part of Germany'; and the German liberal spokesman at Frankfurt said of western Poland: 'Our right is that of the stronger, the right of conquest'. This phrase supplied the basic theme of German history, until it turned against Germany a century later.

Resistance to German claims was not delayed until the twentieth century; it was the motive of the Slav Congress which met at Prague on 2 June 1848. The Slav peoples of eastern Europe were individually too small to hold out against German pressure; therefore, improving on the German model which had made language the basis of nationality, they tried to find a bond of alliance in ethnography and philology. The Slav Congress had practical motives of defence against German nationalism and had no time to trouble about the virtues of the Slav character. Still, even at Prague, Bakunin, one of the inventors of Slav solidarity, found in the Slavs 'an amazing freshness and incomparably more natural intelligence and energy than in the Germans'; and he expected them 'to renew the decadent Western world'. The Slavs of the Austrian and Turkish Empires had enough to do renewing themselves and thereafter quarrelling with each other. The only contribution Russia made to the Western world in 1848–9 was to crush the revolution in Hungary. But the spirit of radicalism was not permanently arrested at the Russian frontier; and Pan-Slavism, which evoked little response outside Russia, became the delayed gift of 1848 to the Russian intellectuals. In the twentieth century they escaped from this ethnic intolerance only with the aid of class intolerance, which was the other legacy of 1848 to mankind.

The revolutions of 1848 dispelled the Utopian dreams of the eighteenth-century rationalists. These had supposed that mankind would attain universal happiness if traditional beliefs were abandoned and traditional authorities overthrown. The experiences after 1789 did not destroy this idea. Social concord accompanied the rule of the *bourgeoisie*, and a true international order was established with the Empire of Napoleon; it could plausibly be argued that achievement fell short of the ideal only because success was incomplete. Had the tricolour really 'toured the world', universal happiness could have been expected to follow. In 1848 no bounds were drawn against revolutionary victory: no European country, except Belgium, escaped, and the established system lost its traditional authority for ever. The outcome was conflict, not concord. The June Days announced class war; the record of the German, Italian and Hungarian revolutions announced war between nations. Peaceful agreement and government by consent are possible only on the basis of ideas common to all parties; and these ideas must spring from habit and from history. Once reason is introduced, every man, every class, every nation becomes a law unto itself; and the only right which reason understands is the right of the stronger. Reason formulates universal principles and is therefore intolerant: there can be only one rational society, one rational nation, ultimately one rational man. Decision between rival reasons can be made only by force. This lesson was drawn by the greatest political genius who observed the events of 1848: 'The great questions of our day will not be settled by resolutions and majority votes – that was the mistake of the men of 1848 and 1849 – but by blood and iron.' After 1848, the idea that disputes between classes could be settled by compromise or that discussion was an effective means of international relations was held only in England and America, the two countries which escaped the revolutions.

The liberals, the moderate men, shirked the problem of authority; it was faced by the radicals. They found a substitute for tradition in 'the religion of humanity', just as their nationalism took the place of the decayed loyalty to kings. Above all, they found a substitute for the hereditary governing class in themselves. 'The aristocracy of intellect' had a limitless confidence in its right to govern; for it spoke 'in the name of the people'. The radical leaders nominated themselves to this post: none of the great revolutionaries – not Marx nor Engels, Bakunin nor Blanqui – ever secured election by a democratic constituency, and, for the matter of that, none of them was sure of a majority even among the circle of his close associates. The greatest radical effort in France was the demonstration of 16 March, which demanded that elections to the Constituent Assembly be postponed until the people were fit to exercise the franchise, that is, until they were willing to vote for the radical leaders. Blanqui, when asked how long the postponement should be, answered: 'For some months, or perhaps years.' By democracy the men of 1848 did not mean the rule of the majority; they meant rather the rule of the discontented, a reversal of the previous order of society. The essence of 1848 was belief in movement; therefore only those elements of the population who desired change were democratic. The theoretical justification for this outlook was provided by Marx; it was his great contribution to history. Marx found the motive force of history in economic change; and this force was now impelling mankind from capitalism to socialism. Since movement and democracy were synonymous, only those who desired socialism were 'the people'. Marx could thus eliminate the peasants from his calculations, though they made up the great majority everywhere in Europe; and democracy could be turned into 'the dictatorship of the proletariat'. Marx was a man of the Enlightenment. He held that every man would recognize his own interest and follow it; therefore every proletarian would be a socialist. The proposition could be more usefully reversed: anyone who was not a socialist was not a proletarian. But the dictatorship was not really to be exercised even by those working men who accepted the theories of the learned Dr Marx. The workers were to be led by the communists, 'everywhere the most resolute and progressive element of the working class'. Since the communists in 1848 consisted of Marx and Engels, this was a satisfactory conclusion – and has proved a satisfactory conclusion for communists ever since. The radical theorists were led inevitably from belief in the people to belief in themselves; and so to advocacy of authoritarian government. Marx was more self-satisfied and despotic than Metternich, the other system-maker from the Rhineland.

Yet these resolute and progressive leaders never displayed their talents in a revolution. The original outbreaks had no recognized leaders; and no one knows the names of the leaders of the June Days in Paris or of the October Revolution in Vienna. The name of an individual leader in the rising of 15 May in Paris has been preserved; he is thought to have been a police spy. Only Kossuth and Mazzini experienced the practical tasks of revolutionary government; and the experience of Mazzini was not very serious. For the most part the self-styled spokesmen of the people were always trying to catch up on revolutions which had taken them by surprise, as Marx and Engels were still correcting the proofs of their revolutionary programme, the *Communist Manifesto*, when the first barricades were already built and the first shots were being fired. Bakunin distinguished himself by arriving in time for the Dresden revolution of May 1849. This was an accident – he was leaving Dresden for an imaginary revolution elsewhere and was prevented from reaching the railway station by unexpected barricades.

There would have been no revolutions in 1848 if it had depended on the revolutionary leaders. The revolutions made themselves; and the true heroes of 1848 were the masses. The radical intellectuals had supposed that, once tradition was overthrown, the masses would acknowledge instead the claims of intellect. Nietzsche expressed later this great illusion of 1848: 'Dead are all Gods. Now the superman shall live.' The masses never responded to the ambitions of the intellectuals. Though the masses, too, sought the superman, they sought in him an extension of themselves. The first of these supermen, concentrating the impulses and contradictions of the masses, was Napoleon III. He was a clever French guess at the future, not the real thing; for France remained too conservative in institutions and social structure to experience the full rule of the masses. The real superman of the masses was Hitler, in whom anonymity was personified; or perhaps even more in the enigmatical *Politbureaus* of the 'new democracies', who have put the superman into commission.

In a deeper sense, the true superman, for whom 1848 prepared the way, has turned out to be the masses themselves. The masses have performed labours greater than those of Hercules and have accomplished miracles more wonderful than those of a divine Saviour; more than any individual superman, they have shown themselves to be beyond good and evil. The age which began in 1848 was the age of the masses: the age of mass production, of mass migration and of mass war. In the pursuit of universal happiness everything became universal: universal suffrage, universal education, universal military service, finally universal destruction. The train which Robert Owen signalled has been driven by the masses themselves; the intellectuals have remained passengers, criticizing – or more occasionally – commending the train's progress. The historic task of the intellectuals was to sever mankind from its roots and to launch it on its career of movement. This was the task which was accomplished in 1848.

6

THE MAN OF DECEMBER

SOME historical characters – I would say most – become simpler as you know more about them. The lines get stronger, clearer; you see a whole man, you know how he will behave, how he will face difficulties, how he will respond to success. In the end he will go into one of those two pigeon-holes that are so jeered at and yet are essential for the moral judgement that we finally have to make: he can be docketed as 'a good thing' – or a bad one. But some few escape us and baffle examination. The more we strip off their disguises, the more new disguises appear. Such was Louis Napoleon, the man of mystery. Conspirator and statesman; dreamer and realist; despot and democrat; maker of wars and man of peace; creator and muddler; you can go on indefinitely, until you begin to think that he had no character at all, that at the heart of him was a gigantic nothing. All the greatest political observers of the time tried to penetrate his secret: Tocqueville, Marx, Thiers, Victor Hugo – all failed to make sense of him. Bismarck called him a Sphinx, and added: he was a Sphinx without a riddle. Was it not rather that he had too many riddles, and riddles to which he himself did not know the answer?

Everything about him baffles inquiry. Was he the son of his father? It seems unlikely. Yet if not, then of whom? He was master of concealment. Whatever his other failings, he left few traces. The letters of Napoleon I fill sixty-four volumes; the letters of Napoleon III, even if they could be brought together, would not fill one. He talked endlessly to a great variety of witnesses, but – like the smoke of the cigarettes that he was one of the first to favour – his talk was vague and intangible; it vanished into the air, leaving only a faint romantic odour, a thin cloud of mystery. He was a creature of the Romantic movement, a Byronic hero gone seedy and rather out-at-elbows. Bulwer Lytton and the young Disraeli had the same touch, both in their writings and in their lives: an artificial excitement, a grandeur of ideas and a triviality of performance. The men who grew up in the thirty years after the battle of Waterloo played out their lives in the shadow of the great Napoleon, Napoleon I. He had done great things; they manufactured great phrases. When Napoleon I called himself Emperor of the French, this was an empire which stretched across Europe to the frontiers of Russia and Turkey. Napoleon III, as Emperor, ruled only over the old Kingdom of France, and all that he added to his empire in nearly twenty years was Savoy and a scrap of Indo-China. This was a typical gesture of the Romantic movement, and its great legacy to our own time: the name on the bottle was more important than the drink inside it; the man who writes the advertisement is more important than the man who makes the goods – as for the goods themselves, they are of no importance at all.

One writer has called Louis Napoleon 'the modern Emperor'; another 'the first mountebank dictator'. Perhaps they are the same thing. The radicals of 1848 had claimed that they were bringing the masses into politics. The response had been disappointing. It was Louis Napoleon who first got the djinn out of the bottle. He said himself: 'Other French governments have ruled with the support of perhaps one million of the educated masses; I have called in the other twenty-nine million.' This determined his policy. Napoleon I did great things and then sought to present them in a striking way; Napoleon III looked for things that would appear striking and only then dressed them up as important. He deceived everyone, including himself. He could be an idealist free trader with Richard Cobden; a respectable sovereign with Queen Victoria; an unscrupulous schemer when he was with Bismarck. But there was also the myth that he had created for himself and which took in even him. He really saw himself as the all-wise dictator, the Caesar who would reconcile all the classes in France and would remake the map of Europe. 'When a man of my name is in power, he must do great things.' He thrashed about like a lion in a cage, convinced that it ought to be ranging the jungle; always looking for great things to do, never finding them. He was no lion; he would have made an agreeable, though untrustworthy, domestic cat.

Great men in public life love power. That is what stamps them. They fight to get it and they use it ruthlessly when it is in their hands. Louis Napoleon would not pass this test of greatness. He loved conspiracy: the process of intrigue by which he moved towards power or the endless plans for using it. But he hated the action which threatened to follow these plans. For instance, the *coup d'état* of 2 December 1851 had been planned months before and put off at least twice. When it came to the point, Louis Napoleon hesitated again and might have put it off once more, had not the politicians of the assembly forced his hands, by beginning to make plans against him. And that, he thought, was unfair as well as being dangerous: like other conspirators, he claimed a monopoly in dishonesty.

The famous meeting at Plombières was a perfect example of his methods: the secret messages through somebody else's doctor; Cavour's trip to Plombières under a false name; the long discussions which left nothing on paper. The two men redrew the map of Italy in a few bold strokes; war and peace, and the future destinies of a nation, were settled between the puffs of a cigarette. Napoleon was roused only when they turned to discuss the trick with which they could provoke war; the conspirator's device was the thing that won his interest and held it for hour after hour. Cavour displayed all his gifts in devising schemes to lure Austria into the war that was to be her ruin; and Napoleon was delighted. It was very different when the time came to put the plans into action. Then Napoleon was all for delay, as fertile in excuses as he had once been in plans, and resentful when Cavour held him to his bargain. Six weeks before the war for the liberation of Italy broke out, he told Cavour that the war would have to be postponed for at least a year; and then no doubt he would have been for further delay. 'You should know how to wait as I do.' But his waiting had no purpose. He preferred to dream rather than to act; to make great plans, not to carry them out. He was a procrastinating adventurer; more of a scoundrel in his thoughts than in his deeds.

It was the same when Bismarck discussed the future of Germany with him at Biarritz in 1865. Napoleon supplied the keynote of the talks: 'We must not make events; we must let them happen.' Imagine a man who has lived by robbing banks saying: 'We must not blow open the safe; we must wait for it to fall open.' Bismarck is often credited with having tricked Napoleon at Biarritz: he got permission to go ahead with his plans for defeating Austria, yet promised Napoleon nothing in return. There was no trickery in this; it was what Napoleon wanted. But, again, not for the sophisticated reason so often given. He did not avoid formulating his demands for German territory for fear that Bismarck would think them too great and give up war against Austria. It was his old line of waiting. He did not know what to demand; he only knew how to wait, or so he thought. The conversations at Biarritz suited him even better than the bargain at Plombières. With Cavour he had had to commit himself to action, however grudgingly; with Bismarck he committed himself only to inaction, a course of policy which he meant to follow in any case. Bismarck was to provide the action; and Napoleon was somehow to profit from it. He was like a man who haunts the gambling-rooms in the belief that, if he encourages others to bet, he will one day draw a great prize.

The twenty years when Louis Napoleon ruled France were a period of great creative activity in every country of Europe. The steam engine and the railway spread across the Continent. In France, too, the Second Empire promised energy and creation; yet it was in these twenty years that France lost the leadership of Europe in politics, in economics, in culture. The Second Empire claimed to be Wagner and turned out to be Offenbach – a frivolous echo of the past, not an inspiration for the future. It was the bastard of the great Napoleon – in name, in policy, even in men. It was said at the time that, though Louis Napoleon was not the son of his father, everyone else at Court was the son of his mother. Morny was his illegitimate half-brother; Walewski the illegitimate son of Napoleon I. Its emotions were sham, also. This system which claimed to care for the masses was run by the most dishonest politicians who have ever governed France. All of them, even Napoleon himself, were convinced that the Empire would not last; and they plundered France while the opportunity lasted. Under the July monarchy Guizot had said to the French middle classes: 'Get rich.' The statesmen of the Second Empire applied this doctrine.

In foreign affairs there was the same contradiction between the phrases and the reality. Napoleon liked to believe that his empire had sprung from the resentment which every Frenchman felt against the settlement of Europe made at Vienna in 1815 after the defeat of his uncle. In reality, this settlement had given France a position of primacy in Europe and had made her secure: if it was changed, France was bound to suffer. Hence Napoleon was constantly driven forward; and as constantly shrank from the results. In Sorel's words: 'His name was his fortune and his undoing. His origins condemned him to success.' Any other Frenchman might have defended the settlement of 1815; a Napoleon could not. Louis Napoleon believed that nationalism was the winning cause in Europe; and he meant to associate himself with its success. Despite his inaction, he could never support conservatism when it came to the point; and he tried to satisfy German and Italian nationalism without injuring France. In the outcome, he failed on both counts. He estranged Italy by holding on to Rome; he tried to make German unity stop at the Main; and by his very inaction took the decisive steps which ended the career of France as the Great Power of Europe.

Yet, with all his cunning, there was great good will. He really cared for Italy; he sympathized with Germany, or at any rate with German romanticism. He dreamt always of a Europe in which there would be 'a peaceful redress of grievances'; and he was the first European statesman in a responsible position to put forward plans for general disarmament. But, of course, they were plans in which the preponderance of France had to be recognized and made permanent. Disarmament, as always, seemed most attractive to the power that was on the decline.

Though he ruined France as a great power, he made France what she still is – as far as looks go. The Paris which tourists admire, the Paris of the opera and the great boulevards, is the creation of Napoleon III. Like every adventurer who has arrived, Napoleon wanted something solid to show, something that would assert his permanence against the facts. And the Paris of Napoleon III has not done badly – better, at any rate, than the Berlin of Hitler or the Rome of Mussolini. Yet even this was a fraud. Its real purpose was to make long, wide streets so that a revolt could be put down easily, hardly a gesture of confidence towards the twenty-nine million. And having tricked others, Napoleon here misled himself. When his empire fell, there was no whiff of grapeshot; not a shot was fired. The boulevards had failed of their purpose.

We imagine nowadays – and even take pride in the thought – that dictators, swindling their way to power and keeping power by a succession of tricks, are a disease peculiar to the twentieth century. But there is nothing new in Hitler or Mussolini: Louis Napoleon had all their cards up his sleeve, except, perhaps, their brutality. He did not need a Nietzsche to put him beyond good and evil; he had arrived at the idea for himself. Certainly he owed his success to the same historic causes. The great French Revolution destroyed the history of France before going on to destroy the history of Europe. Destroy tradition; destroy the political values on which a community has been built up, and only class war remains.

Marx did not discover this class war. He observed it in France and then generalized it as a formula for the future. That is the only way of the prophet: to foretell as the future what has already happened. Marx's prophecy has come off better than most, but in one vital point he went wrong. He supposed that the class war would be fought to a finish, that one side would win. And, since the *bourgeoisie* could not exterminate the proletariat, the proletariat would exterminate the *bourgeoisie*. There has been a different outcome: someone has slipped in between, played off one class against the other and exploited both. This, not his ragbag of ideas, was the great historical innovation of Louis Napoleon. He appealed to the fears of the middle classes when he made the *coup d'état* and presented himself as 'the Guardian of Order'. But he was also, in his muddled way, a socialist; he did more for the French working classes than any other French government before or since; and when he died a trade-union representative was the only man to come from France to his funeral.

But there was also another France, the France that had been created by the Great Revolution after what had been destroyed: the France that cared for liberty and the Rights of Man. This made the great difference between Louis Napoleon and his twentieth-century successors. The generals and civil servants and business men of Germany no doubt thought Hitler a barbarian; but once he had gained power, they licked his boots. The writers and political leaders of France never forgave Napoleon for the trickery and violence by which he had come to power. They turned their backs on him and condemned him to rely on his fellow-gangsters. It is not surprising that many Frenchmen supported Napoleon, especially in his hour of success; what is surprising and honourable is that so many Frenchmen opposed him from beginning to end. It was easy to be against Napoleon when he turned out to be the man of Sedan. It was his doom that he was branded from the start, and branded in history, as the man of December.

7

CRIMEA: THE WAR THAT WOULD NOT BOIL

JOHN BRIGHT, with ponderous Victorian wit, called the Crimean War 'a crime'; most historians have presented it as a bewildering series of diplomatic and military blunders. With the experience of the last few years to enlighten us, we should do better: we know that the diplomatic tangles since 1945, which may seem bewildering to the future historian, conceal the reality of 'the cold war'. The Crimean War was the cold war in an earlier phase. Two world systems, mutually uncomprehending, lurched against each other, each convinced of its defensive good faith. The struggle between them was fought in a ragged way at the edges. Both sides shrank from the head-on collision which would have produced a war to remake the world – Russia from lack of strength, the Western Powers from lack of conviction. Though the Crimean War seemed indecisive, great decisions followed from it. Without it neither Germany nor Italy could have been united; without it Europe would never have known 'the liberal era', that halcyon age which ended in 1914 and which, for centuries to come, men will regard as 'normal times', just as the barbarians looked back to the peace and security of Augustan Rome.

The Crimean War is often treated in England as a war over the Eastern Question, a war to secure the route to India, and thus a rehearsal for Disraeli's 'peace with honour' campaign in 1878. This is to err both in time and place. The war had little or nothing to do with the security of India. The Suez Canal was not built; the overland route catered for a few travellers in a hurry; for that matter Russia's land-route to India was still in the future. The Crimean War was fought for essentially European considerations – against Russia rather than in favour of Turkey. It was fought for the sake of the Balance of Power and for 'the liberties of Europe'; more positively, it aimed to substitute diplomacy by agreement, the Concert of Europe, for the settlement of affairs at the dictation of a single Great Power. Disraeli was a consistent disciple of Metternich when he criticized the Crimean War and yet opposed Russia in 1878: the Crimean War had general altruistic motives, the crisis of 1878 was caused solely by the defence of Imperial interests. In other words, 1878 was a Tory affair; the Crimean War, with all its muddle, sprang from Whig principles, the last fling of a dying party.

British policy in the Near East had not been consistently anti-Russian before the Crimean War, though it became so afterwards. Canning, for instance, co-operated with Russia throughout the Greek war of independence; and though Palmerston thought of working with France against Russia in the Near East in 1833, he ended up by working with Russia against France in 1839 and 1840. Throughout the eighteen-forties, and indeed until the beginning of 1853, British suspicions were turned against France both at Constantinople and in Egypt; and Great Britain and Russia often made common cause in resisting French encroachment. Nor can there be any easy dividing line in their attitude to the Ottoman Empire, as though Russia wanted to break it up and Great Britain wished to preserve it. Both Powers found it a convenience; and both Powers doubted its capacity to survive. Their difference was in timing, not in judgement of the situation.

The British attitude to Russia was very different when it came to Europe; hence the Crimean War makes sense only with a European background. Ever since 1815 British statesmen had been obsessed with the thought that, if France ceased to dominate Europe, Russia would take her place; as Napoleon had said, in fifty years all Europe would be either Republican or Cossack. Hence Castlereagh's rather absurd alliance with France and Austria in January 1815; hence Canning's calling in of a New World to redress the balance of the Old (though the New World did not respond to his invitation); hence Palmerston's welcome to the July monarchy in France and his Quadruple Alliance with Spain and Portugal as well in 1834. This was one side of British policy: to maintain France as a Great Power and yet to keep her harmless – just strong enough to check Russia's domination without reviving the same taste in herself. The other element in British policy was to develop the independence of Central Europe, so that it could hold its own against both Cossacks and Republicans without constant alarms or war. This was what was meant by the favourite description of Prussia and Austria as Great Britain's 'natural allies': they were serving the purposes of British policy without any effort on the British side. Curiously enough, Metternich and Palmerston, who were supposed to hate each other so much, were pursuing the same aims and served each other's needs. So long as the 'Metternich system' worked, Central Europe was independent of both France and Russia; and the Balance of Power in Europe freed Great Britain from European commitments.

The revolutions of 1848 ended this finely drawn policy. The fall of Metternich was a disaster to the British position; and it was little consolation to make out that he had fallen because of his refusal to take British advice. The revolutions of 1848 seemed to make France more powerful than before; to weaken Prussia; and to threaten Austria with elimination from the ranks of the Great Powers. Europe would become either Republican or Cossack. Though this bitter saying was not at once fulfilled, it seemed at most postponed. On the one side, France emerged from the revolutionary year under the rule of a new Bonaparte, inescapably committed to the overthrow of the treaties of 1815 and almost as much to the restoration of French domination in Europe. On the other, the revolutions in Central Europe – in Germany, in Italy and in Hungary – were defeated only with Russian backing; so far as Hungary went, only with Russian military aid. By 1850, Francis Joseph of Austria and Frederick William IV of Prussia seemed to be Russian dependants, subservient not only from ideological similarity, but from their inability to hold their monarchical power except with Russian support. The Holy Alliance was the Cominform of Kings.

The defeat of the revolutions of 1848 with Russian aid had a profound effect on British public opinion. Before 1848 fear of Russia had been a diplomat's calculation; there had been no 'Russian bogey'. After 1848 British liberals picked up the habit of continental radicals and began to regard Russia as the tyrant of Europe. War against Russia was regarded as the preliminary to any radical success elsewhere. The old diplomatic apprehension of Russia now seemed tepid and half-hearted. In radical circles, for instance, it was common doctrine that Palmerston was in

Russian pay; the proof was found in his reluctance to launch the great European 'war of liberation'. This theory can be found worked out in the essays which Karl Marx wrote on *The Eastern Question*; he learnt it from the pro-Turk lunatic, Urquhart. Except among radicals and exiles, fear of France still predominated in England until the spring of 1853. Indeed, belief that the British were more apprehensive about Belgium than about Turkey was one of the factors which led Tsar Nicholas to act so carelessly and so provocatively in May 1853, when the war-crisis first began to stir.

There was, of course, another and more obvious cause of Russian confidence. A coalition ministry had been formed in England at the end of 1852 under Lord Aberdeen; and Aberdeen, though a free trader, was an old-fashioned Tory. He had no sympathy with radical hostility to Russia; great confidence in the Tsar's good faith; and great distrust of Napoleon III. If Aberdeen had had his way there would have been no Crimean War. Russia would have strengthened her position in Turkey, consolidated her reactionary hold over Europe; and Great Britain would have consoled herself by taking Egypt. This would have been a reasonable, though not an idealistic, solution; hence the later regrets of Lord Salisbury, a reasonable man without ideals, that it was not adopted. It could only have been adopted by a purely Tory cabinet; and from such a cabinet Aberdeen was barred by his free-trade doctrines. Instead, he was saddled with Whig colleagues, Palmerston and Russell, who were both in their way friendly to France and who both, without yet distrusting the Tsar, wished to draw a sharp line against any new Russian advance. Russell had been Prime Minister; Palmerston was going to be. They were both pretty clear that a firm line against Russia would be a winning card in the game for public favour which they were playing against each other. Here too, if Palmerston and Russell had had their way, there would have been no war. The Tsar would have stepped aside from the Eastern Question before his prestige was involved and waited for a more favourable opportunity. Perhaps even, as we go on dreaming nowadays, Russian despotism would have saved everyone the trouble of a war by crumbling from within. It was this mixture of conciliation always too grudging and firmness always too late which, on the British side, produced the Crimean War.

There was, however, another principal in the war, one often forgotten in British and even in Russian accounts. Neither the Tsar nor the British Government wanted war; Napoleon III did. Not necessarily the Crimean War as it worked itself out, but a war which would disrupt the existing structure of Europe. Thus Great Britain became involved in war in order to preserve the Balance of Power and to defend the liberties of Europe; Napoleon III pushed into war in order to overthrow the Balance of Power and to clear the way for French domination. After all, it is a simple calculation that if the allies of a Great War fall out the defeated party will come into his own. In 1853 the calculation was made in Paris; now it is made in every German village. The Crimean War was not a good war from Napoleon III's point of view; a war in Poland, in Italy, or on the Rhine, would have been much better. But it was better than no war at all. On the other hand, Napoleon III had learnt from his uncle's failure – had learnt, that is, in the scrappy, illogical way, in which men use the past to prop up their own prejudices. Napoleon III supposed, though wrongly, that his uncle's great mistake had been to quarrel with England; his key to success was therefore to be the British alliance, and the Crimean War was welcome to him in that it gave him this alliance. In the long run, however, Napoleon III did no better with the British alliance than his uncle had done without it – unless it is better to die in Chislehurst than at St Helena.

By the summer of 1853 France, Russia and Great Britain were all tugging themselves into war in their different ways. The Tsar, though with no deep-laid plans for encroaching on Turkey, had grown too confident; regarding Prussia and Austria as his satellites, he supposed that he could display his prestige at Constantinople without risk. When this proved mistaken, he – like the Russians generally when they are challenged – felt genuinely threatened with aggression; and in Russian eyes the Crimean War was a defensive war. The British Government, though also without deep-laid plans, would not allow the Tsar's claims and, in their anxiety to win the alliance of France, often acted more firmly than Napoleon III expected or desired. Napoleon, on his side, wanted to shake Russia's prestige and to build up his own;

but most of all, he wanted to keep in step with the British, who, with the same motive, constantly quickened the pace until the two fleets tumbled into the Black Sea more to prove mutual good faith and enthusiasm as allies than to oppose Russia. As a matter of fact, when the British and French fleets entered the Black Sea at the end of 1853, the Crimean War, not yet started, had already been won so far as the original causes of war, or excuses for it, were concerned. That is, the Tsar was quite prepared to drop his immediate claims on Turkey, once it became clear that England and France intended to resist them. This did not satisfy the western allies. With their public opinion roused and their resources mobilized, what they wanted was a decision, not merely the withdrawal of the present Russian demands. The problem of the Crimean War, never solved, lay here. The Russians had dropped their demands because the British and French fleets had entered the Black Sea. How could the renewal of these demands be prevented when the British and French fleets went away again?

The problem had two sides, military and diplomatic. The military problem was, how to get at the Russians, in order to inflict on them the defeat which would make them accept the terms needed for Europe's security? The diplomatic problem was, what were the terms which should be imposed on the Russians when they were defeated? The two problems were mixed up throughout the war. Sometimes the allies tried to devise terms which would make a defeat of the Russians unnecessary; sometimes they dreamt of a defeat so decisive as to spare them the trouble of devising terms. At bottom the problem was insoluble. The Western Powers could not alone inflict on Russia a decisive and lasting defeat; nor, even were she defeated, could they devise terms which would ensure against a renewal of her expansion. It would have been a different matter if Austria and Prussia, the states of Central Europe, could have been drawn into the war. Hence the real decision of the Crimean War came from the two Germanic powers when they decided to stay out of it. Austria and Prussia were 'the third force'. Their persistence in this line of policy both caused the Crimean War and led to its being indecisive. Until the beginning of 1854 the Tsar had regarded them as reliable satellite states, dependent on his support. As soon, however, as he depended on their support, they ceased to be satellites.

He could no longer keep France out of the Near East by a threat from Prussia on the Rhine and from Austria in Italy.

The Western Powers imagined that 'the third force' had come over to their side and that a full-scale defeat of Russia was in sight. Certainly a coalition of all the Great Powers of Europe against Russia would have excluded her from Europe, might even have destroyed her as a Great Power. Poland would have been restored, Turkey secured; Louis Napoleon would have become master of Europe. This was an outcome more unwelcome to Prussia and Austria even than Russian domination of Turkey. Whereas the Western Powers wanted a decision, the Central Powers wanted no decision; and they got their way. Prussia had the great advantage that she was indifferent to the affairs of the Near East, though concerned with the general European balance. Hence her neutrality was genuinely impartial. Her only aim, which seemed craven enough, was to ensure that no fighting took place on Prussian soil. This no doubt benefited Russia and won her gratitude; but since Prussia did not promise anything to the Western Powers, she did not disappoint them either. When the war ended, Prussia was not at first invited to the Peace Congress at Paris. This seemed a humiliation; later events showed the enormous gains to be won from keeping out of other people's quarrels. Any contemporary statesman who wishes to reap the advantages of the third course should study the policy of Prussia during the Crimean War.

Austrian policy is equally instructive: it shows the disadvantages of a neutrality which offends both sides. Whereas Prussia was neutral from indifference, Austria was neutral from being too deeply committed. She had her own grounds for opposing Russia. Russia's control of the mouth of the Danube, where her troops had established themselves in 1853, cut one of Austria's main economic arteries with the outer world. Thus the practical aim of Austrian policy was to get Russia out of Rumania and to get herself in. But there were complicating factors. If Austria entered the war on the side of the Western Powers, she would bear the brunt of the fighting; worse, an allied victory, expelling Russia from Europe, would make Napoleon III supreme and thus clear the way for the national principle. Austria would win Rumania at too high a price if she lost her

Italian lands, the symbol of her Imperial greatness. Yet, apart from her anxiety about Rumania, Austria dared not favour Russia nor even keep a resolute neutrality, for fear that Napoleon III would explode Italy against her. As a result Austria followed the worst of all policies. She offended the Tsar by refusing to promise a secure neutrality; she offended the Western Powers by refusing to go to war. She pressed her alliance on England and France in order to conciliate them; she failed to operate it and left them more estranged than before. Neutrality, like virtue, has its merits if maintained inviolate; it can also be sold for a high price. The one impossible thing is to be up for auction and to remain virtuous at the same time.

The first stage of the Crimean War was the stage when the Western Powers imagined that 'the third force' could be drawn into the war and a real decision thus produced. This stage lasted until the summer of 1854, by which time Prussian neutrality was certain and Austrian belligerence uncertain. The Crimean War, in the strict sense of the term, followed – the war with all its blunders and muddles which perplexed contemporaries and baffled posterity. Yet the confusion had a simple cause – how could the allies get at Russia when the great neutral buffer of Central Europe was interposed between them? The allies had hoped that the Russians would obligingly remain in Rumania in order that they might be defeated there; instead the Russians withdrew from Rumania in July 1854. In their perplexity the allies decided on Sebastopol, the Russian naval base in the Crimea, which was supposed to be vulnerable to an amphibious operation. As a matter of fact, it took nearly a year's fighting and the mobilization of armies on a continental scale for this amphibious operation to succeed.

It takes two to make a war. Russian strength in the Near East lay in her proximity; her strength in the European balance lay in her army. Her naval power in the Black Sea was a secondary affair; and it could always be checked if the British and French fleets, or even the British fleet alone, passed the Straits. If the Russians had abandoned Sebastopol and sealed off the Crimea, the western allies would have scored a success of prestige; but Russia would have been no weaker than before. The allies would have cruised undisturbed in the Black Sea until their position became ridiculous; they would then have retired, and Russia's pressure on Turkey could have been resumed. But autocratic monarchies also have their prestige. The Tsar did not grasp that if the allies failed to defeat him, he had won; whereas, whatever efforts he made at Sebastopol, he could not defeat the allies. Russia's military strength lies in withdrawal; but this has always to be imposed upon her by her enemies, instead of being a conscious choice. Alexander I fought Napoleon at Austerlitz and even wanted to fight on the frontier in 1812; Stalin was only saved from catastrophe on the frontier in 1941 by being caught unprepared. In the Crimean War, the Tsar obligingly provided the maritime powers with the battlefield which they could never have found for themselves. Instead of being withdrawn, the Russian armies in Sebastopol were reinforced; and Russia exhausted herself for the sake of the maritime powers. The allies lamented that they had not taken Sebastopol by a *coup de main* when they landed in 1854; if they had, there would have been no Crimean War and nothing would have been achieved at all. For the essence of war is not to take this point or that, but to destroy, or at least to weaken, the military strength of the enemy. This was accomplished by the year's fighting in front of Sebastopol. The Russian armies were greatly weakened; Russia's military prestige lessened; most of all, Russia's economic resources were intolerably strained. It took Russia a generation to recover from the effort of the Crimean War; and in this generation Europe was remade without Russian interference.

The defeat of the Russian armies, and the weakening of Russian power, were the real result of the Crimean War; but this was a result too vague to satisfy the victorious allies. Their victory had to be translated into a treaty of peace; yet they had no clear idea what this treaty should contain. As on other occasions, the Western Powers knew what they were fighting against, not what they were fighting for. They were fighting against Russia; and their real wish was that Russia should cease to exist or – what amounts to the same thing – become a modest and satisfied member of an Anglo-French world. Napoleon III was prepared to accept the logic of this wish. When Sebastopol fell, he proposed to the British Government a programme which would sweep Russia from Europe and destroy her as a Great Power – the programme of full national reconstruction, especially of Poland, which would incidentally make France supreme in Europe. The British Government had the exactly opposite aim: they had wished to destroy Russian supremacy in Europe without putting French supremacy in its place. Yet on the other hand they were the more eager of the two to continue the war until a 'decision' had been reached. A characteristic compromise followed. Each accepted the other's negative: the war was brought to an end, without any positive war-aims being drawn up.

This is not to say that the Crimean War accomplished nothing, or even that the Treaty of Paris contained nothing of moment. Apart from the weakening of Russian power, which could not be put into a treaty, the Crimean War had two achievements, one which lasted for nearly eighty years, the other for fifteen years. The more permanent outcome, as things go in international affairs, was the independence of Rumania, freeing the mouths of the Danube from either Russian or Austrian control. The Russian army had withdrawn in July 1854; the Austrian army had taken its place, and the Austrians had hoped to annex Rumania. But they would not pay the French price, which was to give up Italy; therefore they had to withdraw in their turn, and Rumania became a genuinely independent state, a buffer between Russian interests and those of Central Europe, until the time of Stalin and Hitler.

The more prized achievement of the treaty of Paris was the 'neutralization' of the Black Sea. Russia was forbidden to maintain a fleet in the Black Sea, or to rebuild her naval arsenals; it is true that the same restrictions were imposed on Turkey, but since the Turks could maintain a fleet in the Sea of Marmora they could always dominate the Black Sea in time of war. The neutralization clauses of the Treaty of Paris were a rehearsal for the demilitarization of the Rhineland in the Treaty of Versailles, and equally futile. Either Russia accepted them because she feared England and France; in that case she would repudiate them when she ceased to fear England or France. Alternatively Russia accepted them because she had changed her ways and given up aggression against Turkey; in that case they were unnecessary. The British and French would not keep their fleets in the Black Sea indefinitely; they were not even sure that they would remain indefinitely on good terms. Hence they tried to make the Russians promise that they would continue to behave as though the allied fleets were still in the Black Sea when in fact they had been long withdrawn. A treaty of peace can only define the conditions of the present; it cannot bind the future. This the Russians demonstrated fifteen years later, when they repudiated the Black Sea clauses of the Treaty of Paris. The British doctrine of the sanctity of treaties was upheld only by the pious pretence of a conference in London, at which the Powers, to no one's surprise, confirmed what Russia had already done. The neutralization clauses taught a lesson which was ignored in 1919: if you wish to perpetuate a military victory, you must perpetuate the balance of forces which produced that victory.

The Crimean War was, in short, a war that did not come off, a war without a decision. But that was itself the decision. Though Russian strength was not broken, Russian influence in Europe was lessened. Though French prestige was increased, France did not become dominant in Europe. Napoleon III thought he had freed his hands in order to remodel Italy and Germany to his own taste; it turned out that Italy and Germany had freed their own hands to remodel themselves against him. Cavour and Bismarck, not Napoleon III, were the real victors of the Crimean War. If there were a moral to be drawn from the Crimean War which might apply to the present, it would be this: in a war between Russia and the west, it is the Powers which keep out who will be the real gainers. Last time it gave Prussia mastery of Germany.

For the British, the Crimean War, though superficially inconclusive, was less of a disappointment than it was to Napoleon III. They had set out to lessen Russian power; and they had succeeded. Later on, they imagined that they had intended to give Turkey the chance of reforming herself; and were correspondingly embittered when no reform followed. Nevertheless, the Crimean War brought real gains to the British. The Balance of Power in Europe was strengthened, not overthrown; and Great Britain did not need to intervene in a continental war for sixty years thereafter. Two generations of peace are something to be thankful for; it is more than we have had in our lifetime.

8

FRANCIS JOSEPH:
THE LAST AGE OF THE HABSBURGS

On 2 December 1848, Francis Joseph became Emperor of Austria. He was to reign for almost sixty-eight years, the longest effective reign of modern times. His life spanned the epochs of history. Metternich had ceased to be Imperial Chancellor less than nine months before his accession; two years after his death Austria-Hungary disintegrated into national States. When he was born, Napoleon's son, the King of Rome, was living in Vienna as an Austrian archduke; when he died Adolf Hitler, still an Austrian subject, was serving in the German Army. His reign opened in revolution and closed in war.

Francis Joseph himself fought two wars: in the first he lost his Italian territories; in the second he lost the hegemony of Germany. He started a third war and did not live to see its end; this end was the loss of everything. He won no wars; he lost more territory than he gained. His success was in surviving at all. He was a symbol of rigidity and of resistance, if not of life, in an Imperial organization which, while it had lost creative power, refused to break in pieces. He called himself 'the last monarch of the old school' and imagined himself at one with Charles V or Louis XIV. Their pride rested on unquestioning self-confidence; his was always conscious of the challenge of 'the revolution'. He represented traditional beliefs and institutions, when these had been forced on to the defensive; like them he lacked faith even in himself. He always expected failure and disappointment, and he always got them.

The manner of his accession set the pattern for his reign. The Court was at the little Moravian town of Olomouc, in refuge from the Vienna revolution of October 1848. The revolution had been crushed, and the counter-revolutionary Prime Minister, Felix Schwarzenberg, wanted to show by a striking gesture that a new era of ruthless power had opened. The mild, half-witted Emperor Ferdinand was therefore pushed aside in favour of his nephew

Francis Joseph, the young pupil of clericalist soldiers. The actual abdication was hurried through in a room of the archbishop's palace before a few Court officials. No one had had time or opportunity to look up the precedents, and the only ceremony was a blessing of Ferdinand on his nephew. Thus Francis Joseph, the personification of monarchical right, ascended his throne in a hole-and-corner manner; this august 'crowned head' reigned for nineteen years without any kind of coronation – and was then only crowned King of Hungary. For though the House of Habsburg could rightly claim to be the most historic dynasty in Europe, Hungary was the only part of the Habsburg Empire with a living tradition; yet this tradition was largely of resistance against the Habsburg rulers.

When Francis Joseph took over the throne he exclaimed: 'Farewell, my youth!' It was his only human remark. From the first he turned himself into an institution. He sacrificed everything for the sake of the dynasty, and he expected others to sacrifice everything too. Though he had a sincere love for his wife, Elizabeth, the most beautiful woman of her age, he would not extenuate the harsh ritual of Court life even for her. Elizabeth's spirit would not be stifled, and she left him, after providing Catherine Schratt, the Emperor's mistress for more than thirty years and the only human being who came into contact with him and remained human. Elizabeth wandered restlessly across Europe from Corfu to Ireland until she was assassinated by an anarchist on a Lake of Geneva steamer. Rudolph, Francis Joseph's only son, was also driven into wild courses by the repressive Court life and committed suicide at the end of a somewhat sordid romance. Francis Ferdinand, the Emperor's nephew and next heir, married morganatically outside the permitted degrees of royalty. When he and his wife were assassinated at Sarajevo in 1914 the first thought of Francis Joseph was that dynastic purity had been saved: 'A higher power has reasserted the rules that I was unable to maintain.'

Francis Joseph had no tastes and no friends. Though Vienna was largely built in his reign he set no mark on it; the Imperial buildings are heavy and lifeless. He did nothing to encourage the arts, not even the art of Johann Strauss or of Lehar. Viennese culture, real though frivolous, had no contact with this conscientious worker at his bureaucratic task. His Ministers experienced even more than the usual 'thanks of the House of Habsburg'. He used them, thrust them forward into conflict, and then, on an impulse or a rumour of failure, would fling them aside. Taaffe, Prime Minister of Austria for fourteen years and the Emperor's boyhood companion, was thus dismissed without explanation or thanks in 1893, and so, in 1906, was Beck, Chief of Staff for thirty years. Francis Joseph ruled without imagination and without winning the hearts of men. After he had been reconciled with the Hungarians and presumably wished to conciliate them he decorated the royal palace at Budapest with scenes of his victories over the Hungarians in 1849. His only thought was of dynastic power. Yet, though rigid in his dynastic aims, he was ready to try any means of sustaining his Empire. He began with military dictatorship and sometimes reverted to it. Taught by defeat, he made concessions to all in turn; the Compromise of 1867 gave Hungary internal independence, and in the same year Austria received a liberal Constitution. Later he sought to win over the Czechs, and finally, in 1907, forced universal suffrage through the Austrian Parliament in order to be able to play off the masses against the middle-class politicians in a vast game of *rouge et noir*. His greatest hatred was for 'liberalism' – the attempt to limit the prerogatives of the Crown. Against this liberalism he would call on any ally and would even invoke the rival nationalisms which were tearing his Empire to pieces.

Clever writers in Vienna tried for more than a century to invent an Austrian 'mission'. This 'mission' was supposed to be the security which the Empire gave to fifty million people, in which they could prosper and develop their cultural life. In the twentieth century this 'mission' took on a predominantly economic tone, and Austria was praised as a great 'Free Trade area'. In truth, the mission was a device by which Hungarian landowners and German capitalists grew rich from the labour of the lesser peoples. It was these two groups whom Francis Joseph took unwillingly into partnership. In his own mind Francis Joseph cared for none of these 'missions'. He did not regard the dynasty as the servant of the Austrian peoples; it was for them to be the servants of the dynasty and to sustain its military greatness. Viennese intellectuals complained that Francis Joseph did not follow the example of Joseph II, the 'people's Emperor'. To do this he would have had to lead peasants against their lords and subject peoples, Slav and Rumanian, against the Germans and Magyars, the two privileged nationalities. Such a course was outside dynastic imagining. Francis Joseph was fated to end his reign as a German auxiliary; the only 'mission' he left to his successor was to be a German agent – or to disappear.

9

CAVOUR AND GARIBALDI

IT used to be the fashion to contrast the unification of Germany and of Italy. In Italy idealism; in Germany *realpolitik*. In Italy the spread of parliamentary liberalism; in Germany the triumph of the Prussian army. Bismarck appeared always in a general's tunic, ruthless, unscrupulous, a master of force and dishonesty. Cavour was the civilian statesman, relying on parliamentary speeches for his success. The failure of the German radicals was lamented; there were few to regret the failure of Mazzini or Garibaldi. They were impractical dreamers who did not understand the greatness of Cavour; and it was a good thing for Italy when they were shipped off, Garibaldi to Caprera, Mazzini back to exile in London. More recently, Cavour has had a bad press. His private correspondence has at last been published (it is now almost complete); and his own words have shown him to be much more like Bismarck, much less like Gladstone, than used to be supposed. He wielded the weapons of traditional diplomacy with incomparable skill, but also with incomparable lack of principle; and Metternich turns out to have been his exemplar as well as his enemy.

Cavour did not care much about the unification of Italy, or at any rate ranked it low in his scale of values. Himself with little national feeling, preferring to speak and write in French, his deepest concern was for moderate liberalism. He wanted a free press, free trade, and a parliament based on limited suffrage, first in Piedmont and then perhaps in northern Italy. But he did not regard the unification of the whole peninsula as a noble idea or believe that it would of itself bring about a moral regeneration. He had nothing but contempt for idealists like Mazzini and could have said with Bismarck: 'The great questions of our day will not be settled by speeches and majority resolutions but by blood and iron'. What he lacked in blood and iron he made up for in deceit. The Italian question was for him a problem in European diplomacy, not a matter of national sentiment. He hardly thought about the Italian people except to fear them. His thoughts were concentrated on Napoleon III. And the later observer must confess that the unification of Italy might well have been impossible, unless Napoleon III had been brought in to defeat Austria in 1859. After all, the victory of nationalism was not inevitable. Poland had to wait until the twentieth century, despite a much stronger national sentiment; the Ukraine waits to the present day.

We still need a history of Italian unification from the European angle. Professor Valsecchi of Milan is writing it; but so far he has only got to the early days of the Crimean war. Meanwhile, Mr Mack Smith has given us a new version of the story at a later stage[1] – the stage of 1860, when Lombardy and central Italy had been united to Piedmont, but when the Two Sicilies and the Papal States (to say nothing of Venetia) had still to be liberated. This was the moment of greatest contrast between Cavour's reliance on diplomacy and the faith of the radicals in their own ideals. Cavour still feared the intervention of 'the Holy Alliance', still pinned his calculations to the favour of Napoleon. Garibaldi believed that the entire peninsula could be brought together by a spontaneous outburst of national enthusiasm; and he thought the prize worth any risk. He was determined to act somewhere – against Austria in Venetia, against Rome despite its French garrison, or, when Sicily rebelled, against the Bourbon kingdom of the Two Sicilies. It used to be held that Cavour secretly encouraged Garibaldi and was in alliance with him. The truth is less creditable. He pushed Garibaldi off to Sicily in order to get him out of the way and in the hope that failure would ruin the radicals once and for all. Instead, Garibaldi succeeded beyond his wildest dreams; and Cavour had to sweep up the pieces of a policy in ruins.

Mr Mack Smith has produced a surprising book to come out of Cambridge. He acknowledges his debt to Professor Butterfield; and one would have expected praise of Cavour and condemnation of Garibaldi from a member of this neo-Machiavellian group. But not at all. With brilliant, though well-founded, perversity, Mr Mack Smith turns things upside down. It is Garibaldi who was the realist, arriving at the right conclusions by instinct, and

1. *Cavour and Garibaldi 1860. A Study in Political Conflict.* By D. Mack Smith.

Cavour who was the dogmatic muddler. Mr Mack Smith is perhaps a little unfair to Cavour. As things turned out, Italy in 1860 was able 'to do it herself', as she had mistakenly boasted she would in 1848; and Europe counted for little. But this could not have been foreseen when the Thousand sailed. Napoleon III still seemed to dominate Europe, his decline lay far in the future; and Cavour was not the only man to fear the might of France. Moreover he was right on one essential point, the question of Rome. Rome dominated the Italian problem; and even Garibaldi went to Sicily principally in order to reach Rome by the back door. Yet the French could be got out of Rome only by diplomacy, not by force; and for the sake of Italy Garibaldi had to fail before he reached Rome, unless the Pope had already withdrawn – and the French along with him. Moreover, Mr Mack Smith underrates the danger that Austria, Prussia and Russia would come together in resistance to 'the revolution'. They nearly did when they met at Warsaw in October 1860; and they were prevented more by the diplomacy of Napoleon III (and hence indirectly of Cavour) than by Garibaldi's success in the south.

Still, by and large, the emphasis is put the right way. Cavour was blinded by his rigid hostility towards the radicals. He saw in them only 'the social peril', and was convinced that anarchy must follow their victory. His primary object was that Garibaldi should fail; only in the second place did he want Italy to be united. This view divided him not only from the radicals, but even from his king, Victor Emanuel, who was ready 'to become simple *monsu Savoia* and clap his hands at Mazzini's success if this sacrifice were necessary for the making of Italy'. Yet Cavour's own policy was more Utopian than that of any radical. He imagined that Italy could be brought into being solely by the moderate liberals – the most useless of all classes in a revolution. Ricasoli's ruthlessness made this policy work in central Italy; but in the south there was nothing between the aristocracy and the masses. The few middle-class lawyers there supported unification only in order to get the courts open again; they would not fight for it, and Garibaldi succeeded by rousing the masses. This was a social revolution against the landowners – a revolution which Garibaldi exploited for the national cause. He had no social programme, despite his emotional sympathy with the peasants and despite

Cavour's suspicions; and he allowed them to fall under the rule of a harsher, more rigid Piedmontese bureaucracy without ever understanding how he had betrayed them.

Cavour always suspected Garibaldi; Garibaldi never suspected Cavour. This is the central theme of the whole affair. Of course, Garibaldi disliked Cavour and resented his cession of Nice to Napoleon III; but he thought that, just as he had dropped his republicanism, Cavour would drop his hostility to the radicals for the sake of united Italy. If the radicals united Italy, this would certainly weaken Cavour and perhaps even lead to his fall; but again Garibaldi, being ready to make the greatest personal sacrifices on his side, could not understand that Cavour would not do the same. Cavour, like Bismarck, regarded himself as indispensable; when he proved unyielding on this, everyone had to give way to him in the last resort – and Italy paid the price. Garibaldi put Italy first; Cavour put himself first. Therefore Cavour was bound to win in the end, despite the great advantages which Garibaldi accumulated in Sicily and Naples.

For they were great advantages. The liberation of the Two Sicilies seems easy in retrospect; we almost fail to notice that it needed a leader of genius to accomplish it. European radicalism produced three great dictators – Kossuth in Hungary, Mazzini in Rome, Garibaldi in the Two Sicilies. Garibaldi was the least intellectual of the three, with few ideas and unable to formulate even these clearly. Yet he was easily the most successful. He evoked from the people and even from the politicians a personal devotion almost without parallel in modern history; again and again he chose the right course by instinct; and he showed himself the greatest general that Italy has ever produced. In the late summer of 1860 Sicily was a true radical paradise, radiating the hope – or perhaps the illusion – that every evil legacy of the past had been swept away. Cavour was not the serpent in this garden of Eden; Garibaldi's success had eclipsed him for the time being. The real trouble was that Garibaldi and the people of Sicily were at cross-purposes. They supposed that he had brought them freedom; he looked on Sicily only as the first halt on the road to Rome. Both alike resisted Cavour's plan for an immediate annexation of Sicily to the kingdom of Sardinia. But the Sicilians wanted permanent autonomy for their island; Garibaldi and his radical supporters wished to use Sicily as a base for further successes. Once Garibaldi had crossed to the mainland and carried all before him, he lost interest in Sicily; and it irritated him to have to return in order to settle its internal conflicts. Even in Naples, he listened impatiently to the republican arguments of Mazzini and the federalist schemes of Cataneo. The march on Rome was the only thing that interested him.

The resistance of the Neapolitan army on the Volturno gave Cavour his chance. He was able to stop Garibaldi just in time. He acted no doubt cynically and basely, discrediting Garibaldi unjustifiably with the king and killing the idealism of the radical movement. But there was something wrong with a radicalism which could think only of further battles. The radicals had an aggressive foreign policy; they improvised casually in home affairs. Mr Mack Smith is inclined to regret that Sicily and even Naples did not survive as autonomous radical states. Was Cavour alone to blame? After all he had only another six months to live; and the radicals had plenty of chance in the future if they could take it. They never made much of it; and Italy has been kept going (so far as it goes at all) by hard-headed officials of Cavour's stamp. Idealists make revolutions; practical men come afterwards and clear up the mess. Garibaldi was luckier than most revolutionary leaders. He remained an idealist to the end of the chapter. If Cavour had not existed, Garibaldi must either have failed or have ended by playing the part of Cavour himself. Perhaps it was Cavour who made the greatest sacrifice after all. Garibaldi returned to Caprera; Cavour remained in power.

10

BISMARCK:
THE MAN OF GERMAN DESTINY

OTTO VON BISMARCK was born in 1815 and died on 30 July 1898. At his birth Prussia was the least of the Great Powers; when he died Germany already overshadowed Europe. This was not his doing. Increase of population and an unrivalled heavy industry made German greatness inevitable; Bismarck's achievement was to keep this greatness within bounds.

A Conservative by origin and by conviction, he hated 'the deluge' as much as Metternich. Only his method differed. Metternich resisted the revolution and fell; Bismarck led the German revolution and mastered it. He used the phrases of demagogy in order to cheat it of results. He claimed to have united Germany; in reality he partitioned Germany with the Habsburgs. He preached the doctrine of military power; in practice he took only the most limited profit from the victories over Austria and France, and gave both Powers another generation of artificial greatness and independence. He instituted universal suffrage in Germany; he manipulated it for the benefit of his own class and, most of all, for himself. While he could not prevent the Germans running mad, he lured them into a strait-jacket which did not work loose until twenty years after his fall and was not fully discarded until forty years after his death.

Bismarck was as deceptive in personality as in policy. 'The Iron Chancellor' was nervous and highly-strung, given to hysterical weeping and racked with sleeplessness. Despising writers and artists, he ranks with Luther and Goethe as a supreme master of German prose and made every political act a finished performance. He denounced ideas and won success by manipulating them; he preached 'blood and iron', and pursued European peace; though a civilian, he always wore military uniform, yet – alone of German statesmen – asserted the primacy of politicians over the General Staff.

Educated in Berlin by a sophisticated mother, he took on in

adult life the rustic airs of his boorish father and paraded a devotion for the family estates which he had rarely seen in youth. From others he demanded absolute sacrifice to duty; he himself as a young man deserted his State post for many months in order to pursue an English girl across Europe and, at the end of his life, betrayed State secrets to the press in order to discredit William II, the master who had dismissed him.

A man of deep emotions, he had no friends, only sycophants. He despised his supporters even more than he hated his enemies, and ruined the happiness of the son whom he loved because of an old personal feud with the family into which Herbert wished to marry. He had a secure and perfect relationship only with his wife; their love was mutual, yet he joked about the religion which was their closest tie. He made loyalty to the House of Hohenzollern the mainspring of his politics, yet spoke of both William I and William II with boundless contempt and said after his fall: 'Were it to do over again, I would be a republican and a democrat.' With true genius he expressed the contradictions of the German spirit.

Bismarck made his real entry into politics in 1848 and remained all his life a man of the revolutionary year. Social upheaval and international isolation were his two nightmares. Security was the motive of his policy at home and abroad; and everything he did was an insurance against dangers, some of them imaginary. For many generations the Powers of the circumference – Russia on one side, England and France on the other – had laid down the law to Central Europe. Bismarck isolated Prussia's neighbours, laid down his law in Central Europe, and finally laid down the law for France and Russia as well.

He became Prime Minister of Prussia in 1862. Within two years, he exposed the sham of the Concert of Europe and imposed his will in Sleswig and Holstein, though this involved the deception of the king, of German national feeling, of Austria – his ostensible ally – and of the Great Powers. Two years later, in 1866, he lured Russia and France into tolerating the overthrow of the Balance of Power between Prussia and Austria, on which their own security rested. The battle of Sadova (Königgrätz) made Prussia supreme in Germany; it did not destroy the Habsburg monarchy. Instead Bismarck preserved the Habsburgs, in association with the Magyars, as a barrier against Greater Germany and thus freed Prussia from taking up the German legacy in the Balkans. Similarly in 1870 and 1871, though he isolated France and organized her defeat, he kept victory within bounds; he neither renewed the attempt of Napoleon nor anticipated that of Hitler.

After 1871 Bismarck was the supreme exponent of the Balance of Power: seeking security for Germany, he gave it to every State in Europe. He would not allow Russia to destroy Austria-Hungary; at the same time he would not support Austrian ambitions in the Balkans. Thanks to Bismarck, the British Empire was never endangered; yet under his patronage France built up an Empire in Africa, and Russia expanded in Central Asia and the Far East. Not only at the Congress of Berlin, but for nineteen years, Bismarck was an honest broker of peace; and his system of alliances compelled every Power, whatever its will, to follow a peaceful course.

Within Germany, too, Bismarck aimed at a balance. With liberal aid he forced concessions from the Junkers, then reined in the liberals with Junker support. He first tamed the Roman Catholics by evoking nationalist frenzy, then used the Catholic Centre as a brake on radical nationalism. Restraining German nationalism was not as easy as restraining foreign Powers. Bismarck's Reich was held together by Junkers who cared nothing for Germany; it treated as enemies the Roman Catholics and the Socialists, who between them represented the German masses. A national State which excluded eight million Germans and a system of universal suffrage which operated against the mass-parties was a political conjuring trick which even Bismarck could not sustain indefinitely. In 1890 he confessed defeat, and William II dismissed him.

Similarly in economic affairs, Bismarck ended in contradiction. He wished to preserve an agricultural Germany of peasants and Junker estates; for the sake of German power, he had to develop German heavy industry, to the ruin of German conservatism, and thus promoted the growth of an urban working-class. Bismarck feared nationalism and socialism; partly by resisting them, partly by compromising with them, he both postponed their victory and made it inevitable.

Bismarck's failure was the failure of conservatism in an age of upheaval. Germany was on the march to world power, and Bismarck could only retard her advance. Nevertheless, no other man could have achieved even his limited and temporary success. The world owes what has been good in the Germany of the last fifty years to Bismarck's policy. In the words of Goethe, *In der Beschränkung zeigt sich erst der Meister*; his greatness lay in his restraint. The history of modern Europe can be written in terms of three Titans: Napoleon, Bismarck and Lenin. Of these three men of superlative political genius, Bismarck probably did least harm.

11

BISMARCK'S MORALITY

HISTORICAL reputations are a sort of political barometer; every generation gets the heroes it deserves. Professor Geyl recently gave a brilliant demonstration of this in the case of Napoleon. In English history, Henry VIII, hero of the late Professor Pollard, is going down; and Elizabeth, courted by Professor Neale and Dr Rowse, is coming up. No doubt, in our era of decline, we prefer subtlety to animal vigour. Bismarck is the German barometer, the test of what German historians think of themselves and of the world. Of course, there are other significant German figures – Luther and Goethe, for example. Luther has gone down with the general decline of religion; unless you take his faith seriously, he was a repellent boor. Goethe is always produced when the Germans are feeling sorry for themselves. He has to act as excuse for the concentration camps and the gas-chambers; after all, a nation which produced Goethe cannot be wholly bad. Goethe was certainly a poet of the highest genius; apart from this, he was a complacent prig, servile and self-satisfied. He won't really do if the Germans are to escape the fate of Sodom and Gomorrah. Bismarck, with all his faults, is a better card for the Germans to play. He has that essential quality of the significant figure: he can be made to sparkle whichever way you look at him.

It is all the more surprising that hitherto there has been no good life of Bismarck. The standard German life by Max Lenx is no more than an enlarged obituary. Grant Robertson's splendid sketch, written during the first German war, gives out in 1871 when Bismarck had nineteen years of high office still ahead of him. During the second German war Erich Eyck, a German living in England, wrote a three-volume life which was published in Switzerland. He has now produced a reduced version in one volume[1] for the English reader. It would be a poor compliment to say that this is the best life of Bismarck; it is the only life of Bismarck and will hold its own for years to come. For one thing, it covers the

1. *Bismarck and the German Empire*. By Erich Eyck.

whole story from beginning to end. Or rather, to be precise, it gives out when Bismarck left office and omits the last eight years when Bismarck conducted a malicious and unscrupulous campaign against William II who had dismissed him. Still, it is more important that Dr Eyck has read and digested the enormous mass of Bismarck literature. Even more than Napoleon, Bismarck has been the victim of too much scholarship. For the first eight years of Bismarck's time in office alone, there are forty-four volumes of published documents from the Austrian, Prussian, and French archives. No one had really sorted them out till Dr Eyck faced them. Then there have been endless works of meticulous research, conducted as solemnly as the study of Holy Writ; every scrap of Bismarck's writing, every fragment of his conversation, have been assembled in the fifteen volumes of his Collected Works; and Bismarck added to the confusion in probably the most misleading work of autobiography ever written. Dr Eyck is the master of his subject. Even though the bibliographical apparatus has been omitted in the English edition, the reader can have confidence that Dr Eyck has examined all the evidence before passing judgement.

This last sentence suggests one of Dr Eyck's defects. He is by training a lawyer, by profession a liberal journalist; and he took up history to relieve the tedium of exile. It is not so easy to become a historian as is sometimes supposed. Dr Eyck gives the impression that he is always out for a verdict; and so far as Bismarck is concerned it is usually a verdict of guilty. Bismarck himself claimed that he kept five balls in the air; Dr Eyck tends to insist that one ball must have been the decisive one and the others just kept spinning to deceive the audience. Bismarck had political genius of the highest order; certainly therefore he knew what he was doing. Dr Eyck interprets this as meaning that Bismarck knew where he was going, a very different matter. The nineteenth century was an age of political optimism, and therefore most politicians thought in terms of objective – even though what they accomplished often turned out very differently from what they intended. Dr Eyck's attitude is all right for them. But Bismarck was not a political optimist. He did not want to go anywhere; quite the reverse, he wished to slow things down. Most of the things that Bismarck accomplished – the war with Austria, the war with France, the so-called unification of Germany – would have been accomplished anyway. What Bismarck really achieved was to make them less decisive than they would have been otherwise. He propped up the Habsburg monarchy for fifty years after its collapse; he preserved France as a Great Power; he retarded German unification until the days of Hitler; within his own limited Germany he staved off the triumph of plebiscitarian democracy.

This criticism leads to the deeper defect in Dr Eyck's approach. His judgements are those of a contemporary, not of a historian. Dr Eyck grew up dreaming of a liberal constitutional monarchy in Germany, associated with the Western Powers and with a liberal German Austria, and pushing Russia far to the east. Bismarck did not share this dream; and therefore Dr Eyck condemns him. For instance, he condemns Bismarck for not making an alliance with England against Russia in 1879; yet such an alliance would certainly have led to war in the Near East. In fact, Dr Eyck is not far removed from the conviction now widespread in the Western world – when is war not wicked, not a crime against humanity, not destructive, in fact when is war not war? When it is against Russia. Yet Dr Eyck expresses a judgement on Austrian politics which is to me much more shocking than anything Bismarck ever did. He condemns Francis Joseph for dismissing his German ministers in 1879 and writes: 'We know now that in fact Francis Joseph brought about the collapse of his dynasty by banishing his faithful German subjects to the wilderness.' In other words Francis Joseph ought to have left power in the hands of the German minority – simply because they were middle-class liberals – and not attempted to conciliate his Slav subjects.

Dr Eyck's verdict on Bismarck is that, though he was a wicked man, he accomplished a glorious work. He describes his enormous achievement – 'the fulfilment of the dream of the German nations, their unification in a powerful and glorious Empire'. Again, 'the critics of his methods and his personality never can, nor will, doubt his singular greatness and his everlasting glory'. Bismarck's reputation for wickedness is a very curious affair. He has become the Old Nick of modern times; yet what did he do that others did not? He treated Austria much more considerately than Lincoln treated the southern states; he used his victory over

France with much more moderation than Napoleon III would have used a victory over Prussia. He bullied Denmark in 1864. Was this worse than the way Palmerston bullied Greece in 1850 or China in 1860? Though he was jealous of political rivals, he was no more jealous than Gladstone was of Chamberlain. It is difficult to discover noble idealists among the European statesmen with whom Bismarck had to deal – Gorchakov? Thiers? Andrássy? Disraeli? Bismarck did not lack morality; what he lacked was uplift. He could not make his voice quaver with unselfish zeal, as Gladstone's voice quavered when he occupied Egypt. Bismarck fought 'necessary' wars and killed thousands; the idealists of the twentieth century fight 'just' wars and kill millions. Bismarck defended national sovereignty, or rather accepted it as a fact; this was no more wicked than to reject the Schuman plan on the same grounds.

Though Bismarck lacked humbug, he did not lack principles. Only they were not liberal principles. They were principles founded in distrust of human nature, principles of doubt and restraint. When men dislike Bismarck for his realism, what they really dislike is reality. Take his most famous sentence: 'The great questions of our time will not be settled by resolutions and majority votes – that was the mistake of the men of 1848 and 1849 – but by blood and iron.' Who can deny that this is true as a statement of fact? What settled the question of Nazi domination of Europe – resolutions or the allied armies? What will settle the question of Korea – majority votes at Lake Success or American strength? This is a very different matter from saying that principles and beliefs are ineffective. They can be extremely effective if translated into blood and iron and not simply into resolutions and majority votes. As a matter of fact Bismarck never underrated the importance of principles; rather he erred in taking the principles of others too seriously. He conducted political war first against the Roman Catholics, then against the Social Democrats, because he thought that they meant what they said – the Catholics that they were loyal only to the Pope, the Socialists that they were revolutionaries. The basis of our modern liberal democracies is that men do not mean what they say. This was indeed the justification for our first liberal act – the emancipation of the Roman Catholics from the penal laws. Nowadays, Mr Attlee does not really believe that Mr Churchill wishes to exploit the poor; and Mr Churchill does not really believe that Mr Attlee would lead the country to ruin. Most of our present troubles with the Russians spring from the conviction of Roosevelt and his advisers that the Communist leaders did not mean what they had been saying for thirty years – at least no more than Roosevelt meant what he said at election time. Unfortunately the Communists are old-fashioned – like Bismarck.

Bismarck was old-fashioned in a more fundamental sense. He came from a peaceful, stable society; and he valued stability above movement. First inside Germany and then in Europe he achieved a balance of opposing forces, and so created a generation of stability. Men fall easily into the habit of taking security for granted; and the generation which flourished after 1878 soon regarded internal order and European peace as normal. In fact the years between 1878 and 1914 – years with no revolutions outside Russia and no wars outside the Balkans – were the most abnormal years in modern history; and whatever the future has in store for us it is pretty certain that we shall never see the like of them again. Instead of dismissing Bismarck as a nasty man, it would be wiser to bear in mind that these years were his doing; that without him the great war of all against all – of class against class, of nation against nation – would have got under way sooner.

Finally, when judging Bismarck as a politician, one has to remember one other thing, which is not obvious to a German writer: Bismarck was dealing with Germans. The personal spite; the raucous evocation of Power; the irritation at opposition – these were qualities which he shared with other German politicians. The restraint; the ability to see into the minds of others; the readiness to risk his own prestige for the sake of peace and moderation; these were the things that Bismarck added. No doubt Germany and German policy in Bismarck's day had many faults; but no German since has done any better. I suspect that Bismarck would have preferred this cool praise to the eternal glory and moral disapproval which Dr Eyck offers him.

12

BISMARCK AND EUROPE

LEGENDS of Bismarck sprawl over the history of the later nineteenth century. First, the contemporary legend – the Bismarck who produced calculated effects on diplomats and politicians, wore military uniform and revealed only late in life that he had done it in order to save the wear-and-tear on his more expensive civilian clothes. Then the legend of German historians who saw in Bismarck the maker of German unity and for whom he could do nothing wrong or even mistaken. And, the reverse of this, the legend primarily of French historians, though often accepted in England too, for whom Bismarck could do nothing right – the man who planned the downfall of France as a Great Power and was responsible for three invasions of 'the national territory'. More recently there has grown up a version, to which I myself have contributed a little, of Bismarck as the thwarted conservative, exponent of the doctrine of 'the lesser evil', of whom one might say that everything he did he did unwillingly and only because anyone else could have done more of it. Though his political offspring were illegitimate, they were 'only little ones'. The study of Bismarck has become a modern scholasticism, each act and each saying combed over and elaborated on as though it were Holy Writ or one of those few documents which, surviving by chance, give medieval historians the illusion that they are engaged in a more scientific discipline than ours.

I have recently been fortunate enough to start examining Bismarck's diplomacy all over again. It would be foolish to pretend that it is possible to shut out of mind the versions of those who have gone before – Sybel and Ollivier, Friedjung and Matter, Grant Robertson and Marcks, Eyck and Srbik. But all of them had some political axe to grind; they were all concerned to show that he had failed or, more rarely, succeeded. I have clean hands. I really do not care – though this may sound untrue – I do not care about the Germans any more one way or the other. I am prepared to believe that Europe is finished; and I am only curious to know what happened to Europe in the second half of the nineteenth century without worrying any more about the outcome. So much of the diplomatic record has now been published that it is possible to write the story virtually from the archives, at any rate so far as Austria, France, and Prussia are concerned. Some details of British diplomacy could, no doubt, be added from further study of the archives, though I do not think they would be details of much moment. Russian policy is admittedly still obscure; and a documentary study of this between 1863 and 1871 would be one of the most welcome tasks which a Soviet scholar might perform. But even here the broad outline is clearer than it was a few years ago. I would add two points of caution or of apology. First, I am only concerned to look again at Bismarck's diplomacy, not at his work in Germany. I am convinced that his decisive achievement was in domestic politics and that the Bismarckian compromise or contradiction within Germany – it comes to much the same thing – is what mattered most in European history. Second, there can be no doubt that Bismarck was a great man. He ran down his predecessors and exaggerated his own achievements; he made more mistakes than he or his admirers would admit; he knocked sometimes at the wrong door and more often at doors that were already open. All the same, it is impossible to read his most casual utterance without feeling that here was someone outsize. It would be a waste of time to try to prove anything else; and equally unnecessary to be reiterating how great he was.

It is a great mistake to begin the story of German unification with Bismarck's accession to power in 1862, or even to treat the events of 1848 as a preliminary without relevance. Everything, including Bismarck's own work, springs from the revolutionary year. It is now widely held that France or Russia or both of them would have forbidden national unification in 1848. There seems little evidence of this. The French radicals supposed that national Germany would be their ally in liberating Poland; and though Bastide, Foreign Minister from May until December 1848, saw no reason to encourage a national Germany, his only approach to Russia was made to deter the Tsar from reviving the policy of the Holy Alliance. The Tsar's policy in 1848 was simple: he was determined not to move his armies beyond Russia's frontiers.

Hence, he refused to intervene even in Sleswig-Holstein, though an important Russian interest – free passage of the Sound – was at stake there. In fact the only Power who threatened action over the Elbe duchies was England, the Power which otherwise favoured German unification. This is what Palmerston meant by his complaint against 'the parcel of children' at Frankfurt. The German liberals, he thought, ought to be creating 'a natural ally' for Great Britain on the continent instead of threatening the security of the Baltic. In any case, whatever the attitude of France and Russia to a hypothetical liberal Germany, neither of them made any objection to the consolidation of north Germany under Prussia. The Erfurt union, which made Prussia supreme north of the Main, was carried through without objection from either Russia or France. It is true that the Tsar's object in intervening in Hungary was, in part, to restore a balance in Central Europe between Prussia and Austria; but he held, as the French did, that this balance was improved rather than the reverse by the strengthening of Prussia in northern Germany.

Russia followed the same policy in the crisis of 1850 which ended with the agreement of Olomouc. Certainly the Tsar wished to prevent a war between Prussia and Austria; but he wanted a settlement without either victors or vanquished. His real aim was to consolidate both Prussia and Austria as a neutral conservative buffer between Russia and western Europe. Hence he declared that he would support whichever was attacked; though, in fact, at the crisis Russia promised Austria only moral support. It was not danger from Russia which led the Prussians to give way; nor, for that matter, was it military weakness. Prince William was confident that Prussia could win; and this opinion was shared by the Russian generals who had seen Austrian troops in action in Hungary. Paskievich, the Russian commander-in-chief, even believed that Prussia would be a match for Russia and Austria combined. Prussia's real weakness was that both Frederick William IV and his conservative ministers regarded war with Austria as 'wicked'. They gave way more from conviction than from fear; and after 1850, as before it, Prussia was committed to the policy of reconciling hegemony north of the Main and partnership with Austria. This was also Russia's policy, as was shown in the spring of 1851, when the Tsar forbade Schwarzenberg's programme of uniting Germany under Austria – the Empire of seventy millions.

Though Bismarck welcomed the settlement of Olomouc, no one has contributed more to the version that Prussia thereafter became subservient to Austria. This version cannot be sustained. There was perhaps subservience when Manteuffel, the Prussian Foreign Minister, made a defensive alliance with Austria for three years in 1851. This certainly implied a Prussian guarantee for Austria's possessions in Italy, which she steadily refused thereafter; but it also barred the way against what seemed more likely in 1851 – an Austrian alliance with Napoleonic imperialism. At any rate, there was no subservience in the alliance, when it was renewed on 20 April 1854. Though it, too, seemed to serve an Austrian purpose – by guaranteeing the Danubian principalities (later called Rumania) against Russia – this was in reality only the bait by which Austria was held from making an alliance with England and France. If Austria had joined the Western Powers in war against Russia, Prussia could not have stayed out. Whichever side she joined, she would have had to bear the main brunt of a war fought probably on her own soil – a war from which she could not possibly have gained and in which she might well have lost her Polish lands. As it was, Prussia performed the great service to Russia by keeping Austria neutral at no cost to herself; and, by advocating neutrality at the Diet, won the leadership of the German states as well. Yet this was the time when Bismarck denounced the incompetence of his official superiors. He opposed the alliance with Austria. At the beginning of the war he would seem to have favoured supporting Russia; at the end of it he preached, in one of his most famous compositions, that Prussia should make a third in the coming partnership between Russia and France. His own action in 1879 is the best comment on this policy. As Imperial Chancellor, Bismarck judged Manteuffel to have been right and himself wrong; but he took care not to say so.

Bismarck overrated all along the dynamism of the Franco-Russian entente. He thought that Napoleon III and Alexander II were set on remaking the map of Europe, both east and west, in the immediate future and that Prussia must hasten to play the jackal with them if she were not to be left out of things. Official Prussian policy, whether under Frederick William IV and Manteuffel or under the Prince Regent and the despised Schleinitz, stuck to its old line: support for Austria once she had recognized Prussian hegemony north of the Main. This policy came within sight of success in the Italian war of 1859. If Napoleon had insisted on his original aim of liberating Venetia as well as Lombardy, even more if Alexander II had taken the opportunity to reopen the Eastern Question – in fact, if France and Russia had been as dynamic as Bismarck supposed – Austria would have had to pay Prussia's price. As it was, she lost Lombardy and thus ended the war without Prussia's help. The real turning-point came in the following year, 1860. In July, Schleinitz and Rechberg, the Austrian Foreign Minister, met at Teplitz and agreed on a defensive alliance between their two countries – an alliance which Bismarck himself quoted as a precedent in 1879. The awkward question of Prussian hegemony north of the Main was postponed to a military convention that was to be negotiated subsequently. All this was a preliminary to a meeting of the two German rulers with the Tsar at Warsaw in September. They believed that Alexander II had taken fright at Napoleon's revolutionary policy and would now urge joint resistance in Italy. When it came to the point Alexander II could not give up his hopes for revising the settlement of 1856 in the Near East with French help and therefore would do nothing against Italy, Napoleon's satellite. The Holy Alliance turned out to be a mirage; and the Prussians were quick to draw the lesson. They screwed up their terms in the military discussions with Austria; and when these broke down, the alliance vanished with them. If there was a decisive moment in the relations between Prussia and Austria, it was in April 1861, and not after Bismarck became Prime Minister.

Bismarck's predecessors perhaps had different allies in mind. Schleinitz counted on the 'liberal' alliance with England, so far as he counted on anything at all. This policy was ruined by the American civil war, which locked up British military resources in Canada. Moreover, the British were increasingly aware that their navy was out of date. These factors, rather than any ideological swing towards isolationism, made Great Britain ineffective during Europe's years of destiny. Bernstorff who followed Schleinitz looked instead to France; his object was to replace Russia as France's continental ally. When Bismarck arrived in October 1862, he certainly meant to play the role of a Prussian Cavour;

but with this difference from Cavour (as from Bernstorff) that he intended to co-operate with Russia as well as with France – a partnership therefore that would be anti-British as well as anti-Austrian. In fact he missed the bus (if there was ever one to catch). He assumed that the Franco-Russian entente was solid; instead it collapsed before he had been in office six months. Almost his first act was to ask in Paris what the French attitude would be 'if things hot up in Germany'. He was too late. Drouyn de Lhuys, enemy of Russia and advocate of alliance with Austria, had just returned to the Quai d'Orsay. Bismarck's query was brushed aside. Three months later the Polish revolt blew the Franco-Russian entente sky-high. Years afterwards Bismarck built up the story that he had pulled off a great stroke of policy by supporting the Russians in Poland and therefore winning their gratitude. This is untrue. The Russians thought they could deal with the Poles alone and much resented Prussian patronage. Moreover Bismarck's step ensured that, if it came to war over Poland, Prussia would have to fight for the sake of Russia's Polish lands; and he had to beg to be excused from the alliance with Russia within six weeks of making it. Even as it was, the quarrel over Poland was disastrous for Prussia. The great hope of Prussian policy had been that the French threat to Venetia and Russian threats in the Near East would so embarrass Austria as to make her surrender the hegemony of northern Germany to Prussia without a war. This hope was now ruined. The Franco-Russian entente had never been a threat to Prussia; rather it gave her security. The entente was directed against Austria; and France would not endanger it by seeking gains on the Rhine. The French threat there, if it ever existed, was created by the estrangement between France and Russia, not by their entente. No doubt Russia was now prepared to tolerate a Prussian war against France; but so she always had been, and this was a very different thing from active support – that the Russians never offered.

The truth is that, once the Franco-Russian entente broke down, Prussia was forced back to friendship with Austria as her only means of security. Here again Bismarck later created a myth – the story that the Sleswig-Holstein affair was a trap for Austria from the beginning. I think rather that, as so often, Bismarck, always impulsive and always exaggeratedly nervous of the aggressive designs of others, rushed himself into a commitment and then had to exercise all his great genius in order to get out of a tangle of his own making. For there is the fact. In January 1864 he made an alliance with Austria which did not include the recognition of Prussian hegemony north of the Main on which his predecessors had always insisted. His motive was fear, not gain; fear that, as in 1848, Prussia would be pushed forward in Sleswig by German feeling and then have to face a coalition of the Powers, reinforced this time by Austria. The Conference of London which tried to settle the Sleswig question showed that these fears were exaggerated. The Russian Government was estranged from the Western Powers both by the Crimean War and, more recently, by the Polish affair. Besides, the Russians did not object to Prussia's gaining control of the Sound so long as she did not do it on a basis of nationalist enthusiasm. They objected much more to Austria's getting a foothold there and would have preferred an isolated Prussian action. Thus, curiously enough, the partnership with Austria – which Bismarck had insisted on as essential – was the one thing that worried the Russians and made them hostile. Still they did not mean to act in 1864 – as, for that matter, they had refused anything but moral reproofs in regard to Sleswig both in 1848 and 1850. The real opposition in the previous crises had come from England; and the British – estranged from Russia by the Crimean War, suspicious of Napoleon III as a result of his annexation of Savoy, and with their forces tied in Canada – had no means of action. It is inconceivable that there could ever have been an Anglo-Austrian alliance to check Prussia in Sleswig; and, short of this, there was nothing the British could do. They twice took soundings for French support, in February and again in June. Both met with the same response. Napoleon would not act against the 'national' principle; Drouyn, who hated nationalism in general and Prussia in particular, demanded concrete gains on the Rhine – a prospect more unwelcome to the British than the Danish loss of the Duchies.

The three non-German Powers were in fact far more suspicious of each other than concerned about what might happen in Germany. The only thing that alarmed them was Prussia's alliance with Austria – Bismarck's own doing. Had he acted alone against Denmark, he would have had the approval of all the Powers except Austria; but he would have had to act on a liberal basis. Prussia's foreign danger, in short, was increased, if not created, by Bismarck's conflict with the liberals. He made the Austrian alliance, not to trick Austria, but to save himself. This is, I think, the answer to the disputed question whether Bismarck was ever sincere in his conservative partnership with Austria. He was a man of extremes. He could conceive a full return to the system of Metternich; hence in August 1864 he pressed on Austria not only a Prussian guarantee of Venetia, but a campaign for the recovery of Lombardy. He could also conceive of a 'revolutionary' alliance with France, by which Prussia expelled Austria from Germany north of the Main while France gained land on the Rhine. What he never foresaw was the moderate outcome – neither reactionary nor revolutionary – for which he has been so much praised. Moderation is said to be the most difficult of policies; it was certainly difficult for Bismarck.

I make no doubt that the offer of an alliance which he made to Austria in August 1864 was genuine. It seemed to him 'in the logic of the situation'. If Prussia was not to follow a revolutionary course, she must follow a reactionary one. Once more he asked less than his predecessors. In his exaggerated fear of French aggression, he offered Austria alliance against France without demanding Prussian hegemony north of the Main. William I, not Bismarck, insisted on this condition; and the Austrians thought Prussia so dependent on their support that they named Silesia as their price. The deadlock drove Bismarck off on the alternative 'revolutionary' course. He screwed up tension against Austria; and in May 1865 spoke openly of his policy as 'war against Austria in alliance with France'. A new compromise followed in August 1865, the Treaty of Gastein. This compromise came mainly from the side of the Austrians; and Bismarck accepted it merely because it was offered. But he was also bewildered by the failure of his 'revolutionary' policy to explode. When he approached the French for an alliance, they refused to display territorial ambitions. Napoleon went ostentatiously into the country; and left policy to be defined by Drouyn the conservative.

In October 1865, Bismarck visited Napoleon at Biarritz in order to clear up the mystery of French policy. It is often said that he tricked Napoleon by vague talk of future French gains in Germany. This is not so. It is true that the two rogues discussed 'advantages which might offer themselves unsought', advantages, of course, in Germany: but this was a casual theme. Napoleon's overriding interest was Venetia; he was determined to complete the work of 1859 and not leave to his son 'a volcano for a throne'. His price was Venetia; and Bismarck paid it. He promised that he would not guarantee Venetia to Austria; and in return Napoleon promised that he would not make an alliance with Austria against Prussia – 'he would not go and stand beside a target'. This was the essential bargain of Biarritz: Venetia for Italy, and French neutrality in a war between Prussia and Austria. Bismarck gave the bargain a positive shape when he concluded his alliance with Italy in April 1866; this ensured Napoleon that he would get what he wanted, and Bismarck was able to wage a limited war against Austria. Napoleon, not Bismarck, made the moderate programme possible and enabled Prussia to win hegemony north of the Main without a general European upheaval. To the very last Bismarck could not believe in his own success. In May 1866 he offered the Austrians peace if they would share the military headship of Germany. The Austrians would have agreed if they could have had in exchange a Prussian guarantee of Venetia; this, owing to his bargain with Napoleon, was the one thing that Bismarck could not give. Venetia compelled Bismarck to go to war. It also compelled Napoleon to favour war – it was the factor which wrecked his proposal for a European Congress. Most paradoxically of all, it even led the Austrians to want war. By May 1866 they had come to believe that the only way out of their difficulties was to surrender Venetia and gain Silesia in exchange. This would win Napoleon as an ally against both Prussia and Russia; it would free their southern frontier; and it would restore their prestige in Germany. But it was only possible by means of war against Prussia. Therefore, in the last resort, it was the Austrians who were eager to bring the war on. It is a curious fact that every European war between 1815 and 1914 was exploded by the Power standing on the defensive: England and France insisted on the Crimean War; Austria on the wars of 1859, 1866, and 1914; and France on the war of 1870. It is also a curiosity how little military considerations weighed in the decision to provoke war or to avoid it. Thus, the

Prussians accepted the compromise of August 1865, although they were confident of victory. There is little foundation for the later story that they put off war until they could clinch their military superiority by making an alliance with Italy. And this alliance, when it was made in April 1866, was concluded for its political effect on Napoleon, rather than to divide the Austrian armies – this again was an advantage which the Prussians only discovered after it happened. On the other side, the Austrians did not provoke war in June 1866 because their military position had improved, but because it had got worse; they could bear the tension no longer. Finally, the French decision not to intervene after the Prussian victory at Sadova sprang purely from considerations of policy; the question whether the French army was capable of intervention was hardly raised. I am not sure whether any conclusion can be drawn from this odd ignoring of the basic facts.

There is another oddity. The war between Austria and Prussia had been on the horizon for sixteen years. Yet it had great difficulty in getting itself declared. Austria tried to provoke Bismarck by placing the question of the Duchies before the Diet on 1 June. Bismarck retaliated by occupying Holstein. He hoped that the Austrian troops there would resist, but they got away before he could catch them. On 14 June the Austrian motion for federal mobilization against Prussia was carried in the Diet. Prussia declared the confederation at an end; and on 15 June invaded Saxony. On 21 June, when Prussian troops reached the Austrian frontier, the Crown Prince, who was in command, merely notified the nearest Austrian officer that 'a state of war' existed. That was all. The Italians did a little better. La Marmora sent a declaration of war to Albrecht, the Austrian commander-in-chief, before taking the offensive. Both Italy and Prussia were committed to programmes which could not be justified in international law, and were bound to appear as aggressors if they put their claims on paper. They would, in fact, have been hard put to it to start the war if Austria had not done the job for them.

The war of 1866 was not the revolutionary war which had been preached by Bismarck until his visit to Biarritz; it was the moderate war as always envisaged by the Prussian statesmen whom Bismarck had despised. It is often regarded as something of a miracle that Bismarck carried it through without intervention from either France or Russia; but in truth neither of them had any objection to a Prussian hegemony in northern Germany which is all that was accomplished. The Russians, in any case, were in no state to intervene. For fifteen years after the Crimean War they almost ceased to be a military power so far as Europe was concerned. Between 1856 and 1863 the annual call-up for the army was not enforced; and the Polish revolt in 1863, itself caused by an attempted call-up, further delayed their recovery. They owed their security during this period of neglect to the Prussian buffer; and were therefore glad to see it strengthened. No doubt they would have expostulated if Bismarck had annexed the states of southern Germany or dismembered the Austrian Empire, but this was never on the programme. His moderation against Austria in 1866 has been much vaunted. Yet even he put up his terms. He excluded Austria from Germany, instead of dividing it with her at the Main. The King and the generals, who grumbled at his moderation, merely wanted some satisfactions of prestige – annexation of some Austrian territory in Silesia or a victory-march through Vienna. They certainly had no thought of destroying the Habsburg Empire. Nor is it true that Austria was reconciled by Bismarck's moderation. The Austrians had burnt their fingers in 1866 and meant to take less risks next time; but they still hoped for a next time. The war of 1866 was a milestone, not a turning-point, in Austro-Prussian relations.

The real turning-point, for all Europe, was, no doubt, that France did not intervene; but even the dramatic nature of this has been exaggerated owing to the fact that history has been written by those who opposed or regretted the decision, while Napoleon, the man who made it, remained silent. He had made up his mind all along; he was on the side of 'the revolution', on the side, that is, of Prussia in Germany, as he had been on the side of Sardinia in Italy. There was no real crisis of decision in Paris between 4 July and 10 July. It was simply that Napoleon, having deceived his ministers from the first, had now to override them. He thought – and perhaps rightly – that the European situation had changed in his favour; Prussia stronger than before and therefore less dependent on Russia; Austria excluded from Germany and therefore freer to balance Russia in the Near East; Italy contented with the acquisition of Venetia; and southern Germany 'internationally independent'. Even if he had known of the Prussian treaties of alliance with the southern States, he would have regarded this as an improvement on the German confederation. Then southern Germany had been guaranteed by both Prussia and Austria; now by Prussia alone, and with her Napoleon had no quarrel. Indeed he took Bismarck's breath away by insisting on Prussia's annexing the whole of north Germany – a victory for the revolution over moderation.

In the summer of 1866 Napoleon supposed that he had at last achieved the revolutionary coalition with Prussia and Italy; and he meant to complete it by resurrecting his entente with Russia. He was of course misled by the analogy with Italy. He supposed that, since the Italians continued to need protection against Austria, Prussia needed it also; and his half-hearted demands for compensation, which culminated in the attempted annexation of Luxembourg in March 1867, were all designed to make an alliance with Prussia acceptable to French public opinion. It is common to speak of these negotiations, and especially the Luxembourg affair, as a trap which Bismarck laid for the French. If it was a trap, why did he not spring it? The truth is simpler. The affair was not of Bismarck's seeking; it was thrust on him by the French and, though no doubt he had to consider German feeling, he would have welcomed an alliance with France, if Russia had been included in it. There, it seems to me, is the real explanation. The key to European diplomacy between 1866 and 1870 is to be found in the Near East, and not on the Rhine or even in Poland. So long as Russia and France were at loggerheads in the Near East, Bismarck could not let Luxembourg go to France without implicitly taking her side against Russia. But equally he refused a Russian offer to keep Austria neutral, because this also involved paying a price in the Near East. In April 1867 at the height of the Luxembourg crisis, he first suggested the solution that was his ultimate favourite: the revival of the Holy Alliance. It was contemptuously refused by both the other parties. Austria would not join without concessions in Germany, Russia would not guarantee the integrity of Austria nor allow her gains in the Balkans. The Eastern Question dictated a peaceful outcome of the Luxembourg affair. France would not allow Russia a free hand against Turkey;

Prussia would not allow her a free hand against Austria. There-fore both botched up the Luxembourg question as best they could. The great turning-point had been reached without design and before anyone noticed it. Both French and German public opinion had taken a hand in diplomacy; and henceforth they were not to be reconciled – perhaps not even to the present day.

There is not much to be said of Bismarck's diplomacy between 1867 and 1870. As always when the Near East took the centre of the stage, he had none except to keep out of the way; or, at most, to act as honest broker when the conflicts of the other Powers threatened to involve Prussia. When the Franco-Russian entente seemed to be working in the Near East during the autumn of 1867, he played in with it; and, with Italy joining in too, this was the last display of the 'revolutionary coalition'. Bismarck backed out of the Near East as soon as the entente broke down, so as not to be left alone on the Russian side. In March 1868, he refused a direct Russian demand for an alliance against Austria-Hungary, though 'of course neither Power could afford to allow the des-truction of the other'. In the autumn of 1868 he used the Hohen-zollern family influence to damp down irredentist agitation in Rumania, so as to avoid having to choose between Russia and Austria-Hungary; and in 1869 he helped Russia and France to wind up the Cretan affair. He never took seriously the talk of an alliance between Austria-Hungary and France; it was, he said, 'conjectural rubbish', as indeed it turned out to be. He calculated quite rightly that the Habsburg government would never dare to offend Hungarian and Austrian-German feeling by supporting French interference in southern Germany; and equally that Napo-leon would not break with Russia for the sake of Austria-Hun-gary. This disposes of the defence put up for Bismarck by some of his admirers that he had to provoke war against France in order to anticipate either an Austro-French or a Franco-Russian agree-ment. There was never any serious chance of the first; and the second offered Prussia advantages, not dangers.

There is a simpler defence of Bismarck's policy in 1870, that is, if he needs one: he did not provoke the war at all, except in the narrowest sense of exploding it at the last moment. Later on, when the war had become a national legend, Bismarck tried to take the credit for it; but it was unearned. Of course the Hohenzollern candidature for the throne of Spain was of his making. Its object was to act as a check on France, not to provoke her into war. His encouragement of or indifference towards the Spanish affair varied inversely with the Franco-Russian entente. When France and Russia were on good terms, this gave Prussia security, both against Austria-Hungary and against being involved in an eastern war; whenever they quarrelled, he looked round for other means of distracting French attention from the Rhine. He first took up the Hohenzollern candidature in February 1869, when Russia and France were in dispute over Crete. He dropped it as soon as they settled the question; and left it alone so long as their entente seemed within sight of renewal. He revived it once more, in the spring of 1870, when the Franco-Russian approach broke down. But the Hohenzollern candidature was primarily not a move in foreign policy at all. Bismarck's overriding concern was with southern Germany; and a Hohenzollern on the Spanish throne – like the project of declaring William I German Emperor which he aired at the same time – was designed to raise Prussian prestige south of the Main. In June 1870 Alexander II met Bismarck and William I at Ems – one of the many legendary meetings at which a war was supposed to have been plotted. In fact war against France was never mentioned. Bismarck expressed disapproval of Habsburg policy in the Near East; and he tried to persuade the Tsar that the South German princes would make a better bargain with William I than if they waited to be swept away by a more democratic wave in favour of his liberal successor. There could hardly be clearer evidence that Bismarck was not expecting the Franco-Prussian war at that time.

Of the actual war-crisis in July 1870 two things seem to me clear beyond all doubt, if one can escape from the layers of myth and prejudice. First, no one could have expected it to explode in the way that it did. According to all rational calculation, Leopold of Hohenzollern ought to have been on the throne of Spain before the French, or anyone else, knew what was happening. The actual leakage was due to the blunder of a cipher-clerk in the German legation at Madrid – an unpredictable event. Second, no one could have expected the French to turn the crisis into a war. Bismarck thought the affair would end in a humiliation for Prussia. That is why he stayed in the country and left William I to do the negotiating. The course of events was a set-back for Bismarck, though he quickly made the best of things. So far as he had a settled policy, it was to incorporate southern Germany with Russian and even French approval – a decisive stroke against Austria and back to the dynamic coalition with France and Russia that he had always favoured. After all, he believed, rightly, that the Empire was the form of French Government most favourable to Prussian interests; and he went on trying to restore Napoleon III even at the beginning of 1871. He had sometimes thought that a French revolution would lead to war; it was quite against his intentions that war led to a French revolution.

It is a further myth that Bismarck's diplomacy secured the neutrality of Russia and Austria-Hungary. Neither Power ever had any intention or inclination to go to war. Bismarck made no promises to the Russians of support in the Near East; and they made no promises to him. The Russians did not mobilize any troops in Galicia – they had, in fact, none to mobilize. They did not threaten Austria-Hungary. They promised the Austrians to stay neutral, if Austria-Hungary did the same; but in view of their military weakness, they would have stayed neutral in any case. For that matter, they did not believe that their interests would be injured by a French victory over Prussia – nor by a Prussian victory over France. The Austrians remained neutral solely from consideration of their own interests also. Beust wished to mobilize in order to intervene after the decisive battles had been fought; and, since he expected France to win that battle, his intention was to protect southern Germany against her. Andrássy, too, favoured mobilization; only he insisted on a declaration of neutrality so that, after the French victory which he also expected, both France and Prussia could be persuaded to join a crusade against Russia. This was as crazy as most of Andrássy's schemes. Gorchakov, the Russian Chancellor, passed the correct verdict on the French dreams for an Austrian alliance when he said: 'Russia did not paralyse a support which had no chance of being realized'. Neither Russia or Austria-Hungary cared which way the war went in western Europe. So far as there was any element of calculation in their policy, it was simply that, once France was out of the way, Germany would no longer be able to follow a neutral line in the Near East – the only topic that interested them.

From Bismarck's point of view, the war of 1870 was a senseless affair; and he admitted as much in his many later apologies to the French. So far as he had any responsibility for it (and he did not have much), this sprang from his desire to weaken German liberalism by making France the national enemy instead of Russia. Whatever the responsibilities, the consequences of dividing Germany with Austria and of quarrelling with France were all that Bismarck had foreseen in his days at Frankfurt. Vienna took Berlin prisoner. In the Crimean War Prussian statesmen had worked to prevent Austria's going to the assistance of the Western Powers; in the Bulgarian crisis of 1887 Bismarck had to implore the British to go to the assistance of Austria-Hungary; and a generation later his successors had to go to her assistance themselves. In 1879 Bismarck, and none other, tied 'the trim Prussian frigate to the worm-eaten Austrian galleon' – tied them together for good, although the galleon was now more worm-eaten by a generation. Was this really a triumph for his diplomacy?

To my mind, the younger Bismarck was the greater one – the Bismarck who modelled himself on Cavour rather than the Bismarck who modelled himself on Metternich, the 'mad Junker' rather than the sane one. He saw clearly that a national reconstruction of Central Europe in co-operation with Russia and France was the wisest course for Prussia. But, when it came to the point, he himself prevented this. He overrated, no doubt, Russian and French dynamism; and when this failed swung away on the opposite tack. But his rejection of his own earlier policy had a deeper cause. The national principle in Europe only made sense on a liberal basis, as Cavour appreciated. Both Bismarck and Napoleon III hated the liberalism which was essential to the success of their foreign policy. Napoleon pretended to accept it; Bismarck hardly troubled to make the pretence. Germany and France could not work together except on a liberal basis; hence Napoleon III and Bismarck between them ensured that they would not work together at all. Everything sprang from this failure. Without French co-operation, Germany could not risk a national remaking of eastern Europe by Russia; therefore she had to prop up Austria-Hungary. The diplomacy of Bismarck's later years was simply an elaborate jugglery to conceal the fact that he had abandoned his earlier visions and had been forced to repeat, or even to outdo, the mistakes of his predecessors. It is curious, and more than a coincidence, that in the very weeks when Bismarck was founding his so-called 'league of peace' by means of the Austro-German alliance, Gladstone was formulating his principles of international co-operation in the Midlothian campaign. Nor is it, I think, an accident that in every subsequent world-conflict, Bismarck's heirs, the boasted real-politikers, have always been defeated by the heirs of Gladstone, those who hope to make the world anew. Once Bismarck had been one of these. He set out to remake Central Europe. Instead he tied himself to the Habsburgs, and, like everyone who follows this path, ended up by believing that peace could be kept by tricks.

13

RANKE

THOUGH standards vary, greatness remains; indeed it is the true mark of greatness that it can survive changing standards. Shakespeare was great to Johnson; great to Coleridge; is great to us. Ranke was a historian of the same grandeur – great to his contemporaries, still great after the passage of a century; if not the greatest of historians, securely within the first half-dozen. Great as a scholar, great as a master of narrative, Ranke has the special claim of having achieved something more than his own work; he founded a school, the school of scientific historians, which has dominated all historical thinking since his time, even when in reaction against it. His wish to present the past 'as it really was' became, in the German phrase, 'a winged word'; one of those pregnant sayings which concentrate the aspirations and outlook of a generation. Indeed the past 'as it really was' can be put with Bismarck's 'blood and iron' as the two most important spiritual legacies left by the Germany of the mid-nineteenth century. A composite picture of the German character would have to include Ranke, just as it would have to include Goethe and Schiller on the one side, Hitler and Himmler on the other. Perhaps Ranke displayed even more clearly than these other representative figures the strength and achievement, also the weakness and the defects, of the German character.

The present revival of Ranke is not simply a publishing accident. The German interest in Ranke is one attempt among many to find normality and self-confidence among their own kind; it is also, however, one attempt among many to evade the responsibilities of the day, as Ranke evaded them, by a sort of political quietism – finding God in history in the hope that He will take the blame for everything that goes wrong. In his life, as in his work, Ranke remains full of lessons for the Germany of the present day and also for the historian in every country.

Ranke has one qualification which he himself regarded as essential for the study of a subject: there is plenty of material. His

works stretch at unrivalled length on the shelves; and his life was
as interminable as his works. Few historians have matured so
young; none other of the first rank has kept going, in full possession of his faculties, until well over ninety. His first published
letter is dated 1814, the last 1886. Both show the same gravity and
self-confidence. These qualities made Ranke a great historian. He
never doubted what he wanted to be and what he wanted to do.
Though he was an affectionate son and brother and, late in life,
an affectionate husband, he was dedicated to the study and writing
of history, accepting without complaint the solitary existence
which that involved. He never sought guidance or instruction;
when he met other historians, it was to discuss questions of
organizing historical studies, not to debate historical problems.
He never troubled about criticism, except when this challenged
the accuracy of his facts. Facts were his guiding star, one might
say his illusion. In a letter to his brother Heinrich in 1831 he
wrote:

> My basic thought is not to accept either one theory or another, not
> even the one which lies between them; but to recognize the facts, to
> master them and display them. The true teaching is in the recognition
> of events.

Forty years later, facts had become even more sacred. He wrote in
1873:

> The historian exists in order to understand the sense of an epoch in
> and for itself and to make it understood by others. He must keep his
> eye with all impartiality only on the subject itself and on nothing else.
> Through everything runs the divine order of things, which certainly
> cannot be precisely displayed, but is to be felt all the same. The signi-
> ficant individuals have their place in this divine order, which is identical
> with the succession of epochs; this is how the historian must compre-
> hend them. The historical method, which seeks only the genuine and
> the true, thus comes into direct contact with the highest questions of the
> human race.

Yet what were these facts which revealed the divine order of
things? Simply the documents which had survived by accident and
which jealous archivists allowed him to see. Time and again he
wrote to the archivists (or, when these proved stubborn, to their
official superiors, even to Metternich) for one more document, one

more 'fact', endlessly confident that with this extra 'fact' everything would at last fall into place and the divine purpose be
revealed. He supposed that in writing documents men record their
motives; he almost assumed that men wrote documents for the
benefit of historians. The supreme consequence of Ranke's
doctrine was the belief, universal after the first German war, that
if the archives were combed through an 'explanation' of our
twentieth-century turmoil would be discovered. Nowadays we
know better and read diplomatic history for purposes of entertainment. 'Facts' have crumbled along with the Newtonian system of
the universe. Ranke would have been bewildered by a judgement
essential to modern science: 'The person of the experimenter is
himself part of the experiment.' Or, to put it in terms of the
historian: 'Impartiality gives a more dangerous bias than any
other.'

Though impartiality is impossible, accuracy is a different matter. A historian can copy a document accurately, though he can
never give to it a full, final and lasting interpretation. Impartiality
would not have carried Ranke so far, if he had not been accurate
as well; and maybe he would not have been accurate without his
worship of the elusive 'fact'. The present-day historian feels his
mouth water as he reads of Ranke's three years in Italy, moving
from one archive to another and seeing them opened for historical
purposes for the first time. Ranke was then a little over thirty,
perhaps the best time for an historian to engage in intensive
research: old enough to know what he was doing, young enough
to have energy and zest. We smile at the assiduity with which
scholars nowadays get their foreign travel at other people's
expense – a week at Monte Carlo at the expense of UNESCO,
three months in America at the expense of some foundation, a
trip round the world at the expense of Andrew Carnegie or Cecil
Rhodes. Ranke did far better than his modest successors: he
spent three years in Italy at the expense of the Prussian State.
No historian without private means has ever had such a stroke of
fortune. While in Italy he bought every manuscript and early
printed book which might be useful to him for the Royal library
in Berlin; on his return he borrowed them as long as it suited
him – a convenient arrangement. For Ranke, though remote from
the world, was not without worldly skill.

It is curious to trace, in his letters, Ranke's growing realization that the historian, especially of modern times, will do well to be on the right side of the authorities. There was no element of dishonesty in this; Ranke had been on the side of authority from the beginning. Though he wrote his letters on a desk that had belonged to Gymnastic-father Jahn[1], and had always a touch of German romanticism in his private judgements, Ranke had no sympathy with the political enthusiasms which spluttered among German students after 1815. His religious convictions were deep; among these was a confidence in the divine mission of the monarchical State. He wrote of a speech delivered by Frederick William IV in 1847:

> I say definitely that I know nothing since the psalms where the idea of a religious monarchy has been expressed more powerfully and more nobly. It has great passages of historical truth.

Since this religious monarchy was a 'fact', Ranke was never troubled by any conflict between his devotion to 'facts' and his loyalty to the Prussian State. It never occurred to him that he might discover a fact discreditable to the Prussian monarchy; and sure enough he never did. Each year, in his old age, Ranke would produce a new volume of history 'as it really was'; and each year a copy of the new volume would be sent to William I with an accompanying letter, emphasizing that the volume was devoted to showing the religious mission of the August House.

Thus Ranke escaped from the problems of intellectual integrity which have troubled many academic figures. His nearest contact with it was in 1837, when the famous 'seven of Göttingen' protested against the abolition of the Hanoverian constitution and were deprived of their chairs. Ranke thought their action unnecessary; on the other hand, he refused to accept one of the vacant chairs. It may be wondered whether his refusal would have been so firm if the offer had come from the House of Hohenzollern. This is not to say that Ranke approved of all that happened in Prussia after 1862. His ideal king was Frederick William IV; and though he tried to turn William I into a pillar of European

---

1. Jahn was leader or 'father' of the Gymnastic Unions (*Turnverein*) which became an expression of student radicalism after the Napoleonic wars.

peace, he had difficulty in striking the right note with Bismarck. Ranke distinguished clearly between States and nations; and he regretted Bismarck's association, however equivocal, with German liberalism. He believed that a divine monarchy must keep finance and the army out of parliamentary control. Bismarck had done this in Prussia; but the Imperial constitution of 1871 made dangerous concessions to liberalism. It is not surprising that Ranke sought escape from Bismarck's policy by editing the letters of Frederick William IV to Bunsen – editing them, as he explained to William I, with the necessary discretion. Between Ranke and Bismarck there was never more than a watchful, doubting truce – a conflict of character rather than of fundamental outlook. After all, Bismarck, too, was engaged in preserving the August House (to his own later regret); and Ranke's disciples, though not Ranke himself, had no difficulty in fitting Bismarck into the divine order of things.

Though Ranke did not ignore domestic events either in history or in politics, his consuming interest was in foreign affairs – the domain of history in which the 'fact' is at once most attainable and most elusive. Here, too, he found a divine order, but of a different kind. Within the State the divine order rested on monarchical authority; in the wider community of Europe it was expressed by sovereign States acting to preserve their independence. Not that Ranke was unconscious of the cultural links which held Europe together; after all, he enjoyed a European reputation. He visited Macaulay (though disapproving of the way 'in which he illuminated the present by the past'); he was on intimate terms with Thiers and had an important conversation with him at the height of the Franco-German war; he appreciated Italian art in his rare moments of escape from the archives. But these cultural issues seemed to Ranke to have little to do with politics; or rather, he regarded the conflict of states as an aspect of European culture. Since he accepted the Prussian army as a special manifestation of divine providence, he found no fault in war as such; he condemned only wars fought to spread 'red republicanism' or to establish the domination of a single Power on the Continent – in other words he condemned wars fought against Prussia. For when one comes to look for other monarchies which would display the divine purpose they are difficult to find.

Ranke was on friendly terms with King Maximilian of Bavaria and even claimed that Maximilian, who died in 1864, would have prevented the Austro-Prussian war. But this was no more than a gesture of appreciation to a generous patron of history; besides, the divine order in this case had a curious origin, for the Kingdom of Bavaria had been created by Napoleon.

Austria was a different matter. Here, too, was an August House, of indisputable historical character, and the traditional opponent of revolution. So long as the Habsburg monarchy co-operated with Prussia, it received Ranke's blessing; when it sought to overthrow the divine balance between the two German Powers, Ranke discovered that Roman Catholic Powers did not understand the workings of Providence. It was no accident that in the same year, 1865, Ranke on a visit to England observed a revival of intolerant Protestantism and was glad of it; 'for positive religion, which rejects the general flight into a vague liberalism, accords with my own beliefs'. Thus, the war of 1866 appeared to Ranke as a war of Prussian defence, meant to restore a divine balance which Austria had threatened to overthrow. Once Austria returned to co-operation with Prussia, she became again part of the 'God-willed' order. Beyond these two German Powers, one so full of defects, the monarchical system seems hardly to have extended. Ranke makes virtually no comment on Russia: only Bismarck understood that German destinies depended on what happened beyond the Vistula. Ranke saw catastrophe to the divine purpose in the French Revolution; though he spoke often of Franco-German co-operation he assumed that this could only follow a repudiation by the French of the revolutionary tradition – a sound judgement, as the story of Vichy shows. He welcomed the war of 1870 as a war both against Jacobinism and against Napoleonic imperialism; it was for him a war of the balance of power, a war of self-defence. This carried him far from the controversies of the nineteenth century. He told Thiers in October 1870: 'The King of Prussia is not fighting any longer against Napoleon, who is a prisoner, nor even against France as such; he is fighting the idea of Louis XIV.' Yet it is difficult to think of any monarchy more divinely appointed than that of the Bourbons. Here again the divine order turns out in practice to mean nothing more than increase of Prussian strength.

Worship of power was the creed which bound Germany to-gether; it is a more repellent creed when decked out with phrases of Christian religion. Ranke's letters are a strange mixture in which love of Nature and sincere religious feelings are com-pounded with sycophancy towards the great and apologies for Prussian power. A reader of them turns almost with relief to those latter-day Germans whose orthodoxy did not shrink from straight brutality and dishonesty. Yet this feeling is as mistaken as the hero-worship of Ranke, traditional in German scholarship. Ranke was by no means a hypocrite. He was a man truly dedicated to his task. In his own words: 'I know that I am born to do what I am now carrying out, that my life has no other purpose. I must go on whether I want to or not.' And again: 'I'm content to know what I live for; my heart leaps with happiness when I foresee the joy that executing an important work will give me; I swear daily to execute it without departing by a hair's-breadth from the truth which I see.'

This dedication was a noble passion. But it rested on the assumption that others were dedicated to public duties as Ranke was dedicated to history. Ranke spoke of historians as priests; he regarded kings as the most sacred of priests. The State could never sin; and if it did, this was not his affair. This was the spirit of the learned classes in Germany which brought Hitler to power. Ranke and his followers were not National Socialists, not even their precursors. They were all dedicated men, simple and pure in their private lives. But they regarded the State, whoever conducted it, as part of the divine order of things; and they felt it their duty to acquiesce in that divine order. They never opposed; they rarely protested. Inevitably, therefore, they usually found themselves apologizing for what the State had done. If Hitler was merely the working-out of historical forces, then how could historians con-demn him? Ranke had 'explained' the revocation of the Edict of Nantes; his successors 'explained' the gas-chambers. Nor can the Western world regard Ranke's political quietism with com-placence. The English or American scientist who believes that he has discharged his duty to society by working devotedly in his laboratory evades responsibility as Ranke did; and will end in the same service of blind power. It is tempting to believe that govern-ment is a special calling and that the calling will always be of God.

If history has any lesson it is that men should resist this temptation and should recognize that no member of a community can escape responsibility for its actions. The historian or the scientist does well to lead a dedicated life; yet, however dedicated, he remains primarily a citizen. To turn from political responsibility to dedication is to open the door to tyranny and measureless barbarism.

14

GERMAN UNITY

WHAT is wrong with Germany is that there is too much of it. There are too many Germans, and Germany is too strong, too well organized, too well equipped with industrial resources. This great Germany is a very recent appearance, created overnight by Bismarck and completed only by Hitler. It is tempting, and perhaps profitable, to look back to the time before this Reich was manufactured, and even to consider whether there are any remnants of a Germany of more normal proportions. The longing for a more manageable Germany accounts for the speculations about German particularism, especially for the theory that German aggression can be explained by the domination of Prussia over the remaining German States. But an historian would hesitate to confirm either this easy theory or these easy solutions.

The mosaic of petty States which conventionally forms the immemorial background of Germany was, in fact, the creation of the Treaty of Westphalia (1648), the outcome of the Thirty Years' War. The Treaty of Westphalia enshrined and made permanent German disunity; but it was not the work of the Germans. Indeed, if Germany had been left to herself the Thirty Years' War would, in all probability, have produced a Germany united under the House of Habsburg. Westphalia was the result of foreign interference, the intervention of Denmark, of the Dutch, of Sweden and, above all, of France. The German States were artificially preserved by a balance imposed from without. Few of these States had much historic background; and few of the dynasties had any individual character or long-standing connexion with the territories over which they ruled. The object of the system of Westphalia was not the preservation of particular dynasties but the maintenance of dynasticism in general.

In the ensuing century and a half dynasties rose and fell in importance; some disappeared altogether, one – the Hohenzollern kings of Prussia – came to rank along with the Habsburg emperors as a European Power. These dynastic shufflings meant little or nothing to the inhabitants of the German States. Their attachment was not so much to particularism as to localism. The inhabitant of Dresden or of Leipzig was proud of Dresden or of Leipzig, not of Saxony; the inhabitant of Heidelberg was proud of Heidelberg, not of the Palatinate. Particularism helped localism to survive; only in that sense did it correspond to any German desire. But German desires were irrelevant; the Westphalia system was maintained, as it had been imposed, from without.

The Westphalia system was also overthrown from without by the armies of the French Revolution and the policy of Napoleon. The French armies defeated first Austria and then Prussia, and so destroyed the balance on which the old system had rested. Napoleon wanted more from Germany than the French monarchy had done. The Bourbons had merely wanted Germany to be harmless; Napoleon wanted active German assistance in the furthering of his European plans. The old system of petty States and Free Cities could not produce either the men or the money Napoleon needed. Quite arbitrarily he eliminated all the smaller units and regrouped Germany into some thirty States of medium size; States impotent to oppose him but respectable enough to be ranked as allies.

These States, though larger, had no more reality than before; in fact, thanks to the ruthless redrawing of frontiers by Napoleon, they had less. The Free Cities and the ecclesiastical States were incorporated territorially in the neighbouring kingdoms; spiritually they remained unaffected. Napoleon said the last word on these royal creations of his when he cut short the attempt of one of them to butt into a conversation with the Tsar Alexander I: 'Taisez-vous, roi de Bavière.' The German princes, grouped into the Confederation of the Rhine, were in law sovereign and independent; in fact they counted in Napoleon's Empire for as much as did Croatia or Slovakia in the Empire of Hitler. Their independence decorated the Empire but degraded themselves.

The defeat of Napoleon brought this short-lived system to an end, and in the general hurly-burly the German States were threatened with total disappearance. But in 1815 a united national

Germany was a Jacobinical solution, unacceptable to the victorious Powers. The German States could disappear only if absorbed into an existing Great Power, and in Germany, there were two – Austria and Prussia. Therefore the petty States continued to exist, their existence dependent on the jealousy of Austria and Prussia, not on their own strength. They were grouped now into the German Confederation, a new edition of Napoleon's confederation, with Austria and Prussia substituted for France as the protecting authority.

Life was pleasant in these little States. The inhabitants escaped the burdens of military service and of taxation which they would have had to bear if their preservation had depended on their own efforts; and they enjoyed an affected sham-constitutionalism which they proudly contrasted with Austrian and Prussian autocracy. Thus there came into being the conception of a 'third Germany', under the leadership of Bavaria, the most respectable of these States: the Germany of culture and art, free from absolutism and militarism – but free also from reality. The system of 1815, like the system of Westphalia, was imposed from without. Austria and Prussia held each other in check but acted together against any renewed French threat or against any attempt to unite Germany by revolutionary means; and the two great neighbours, Russia and France, were always alert to see that the balance was maintained. The German States owed their existence not to German sentiment but to the determination of the Great Powers.

In 1848 German liberals of the middle class attempted to unite Germany by peaceful constitutional means. They failed: there was no force in the 'third Germany' and without force Austria and Prussia could not be eliminated. After 1848 Karl Marx wrote: 'Unless the radicals unite Germany by revolutionary means Bismarck will unite it by reactionary Junker means.' The reverse was also true: Bismarck set out to conquer Germany for Prussia in order to prevent a radical Germany which would conquer Prussia. Bismarck talked nationalism; he thought only of the Prussian landed class. This explains the paradox that he allowed the States to continue to exist when he could, apparently, have ended them altogether. If the German States disappeared Prussia too would be swallowed up in a liberal-national Germany; the sham existence of the other States was the guarantee of the continued real existence of Prussia and her Junker lords.

Bismarck had to eliminate one by one the forces which had imposed the settlement of 1815. Russia was bought off, partly by support for Tsarist tyranny in Poland, mainly by acquiescing (or rather appearing to acquiesce) in her Balkan plans. England did not need to be bought off: absorbed in the pursuit of wealth, she had renounced interest in continental affairs. Austria was isolated and, in 1866, defeated in war. The German Confederation ceased to exist; most of the north German States were annexed to Prussia and the other States north of the Main were incorporated into a new federation, which amounted to annexation to Prussia in all but name. The military efforts of the southern States in 1866 had shown that by their own strength they could not exist for a day. But Napoleon III insisted that they should remain independent, and on French orders they enjoyed four years as 'internationally independent States'.

In 1870 Bismarck dealt with France as he had dealt with Austria: isolated diplomatically, she was then defeated in war. For the first time since the early seventeenth century a single authority ruled in Germany, secure from foreign interference, and could dispose of Germany as it wished. But Bismarck wished for a conservative Germany, a Germany of princes and nobles, not an egalitarian Germany of nationalist liberals. All Germany could, no doubt, have been incorporated in Prussia; but then Prussia would have been incorporated in Germany. Prussian needs kept the German States in existence.

The States which joined the Empire in 1871 received greater concessions than had been given in 1867. Bavaria in particular kept not only her own postal system but controlled her own railways and had, in peace-time, a separate army command. The Federal Council, nominated by the State Governments, was, in theory, the governing body of the Empire, in which policy was decided; the Reich had limited defined powers; apart from the yield from Customs dues it had no independent income, but was dependent on deficiency grants from the member States. In form, indeed, the Reich was no more than a federation of princes, with the King of Prussia as President. But it was a federation in which the President could always call the tune: he commanded the armed forces, he nominated the Chancellor, for all practical purposes he could interpret the Constitution as it suited his needs, the deficiency grants had to be provided. The States survived just as long as their existence suited the aims of the Prussian governing class.

The First World War exposed the artificiality of this federal structure. The States were told nothing of the causes of the war, nor of its aims; and Germany fought the war under the dictatorship of the High Command without ever noticing that the States still existed. In 1918 defeat destroyed the basis of Bismarck's elaborate compromise and seemed to give a new chance to the liberal forces which had failed in 1848. The Left majority of socialists and liberals in the Constituent Assembly at Weimar desired a unitary Germany; they knew that the States expressed the class structure of old Germany, not the sentiments of the peoples.

But this Left majority, though sincere in its beliefs, was even more anxious to conciliate the Right parties and so to present a solid 'national' front against the victorious Allies. The Right feared a Socialist Germany and therefore defended the States, Bavaria above all, as a means of limiting the democracy of the Central Government. The States were advocated as a deliberately reactionary measure; and hostility to 'Versailles' made the Left abandon their liberal convictions. Once more the States owed their existence to external forces. An attempt was made to regroup the States on regional lines; but the project came to nothing, and the States remained, more senseless than ever; explicable only on dynastic grounds, they had lost their dynasties and yet continued to exist.

The German States under the Weimar Republic had no real power. Only Bavaria aspired to play an independent role, half-farcical, half-gallant, as the rallying-point of the conservative and 'national' forces against the 'Marxist' Reich. The high-water mark of this performance was Hitler's attempt at a national revolution in Bavaria in 1923. But Hitler's coup came too late (and too early). Germany had now a strong Government under Stresemann; and his first action was to explode the myth of Bavarian separatism. After 1923 the Weimar Republic was a unitary system, the States enjoying a twilight existence only because of the respect felt by the Parliamentary politicians for the letter of the Constitution.

Once this respect vanished the States vanished too. In 1932 the Socialist Government of Prussia was brusquely ordered out of existence by Von Papen; it protested – and obeyed. In 1933 Bavaria tried to revive its independent performance, this time as the rallying-point for the forces of legality; the performance did not last twenty-four hours. In May 1933, Hitler brought the German States to an end: they remained as administrative units, and that only for some purposes, but in a Germany without rights the States were without rights too.

Thus the German States have always been as much artificial, as much manufactured, as the Reich; they have always been imposed upon Germany from without. It is sometimes proposed to revive them in order to save the victorious Allies the burden of policing Germany, but the moment the Allies cease to police Germany the revived States will collapse. It is more practicable to make Germany's neighbours strong than to make Germany weak.

15

THE FAILURE OF THE
HABSBURG MONARCHY

THE Habsburg monarchy was the toughest organization in the history of modern Europe; no other has stood up so long to such battering from so many sides. The Habsburgs rode out the storm of the Reformation; withstood the impact of the Turks; challenged Louis XIV; and survived the French Revolution. The age of nationalism was their doom. This reason alone would justify a new analysis of the national problem in the Habsburg Empire. And there are others. In 1919, after the First World War, the national State seemed to be the pattern for the future. Now we are not so sure. Even the old-established national States of western Europe are drawing together in terms of incipient federalism; how much less likely is it that the national States of Eastern Europe will survive in undiminished sovereignty. Thirty years ago writers tended to regard the great Habsburg Empire as the 'normal' civilized order from which the national States were an unfortunate decline; then, for a short time, men regarded the national States as something equally 'normal' and yet more final. Now we are coming to recognize that both were transitory like all else in history; Francis Joseph could not live for ever nor could the world stand still in 1919. The present system in Eastern Europe has elements of federalism, mixed up in its communist dictatorship; and it is almost certain that no future swing of events will bring back either the Habsburgs or the national States with unrestricted sovereignty. Thus it is rewarding, at any rate as a preliminary exercise, to analyse not only the national problem in the Habsburg monarchy, but also the attempts to reconcile nationalism with a supranational structure.[1]

This is what Professor Kann has attempted to do in his two formidable volumes. They provide more material for a study of

1. *The Multinational Empire*. Nationalism and National Reform in the Habsburg Monarchy, 1848–1918. Volume I: Empire and Nationalities. Volume II: Empire Reform. By Robert A. Kann.

the problem than has hitherto existed in any single book in English. His work, it must be admitted, is rather uncritical. It is an anatomy in Burton's sense, not an analysis. Material is accumulated; quotations are piled one on top of another without discrimination. Altogether his book illustrates the modern delusion that if only we know enough facts we shall arrive at the answer. This is particularly true of his first volume, which sets out to present the national problem. Kann recognizes, of course, that nationalism is tangled up with history; and he elaborates two principles that are common to all discussions of the Habsburg monarchy. One is the division between the nations with a history – the Germans, the Magyars, and even the Czechs – and the nations whose cultural tradition had been completely broken, such as the Slovaks or the Ruthenes. The other is the doctrine of the 'historico-political individualities', by which historical units, such as Hungary or Bohemia, were identified with national claims (Magyar or Czech) which did not in fact correspond with them. Thus history bedevilled the national problem in a twofold way. The nations with a history despised the nations without a history; moreover, they tried to enforce against them, or even against other nations with a history, claims based on history, not on national right. The Magyars insisted on the unity of Hungary against the subject races; the Czechs insisted on the unity of Bohemia against the Germans; the Germans, for that matter, tried to maintain the unity of a German-controlled empire against all comers.

Kann further recognizes that there were in the Habsburg monarchy two sorts of nationalism; the nationalism of landowners and the nationalism of professors – the one traditional, the other academic. But he does not push this analysis far enough. Like most liberal writers, he dismisses Magyar nationalism as 'feudal' and never makes the vital point that its real standard-bearers were the petty gentry, not the great aristocrats. If Hungary had had to depend solely on the Andrássys and Apponyis, its nationalism would have been as artificial as was the Czech movement in the days when it looked to the Thuns and Clam-Martinics. When we come to academic or cultural nationalism, the distinctions are more complicated and more essential. The first age of national awakening is strictly academic. It is led by university professors and is concerned with such things as the study of medieval manuscripts, the evolution of a national language from a peasant dialect, and the rewriting of history on national lines. The second stage comes when the pupils of the professors get out into the world. Then it is a question of the language used first in secondary, finally in elementary schools; the battle is fought over popular newspapers, not over learned works of research. Finally, the elementary school-teachers themselves have pupils: men of some education, who remain peasants or factory workers. We have arrived at mass-nationalism; what Kann calls, without analysing it, the integral nationalism of the twentieth century.

Each of these nationalisms is different in character, in its demands, in the weight of its support. Incredible as it may seem, Kann does not attempt these distinctions; he does not even attempt to estimate the numbers of supporters that any national movement had at any particular moment. Yet there can never be a time at which, say, the equation 'German equals German nationalist' is true. Kann accepts the consequences of this without understanding the reasons for it. He discusses the two non-national movements of the Social Democrats and the Christian Socials; but the point is lost. Yet it is a simple one. Only when nationalism becomes a mass movement do the mass movements become important. On the other hand, at this very time, they begin to lose their non-national character. In the last decade of the Habsburg monarchy both international socialism and international clericalism were beginning to disintegrate under the impact of nationalism; and the process was carried further in the inter-war years. Nowadays even communism is shaken by the nationalist heresy.

The second volume of Kann's book deals with the attempts at reform. But, since there has been no real diagnosis, the reader is constantly puzzled by the question: 'What is it they were trying to solve?' Of course, the men of the time were equally puzzled by this question; hence perhaps their failure. It was commonly believed that the national question was a question of administration. If men could have officials, teachers, and judges using the national language, they would be satisfied. The example of Hungary was decisive and misleading. There can be no dispute that autonomous local administration in the *comitats* was the secret of Hungary's success both in surviving as a nation and then in defeating Habsburg encroachments. But it did not follow from this that, if other nationalities got autonomous local government, they too would automatically repeat Hungary's success. In fact, under dualism, Hungary became a centralized modern State and the *comitats* an empty form, at the very time when centralization was being weakened in the rest of the Empire for the sake of local autonomy. The explanation was simple. Local autonomy was a vital weapon so long as it was a question of resisting the central government; as soon as this battle had been won, it became useless and even an embarrassment. If the *comitats* had remained genuinely autonomous they would have been captured by the nationalities; and Hungary would have ceased to be a Magyar State.

In the last resort the national question is not a question of schools or of government officials – these are mere preliminaries. It is a question of power. Men wish to decide their own destinies. In a national State this leads them to resist kings and emperors and to demand democracy. In a multinational State they resist the rule of other nationalities as well. The Czechs or Rumanians or Ruthenians did not wish merely to use their own languages in school or in the courts; they were determined not to be involved in wars for the sake of German supremacy or for Magyar and Polish causes. The most extraordinary thing in all the discussions about the 'Austrian problem' is the question always left out: who was to rule? Or rather, the omission was deliberate. Every so-called solution assumed that the Habsburgs would remain in supreme control in Vienna; hence the only problem to be solved was that of local administration. Anybody can think of satisfactory schemes for chopping up the empire into national units or historical units or a mixture of both, which would have done quite well if they had settled the essential problem; in reality they were remote from it. The more perfectly the central parliament represented the different nationalities of the empire the more futile it became; for the more it was divided. The basic misunderstanding can be seen in the very title of Kann's book. The Habsburg monarchy was not a multinational empire; it was a supranational empire. Nations can perhaps co-operate if they have a common loyalty to bind them together; they cannot co-operate, at any rate within a single State, merely for the sake of co-operating. The Habsburgs had once provided the common loyalty; in the nineteenth century they failed to do so any longer, and it was this Habsburg failure, not the rise of the nationalities, which doomed their Empire.

The Habsburgs are missing from Kann's book – missing that is as a principle and a cause. Francis Joseph appears merely as ruler, playing the same role as, say, a President of the United States. But Americans are not loyal to President Truman as such; they are loyal to the constitution, to the American 'idea'. The Habsburgs failed to find 'an idea'. How could they be expected to find one? For them, as much as for the nationalities, politics was a question of power; and, so far as they were concerned, it was a question of foreign power. One of the great blunders of modern political thinking is to invent an abstract entity called the State. Many States can be organizations for welfare or internal order, or whatever else suits the theorist. But some half-dozen States, called the Great Powers, are organizations primarily for power – that is, for fighting wars or for preventing them. Hence all analogies between the Habsburg monarchy and, say, Switzerland break down. The Habsburg monarchy was a Great Power or it was nothing. If it could have survived in war against other Great Powers it would not have undergone national disintegration.

The practical historian is thus driven back to analysing the failures of Habsburg power – failure in its armaments, failure in its system of communications, failure in its food supplies, above all failure in its foreign policy. The Habsburgs were fond of finding their doom in a 'Piedmont'; first in the original Piedmont, which nearly brought disaster to them in 1859; then in Serbia, which was the 'Piedmont of the South Slavs'. This analysis, correct enough in its way, has been much misunderstood. The essence of a 'Piedmont' was not that it represented a national challenge; the Habsburgs could deal with such. A 'Piedmont' rejected any need for the Habsburgs at all; it was a rival Power. Both Italy and the South Slav State wished to destroy the Habsburg monarchy, not to reform it; both would have turned with a smile from the elegant plans of reform catalogued by Kann. It is ironical that they should now be the two States which feel most acutely the consequences of the monarchy's disappearance: both have Russia on their borders. In the last resort the Habsburg monarchy was not a device for enabling a number of nationalities to live together. It was an attempt to find a 'third way' in Central Europe which should be neither German nor Russian. Once the Habsburgs became Germany's satellites in war they had failed in their mission. Their doom was of their own making.

16

MARX AND LENIN

UNIVERSITIES nowadays have Professors of almost everything –
Brewing at one, Race Relations at another, Town Planning at a
third. Yet there is still room for a pious benefactor. No university
has a Professor of Marxism; and the theoretical background of
the only religion which is still making converts on a grand scale
remains neglected. Mr Plamenatz will be a strong candidate for
this Chair when it is created. It may seem unlikely that anyone
should write at this time of day a book about Marxism which is
both new and sensible; but Mr Plamenatz has done it.[1] The existing books are special pleading, almost without exception. They
start by assuming either that Marx was right or that he was
wrong; and they go on developing one or other of these assumptions at interminable length. Mr Plamenatz has merely assumed
that Marx was a political thinker of the first rank, who should be
taken seriously; and he has then examined Marxist doctrine with
detached common sense. He treats Lenin as a master of practical
politics, not as a serious thinker, and shows how Bolshevism
transformed Marxism, somewhat as Paul is said to have done with
the teachings of Christ.

Though this is a good book, it is not the book that Mr Plamenatz set out to write, if his title is any guide. The first and more
important part is about Marx, not about German Marxism. But
Marx cannot be treated as a purely German thinker even in his
methods. He himself claimed to have combined German philosophy, English economics, and French politics; and this is a
good deal nearer the truth, though it would be still truer to say
that he rode three separate horses and never got them teamed together. The only German quality in Marx was the 'dialectic'
framework which he learnt from Hegel; and, as Mr Plamenatz
shows, this was a gigantic nuisance which Marx increasingly abandoned when he wrote on serious questions. Marx's economics
derived solely from English writers, principally from Ricardo;

1. *German Marxism and Russian Communism.* By John Plamenatz.

and the practical basis of them – made into a generalization of universal application – was capitalist England of the textile age. His political outlook was that of an extreme French radical; and the only political events on which he made any valuable observations were the French revolution of 1848 and the Paris Commune of 1871. The English Labour party has come nearer than any other to applying the economic part of Marx's programme; just as the French and those who have learned from them are the only ones to have a genuinely revolutionary proletariat.

Neither Marxist economics nor Marxist politics suited German conditions; and the German Marxists had to adapt these doctrines to quite different conditions, a process in which Engels himself led the way. How they did this would make a fascinating study, never yet attempted. It is not enough to mention Bernstein's revisionism or to assert that the German Social Democrats wanted a welfare state, not social revolution. Such a study would have reinforced the argument of Mr Plamenatz's book; for it would then have appeared that the Germans set the example which the Russians followed. Kautsky first built up a Marxist orthodoxy devised for German conditions; and Lenin learnt the trick from him. Both were forcing a given theory to fit into existing conditions, instead of deriving their theory from these conditions – a confusing, but very usual, process. Mr Plamenatz sees this clearly enough with the Bolsheviks. They made a revolution, established themselves in power, and then asked: 'how can Marxism be used to justify what we have done?' But the Germans had done exactly the same; and if Mr Plamenatz had brought this out, he would then have realized that it applied to Marx also. Marx wanted certain things; and he therefore devised theories which proved that they would happen. Principles and actions came before theory in Marx's case, as in everyone else's.

Of course Mr Plamenatz goes some way to recognizing this. Indeed much of his book is given over to a careful logical demonstration that Marx's theories were dogmas, which could not be justified by the facts. For instance, Marx insisted that the number of labourers increased faster than the machines which employed them; therefore 'the reserve army of the unemployed' would grow ever larger. He expressed this by a mathematical formula which is made more telling by being repeated again and again. But the formula could be proved true only by statistics which Marx did not possess and which indeed do not exist. As a matter of fact scientists often proceed in this way. It is a great mistake to suppose that they generalize only from a random body of experience. More usually they first formulate a theory and then collect the evidence to prove that it is true. The great scientist is not distinguished by guessing less, but by guessing better. The process is much more difficult to apply in history. The natural scientist can make his laboratory produce the necessary evidence to justify his theory. The historian can only turn to the records; and these were never kept to answer the questions which he had in mind. Hence it has been plausibly maintained that no serious history can be attempted before about 1850, when accurate statistics begin; and even these are so faulty that some dismiss the possibility of rigorous history before the outbreak of the Second World War. All historians before then, including Marx, were literary artists – a description which most historians of the present day certainly do their best to avoid.

Marx's generalizations about history can never be shown to be either true or false. They are merely curious. It would be more rewarding to explain how he came by them and what results he expected from them. In fact what we want is a Marxist analysis of Marx. Mr Plamenatz has a mastery of Marx's writings which would enable him to do it. Unfortunately, like most political theorists, he will not condescend to the routine task of learning history. He treats Marx in detachment without much reference to the intellectual climate of the time. He has therefore missed a discovery of the first importance, though he is constantly on the edge of it. For though Marx was the greatest of socialist writers and the founder of modern Socialism, he was as a thinker the last flower of Individualism. He achieved Socialism simply by taking *laissez-faire* economics and rationalist psychology and standing them on their heads; but despite this inversion they remained individualist theories. Take, for instance, the class struggle, which is the central point of his doctrine. This is true only if we accept the principle – universally assumed in the middle of the nineteenth century – that every man recognizes his economic interest and pursues it. Every proletarian fights his employer and co-operates with every other proletarian; every peasant or shop-keeper knows that he belongs to a dying class and therefore joins the rising one. If rationalist individualism is true, then Socialism must follow from it. It is not true; and that is why we have not got Socialism.

In exactly the same way, Marxist economics are individualist economics. They assume the working of 'economic laws' and project them into the future. Mr Plamenatz finds it puzzling why Marx thought that a capitalist should pursue higher profit when he had plenty already. But, given the contemporary assumption that capitalists were capitalists all the time, it must necessarily follow. If a man stopped behaving as a capitalist even for a minute of the day, economic laws would break down, as they always do in practice. Again, it seems an extraordinary thing that Marx had no theory of foreign trade; and the lack of it has handicapped socialists from then until now. But in the era of Free Trade, no theory of foreign trade was necessary; or rather it was there already. Marx merely assumed that Socialist communities would go on trading with each other according to the best principles of the division of labour. Indeed, he even assumed that Socialism would work without planning or conscious forethought; and so it would, if every man followed his own economic interest logically.

Similarly, when Marx came to politics, he shared the individualist radicalism of his time. He, too, assumed that it was highly desirable to strangle the last king with the bowels of the last priest; and he believed that inestimable benefit would follow from this. His only novelty was to show that the last capitalists (and by Marxist laws these would be few) should be strangled at the same time. Mr Plamenatz keeps asking impatiently: 'but why should Utopia arrive merely because this curious operation has been carried out?' Marx would have answered: 'Because every serious political thinker of my time from Bentham to Mazzini says so.' Marx was superior to his contemporaries in seeing that democracy could not work without a social revolution; but, living in the age of rationalism, he could not be expected to see that it needed a psychological revolution also.

This surely explains Lenin's creation of a new Marxist theory. Mr Plamenatz makes it clear that he was a different sort of man;

but this is not an interesting discovery – all men are different, as well as being the same. The important thing is that he was a man of a different age. Marx was a rationalist, believing in Progress and anxious to discover its laws. He was satisfied when he showed that progress was going in the same direction as himself. Lenin belonged to the age of collective man and of the struggle for power. He himself once said that the only interesting question in life was 'who whom?' Who exploits whom? Who sentences whom to death? He was not interested in where history was going. He wanted to know how to get to the right end of a gun and stay there. This is not an attractive question for the political theorist, but it has its importance in certain societies and at certain moments. Leninism is not a political philosophy; it is a guide to political practice in the era of gangster-warfare, the sort of guide that Marx often tried to write but never succeeded. Mr Plamenatz suggests that Lenin vulgarized Marx's theories and perverted them. But he believes this only because he prefers the age of rational individualism to that of the gangsters. Everyone can have his private tastes, but they have no place in historical study. John Stuart Mill has long been in his grave; and we have to live with the secret police, the televised politician and the hydrogen bomb. 'Who whom?' is a question that will last our time.

17

THE SECOND INTERNATIONAL

THE nineteenth century travelled hopefully. We have arrived. Everyone is prosperous, secure: television sets and second-hand cars firmly embedded as a cost-of-living. The will of the people prevails at every general election – a will no doubt accurately expressed in a precise balance between two equally ineffective parties. Keynesian principles guard us against every economic ill; and now the hydrogen bomb, it is said, guards us against war. We are in the earthly Paradise. The only price we have paid is to cease to believe in it. Progress has been the great casualty of our age. There is no longer a MacDonald to hold out the prospect of 'up and up and up and on and on and on'. There would be no audience even if a new MacDonald appeared. To recapture the belief in Progress we must return to the twenty-five years before the First World War, years in which European civilization reached its zenith. These years were exactly spanned by the Second International, the subject of the third volume in G. D. H. Cole's *History of Socialist Thought*.[1] Its thousand pages present a theme now remote and unsympathetic – futile debates, empty phrases, barren and impotent leaders. Yet there was in it deep tragedy – the tragedy of disappointed Hope and the greater tragedy of Hope Fulfilled.

In Cole's earlier volumes there were few Socialists but much thinking. In the present volume there is a great Socialist movement and virtually no thought. Take away Rosa Luxemburg, and everyone – reformist or revolutionary, Fabian or Bolshevik – scrabbled over phrases, while throwing his real energy into winning votes or enlisting members. All were convinced that the victory of Socialism was inevitable and that it would be achieved in a democratic way. The German revisionists and English Fabians indeed held that the victory would be imperceptible: there would be no precise moment at which capitalism ended and Socialism

1. *The Second International*, 2 volumes. Volume III of *A History of Socialist Thought*. By G. D. H. Cole.

began. The orthodox continued to believe in 'the revolution'. There would be at some point a jerk, a change of gear, when the Socialist commonwealth could be acclaimed. But for them, too, the revolution was simply part of an inevitable process; in democratic countries it would be little more than the appearance of a Socialist majority in Parliament. Even in countries not yet democratic – Germany in particular – the revolution would be political, not economic: the Social Democrats would insist on a change in the constitution once they got a majority, and thereafter Socialism would flow inevitably on. Kautsky, the high priest of Marxism, postulated in *The Way to Power* that the secret of success lay in doing nothing: the longer the Social Democrats sat tight and allowed their supporters to accumulate, the greater and more irresistible would be their triumph when it came.

The greatest handicap of the Social Democrats was their adherence to the Marxist scriptures. Their adherence was selective. They suppressed or ignored Marx's advocacy of violent revolution; and therefore clung the more obstinately to his economic analysis. This was not surprising. Marx saw more deeply than any previous observer; but he drew from the Lancashire textile industry generalizations of world-wide application. The capitalists would grow fewer and richer; the workers poorer and more numerous. In the end there would be nothing in between. Hence the working-class party would inevitably become 'the democracy' by the mere passage of time. The prophecy worked satisfactorily until just before the First World War. Then the German Social Democrats realized that their rate of increase was grinding to a stop, as that of the British Labour Party has now done. The insoluble dilemma was approaching; do we abandon Socialism or Democracy? The Bolsheviks, never having enjoyed Democracy, were to choose Socialism; others, doubtful in any case about Socialism, preferred to wait for the majority that never came.

This was not the only gap in Marx's teaching. He had always promised to provide the equation demonstrating the collapse of capitalism; but he never found it and for this reason left the second volume of *Capital* unfinished. He had nothing to say about the peasants except that they must be destroyed. Later Socialists have improved on this only by proposing (as Lenin did) that the peasants should be gulled until the moment for their destruction arrived. Again Marx had no answer to the national question except that it did not exist: 'The workers have no country.' The German leaders of the Second International interpreted this to mean that, since they had achieved their national freedom, the other peoples of Central Europe should be delighted to become Germans also. When this bargain failed to attract, the 'Austro-Marxists' of Vienna invented the legend of the Habsburg monarchy as a great Free Trade area, an International in miniature; and their example has been loyally followed by Socialist enthusiasts for the British Commonwealth in our own day. The Second International was a combine of master-nations, secure in their own rights and bewildered by the claims of others. Even more striking, the International was a purely European affair with a solitary Japanese representing nobody. The few Socialist parties outside Europe were the work of immigrants and usually faded away with the second generation. Professor Cole includes a chapter on China for the sake of Sun Yat Sen. It is modelled on Johnson's chapter on snakes in Iceland: there was no Socialism in China. In this the International reflected the universal assumption of the time. Europe was civilization; therefore no Socialist movement could flourish outside it.

The Second International carried belief in Progress to its highest point. Progress was both the inspiration of Social Democracy and its ruin. Marx shared with Samuel Smiles the belief that if men pursued their material betterment persistently enough Utopia would arrive. The only difference was that Marx preached this doctrine to the working class instead of to the entrepreneurs. But the principle was the same: demand higher wages, shorter hours, and International Socialism will be here in no time. The Social Democrats discovered to their confusion that the workers, having secured high wages and shorter hours, now demanded wages still higher and hours still shorter, and that Socialism was further off than ever. This outcome affected the Social Democrats themselves. Once the German Social Democrats had built up a gigantic party-machine for class war, they shrank from using it for this or any other purpose. The party bosses came to regard themselves as the purpose of the party-machine long before the Russian Communists made the same discovery. Ebert, Viktor Adler, or

Arthur Henderson might well have said: 'We are all Stalinists nowadays.'

The same law operated between nations. The peoples of Europe had once been oppressed. By the end of the nineteenth century they were living on the plunder of the rest of the world as they still do. The more hard-headed Social Democrats proposed that the workers should enter into a junior partnership with their own capitalists for the exploitation of others – a line taken by some German Social Democrats during the First World War and by Ernest Bevin in England after the second. Most Socialists shrank from the cynicism, but they were not altogether at a loss. The Fabians, in particular, were delighted to demonstrate that the exploited peoples were being plundered for their own good. They differed from their rulers only in holding that the Powers should not run into conflict as to which should shoulder the greatest share of 'the white man's burden'. The international 'consortium' was a happy invention before the First World War; the international 'mandate' an even happier after it. The Second International held fast to its high principle: fair shares, at any rate for the Big Brothers.

Imperialism landed the Social Democrats in the problem of war, much to their surprise. Marx had given them no warning. He had blamed capitalism for being too pacific, not too warlike. The capitalists of Cobden's day had refused to fight the great war of liberation against Russia which Marx passionately advocated. Even now the Social Democrats went on dreaming that the magnates of finance would pull off a great merger at the last moment. Still they tried to discharge their responsibility. The Second International discussed the problem of war again and again. It laid down a simple truth: the workers could prevent war if they wished to do so. But suppose they did not wish to prevent war, what then? Viktor Adler gave the answer in 1914 when he supported Austria-Hungary's attack on Serbia the moment that the crowds in the streets of Vienna demonstrated in its favour. It is often said that the World War ruined International Socialism. A more careful reading of the record shows that it was the other way round. The Second International was already torn wide apart before the crisis of 1914. If it had possessed the unity and strength even of ten years before, the outbreak of war would have been impossible. Success ruined the Social Democrats. They thought that it was essential to be on the winning side; for, by definition, Progress means simply the side that wins. Things are much easier now that Progress has come to an end. Who cares about Success? Right is still Right though the heavens fall. And, by the way, the ones who stuck to their hopeless principles got Success as an unlooked-for bonus. Lenin achieved supreme power; the German Social Democrats never got anywhere. The more ruthless, extreme, and uncompromising your politics, the greater will be your reward in this world as well as in the next. A most consoling conclusion, though not perhaps for the Rt. Hon. Hugh Gaitskell.

18

THE ENTENTE CORDIALE

THE agreements which gave formal expression to the Anglo-French entente were published on 8 April 1904. British opinion welcomed the agreements enthusiastically, but saw in them colonial arrangements and nothing more. 'We have settled our differences with France' was the common phrase. England had made a good bargain: apart from the sorting out of many minor disputes she had made her control of the two ends of the Mediterranean secure from French interference for ever. At the one end France recognized British predominance in Egypt and finally renounced her own claims; at the other end France gave new guarantees for the invulnerability of Gibraltar, for she agreed, as the condition of her bringing Morocco into the French Empire, that the Moorish coastline opposite Gibraltar should pass to Spain and should be preserved unfortified by the three Powers.

No wonder the British welcomed the agreements: in cheering the French they were, in characteristic British fashion, cheering a good loser. The heirs of Napoleon were acknowledging finally the victory of Nelson. There was on the British side hardly a shade of precaution against Germany. The British were, of course, glad to escape from the attitude of dependence on Germany into which the danger of conflict with France had sometimes led them. But they did not fear Germany, nor had they any cause of conflict with her: the trivial colonial disputes were long ended, and although the building of the German fleet was a nuisance the British were confident that they could always hold their own at sea unaided – after all, in 1905 the British Navy attained a superiority over the combined naval forces of all other Powers unparalleled in our history.

Still less was there on the British side any great principle, any idea of co-operation between the Western democracies against German militarism. Lord Lansdowne, the Foreign Secretary, had worked as hard in 1901 for an alliance with Germany as in 1903 and 1904 for an entente with France. It would be difficult to see in the Irish landowner who resigned from Gladstone's Government in 1880 rather than acquiesce in Irish land reform and the Tory die-hard who defended the House of Lords in 1910 a champion of democracy; and the author of the Lansdowne peace letter, who in 1917 advocated a *status quo* peace (for the sake of social order) and even then saw no need for Germany to atone for her crimes, detected no threat to civilization in the Germany of 1904.

With the French it was far otherwise: there the advocates of the entente knew what they were doing, knew that they were staking the future of France for the sake of western democratic civilization. For more than two hundred years the French had carried on colonial conflicts with England, and for more than two hundred years French ambitions in Europe had made her the loser in these colonial conflicts. French domination in Europe was ended at Leipzig and Waterloo, and its last echoes were silenced at Sedan. After 1871 necessity left France free as never before to pursue colonial aims and to find a substitute for lost European glory in the Mediterranean empire which was the legacy of Bonaparte's expedition to Egypt in 1798. Germany, as Bismarck was constantly urging, was eager for reconciliation, and if France had been reconciled with Germany as Austria-Hungary had been after 1866 she could have had German support against England in Egypt as Austria-Hungary had it against Russia in the Near East.

Reconciliation was the logical, easy course, but it was not taken. Only a small unpopular minority advocated revenge. The great majority recognized that France had been irretrievably defeated, yet they would not accept German patronage. For almost thirty years France refused to acknowledge the inevitable; she tried to oust the British from Egypt without German support. The Fashoda crisis of 1898 showed that the attempt was impossible, and Delcassé, then newly Foreign Minister, determined the future destinies of France when, without appealing for German assistance, he ordered Marchand to withdraw.

For the English the entente had no anti-German point, but the French knew that in making the entente they were becoming the hostage of democracy on the continent of Europe. They had no hope of winning British assistance for a war of revenge. Indeed in the then state of the British Army they did not even value British assistance for a defensive war; the army of their Russian ally remained their sole military support. But the French were determined not to become partners in the German order. To renounce Egypt was a crime against the memory of Bonaparte; to renounce Alsace and Lorraine would be a crime against the national principle, an infringement of the Rights of Man.

The French hesitated for thirty years, but at the crisis of their destiny they remained faithful to the ideas of the Revolution. Relinquishing material gain and Mediterranean empire, they chose to remain independent and to remain democratic; they continued to be the standard-bearers of western civilization against militarism and autocracy. They chose with their eyes open; they knew that if they held out against German temptation it was on them that the German blow would fall. By making the Anglo-French entente the French brought on themselves the sufferings of 1914–18 and of 1940–44, but in 1904 the prospect of a German hegemony of Europe achieved by peaceful means vanished for ever.

Small wonder that the French hesitated. Small wonder that the entente was not received on the French side with the easy popularity which it evoked in England. Small wonder that at first the nerve of the French almost failed and that, fifteen months after the conclusion of the entente, Delcassé, its author, was driven from office on German orders. Yet the work of Delcassé was not undone. France looked the dangers in the face and, when the time came, accepted them. Many Frenchmen contributed to this decision. Yet Delcassé was more than their spokesman. He was not a great man; indeed, in some ways he was foolish and hot-headed. He offended his own colleagues and injured his own cause. But he had in him the flame of loyalty to the ideas of 1789, to the principles of national independence and of human equality. He was determined to keep France free, both at home and abroad. The entente was perhaps no more than a new expression of the unity of Western democratic civilization, but Delcassé gave it that expression. Forty years after, all those Englishmen who recognize the difference between French civilization and German order may well say: 'Homage to Theophile Delcassé!'

19

THE SECRET OF THE
THIRD REPUBLIC

THE Third Republic puzzled contemporary observers; now it
baffles the historian. The revolution, the empire or the monarchy
of July can be reduced to a formula; the Third Republic defies
definition. It is much easier to describe the forces which threatened
it than to discover those which preserved it; hence French
historians have written brilliantly on Boulangism, on Royalism
or on the revolutionary Syndicalists. It is even possible to explain
the origins of the Third Republic; but its founders, whether Thiers
or Gambetta, would have been astonished at its development.
Inaugurated with radical phrases, it gave France the most conservative system of government in Europe; established by the
massacre of Parisian workers, it was the first Great Power to
have Socialist ministers, and at the beginning of the twentieth
century the leader of the Socialist party was its greatest parliamentarian; repudiating the empire that had preceded it, it
made France the second Imperial Power in the world; born of
defeat, it recovered for France the Rhine frontier which two
Emperors had lost. Despite its feeble origins, it gave France within
fifty years the highest position she had held in Europe since the
days of Louis XIV. Twenty years after this achievement, it
brought France lower than she had ever been in modern times.
The Third Republic went from the greatest success to the worst
defeat; yet it had no other aim than compromise and a quiet
life.

The most baffling period in this baffling story is that of the
national revival between 1912 and 1914. Within these two years
France abandoned the policy of conciliation towards Germany
and claimed again the position of a Great Power; thus she acquired the vitality which enabled her to withstand not only the
first shock of the German attack, but still more the shock of
Verdun and of the failure of Nivelle; to survive, despite many
alarms, until at last the elderly Clemenceau seemed to give her at

THE SECRET OF THE THIRD REPUBLIC   147

last a new youth. Clemenceau became war-dictator; all the same Clemenceau was not a characteristic figure of the Third Republic, and the study of his career throws no light upon it. Rather he was the enemy of all that the Third Republic represented and passed his life attacking its ministers. When he was criticized for this, he replied: 'Bah! I have always overthrown the same ministry.' The antagonism was clear to him, though not always to his opponents.

It is Caillaux, not Clemenceau, the 'traitor', not the dictator, who should be studied; it is Agadir, not the victories of 1918, which express the spirit of the Third Republic. Its secret, if it is to be found anywhere, will be found in Caillaux's *Memoirs*,[1] the two first volumes of which were published during the occupation and the third in July 1947. This is not an impartial contribution. It is a subtly delayed revenge against the men who brought Caillaux to ruin, above all against Poincaré and Clemenceau who, according to Caillaux, by asking too much of France ruined the Third Republic. Caillaux promises revelations; all he gives is the warmed-up gossip of the Palais Bourbon. The reader, half-recollecting Caillaux's story, opens the book full of sympathy for its author; by the end he has almost been convinced that the charges made against Caillaux must have some foundation.

Caillaux, however, does not present himself as a topic of controversy; rather, caught in the storm, he has tried to brave it. The first volume is the story of the days of easy success, when nothing seemed to threaten the stability of the Third Republic. Caillaux was not a Republican by family origin or by education, and still less a radical Socialist. His father had been a minister in Broglie's government of '16 May' (1877); Caillaux himself began in the Inspectorate of Finance. He was essentially a man of order, hating excess and violence, whether Bonapartist or Republican; he became a radical, when he saw that the lower middle class and the peasants had become the governing classes. His father approved this step: 'One must go with the governing forces of one's country.' The same argument would have made Caillaux a loyal servant of the Bourbons or of the Directory. Caillaux entered politics as a 'government man'; he had the good luck to become,

1. *Mes Mémoires*. I. Ma Jeunesse orgueilleuse, 1863–1909. II. Mes audaces. Agadir 1909–12. III. Clairvoyance et force d'âme dans les Épreuves, 1912–30. By Joseph Caillaux.

almost at once, Minister of Finance under Waldeck-Rousseau. Caillaux perhaps exaggerates the work and character of this parliamentarian whom he presents as a great man. He hints at an apostolic succession of radical leaders: Waldeck-Rousseau, Rouvier, Caillaux, patriots though pacific, whose work was destroyed by ambitious 'warmongers'. Certainly if Caillaux is to be judged by his own account of the years between 1898 and 1909, he must be recognized as the best Minister of Finance in the Third Republic. There is one surprising point: from 1906 to 1909 Caillaux was a minister in the government of Clemenceau. He supposed that Clemenceau had been tamed by the bitter years which followed the Panama scandal; he thought that Clemenceau had become, like the others, a good Republican. Despite this, Caillaux strikes a false note. He cannot refrain from anticipating later events and from producing in advance the stories that he had accumulated over the years. He claims that in 1928 Briand told him that the faults of the Treaty of Versailles were due to the fact that 'Clemenceau was not free in relation to England'. It is difficult to decide whether this story reflects more discredit on Briand or on Caillaux; and it is typical of the 'proofs' which Caillaux claims to furnish.

One episode disturbed the quiet of the first decade of the century: the Moroccan crisis of 1905. Caillaux passes rapidly over this topic, attributing the dispute entirely to Delcassé's failure to inform Germany of his Moroccan plans. This is essential to his later argument. If he once admitted that the German object in 1905 was to reduce France to a position of dependence, the policy of Agadir would be condemned in advance. Agadir is the subject of Volume II, the least interesting of the three volumes. The revelations, for what they are worth, have already appeared in Caillaux's earlier book on this subject; they are merely repeated here with more bitterness. Caillaux was at least consistent: having once taken up a line of defence, he neither changed nor added to it, even in a book to be published after his death. Thus there is nothing new concerning the unofficial approach which he made to Germany; nothing on the projects of economic collaboration between Germany and France to which he aspired; and very little on his schemes for acquiring Spanish Morocco with German assistance. His attitude towards England is the strangest feature in his account of Agadir. The English statesmen aimed to show their firm determination to support France; Caillaux represents himself as abandoned by England and extracting from the English statesmen only a reluctant acquiescence. The Agadir crisis was certainly a turning-point in British foreign policy: the moment at which British opinion in general became convinced that it was Germany's ambition to dominate Europe. Caillaux cannot admit this ambition; therefore in his defence he talks only of Morocco, which he justly claims to have won for France without a war. This was not as great an achievement as he makes out. France could have had Morocco whenever she liked on Germany's terms; and Caillaux seemed to have accepted those terms.

This should have been his real defence, except that it was impossible to use it after all that followed. It was the logical development of the beginnings of the Third Republic that France did not challenge the position of Germany in Europe, but contented herself with empire in Africa; this was the policy of Gambetta and of Ferry, the one policy that could combine glory and peace. Caillaux is in the right when he represents his Agadir policy as that of a good Republican in the old sense; even his secret negotiations had their precedents in Gambetta's advances to Bismarck. But times had changed. Instead of being hailed as a great Republican statesman, Caillaux was driven from power, never again to be Prime Minister. French history reached its most dramatic and unexpected turning-point since the Revolution. Caillaux explains his defeat by intrigue and corruption. These played their part, but far more decisive was the unconscious refusal of French sentiment to accept a subordinate place in Europe.

This was shown by the sequel. Caillaux never realized that his chance had passed. In 1914, he was still dreaming of a pacific coalition between Radicals and Socialists, the coalition of Jaurès and Caillaux; this, he claims, would have refused to support Russia in the Balkans and so prepared the way for a Franco-German co-operation to impose peace on Russia and Austria-Hungary. Jaurès was blinded by his preoccupation with electoral reform. Nevertheless, Caillaux insists, the coalition would have been made, had it not been for the calumnies of Calmette and his assassination by Mme Caillaux. It is typical of Caillaux's vanity

that he should find in his private affairs the cause of the first
German war, typical also of that lack of a sense of reality which
finally brought the Third Republic to disaster. The story of
Calmette is told in detail, the most surprising element being the
affirmation that the press campaign was inspired by Poincaré,
Barthou and Klotz (the last name being added to make the first
two seem less improbable). Certainly Poincaré and Barthou were
glad to see Caillaux excluded from public life. In May 1913
Poincaré said to Paléologue: 'Clemenceau detests me.... Yet
despite his great faults of pride and jealousy, of resentment and
hate, he has one quality which earns him forgiveness, a quality
which Caillaux lacks: he has, in the highest degree, national fibre,
he is a patriot like the Jacobins of 1793'. Caillaux never understood that between 1912 and 1914 France transcended the Third
Republic and rejected for ever his policy of conciliation towards
Germany.

Curiously enough his energy and self-confidence flag when he
comes to talk of the period of the war. Yet it was in 1916 and not
in 1914 that Caillaux offered a terrible alternative to the policy of
making war. In 1914 all France was determined to resist German
domination; by the end of 1916 her effort seemed exhausted. A
party of peace came into existence with Caillaux at its head. If
Poincaré had appointed Caillaux instead of Clemenceau, a compromise peace would have been attempted. It is inconceivable that
Caillaux did nothing, that he attempted no peace propaganda,
that he made no contact, however indirect, with the Germans.
There is not a word of it in his *Memoirs*. Even stranger, Clemenceau, though still hated, becomes in Volume III a great figure
beyond the reach of insults and, almost, the saviour of his country.
It is as though Caillaux acknowledged the greatness of his ad-
versary and admitted defeat. Henceforth he reserves his spite for
Poincaré, certainly a figure of less importance, but who also had
his moment of greatness when he determined to place Clemenceau in power. The story of the peace that failed, the negotiations
of 1917, has still to be written; when it is written Caillaux will fill
a larger place in it than he claims for himself in his *Memoirs*.
This was the last chance of the old Europe and of the historic
Great Powers, of Austria-Hungary and France. To succeed,
Caillaux would have had to be very different from what he was:

less intelligent and less subtle, but also more honest and more patriotic.

Where Caillaux failed after Agadir, Briand succeeded at Locarno and Bonnet at Munich – both attempts to save the continent of Europe by a reconciliation between France and Germany. Caillaux could have claimed to be the John the Baptist of these two strokes and even of the policy of Montoire, which was their last version. Yet though a 'government man', Caillaux had in him a strange streak of obstinacy and contradiction. A financier from the upper middle class, he had turned against his origin and, becoming a Radical, had represented a peasant constituency; he had preached reconciliation with Germany at the moment of national revival; he had intrigued for peace during the first German war. Towards the end of his life, he refused to believe in the policy of collaboration with the Germany of Hitler, although this was the official policy of the governing class. Certainly he had no faith in French resistance or in the return of past glory. Like many others, he accepted the government of Vichy and hoped that France, once liberated by her great allies, would then be reconciled with a more civilized Germany. Thus he remained to the end faithful to the policy of Agadir; and to the end he saw in his opponents only warmongers bent on the ruin of Europe.

Only a Franco-German reconciliation could have given Europe peace and stability; this was the core of truth in the policy of Agadir. The mistake was to suppose this reconciliation possible. The Third Republic was radical though pacific, and its leaders, whether Ferry, Caillaux or Bonnet, believed that in Germany too the policy of war was supported only by a few militarists and by the Kaiser. In reality expansion, if not war, was essential to the German system, and every step towards the rule of the masses increased German violence. A peaceful collaboration was possible only with the German Conservatives, as between Ferry and Bismarck or Caillaux and Kiderlen. This class was losing ground, and there was no Conservative with whom Bonnet could collaborate: he had to pretend to find an aristocrat in Ribbentrop and Bismarckian moderation in Goering. The Third Republic had to choose between Radicalism and Pacifism. In 1914 and 1917, in the strange atmosphere of the national revival, it gave up

Pacifism, and Caillaux represented the defeated party. In 1940 it gave up Radicalism and, in fact, ceased to exist for the sake of reconciliation with Germany. This sacrifice only served to show that the policy of Agadir could not have saved the Third Republic and its contradictions. If France had followed Caillaux in 1911, in 1914, or in 1917, she would have been cut off from England and Russia and would have given Germany the mastery of Europe without a struggle. It needed two German wars to repudiate the policy of Agadir, wars which brought the ruin of France, but which ruined Germany as well. The stability of the Continent was and remains possible only at the price of German hegemony. This price France refused to pay, whatever the consequences to herself. The French decision saved Europe from German domination. It was the last great service which France performed for European civilization before herself ceasing to be a Great Power.

20

HOLSTEIN: THE MYSTERY MAN

THE First World War has always been a happy hunting-ground for theories of the 'Hidden Hand' – men of mystery behind the scenes who manoeuvred human destiny. Even before 1914, many English radicals held that Sir Edward Grey was the prisoner, perhaps unwitting but certainly helpless, of the Foreign Office. The Foreign Office was not condemned alone. The Quai d'Orsay and, still more, the Wilhelmstrasse fell under the same verdict. The Wilhelmstrasse had a special feature. All its members were wicked, but one was more wicked than others. Friedrich von Holstein – the spectre, the evil genius of the Wilhelmstrasse, the man with hyena eyes, blackmailer and psychopath, the perfect man of mystery.

Holstein died in 1909, five years before the outbreak of war. He had retired from the Foreign Office in 1906. He could hardly, therefore, be blamed for the war itself. What he got was the blame for the decline in Germany's position: she was the decisive factor in Europe when Bismarck left office in 1890 – 'the tongue in the balance', he called her. By 1906 she had become isolated and 'encircled', no ally except the moribund Habsburg monarchy, war soon to be forced on her, and defeat following. And Holstein had done it. He manoeuvred himself into the dominant position in the foreign ministry; planted his creatures out in the leading embassies; and then ruined everything by his insane suspicions. His first act as adviser in 1890, when Bismarck went, was to stop the renewal of the Reinsurance treaty with Russia and so force her into the arms of France. Then he followed a policy of irritating pin-pricks towards England, trying to blackmail her into a formal alliance; but when the British statesmen came along with an offer in 1901, he answered with, according to the title of one book about him, 'Holstein's Great No'. So there we are: the Anglo-French entente as well as the Franco-Russian alliance was all his doing.

His evil influence was not shown only in affairs of grand policy; he was also a corrupter of individuals. Sitting at the centre of his spider's web in Berlin, corresponding privately with ambassadors and spying on them, he taught them to be servile – as though Germans needed any teaching in that – uncritical, unreliable. He got hold of scandalous secrets about Princess Bülow, the Chancellor's wife, or, according to another account, about Bülow himself, and he used these secrets to blackmail the Chancellor, not only keeping himself in office but dictating policy to suit his whims. Even when he was got rid of, he released scandal against Prince Eulenberg, the Kaiser's closest friend. The scandals ruined Eulenberg and discredited William II into the bargain. Certainly a fine record of destruction. The papers from the German foreign ministry did not show much of this when they were published in the nineteen-twenties. Holstein appeared as a hard-working official, very competent technically, perhaps rather inclined to see the weak points in any policy rather than its advantages, but not malignant or destructive. Still, the legend survived. It was known that Holstein had carried off most of his private papers; and these hung like a dark cloud over the record, scholars rubbing their hands and saying: 'Wait until they are published. Then we shall see something!'

I have no doubt about the importance of Holstein's career. The years between 1890 and 1906 were vital in the history of Germany, years of decision at their most intense. 1906, I am tempted to think, is the real beginning of contemporary history so far as Europe is concerned; certainly it began the era of the German wars, an era perhaps now closed. The real question of interest in regard to Holstein is not whether he blackmailed people, but how far he contributed to the changes in Germany's position. On the personal side the first volume of his papers, which has just been published,[1] is disappointing. There may be more excitement in the later volumes which will contain his private letters.

This one turns out to be very much a damp squib. It contains his so-called 'memoirs', partly scraps of recollections, from his early years, some amusing anecdotes about Bismarck, spiteful and less amusing remarks about his colleagues; and partly reflections on policy put down after his retirement – German relations with the principal Great Powers, the influence of William II, and so on. There is nothing new here, certainly nothing sensational.

1. *The Holstein Memoirs.* Cambridge University Press.

Holstein had always been an assiduous worker. Thrown out of his job, he was bored, restless, perhaps resentful; and he obviously meant to write a vindication of his career, much as Bismarck had done in similar circumstances fifteen years before. But, like most professional diplomatists, like Bismarck himself, he could not manage a sustained narrative. It is all a rigmarole, just like all the other memoirs by professional diplomatists since the world – their world – began: gossip; personal trivialities; the same grievance or episode repeated again and again. You end by being sorry for Holstein. He obviously had not much idea of what was going on in the world beyond his official desk. But then it has always puzzled me why people should expect members of a foreign office, German or other, to understand what is going on in the world. They are a monastic order – cut off from their own country by always having to deal with foreigners and foreign questions, and yet cut off from the foreigners by belonging to their own country. They have to translate hard, often unpleasant, facts into artificial, fine-spun formulas; and they often mistake the formulas for the reality. It is a profession that both attracts neurotics and produces them. They have their uses so long as we remember this, so long as we accept them as advisers and experts, never as the men who determine policy.

Holstein perhaps stepped over the line here, though I am not sure about this. If you look at the advice he gave, it does not seem to me markedly more suspect, pathological, destructive – whatever you like – than the advice given by similar diplomatic officers in other countries: by Eyre Crowe, for example, his contemporary in the British Foreign Office. In fact, I think Eyre Crowe was even quicker on the draw in spotting traps and frauds in every seemingly innocent German proposal than Holstein was with English ones – perhaps justifiably, of course. To make a case against Holstein you need something more than his advice, however pathological; you have to get him on the charge of deciding and directing policy, without being officially responsible for it. And there is something in it – though Holstein was not by any means the only one. He did sometimes go behind the back of the Chancellor, particularly in the days of Bülow; he certainly tried to keep affairs away from William II, who was theoretically the supreme authority. But for the most part he stuck to advice; and if his superiors usually swallowed his advice, it was because they were not capable of anything better on their own.

Bülow, for instance, the man whom the liberals wanted as the saviour of Germany as late as 1917, though a brilliant orator in his way, had to have every word written out for him beforehand; even his celebrated impromptu replies to interruptions had to be rehearsed. There was no guiding hand in Germany, no one truly responsible, between 1890 and the outbreak of the First World War (nor, for that matter, after it). But the blame, if you want to put it at someone's door, does not rest with Holstein. It was Bismarck who had destroyed every independent, outstanding figure in politics except himself; or perhaps there never were any. It certainly must have been nerve-racking to work under William II; and I have little doubt that Holstein would have liked to turn the Kaiser into a harmless constitutional monarch, but I do not think he did much more than grumble. And I cannot get up much interest in the other personal affairs that Holstein was supposed to be involved in.

The real interest of Holstein's career, it seems to me, is of quite a different kind: not the mystery, the shady stories, the melodrama, but the policy he advised and perhaps conducted. There certainly was a great change in Germany's European position between 1890, when Bismarck was overthrown, and 1906, when Holstein left office. Her relations with Russia and with England were certainly less intimate. But was this change really owing to personal whims and misunderstandings on one side or the other? Did Holstein help to wreck the Reinsurance treaty simply because it was associated with Bismarck and he wanted to prevent the Bismarck family returning to office? Did England and Germany drift apart in 1895, as Holstein suggests in one of the present essays, simply because Lord Salisbury failed to keep an appointment with William II one summer morning at Cowes? Or, to take the biggest point of all, was the alliance of England and Germany, which was constantly proposed by British statesmen, especially Joseph Chamberlain, between 1898 and 1901, prevented simply by Holstein's unbalanced suspicions? I do not believe a word of it. Look at the Anglo-German alliance which British and German liberals so lamented when the story became known. What the British wanted was an ally against Russia in the Far East. They would provide a navy; and the ally would provide the men. Very nice for the British. But from the German point of view it was an insane proposition – to use that favourite word again – to commit themselves to a large-scale war, a war of life and death, for the sake of British investments in Shanghai and the Yangtse Valley.

The key to Holstein's policy is simple. His attitude, like Bismarck's before him, was purely European. Though he knew the outside world unusually well – spoke perfect English and lived for some years in the United States and in South America – he had no sympathy whatever with what contemporaries called 'World Policy'. Most Germans, indeed most people all over Europe, thought that European conflicts were finished and Europe was settled for good. The future conflicts were going to be for world markets. Holstein would have agreed with Bismarck when he said to a colonial enthusiast: 'Here is Russia, and here is France. That is my map of Africa.' Bismarck had kept German ambitions under control. Holstein could not. But he claimed quite rightly to have opposed every step of Germany's world policy which estranged the two World Powers, England and Russia. Perhaps 'opposed' is too strong. Holstein was not in a position of power where he could oppose anything. But he did not have anything to do with these steps, and he warned against them. He did not favour the Baghdad railway, which helped to estrange Russia. He was in no way responsible for the Kruger telegram, which challenged the British in South Africa. And he did what he could against the plans for a great German navy. Of course, his opposition was futile; and even more futile was his line with British statesmen and journalists that, since he disliked Germany's world policy, they should not resent it – even though it was happening. He was a brake that failed to work, a melancholy position, as he himself came to recognize.

He wanted solely to rely on the German Army and to give Germany security in Europe by means of 'the free hand'. This really was not very different from Bismarck's policy, though he used rather different ways of doing it. I do not believe that he ever intended for a moment to make a binding alliance with either England or Russia, whatever his talk of making them bid higher. He held – quite rightly from Germany's point of view – that she had everything to gain by letting England and Russia quarrel and

remaining uncommitted in the middle. As European policy this
was foolproof. What wrecked it was the German insistence on
having a world policy as well: to be a great imperial Power in the
Far East, in Africa, and on the seas. For this annoyed England
and Russia, and pushed them together. Alliance between Russia
and the Western Powers is the worst of situations for Germany,
just as estrangement between them is the best.

There was, and is, only one way out for Germany. If she is
going to challenge the world Powers, she must become not *a*
European but *the* European power. She must start with the whole
continent under her control. Hitler held this doctrine; so, I
think, do the present German advocates of European unification.
Holstein arrived at it also, towards the end of his life. Since he
could not prevent world policy, he would make it possible. In
1905 he launched the first Moroccan crisis with France with the
deliberate object of turning her into a German satellite – perhaps
by threats, if not by war. Again, in 1909, he pushed Bülow into
standing 100 per cent behind Austria-Hungary in the Bosnian
crisis, with the object of making Mitteleuropa at any rate a solid
military block. His policy did not come off. But it was the only
way out for Germany if she wanted to be a world Power.

The moral of the story? A personal one: it is a sad life being a
private adviser who cannot direct events, but that is a risk private
advisers always take. A literary one: the secrets of the archives
are mostly humbug. Government departments guard their records because it flatters their self-importance, not because there is
anything startling to be revealed. Most of all, a political moral:
when Russia and the Western Powers are on bad terms, Germany
is the only gainer. Holstein could play his tricks at the beginning
of the century; the present rulers of Germany do much the same
now. Very nice for the Germans no doubt, but I have never been
able to understand why we or the Russians should get any pleasure from it.

21

THE RULER IN BERLIN

ON 31 July 1914, Berchtold, Austro-Hungarian Foreign Minister, was dismayed by advice from Bethmann, the German Chancellor, to act with restraint and not to give the signal for war. His distraction was interrupted by Conrad, Chief of the Austrian General Staff. Conrad showed him a telegram from Moltke, Chief of the German General Staff, which urged that Austria-Hungary should at once mobilize against Russia and so launch a European war. Berchtold, with his irresponsible giggle, exclaimed: 'That beats everything. Who rules then in Berlin?' This flippant remark was a profound judgement on the Germany of William II, and for that matter on the work of Bismarck. The question baffled contemporaries and has baffled later observers.

Between 1871 and 1890 it had seemed possible to answer the question. Bismarck ruled in Berlin. He devised legislation, determined policy, controlled even the military leaders; his decisions settled Germany's course. Yet Bismarck himself did not give this answer. He always insisted that Germany was ruled by the King of Prussia; and claimed that this was the core of his achievement. Bismarck's answer was not a mere pretence; even he, the greatest of political Germans, shrank from ultimate responsibility and shouldered it on to a 'King by the Grace of God'. All the same, the version was nonsense in practice, and largely even in theory. Germany could not be ruled by the King-Emperor, as Prussia had been ruled by Frederick the Great or even by Frederick William IV. Men may obey their king, even in a period when monarchical sentiment is declining; they will not obey someone else's king, and the King of Prussia was the king of others for the majority of Germans. The King of Prussia was German Emperor by conquest, by invitation of the German princes, by political intrigue, by constitutional arrangement, by everything except 'the Grace of God'. The German Emperor had no coronation – hence no religious sanction. Right still counted for much in Germany;

and the Emperor's right rested on national sentiment, not on divine appointment.

Bismarck's creation deserved its name of 'the second Empire'; its spirit was, in truth, nearer to the demagogy of Napoleon III than to the mystic tradition of 'the Holy Roman Empire of the German Nation'. After 1806, when the Holy Roman Empire ended, German authority could rest only on the masses. Bismarck had concealed this fact, as the titanic figure of Napoleon I had concealed it in France in similar circumstances. With the fall of Bismarck it could be concealed no longer. The question, 'Who rules in Berlin?' was stated with ever-increasing urgency, until it found an answer in 1933.

William II had perhaps supposed in 1890 that he himself would rule in Berlin. This view was held later by those who wished 'to hang the Kaiser'. The fault of William was his failure to rule, not that he ruled wrongly. Dr Eyck, his latest historian,[1] is nearer the truth when he draws a parallel with the system of English government in the reign of George III. George III, too, used to be accused of personal rule; this is a myth no longer believed by anyone. On the personal side it is unfair to compare William II with George III. William had considerable political gifts, to say nothing of his gift for phrase-making. Theodore Roosevelt said to him in 1910: 'In America you would have your ward behind you and would lead your delegation at your party's national convention.' In fact, William was a first-rate 'key-note' speaker. On the great issues of politics he often saw farther than his professional advisers. In 1890 he was right to reject Bismarck's programme of a *coup d'état* in favour of reconciling the working-classes to the Reich; in 1905 he was right in opposing Holstein's policy of the Tangier visit; he was right (from the German point of view) in promoting the Baghdad railway; he was right in distrusting the moribund Habsburg monarchy and, at the end, in advocating concessions to Rumania as the one way of staving off disaster; even his advances to both Russia and England did more good than harm – without such a gesture, for example, as his visit to the deathbed of Queen Victoria, estrangement between England and Germany would have come even sooner than it did. While the

1. *Das Persönliche Regiment Wilhelms II.* Politische Geschichte des deutschen Kaiserreiches von 1890 bis 1914. By Erich Eyck.

German Foreign Office was confidently snubbing all the Great Powers in turn, William II saw the dangers of 'the free hand' and never ceased, though by erratic impulses, to seek for some great political combination.

His immediate reactions, no doubt, were often as wild as his longer vision was sound. He would scribble, 'We must mobilize at once' on the news of some colonial dispute; and even proposed to arrest the transference of the British Fleet to the North Sea by an ultimatum. He exploded repeatedly against Austrian failure to destroy Serbia; yet he realized more clearly than any German diplomatist that this was a futile programme and, in his serious moments, urged reconciliation. His marginal notes, which made so much stir when published, were written for pleasure, not for action; and no action ever followed from them. They were the outbreaks of a man knowing himself, and known to be, irresponsible. The Kruger telegram is a case in point. This was certainly a watering-down of William's original idea of landing marines at Delagoa Bay. All the same, it would never have been sent, had it not suited Holstein's scheme of frightening England with the shadow of a Continental League. When this scheme failed, Marschall and Holstein shifted the blame to William, though the policy underlying it was theirs. So later, in the great crisis of the reign, Germans of all classes, from Bülow downwards, used the *Daily Telegraph* affair as a means for shifting on to William II all the consequences of German arrogance and power.

William II was not a ruler; he was a medium. He reflected the political mind of Germany and expressed it with genius. Contemporary observers were much at fault when they attributed the great German Navy to a personal whim of William II. The Navy was a demagogic cause, promoted by Liberal professors and popular even among Socialist and Roman Catholic voters. Had William surrendered altogether to his demagogic impulses, he would have anticipated Hitler's undisputed power. As it was, his upbringing and conscience reined him in; the King of Prussia restrained the German Emperor, as Prussia, in Bismarck's conception, restrained Germany. These negations were not a solution; and since William failed to lead, the problem was returned to the Chancellors. Here, indeed, is the profound political interest of the reign of William II – the search for a principle of authority and responsibility when this could no longer be provided by the Crown. To return to the analogy with George III: Dr Eyck supposes that George III was defeated by 'the opposition of Charles Fox', and blames the Germans for not producing a liberal figure of similar eminence. This does that charming gambler too much honour. Growth of a sense of responsibility, not of an opposition, transformed the British Constitution; and this responsibility rested on a governing class which was truly representative of 'the political nation'. In Bismarckian Germany the governing classes, military and civil, were not merely out of touch with the masses who had become the nation: they were actively and consciously opposed to everything that was dearest to national ambition. Bismarck's greatest achievement was his defeat of Greater Germany: he preserved the Habsburg monarchy and insisted that his truncated Germany was a 'satiated State'. This flew in the face of national sentiment. The only binding force in the governing classes was resistance to the popular will. Liberal observers, misled by Western analogies, thought that this implied principally resistance to a constitutional system; but the national masses demanded most of all a truly united Germany.

The reign of William II saw two attempts to break the deadlock between the governing classes and the nation; in different ways both Caprivi and Bülow aspired 'to rule in Berlin'. Caprivi took the way of Liberalism; Bülow attempted to wield the bow of Bismarck and to create a new Bismarckian compromise by agility and intrigue. Caprivi, who followed Bismarck as Chancellor, has been neglected by historians; yet he was the most significant of Bismarck's successors, for he conducted the experiment in Liberalism which later writers often suggested as the 'solution' of the German problem. In fact Caprivi was the only parliamentary Chancellor of Imperial Germany. Though appointed by the Emperor, he thought in terms of a parliamentary majority, and this could be created only by means of a 'national' programme. Hence Caprivi gave up Bismarck's negative foreign policy and supported the German cause in south-eastern Europe: domestic and foreign demagogy went hand in hand. Caprivi justified the imperial military programme by reference to Russia, instead of to France; and the climax of his policy came in 1893 when he carried the increased Army grant with the votes of Roman Catholics,

Poles and some Progressives. As Dr Eyck rightly says, the split in the Progressive party which followed this vote marked the end of Liberalism as a political force in Germany. Dr Eyck calls it suicide; suicide is sometimes the only solution. Liberalism had no future if it failed to support Caprivi; equally it had no future if it supported him. For Caprivi himself had no future. In 1894 he ran into conflict with Botho Eulenberg, Prime Minister of Prussia. Caprivi wanted a democratic reform of the Prussian suffrage, Eulenberg a revival of the anti-Socialist laws. William II took the only course and dismissed them both. The decisive answer was given: no one could rule in Berlin.

This answer was accepted by Hohenlohe, the next Chancellor. Dr Eyck speaks contemptuously of his age and feebleness; these were the necessary conditions of his existence. As a Bavarian, he would not restrain Germany for the sake of Prussia; as a Conservative, he would not break Prussia for the sake of Germany. With little power over events and no influence in the Reichstag, he tolerated all the decisive lurches in German policy: the Baghdad railway, the great Navy, the establishment in China were all Hohenlohe's doing, or rather consequences of his lack of doing. He deliberately avoided asking the great question, let alone attempting to answer it. Yet it was a question which demanded an answer. The man who attempted to answer it in the reign of William II was Bülow, Chancellor from 1900 to 1909. Bülow's name is weighed down by his *Memoirs*, the most trivial record ever left by a man who has occupied high position. Nevertheless he dominated the history of Wilhelmine Germany. Bülow was the only Imperial Chancellor after Bismarck to count in German politics – the only one who made effective speeches and to whom men looked for a 'policy'. Still more, 'the Bülow *bloc*' of 1906 was the first stable parliamentary combination behind the Chancellor since Bismarck broke with the National Liberals in 1879, and it was a more reliable coalition than any created under the Weimar Republic. Finally, in 1908, Bülow – whether deliberately or not – used the *Daily Telegraph* affair to eject William II from politics and to impose upon him the limitations of a constitutional monarch. William II never recovered from this blow; it ended whatever fragments of 'personal rule' remained.

Bülow's success was barren. It served only to reveal that the problem of German government lay deeper than in William's character; it was rooted in the foundations of Bismarck's Reich. The humiliation of William II left Bülow face to face with the Prussian Conservatives; and once more, as with Caprivi, it became clear that the twin causes of 'world policy' and internal democracy could be achieved only after the defeat of the classes which Bismarck had preserved, the forces of old Prussia. Bülow declared to the Conservatives who brought him down: 'We shall meet again at Philippi.' The engagement was not fought in Bülow's lifetime; it was won by his demagogic heir in 1933 and completed by the massacres which followed 20 July 1944. Bülow's fall led to another, more fateful, interregnum, the Chancellorship of Bethmann Hollweg. Hohenlohe had allowed policy to be made without him; Bethmann Hollweg had it made against him. It was a grotesque, though inevitable, conclusion to Bismarck's work that the Chancellor should be helpless both in the Reichstag and in the Prussian Landtag; universal suffrage and privileged class-franchise alike rejected him. Yet for this very reason he was the only possible Chancellor. As in Metternich's Austria, 'administration had taken the place of government'.

A solution of a sort was found, perhaps against Bethmann Hollweg's will: a solution of foreign policy. German foreign policy of the 1890's had been 'cabinet diplomacy', even though it made an occasional demagogic gesture. The last display of this 'cabinet diplomacy' was the first Moroccan crisis of 1905; a crisis deliberately engineered by Holstein without any preparation of public opinion and hence ending in failure for Germany. Once more, in the Bosnian crisis, Bülow was the man of the transition: demagogue enough to back the German cause in south-eastern Europe, Bismarckian enough to regret having done so. In 1911 national opinion came into its own: the Agadir crisis was fought with public backing from start to finish. Nevertheless, Agadir was a false start, a red herring: it was deliberately designed by Kiderlen, last of the Bismarckians, to distract German chauvinism from eastern Europe and so from the mortal conflict with Russia. Until Agadir, Germany had remained a Power which, if not 'satiated', could still be satisfied with colonial gains; after Agadir, Germany had to bid for the mastery of Europe. This inescapable fate determined the diplomacy of 1913 and

1914, which Dr Eyck describes in full detail: German policy sought in vain to avoid the mission of conquest which was being thrust upon it. Few historians will quarrel with Dr Eyck's verdict that the German statesmen and generals did not deliberately plan the outbreak of world war in July 1914; yet a war of conquest was the only possible outcome of German history. Bethmann Hollweg had been the only Imperial Chancellor to be censured by the Reichstag; he was also the only Chancellor to receive from the Reichstag a unanimous vote of confidence. Certainly in August 1914 Bethmann Hollweg did not 'rule in Berlin'; what ruled at last in Berlin was the will of the German people for power.

The German problem, past and present, is the problem of German unity. Though this does not exist now, we are tempted to think that it existed in some Golden Age of the past. Dr Eyck's book is a reminder that this Golden Age cannot be found in the age of William II. Imperial Germany was never a united national State, in the sense that France was united and made a nation by the Great Revolution. In Imperial Germany, almost as much as in the Holy Roman Empire, there was a balance of authorities and classes; instead of authoritarian rule there was 'organized anarchy'. Germany had, in some sort, a 'governing class' – the Prussian army officers and Prussian administrators. Though this class held Germany together, it was even more concerned to hold Germany back; while offering Germany a corset, it strapped on a strait-jacket. The first German war weakened this class; the Hitler revolution completed its destruction. There are now no forces within Germany to resist the full programme of German unification, and the present partition rests solely on the occupying armies. This gives it a unique and precarious character. A Germany free from foreign control will seek to restore the united Greater Germany which Hitler achieved in 1938; nor will democracy provide an automatic safeguard against a new German aggression. In the reign of William II every step towards democracy was a step towards general war. The Navy was popular, 'world policy' was popular, support for the German cause in eastern Europe was popular. Attempts at reconciliation with others were unpopular; and William's prestige was ruined in 1908 when it became known that he favoured friendship with England.

The harsh truth of German history is that the solution of the

Germany question cannot be found within Germany. Partition cannot be maintained as a permanent policy; yet a united Germany will keep Europe in apprehension, and would be tolerable only in a world of United Nations. Wilhelmine Germany overshadowed her neighbours by playing off East and West; any future Germany will seek to do the same. If the Great Powers were on friendly terms, there would even now be no German problem; so long as they remain estranged, Germany will offer the occasion, and may be the originator of future wars. 'Who rules in Berlin?' The question once dominated German history; now it torments all the world. In our impatience and anxiety we are led to hope that one day the German people may rule in Berlin. That outcome is, in the long run, unavoidable; it will be tolerable only if there also rules in Berlin awareness of a community of nations. It is for the Germans to seek unity on a democratic and pacific basis; the Great Powers must ensure that the Germans do not promote unity by a programme of foreign aggression. At the present time, both the Germans and the Great Powers are failing in their task; and the question, 'Who rules in Berlin?' has lost nothing of its menacing character.

22

THE RISE AND FALL OF
DIPLOMATIC HISTORY

HISTORIANS have been writing diplomatic history for a long time, indeed ever since they penetrated into the archives of state. Ranke spent his happiest and most profitable years examining the papers of the republic of Venice. Sorel wrote a masterpiece, *Europe and the French Revolution*, which bears in its title the evidence that it is in part diplomatic history. Vandal reached the same supreme level in his study of *Napoleon and Alexander I*. These themes were relatively remote from the date when the books were published. Moreover, the evidence from the diplomatic papers was subordinated to a general narrative. Political ideas and the personalities of statesmen counted for more than 'what one clerk said to another clerk'. The novelty some forty years ago was twofold. Historians set out to write the history of international relations purely from foreign office archives. More important, they claimed to be able to write about contemporary events with as much detachment as they had written about more distant periods. Their claim may have been justified. But it would be foolish to pretend that their sudden interest in contemporary history was detached and 'scientific'. It was a political interest, forced upon them by events and in particular by the event of the First World War. The twentieth century would have shown less concern with diplomatic history if the Bismarckian peace had endured. The diplomatic history of our time has always been a study of war origins, by no means to its advantage.

Historians seek to be detached, dispassionate, impartial. In fact no historian starts out with his mind a blank, to be gradually filled by the evidence. Is it conceivable, for example, that any document would have induced Macaulay to confess that the Glorious Revolution had been after all a great mistake? Or even conceivable that Ranke might have come to regret the rise of Prussia as a Great Power? The historians of the early twentieth century had lived through the First World War; and nearly all of them lamented it. Their reaction took different forms. German, and to some extent French, historians were anxious to prove that their Governments had been right. British and American historians were anxious to prove that their Governments had been wrong. Soviet historians were a class apart. They were delighted to distribute the blame among all 'imperialist' Governments, the old Russian Government perhaps most of all. But even they trimmed their sails to political convenience.

Diplomatic history was pushed to the front both by the way that the First World War started and by the way that it ended. The European crisis of July 1914 was peculiarly an affair of diplomacy. Few maintained then, and fewer would maintain now, that the outbreak of war was deliberately foreseen and planned by any Power or even by any general staff. Lloyd George expressed the general opinion: 'We muddled into war.' The outcome had been determined by what diplomatists said, or failed to say, to each other. Moreover, what they said seemed to have been shaped by the existing diplomatic structure – the Triple Alliance, the Franco-Russian alliance, or the vaguer commitments of Great Britain to France. Every Great Power sought to justify itself by publishing a selection of its diplomatic papers; and the very inadequacy of some of these suggested that the truth would emerge from a fuller, franker publication. The peace settlement reinforced the demand for impartial inquiry. The treaty of Versailles followed on the defeat of Germany; but its moral justification was that Germany had been solely 'responsible' for the outbreak of war, either deliberately or from negligence No doubt the statesmen at Paris would have made much the same arrangements even if they had been convinced that all the Great Powers were equally at fault; but they would have had a harder time with their consciences, and still more with those of others.

It is not surprising therefore that German historians took up the struggle against 'the lie of war-guilt'. They did not need to prove that Germany had always been right; it was enough for them to show that she had not always been wrong. The first republican Government employed Kautsky to make a very full publication of the German records on the events immediately preceding the outbreak of war. This did not serve the German purpose. For it seemed to show that, whatever the faults of others, the German Government was very much to blame. The German historians therefore shifted their ground back from July 1914 to the diplomacy of the preceding years and ultimately even to the epoch of Bismarck. Within less than a decade after the peace treaty Thimme published fifty-four volumes of diplomatic documents running from 1871 to June 1914. It was not the first publication of the kind. The French were doing it for the origins of the Franco-Prussian War. But the French proceeded slowly – they finished their task only in 1930; the events with which they were concerned were already distant and somewhat parochial. The German publication eclipsed the French series in size and excitement. Historians all over the world, and not only in Germany, took their version of events from it. Even today a historian will catch himself following its pattern even when he resolves not to do so; and the 'received idea' of the world before 1914 still rests on *Die Grosse Politik*, though this origin is forgotten.

Die Grosse Politik was the first and most grandiose publication of documents on the origins of the First World War. There is another reason for its success. The interpretation underlying it corresponded to that which British and American historians had already formed in their minds. It is perhaps a special Anglo-Saxon characteristic to see the virtue in the other side of the case, and even to start out with a prejudice against one's own Government. The official case had been challenged in England from the beginning. The Union of Democratic Control had been founded in September 1914; and its central doctrine was that 'secret diplomacy' caused the war. E. D. Morel, who inspired and led it, had already exposed secret diplomacy in Morocco; his *Truth about the War* soon followed, with the clear implication that earlier versions had been lies. Some of the diplomatic historians in England, such as Lowes Dickinson and Dr G. P. Gooch, were members of the U.D.C.; none escaped its influence. The Englishmen who wrote on contemporary history were as much cut from E. D. Morel's cloak as the Russian novelists were from Gogol's. This spirit soon spread to the United States. There was the same desire for fair play; the same readiness to distrust the national Government; and American historians had always been more closely linked to German scholarship. Apart from this, the American people as a whole shook off sooner the passions of the war years and came to distrust an outlook associated with the spirit of Versailles. American historians were following a national trend; British historians were helping to make it.

The years between the peace settlement and Hitler's victory were great days for the 'pure' diplomatic historian. Men wanted to understand the contemporary world; and historians assured them that they could do so if all diplomatic secrets were 'revealed'. The British documents were published from 1898 to 1914; the French plodded laboriously on (as they are still doing) with a publication of documents from 1871 to 1914. The Italians asserted themselves as a Great Power by refusing to publish anything. More recently they have turned round and made the same assertion by proposing to publish everything from 1861 to 1943. Even the Russians abandoned their traditional secrecy and began to publish on a grand scale; then, repenting their frankness, abandoned the enterprise and tried to suppress what they had revealed already. If the diplomatic archives really contain the key to history, then the door was decisively unlocked. Yet the result was curiously disappointing. For the most part the spate of documents confirmed what men thought already. The Germans and the former members of the U.D.C. demonstrated that Germany had not caused the war; Soviet historians continued to blame capitalist imperialism; and the cynical were still convinced that all statesmen lurched in a fog from one blunder to the next. What was wrong? Why had the golden key jammed in the lock? Perhaps the revelations had not been complete enough. Some discovered defects in the *Grosse Politik*; and these existed, though dwarfed by its great merits. The British Government confirmed half-formed suspicions by imposing a hocus-pocus of secrecy on the so-called 'Cabinet papers'; and some future generation of historians will be disappointed to find what trivialities these contain.

The doubts about diplomatic history went deeper. It was not merely that we had missed some revelation or were being denied some material. We were asking the wrong questions, using the wrong method. We must turn from the Foreign Offices to the more profound forces which shape the destinies of men. Even

Professor Renouvin, the leading French diplomatic historian of the day, has done this recently, though with some backsliding. There was from the start an undercurrent of opinion which tried to give diplomacy an economic interpretation – an opinion partly Marxist, but also stemming from English radicals such as J. A. Hobson. Markets and raw materials, not alliances, had caused the war. This view, though also held by some members of the U.D.C., took longer to become respectable. Teachers of history put the works of Dr Gooch or Professor S. B. Fay on the top of their table and consulted Brailsford's *War of Steel and Gold* under the desk. The economic interpretation did not win the field until the days of the Left Book Club; and even then it was not much applied in detail. Historians setting out to describe an 'imperialist' conflict, lost their balance in the flood of diplomatic documents. Some of them even reached the conclusion, perhaps correctly, that conflicts such as Morocco or the Baghdad railway had more to do with power and less with profits than they had originally supposed. Certainly it is difficult to point to any really successful work of scholarship applying this economic interpretation, even by a Russian. There is, of course, always the excuse that, whereas Foreign Office secrets have been revealed, those of the counting-house and the company promoter have not; and the unknown is always a safe source to look to for further enlightenment.

There have been other and wider forms of retreat from 'pure' diplomatic history. It is fitting that historians in what is called the age of the masses should abandon the archives for the study of public opinion – a study, however, more easily preached than practised. How can we take a Gallup poll among the dead? The study of public opinion has changed only too often into a study of newspapers – a subject also of great interest but one attended with more difficulties than the unworldly historian supposes. Do newspapers voice public opinion or make it? Do they lead or follow? Often neither. They obey the directive of a government agent; dance to the whims of a proprietor; or, more rarely, express the policy of a great editor. Most frequently of all, they put in enough news and articles to fill the space. Little of this was recognized by the earnest scholars, usually American, who pursued the trail of public opinion. How surprised Frank Harris would have been, for instance, to learn that he had supplied the evidence for British hostility to Germany by a single leader in the *Saturday Review*. Some outstanding work has indeed been done in this field. Eckart Kehr wrote an amazingly brilliant book years ago on the building of the German navy and party politics – so brilliant indeed as almost to make one forget that the German admirals must have had something to do with it. More recently Professor Chabod has dissected with infinite subtlety what the Italians thought of foreign affairs in the year 1870. The intellectual achievement could hardly be bettered. But our shelves will groan if every nation is to require 600 pages for each year of its public thoughts.

Historians have run too eagerly after some subjects, and passed others by. It is curious that a generation which experienced two world wars should still neglect the papers of the service departments. No muckraking Radical has penetrated their secrets; even respectable historians have only been allowed a selective glance. The generals and admirals have defended the secrets of their enemies as zealously as they defend their own. The records of the German Admiralty have been reposing in London since 1945, inviolate from any prying eye. The Americans have not done much better with the records of the German General Staff which they carried off to Washington. We know what Hitler planned to do in war; how far was the German Army equipped to carry out his intentions? The answer would be not without interest. Solidarity, worthy of a trade union, ensures that we shall not learn the answer.

Wars are the eclipse of diplomacy, and therefore of diplomatic history. This, no doubt, explains why there are few books on the diplomacy of the First World War and why the archives for this period are still rigorously sealed, even though the documents of the inter-war period are being published. More specifically we continue to live in a war atmosphere in the immediate present – first the Second World War against Germany, then the more insidious 'cold war', which seems equally impervious to diplomacy. The arguments and manoeuvres of diplomatists have become little more than an entertainment, imperfectly cloaking the 'out-door relief' for members of the ruling class which John

Bright regarded as the object of all foreign policy. What goes on at Lake Success is of little moment; therefore, we think, diplomacy never mattered, and the diplomatic historian is wasting his time as well as ours.

This depreciation of diplomacy started even before the Second World War. The dictators, Hitler and Mussolini, refused to play according to the accepted rules. What was the sense of negotiating, still less of making agreements with them? And therefore, even more, what sense is there in writing about these barren negotiations and meaningless pacts? The 'pure' diplomatic historian has been perhaps too readily discouraged. It was the outbreak of the Second World War, not the first, which led Sir Lewis Namier to write a masterpiece – largely from diplomatic documents of the most formal, dreary kind. Foreign policy of a sort will go on so long as there are sovereign States, even though its instrument may be an atomic test instead of a dispatch. Diplomatic historians may have to learn new tricks and to lament their vanished 'purity'. Certainly the records of Foreign Offices no longer arouse much curiosity. Once it was believed that they contained as much explosive matter as Pandora's box. Now it appears that the patron saint of the archives is Joanna Southcott.

23

TROSTKY

ONE early morning, in October 1902, Mr and Mrs 'Richter' were still abed in their lodgings near King's Cross. There was a violent knocking at the door. Mrs Richter, opening it, called out: '*The Pen* has arrived!' In this way Trotsky, 'the young eagle', burst – under his first pseudonym – into Lenin's life. The meeting was a symbol of their future. Lenin was orderly, quiet in speech and habit, hardly to be distinguished from his neighbours. Trotsky rode contemptuously over the conventions, knocking violently at doors and expecting them to open at the impact of his genius. He was at a loss when there was no door to force open. Lenin was to end as a sacred mummy, in the silence of death still dominating the lives of two hundred million people. Trotsky was to be murdered far from Europe and – what would seem worse to him – his very name has been erased from the history-books. Mention Bronstein, and men think you are referring to a chess player. The greatest writer and perhaps the greatest leader that revolution ever produced is forgotten; and the younger generation of readers will puzzle why a book has been devoted to him.

Mr Deutscher has done a striking work of rehabilitation.[1] This is the story of Trotsky's triumph. It carries him through the victory of the revolution and the civil war to his highest moment, when he seemed the predestined successor of Lenin. A further volume will tell the story of his fall and of his unquenchable resistance until he was rubbed out by an ice-pick. Mr Deutscher has mastered all the printed sources and has been the first to use extensively the Trotsky archives now at Harvard. Yet it may be questioned whether he is the right man for the subject. We can perhaps get over his ponderous style, suitable enough when he is pontificating on Bolshevism in the columns of the Astor press. But, like all Marxists – even the lapsed ones – he wants always to discover profound historical forces where there was only the will of men. He writes of the early Bolsheviks: 'Lenin's party had its roots deep in Rus-

1. *The Prophet Armed: Trotsky 1879–1921.* By Isaac Deutscher.

sian soil'; this of some two or three thousand men, bewitched by an academic ideal. In 1917 'the whole dynamic of Russian history was impelling Lenin and Trotsky, their party, and their country towards the revolution'; when it would be truer to say that these two wrenched 'history' (whatever that may mean) violently from its course. In the most preposterous passage of all he describes the Russian working class of 1917 (who, poor chaps, had no idea what was happening to them) as

one of history's wonders. Small in numbers, young, inexperienced, uneducated, it was rich in political passion, generosity, idealism, and rare heroic qualities. . . . With its semi-illiterate thoughts it embraced the idea of the republic of the philosophers.

The reader must put up with this hocus-pocus for the sake of the gigantic individual who overshadows it.

Trotsky himself used to claim that history was on his side. When he came to the Congress of Soviets fresh from the conquest of power, he called to the protesting Mensheviks: 'You have played out your role. Go where you belong: to the dustheap of history.' Yet no man ever chose his role in greater isolation or followed a course of more determined individualism. Trotsky carried to its peak the era of individual greatness which had begun with the French Revolution. His was a more powerful voice than Danton's, self-educated, self-made, self-advised. One could say of him as of Napoleon: 'his presence on the battlefield was worth ten divisions'. It is ironic that Trotsky, the greatest of revolutionary Socialists, should have owed his success to liberal enterprise and capitalist freedom. The age of the individual was finished when men were eclipsed by machines – and nowhere more decisively than by the machine of the great political party. In the First World War genius still counted. Lloyd George, Clémenceau, Trotsky, were each in their separate ways the saviours of their countries. It is no accident that the careers of all three ended in barren failure when the war was over. The leaders of the Second World War needed bureaucracies and party organizations. Even Winston Churchill had to become leader of the Conservative party; and only backward countries, Yugoslavia or France, could produce heroes – a Tito or a de Gaulle. Trotsky came just in time. Now he could never rise from provincial obscurity.

Trotsky had no background of Marxist training or of party experience. Mr Deutscher writes: 'He diligently studied Marxism, which in this its golden age gave the adept a solid mental equipment.' In reality Trotsky learnt from Marxism only that capitalism was doomed – a fact which he knew instinctively already. His own writings that have survived never dealt with economic developments; they were concerned always with political strategy, owing more to Clausewitz than to Marx. He never adapted himself to the needs of practical work in a party. When he first came to London in 1902 it was as a detached individual; and he stood outside the conflict between Bolshevik and Menshevik. Though himself a revolutionary, he opposed Lenin's exclusiveness; and always hoped to close the breach between the two Socialist currents. Even after the revolution of 1905, when his actions had outstripped Bolshevik theory, he kept up a tolerant association with the Mensheviks; and the outbreak of the First World War found him more solitary than ever. He joined the Bolshevik party only in the summer of 1917, some two months before he was to carry it to supreme power. The exact date is unknown; and the possession of a party-card meant nothing to him. His position in the world did not depend on the accuracy of a filing-cabinet.

In the slovenly decay of imperial Russia Trotsky's voice could fill a continent. When the revolution of 1905 broke out, he was an unknown youth of twenty-five. At St Petersburg, knowing nobody, representing nobody, he forced himself on to the Soviet; and before it ended he was its dominating figure. At the final meeting he even ruled out of order the police officer who had come to arrest the members: 'Please do not interfere with the speaker. If you wish to take the floor, you must give your name.' In those days words were more powerful than armies. It was the same on a more gigantic scale in 1917. The Bolsheviks did not carry Trotsky to power; he carried them. Lenin made the party resolve on insurrection, but he was still in hiding when it broke out and at first could not believe in its success. The seizure of power in October was Trotsky's work; and Lenin acknowledged this immediately afterwards, with supreme generosity, when he proposed that Trotsky be put at the head of the new revolutionary government. One may even ask – what did Lenin and the Bolsheviks do during the civil war? They held on clumsily to the reins of civil power in Moscow. It was Trotsky who created the armies; chose the officers; determined the strategy; and inspired the soldiers. Every interference by the Soviet Government was a mistake; and the greatest mistake was the campaign against Poland, which Trotsky opposed. The achievement was not only one of organization. It was the impact of a fiery personality, the sparks from which flew round the world.

The man of action in Trotsky was always second to the man of words, even at the greatest moments of decision. He was never happy over a victory until he had written about it; and in later years literary triumph seemed almost to atone with him for the bitterness of defeat. Bernard Shaw said that, as a political pamphleteer, he 'surpassed Junius and Burke'; what is even more to the point, he is the only Marxist who has possessed literary genius. Time and again the force of this genius posed problems that were still unperceived by others and even pointed to solutions that were unwelcome to Trotsky himself. Immediately after the revolution of 1905, when he was still in prison, he discovered the central dilemma which a victorious Russian revolution would face and which indeed the Soviet Union still faces. How was revolutionary Russia to maintain itself in a hostile world? Backwardness made revolution easy, but survival difficult. Trotsky gave already the answer to which he adhered all his life: permanent revolution. The Russian revolution must touch off revolutions elsewhere. 'The working class of Russia will become the initiator of the liquidation of capitalism on a global scale.' It was in this belief that Trotsky led the revolution of 1917, defied the German empire at Brest-Litovsk, and composed the most ringing phrases in the foundation manifesto of the Communist International. But what if the more advanced proletariat failed to respond? It was useless to maintain for long Trotsky's earliest answer: 'luckily for mankind, this is impossible'.

The impossible is what men get from events – and often at its most unwelcome. Trotsky foresaw even in 1905 the conflict that would follow between workers and peasants, if they were ever cooped up together in isolation. Once more he fell back on pious hope. The working class would remain by its very nature enlightened, progressive, tolerant. Somehow 'proletarian dictatorship' would escape the evils which other forms of dictatorship had always produced. Did Trotsky ever believe this? It seems unlikely. In the early days of doctrinal dispute he always preached toleration, despite his own sharp and wounding phrases. Lenin had an easier time of it. Both men understood the virtue of intellectual freedom. But for Lenin it was one of the many bourgeois virtues that he was prepared to discard – confident that Communism would resurrect it in a higher form. In just the same way he was ready to write off the greatest artistic achievements of the past. The very wonder of them was an embarrassment in the present. Trotsky could never bring himself to renounce European civilization. He recognized Russia's backwardness and resented being associated with it – an attitude possible for a Jew, but repugnant even to Lenin. As the net of intolerance drew tighter, as the European revolutions failed and the Russian masses became increasingly discontented, Trotsky grew more explosive.

His response was characteristic. At one bound he reached totalitarianism in its most ruthless form. His own gifts betrayed him. A dictator lurks in every forceful writer. Power over words leads easily to a longing for power over men. Trotsky could never resist a challenge. He wrote *The Defence of Terrorism* at the height of his labours during the civil war; and he justified the conquest of Georgia against the Social Democrats of western Europe, though he had himself opposed it. Now in 1921 he preached the militarization of labour and permanent dictatorship of the Communist party. Lenin restrained him. But the weapons which Trotsky forged then were soon to be turned against him by Stalin. He was to purge his betrayal of freedom by many years of resistance and exile. The glories of his revolutionary triumph pale before the nobility of his later defeats. The spirit of man was irrepressible in him. Colonel Robins, the American Red Cross representative at Petrograd, pronounced history's verdict: 'A four-kind son-of-a-bitch, but the greatest Jew since Jesus Christ.'

24

THOMAS GARRIGUE MASARYK

T. G. MASARYK, the Founder-President of Czechoslovakia, was born on 7 March 1850. Though the centenary of his birth will now pass unnoticed in the country he created, nothing can weaken his position as one of the great men of our century; even if his work prove barren, he demonstrated the nobility of the human race. His political career began in earnest when he had already been superannuated as a university professor. If he had died at the age of sixty-five, he would have been remembered only as a sociological writer who exposed some judicial scandals in Austria-Hungary.

His extra years turned him into a maker of history. Between 1915 and 1918 Masaryk brought nations into being and drew the lines for a new map of Europe. Yet Masaryk was not an extreme nationalist. He incurred the hostility of the Czechs by exposing their most famous medieval manuscripts as forgeries; and before 1914 he was one of the few Czechs who strove sincerely to transform the Habsburg Monarchy into a democratic federation of peoples.

Unlike most nationalist leaders Masaryk understood power. He called himself a realist and practised 'Realpolitik' in the Bismarckian manner. Indeed he was more of a realist than Bismarck, for he knew how to use the force of ideals. He said late in life: 'Democracy is the rule of the people, but there can be no government without obedience and discipline.' His predecessors had demanded obedience from hereditary right; he claimed it from force of character. For Masaryk was a man born to rule.

Fear of Pan-Germanism, and the determination to be rid of it, were the motives of his political actions. Certainly he desired freedom for his people; but he would have been less uncompromising in his resistance to Pan-Germanism if he had not believed that it rejected the values of European civilization. He did not hate Germany; he wished 'to force Germany to be human' by preventing her rule over others. The events of 1914 convinced him that the Habsburg monarchy had lost all independent existence; it had become merely an instrument by which Slav peoples were forced to fight for the German domination of Europe. Thus he sought an alternative to Austria-Hungary, something which would perform the Habsburg 'mission' more successfully. He found this more effective barrier to German mastery in the small nations of Central and Eastern Europe; and claimed that national freedom was the only way of organizing this great middle zone.

Masaryk tuned his arguments to his audience when he set out to convince the statesmen of the Western Powers: spoke of the rights of nationalities, of the cause of democratic freedom, and of great moral principles. These, though genuine convictions, represented only part of his realistic approach. He was well aware that the small nations of East-Central Europe could not hold their own unaided against German power; and his aim was to combine national freedom with security, not to let nationalism run riot.

Masaryk sought to overcome the weakness of Germany's neighbours by national amalgamation. He did not merely voice national claims; he invented nations. Arguing from the case of partitioned Poland, he represented the Czechs and Slovaks as a single people who would come together as Czechoslovaks when partition was ended; and he had the same programme for the Serbs and the Croats. Himself a Slovak, though born in Moravia, he genuinely believed that the Slovaks would gladly accept Czech history as a substitute for that which they lacked themselves and would regard Hus and Comenius as Slovak heroes. Similarly, he expected the Serbs and Croats to overlook the religious and historical differences which had lasted for a thousand years. It is curious that a professor even of sociology should have been so contemptuous of history; but for Masaryk culture was humanistic, not historical. He admired Hus and Comenius because of what they stood for, not because they were figures in Czech history; and he expected others to do the same.

He thought that nations could be remade at will, if the will were sufficiently noble; and his will was so noble that he partly succeeded. Though Yugoslavia could never be more than a federation of nations, Czechoslovakia became in some sort a genuine national State bound together by common loyalties. But this ideal of a humanistic nationalism was confined to the 'humane' classes; it lost its hold when the agrarian and urban masses came to determine the shape of politics.

Masaryk never supposed that the national amalgams could face out the German threat without assistance. Czechoslovakia and the other succession States were to give the middle zone internal peace; but their existence was to be underwritten by the support of the victorious Allies. In 1914 opinion in Western Europe had only a vague sentiment in favour of national freedom; Masaryk turned this sentiment towards concrete reality. With some justice, though with less than was supposed, he represented the Czechoslovaks as 'peoples struggling to be free'. But his plans were not based solely on support from France and the Anglo-Saxon Powers. He wrote in March 1917:

Will Great Britain join forces with Russia, or does she consider Germany to be less dangerous to her world empire than Russia? This is the question which Great Britain has to decide, and on her decision will depend the future of the Old and the New World.

It was a disaster for Masaryk when West and East were estranged by the Bolshevik revolution; and he never gave up trying to bring Russia back into European affairs – sometimes by seeking to be reconciled with the Bolsheviks, sometimes by preparing their overthrow. For though always a man of Western culture and never sympathetic to Pan-Slavism, Masaryk was realist enough to know that Germany and Russia would partition Eastern Europe unless Russia was on good terms with the Western Powers.

Except for the name of Czechoslovakia little now seems to remain of Masaryk's work. The national amalgams have not held: Czechs and Slovaks, Croats and Serbs are separate peoples; federalism in Yugoslavia, not national union in Czechoslovakia, has been successful; and all Eastern Europe, except for Yugoslavia, has escaped from German tyranny only to fall under Russian control. For this Russia is not alone to blame. If Western countries saw the peril of Pan-Germanism as clearly as Masaryk did we should not be in our present position. The essential condition which Masaryk laid down, though perhaps now unattainable, remains true: only co-operation between Russia and the

Anglo-Saxon Powers can give Europe peace and security. And in spite of the failures of the present there is in Masaryk's life a deeper lesson: nationalism without humanism is harsh and destructive; humanism without nationalism is academic and barren. If there ever is a federation of Europe or of the world it can be based only on free national States, not on the domination of a single Great Power.

25

THE OUTBREAK OF
THE FIRST WORLD WAR

ON 4 August 1914, this country declared war on Germany. The European war had already started. Austria-Hungary declared war on Serbia on 28 July. Germany declared war on Russia on 1 August, and on France on 3 August. The Austrians, late as usual, declared war on Russia only on 6 August; Great Britain and France answered by declaring war on Austria-Hungary on 12 August. This delay was significant. Though the Austrians had wanted a war against Serbia, a general European war was not part of their plan, and their empire became its principal victim. Their little Balkan war was swamped in a struggle of the European Great Powers; and there began a general upheaval in Europe which destroyed its stable civilization – an upheaval which has lasted to the present day. The First World War caused vast destruction and the slaughter of more human beings than anything since the barbarian invasions. But its moral impact – the thing which made it difficult for men to think rationally about it – was that it came after a longer period of peace than any known in the recorded history of Europe.

Great Britain had not been involved in a general war since the battle of Waterloo in 1815. The last war between two European Powers had been the war between France and Germany which ended in 1871. There had been colonial wars; and there had been Balkan wars – the last in 1912 and 1913. But these had all been a long way from what was regarded as civilized Europe. Men went on talking about war; there were diplomatic crises; and every Great Power had vast armaments by the standards of the time. The British Navy had never been so powerful; and every Continental country had millions of men trained to enter the field. All the same, the reality of war was remote from men's minds. Everyone assumed that the system, or lack of it, would go on working, as it had worked for so long. There would be alarms and even mobilizations; but somehow peace would come out of it. War, in the phrase of the time, was unthinkable.

So, when war came everyone demanded an explanation; and the search for this has been going on ever since. Special institutes were set up for the study of war-origins; periodicals devoted solely to it were published. Every Great Power published thousands of diplomatic documents. A full bibliography, if one were ever made, of war-origins would run into thousands of volumes. We know what happened between 28 June and 4 August 1914 in more detail than we know of any other five weeks in history. Indeed, if we cannot understand these events and agree about them, we shall never understand or agree about anything. The problem was not merely historical. It went on being of burning political importance. The victorious allies insisted on Germany's war-guilt. The Germans challenged this; and the evidence which they produced shook many scholars, particularly in England and America. Germany, it was felt, had been harshly treated, hastily condemned; and these feelings made many people sympathize with German grievances even when they were voiced by Adolf Hitler. In fact the controversies over the origins of the First World War helped to bring about the second.

These controversies centred at first on the events which followed the murder of Archduke Franz Ferdinand of Austria at Sarajevo on 28 June. Soon men went much farther back. The Germans blamed the Franco-Russian alliance which had been concluded in 1894; the French blamed the policy of Bismarck, although he left office in 1890. Others blamed things in general – the structure of alliances or the armaments of the Great Powers. Some blamed more specifically the armament manufacturers. Lenin and other Marxists after him blamed capitalist imperialism. Psychologists blamed the pugnacity of human nature. The worst of such general theories is that they will explain almost anything. The very things that are blamed for the war of 1914 – secret diplomacy, the Balance of Power, the great Continental armies – also gave Europe a period of unparalleled peace; and now we are often inclined to think that, if only we could get back to them, we should have peace again. If we are going to probe far back into history, it is no good asking, 'What factors caused the outbreak of war?' The question is rather, 'Why did the factors that

had long preserved the peace of Europe fail to do so in 1914?'
Perhaps then we should conclude that diplomacy was not secret
enough; that the balance did not balance properly; that the
expenditure on armaments was too small.

I would point to one factor which has not perhaps been sufficiently explored. Men's minds seem to have been on edge in
the last two or three years before the war in a way they had not
been before, as though they had become unconsciously weary of
peace and security. You can see it in things remote from international politics – in the artistic movement called Futurism, in the
militant suffragettes of this country, in the working-class trend
towards Syndicalism. Men wanted violence for its own sake;
they welcomed war as a relief from materialism. European civilization was, in fact, breaking down even before war destroyed it.
All the same, we have tended to look too much for the deeper
causes of war and neglected its immediate outbreak. Despite these
deeper causes individual men took the decisions and sent the
declarations of war. You may say that they should not bear all the
responsibility, but they had some. If two or three men had acted
differently, war would not have occurred at that particular
moment. And we have a new guide. A famous Italian publisher,
Luigi Albertini, when Mussolini excluded him from politics,
turned to the study of war-origins. For nearly twenty years he
studied the documents and interviewed the surviving statesmen.
Two massive volumes of his work have been translated into
English; with a third to come. It is unlikely that we shall ever
know more of the political and diplomatic events which preceded
the war of 1914. We might learn something more from the military
records, particularly in Germany and Austria-Hungary, but not,
I think, much.

Let me take the events as we know them. The starting-point
was the assassination of Archduke Franz Ferdinand at Sarajevo.
Why was he there at all? As a gesture of defiance against Serb
nationalism; as a demonstration that Bosnia, though inhabited by
Serbs and Croats, was going to remain part of the Austrian
empire. That explains, too, why Princip and his friends set out to
assassinate the Archduke. They were Bosnian Serbs who wanted
their national freedom; and far from being encouraged by Serbia,
still less acting under Serb orders, their activities were most

unwelcome to the Serb Government. Serbia was just recovering from the Balkan wars of the previous year; she had not absorbed her new lands; and war with Austria-Hungary was the very last thing that the Serb Government wanted. No one has ever managed to show that the Serb Government had any connexion with the plot, though they may have had some vague knowledge. Indeed it was easy to guess that an Austrian Archduke would be shot at if he visited Sarajevo on 28 June, Serbia's national day. One Serb knew all about it – Colonel Dimitrevic, or Apis, as he was called, the head of a secret national society. But though he approved the plans, he did not initiate them, or give much serious help. The plot was the work of six young high-minded national idealists. Two of them are still alive. One is a professor at Belgrade University; the other curator of the museum at Sarajevo.

The plans of such young men are not very skilful. In fact all six of them missed their mark. Princip, the strongest character among them, was standing disconsolately on the pavement about to go home when an open car, with Franz Ferdinand in it, stopped right in front of him. The driver had taken a wrong turning and was now about to back. Princip stepped on to the running-board, killed Franz Ferdinand with one shot and, mistakenly, the Arch-duke's wife with the other – he had hoped to kill the governor of Bosnia. This was the crime of Sarajevo. The Austrian Govern-ment were not much concerned to punish it. They wanted to punish a different crime – the crime that Serbia committed by existing as a free national state. The Austrians wanted to prove that they were still a Great Power and somehow to destroy Serbia. They decided to go to war with Serbia, whatever her excuses and apologies. This was the first decision which brought about the world war. The man who made it was Count Berchtold, a frivolous aristocrat, but the Foreign Minister of Austria-Hungary.

He needed the approval of his German ally; and on 5 July he got it. William II, the German Emperor, agreed over the lunch table: Austria-Hungary, he said, must act against Serbia, even at the risk of war with Russia. Bethmann Hollweg, the Chancellor, turned up during the afternoon: and he approved also. There was no formal council, no weighty consideration of the issues. Of course the Germans were bluffing. They thought that Russia would let Serbia be destroyed. But, if not, they were ready for war. The German army was at the height of its strength; the French army was being reorganized; the Russian army would not be properly equipped until 1917. The German line was: if there is to be war, better now than later. William II often talked violently, though he usually repented soon afterwards. The new factor was that Bethmann also supported a policy leading to war. Hence this worthy, pacific man must bear more responsibility than any other individual for what followed. He alone could have stopped the war; and instead he let it happen.

After 5 July, nothing followed for nearly three weeks. The Austrians prepared an ultimatum to Serbia in their usual dilatory way. The other Powers were helpless; they could do nothing until the Austrian demands were known. All sorts of wild guesses have been made about French and Russian activities. But there is not a scrap of evidence that Russia promised to support Serbia or that France promised to support Russia. In fact Serbia agreed to nearly all the Austrian demands. It was no use. The Austrians broke off relations and on 28 July declared war. They did this deliberately, to make a peaceful outcome impossible. Now Russia had to do something. The Russians had no aggressive plans in Europe. In fact they had no interest in Europe except to be left alone. But they could not allow the Balkans, and so Constantinople and the Straits, to fall under the control of the Central Powers. If they did, their economic life, which in those days depended on the outer world, would be strangled – as indeed it was during the war. They tried to warn Austria-Hungary off Serbia. When that failed, they announced their mobilization, first against Austria-Hungary alone, then on 30 July a general mobilization. This was not an act of war – the Russian armies could not be ready for at least six weeks. It was a further gesture of diplomacy – a warning that Russia would not stand aside.

But it was also the last act of diplomacy. The German plans depended on getting in their blow first. If war came, whatever its cause, they must knock out France in the first six weeks and then turn with all their strength against Russia. The plan had been made by Schlieffen, who died in 1913. It made certain that any war in Europe must be a general war – it could not be localized; and it also made certain that, once Germany began to mobilize, war was inevitable. People everywhere had the habit of saying

'Mobilization means war'. This was only true of Germany; other countries had mobilized in the past without war: the British Navy in 1911, the Austro-Hungarian army in October 1913. And it was true of Germany only because Schlieffen had said it must be true. In this sense a dead man had the deepest responsibility of all for the European war. On 31 July Germany began to mobilize. With this step effective diplomacy ceased. The diplomatists, and even the kings and emperors, went on trying; but there was nothing they could do. Once the German armies mobilized, war had to be brought on, not averted; and the German diplomatists had to do what they were told by the German soldiers. They were not being consciously more wicked than other diplomatists; they had been told for years that only the Schlieffen plan could save Germany, and they believed what they were told.

Russia was asked to stop mobilizing. When she refused, Germany declared war on her on 1 August. France was asked to promise to stay neutral and to surrender her principal fortresses as security. The French evaded this demand; and on 3 August the Germans declared war on them also. It is often said that the alliances caused the war; but the alliances were not observed in 1914. Germany had promised to aid Austria-Hungary if she were attacked by Russia; but in fact Germany declared war on Russia without this happening. France had promised to aid Russia if she were attacked by Germany. But in fact the French were attacked by Germany before they had made a decision of any kind. No doubt they would have decided to aid Russia; and maybe Russia would have attacked Austria-Hungary. As it was, neither of these things happened. The German rulers launched a preventive war.

As to Great Britain, the German generals never gave her a thought. She had no army on a Continental scale; and they never considered the British Navy. The German armies had to go through Belgium as part of the Schlieffen plan in order to knock out France; and it was the German invasion of Belgium which brought Great Britain into the war. People then and since said that this was not the real reason – that we were pledged to France or that we had encouraged Russia. The fact remains that, but for the invasion of Belgium, British policy would have been much more confused and hesitant, the British people certainly not united. As it was, the British action was not much more than a moral gesture. Their army contributed little: it was the French, not the British, who won the battle of the Marne.

Could the war of 1914 have been averted? You can make all kinds of conditions: if Austria-Hungary had given her peoples more national freedom; if nationalism had never been thought of; if Germany had relied more on her economic, and less on her military power. But in the circumstances of 1914, Great Britain could have kept out of war only if she had been prepared to let Germany defeat France and Russia. France could have kept out of war only if she had surrendered her independence as a Great Power. Russia could have kept out of war only if she had been willing to be strangled at the Straits. In short, they could have avoided war only by agreeing that Germany should become the dominant power of the Continent. None of these Powers decided on war. The three men who made the decisions – even if they too were the victims of circumstances – were Berchtold, Bethmann Hollweg, and the dead man Schlieffen.

26

THE GERMAN ARMY IN POLITICS

MR GORDON CRAIG, of Princeton University, has written a fascinating book on the part played in German politics by the Army from its foundation by the Great Elector in 1640 to the disintegration of both Army and State in the defeat of 1945.[1] Most of it is based on well-known printed sources, though it is none the worse for that. Narrative is the lifeblood of history; and scholars err grievously if they think they have discharged the historian's task by writing articles or books of learned detail. Mr Craig has also some new material which is worth special notice. He has had a free run of the German military archives which the Americans carried off to Washington in 1945. It is exasperating to reflect that the German naval archives were similarly carried off to London (where they still are) but that no British historian has been able to use them. Think what we might have done with them! We might, for example, have found out whether there was any truth in the stories of German acceleration which launched the great 'We want eight' naval scare of 1909. But British Government departments regard historians with suspicion and guard German secrets as eagerly as they guard their own.

Mr Craig's 'plums' come from two periods when the Army was faced with a challenge from liberalism. The first is the years 1862–4, when Bismarck came to power. Everyone knows that Roon, as Minister of War, defended the Army from the attempts by the Prussian Chamber to determine its size and character. Mr Craig shows from Roon's papers that he was also threatened from the other side by even more reactionary generals, particularly Edwin von Manteuffel, who wished to destroy the Prussian Constitution altogether. Bismarck certainly defeated the Chamber; but he and Roon also defeated Manteuffel, and their skilful diplomacy finally removed him from close personal contact with the king. Bismarck takes on a new appearance when he is shown as the saviour of the constitutional balance against liberals and

1. *The Politics of the Prussian Army, 1640–1945.* By Gordon A. Craig.

generals alike. Indeed, though Bismarck always resisted parliamentary sovereignty, he successfully asserted civilian authority (his own) against the Prussian generals. The complicated structure of evasion and confusion which the German generals built up after 1871 was designed to thwart none other than Bismarck. He was too much for them. The elder Moltke was never allowed to influence policy. It needed the feebleness of later Chancellors and the fickleness of William II for Schlieffen to be free to dictate plans which made a general war inevitable. In this sense William II and Bethmann were the true 'war criminals' of 1914.

The most substantial of Mr Craig's revelations concern the Weimar Republic. The papers of Groener, Seeckt, and Stresemann are his principal sources. Here again much of the story is already known. Other writers have described the pact between Groener and Ebert, by which the Army agreed to defend the Republic on condition that the Republic should protect the Army. Groener's manoeuvres against the peace treaty are, however, new. When he first read the terms he noted: 'The proposals will be contested all the easier because they are so laughable.' He imagined that the Germans would be allowed to take part in the negotiations and that it would be easy to play on the differences between the Allies – hence his secret discussions with an American representative, Colonel Conger. His second, stronger card was to offer to the victors a German alliance against Soviet Russia. His calculations proved totally wrong; and it must be said in his honour that he faced the duty of accepting the Treaty of Versailles. He told the officers of the Supreme Command: 'I have undertaken great responsibility by my action, but I will know how to bear it.'

After Versailles Seeckt organized the new force of 100,000 men which was to keep the German Army alive for the future. Curiously enough the very limitation of the Army made Seeckt the most independent and arrogant of all German generals. In a mass army the rank-and-file were loyal to the symbol of the State – in the old Army to the Emperor, after 1933 to Hitler. Seeckt's men were pure 'legionaries' who looked only to their commanders. The tragi-comedy of Seeckt's successors, from Fritsch to the 'resisters' of 1944, was that they went on imagining that they could behave like Seeckt when Hitler had really stolen the Army from them. If the generals had come out against Hitler the troops would have refused to obey them. This, and this only, is the truth about 'the revolt of the generals'. Seeckt, however, could adopt an attitude of neutrality towards the Republic; he could even dream of making himself dictator. But in the end a civilian brought him down. Seeckt wanted to stake all German policy on an alliance with Soviet Russia; Stresemann balanced between West and East without committing himself decisively to either. When Seeckt opposed Locarno Stresemann got rid of him.

After 1928 the weakness of the politicians brought new opportunity to the generals – or perhaps imposed it upon them. Mr Craig shows how Groener, now Minister of War, and his assistant Schleicher were the real makers of Bruening's Cabinet. They imagined that it would stand above party intrigue and give Germany 'strong' government. Groener wrote of Bruening: 'His attitude in Parliament towards the babblers is nothing short of an aesthetic pleasure. I have concluded a firm alliance with him.' And again: 'I have never known a statesman, Chancellor, Minister, or general who combined in his head as much positive knowledge and political clarity and adaptability as Bruening.' What ruined Groener was his attempt to suppress the S.A. Schleicher thought that he was 'keeping the Army out of politics' when he organized Groener's fall. Six months later Schleicher became Chancellor himself, only to fail still more catastrophically. He is often said to have tried to keep Hitler out of power. On the contrary, Schleicher regarded the return of Papen as a far greater danger and strained every nerve to create a Hitler Government. The ironical outcome was a Government which contained both Hitler and Papen – the Army's last gift to the German people.

There is a more general point. We often talk of 'Junker' general and officers. Only half the officers were of Junker origin before 1914; only one in five after the First World War. The old Army, say before 1870, perhaps existed in part to defend the interests of the Junker landowners. The twentieth-century Army merely defended itself, like any other bureaucracy such as the Coal Board or British Railways. The more one studies Mr Craig's book the more one reaches the conclusion that the faults of the German Army sprang less from the arrogance of its generals than from the weakness of the politicians. Bismarck kept the generals in order; and so did Hitler after him under very different conditions. If the Germans ever produce liberal statesmen of any guts the Army will give no trouble. As it is, the picture of German generals once more at Supreme Headquarters is bound to stir an anticipatory shudder.

27

NIETZSCHE AND THE GERMANS

EVERY artist wants to live for ever. Though he creates primarily because he must, still he expects his creation to win immortality for him. There are many paths to this heaven, all of them difficult; the most certain of them is when men can say – 'this is the phrase that launched a thousand ships'. It does not matter if the phrase is misinterpreted, torn from its context, made to do work for which it was never intended. The great thing is to crystallize the beliefs and delusions of a generation in a single sentence. Rousseau would have been appalled by the terror which was conducted in the name of the Social Contract; Darwin was bewildered by the political doctrines which were built round the survival of the fittest; Marx would have railed against the dictatorship of the proletariat as it is practised in Russia. For that matter, Jesus Christ would have been dismayed by the doctrines and, still more, the practice of the Christian churches. Every great movement crucifies its founder; and in so doing gives him immortality.

Nietzsche has had the same fate, or achieved the same destiny. He was captured by the dictators of our time. Hitler kept a bust of him on show and consoled Mussolini for the disasters of 1943 with a set of his complete works. Nietzsche's great phrases seemed made for Fascism; it was inconceivable without them. The Will to Power, the Master Race, the Superman – Fascism did not need to look farther for its philosophy. Plenty of others lived by picking up the sweepings of Nietzsche's study. Freud declared that he had avoided reading Nietzsche in order to preserve his open mind – a sure confession that he looted from him. Bernard Shaw, always tawdry when it came to systematic thinking, could never have got along without the ideas he took over from Nietzsche and from his English contemporary, Samuel Butler. Nietzsche would certainly have repudiated his disciples. For one thing, he detested the Germans; he tried to make out that he was of Polish descent, and wished that he could write his books in French. He called himself 'a good European' and perhaps he was right to lecture in Switzerland. Dr Oscar Levy, his English translator, used to write protestingly to the newspapers whenever Nietzsche was blamed for the behaviour of the Germans or of the Nazis; and now an American, Professor Kaufmann, has carried out a mission of rescue on a larger scale.[1] This is the most sensible exposition of Nietzsche's philosophy ever made; it if fails to reveal the full secret it is because it forgets that Nietzsche, as well as being a philosopher, was something more important – a writer of the highest genius.

Nietzsche knew it himself. He said with perfect truth: 'One day it will be recognized that Heine and I have been by far the first artists of the German language – at an incalculable distance from everything that mere Germans have done with it.' Nietzsche invented a style so personal and so powerful that it can be recognized in a single sentence or even in a single phrase. Carlyle did the same; and Nietzsche admitted the likeness, though he dismissed, rightly, the triviality of Carlyle's ideas. It is, after all, very rare for a great writer to be a great thinker; and anyone who has ever tried to read any philosophy must know that the other way round it is rarer still. Nietzsche liked to think that he was a philosopher first of all. He wrote of *The Will to Power*: 'a book for *thinking*, nothing else; it belongs to those to whom thinking is a *delight*, nothing else'. Yet even this phrase gives him away. Whoever the reader may be, the writer is obviously getting a *delight* in expressing his thoughts, as well as thinking them. In fact Nietzsche's genius was his curse: if he had written less well, he would have never won the admiration of those solitary souls, the dictators.

It was Nietzsche who made the great discovery: 'God is dead.' This was not a declaration of atheism. In that case Nietzsche, always accurate, would have said: 'God does not exist.' He was announcing the end of faith in the supernatural and, still more, the end of the spirit-body dualism on which all Western morality had been based. How were things to be kept going when the sanctions of tradition and the supernatural were removed? Nietzsche was the first to answer: 'Become who you are.' Develop according to your own rules and not according to rules made up outside

1. *Nietzsche: Philosopher, Psychologist, Antichrist.* By Walter A. Kaufmann.

by others. Nietzsche also thought that he had discovered this rule of development; in formulating it, he made the great mistake which opened the door to every misunderstanding. The motive of human action, he supposed, was the Will to Power. The phrase, as Nietzsche designed it, was a provocation, almost a joke; it was a jeering reference to the contemporary German craze for the power of the state. Though a reference, it was also a repudiation. Far from wanting power over others, Nietzsche's man should want power over himself; or, to put it another way, should want to develop his powers. Nietzsche spoke constantly of 'over-coming'; but the most important sort of overcoming was to overcome yourself. Even the 'overman' has the same signifi-cance: though a conqueror, he is primarily a self-conqueror. This is, too, the only sense in which the superman is 'bred': he breeds himself. Nietzsche was as knocked over as all his contem-poraries by Darwin's supposed discovery that man was an ani-mal. He was not, however, so silly as to try to escape from this by turning man into a superior animal. Nietzsche's superman is not a biological type at all: he is the individual who has lifted himself out of the animal ruck by heaving at his own shoestrings. How do you tell the superman? Nietzsche's answer at last gives him away and shows that he was a great writer more than a great philoso-pher. For the answer is a joke on a cosmic scale. It is the doctrine of 'eternal recurrence': everything has happened before and will go on happening over and over again. Only a superman could stand such a doctrine; therefore you present it to him like a piece of litmus paper. If he is not a superman, he will go off his head. And this is exactly what Nietzsche did; as a last and colossal joke, the litmus-test produced a result of a most surprising kind. Or was Nietzsche's madness the effect of the disease with which he is alleged to have deliberately infected himself in his only sexual encounter? This too would be a joke of a Nietzschean character: 'boshaft', meaning malicious and sarcastic at once, was his favourite word for such pranks.

Nietzsche's doctrines had a logical form and can be presented in a logical way. Since he was the first modern thinker to face a non-theological universe, he anticipated most of the ideas that have come after. He anticipated psychoanalysis; he anticipated existentialism; even eternal recurrence is now a commonplace in the scientific world. He prided himself most on his methods, not on his results; and his method was that of ceaseless inquiry. He imagined himself as a latter-day Socrates; and what he hated in Christianity was its dogmatism, its elevation of faith over reason. 'Convictions are prisons.' His ideal was Goethe: 'the man of *totality*: he fought the mutual extraneousness of reason, sensuality, feeling, and will . . . the man of tolerance, not from weakness, but from strength'. Indeed he chose the title of his last work, *Ecce Homo*, as an echo of Napoleon's remark when he met Goethe: *voilà l'homme*. Yet when every effort has been made to turn Nietzsche into a man of balance and reason or the great Stoic of our times, doubt raises its head; the Socratic questioning starts again, this time at Nietzsche's expense. Certainly Nietzsche disliked the Germans, hated anti-Semitism, despised those who lived for public success. All the same, he gave them plenty of openings. As he exposes himself to perversions, he has the air of the elderly woman anxiously demanding of the enemy officer: 'When does the raping begin?' Carlyle preached silence in forty volumes; Nietzsche preached sanity and tolerance in works that were raving mad and savagely intolerant from the beginning.

It will not do to blame all the misunderstanding on his sister, as Professor Kaufmann and others have done. Certainly Frau Förster-Nietzsche set out to capture Nietzsche for German nationalism at its most nonsensical; and she spent forty years editing his works in such a way that his subversive thoughts were obscured. But he had given her the excuse and the opportunity. From Luther to Hitler the Germans have always wanted an iron framework of discipline to keep them in reasonable order; when they lose this, they go mad, as Nietzsche did, and it was only to be expected that the Germans would follow his example rather than his teaching. Nietzsche himself felt detached from the community; he was an individual in the void, and he supposed that he was preaching to a few individuals equally detached. His success came when a whole society lost its bearings and threatened to disintegrate. It is all very well to call for the superman so long as you can be sure that the right kind of superman will respond to the call. If Mussolini and Hitler turn up instead, who is Nietzsche to say they do not conform to the terms of the advertisement?

Nietzsche himself said of Napoleon: 'the revolution made Napoleon possible; that is its justification. For such a prize the anarchical crash of our entire civilization is welcome.' The words could be written up over the bunker, if it still exists, of the Chancellery in Berlin. If the Fascists and Nazis, with their will to power and their freedom from slave-moralıty, beyond good and evil, were not the supermen of Nietzsche's imagination, they were too near to it to be comfortable.

The truth is that the individual judgement, with all its enterprise and courage, needs to operate in a settled community. The pioneer must be ahead of his fellows, but not out of sight; otherwise he goes mad or they do – probably both. Blake wrote in much the same style as Nietzsche and with much the same drift; but this never provoked Gladstone, or even Neville Chamberlain, to set himself alight in the cellars of 10 Downing Street. Everyone who has escaped from religious dogma must have been captivated by Nietzsche at some time or other; but most escape the thraldom and discover that it is individualism run mad. It is the philosophy of the *rentier* who imagines that he owes nothing to society, though society owes much to him. Perhaps this is only another way of saying that the job of court-jester is attractive only so long as there is a court to laugh at the jests. Anyone who sets out to be a heretic had better postulate first a society tolerant yet respectable; in fact he had better be an Englishman.

28

THUS SPAKE HITLER

THOUGH Hitler finished as a charred corpse soaked in petrol, he achieved his deepest wish: he staked out his claim in history and eclipsed his rivals. The other dictators of our time – Mussolini, Stalin, even Lenin – seem commonplace in comparison; industrious politicians with a different set of tricks. Hitler had a depth and elaboration of evil all his own, as though something primitive had emerged from the bowels of the earth. At the same time, there was a superb cunning, which enabled him to exploit others. Perhaps there has never been a man who understood power better or who turned it to baser uses. It is loathsome to read of his actions, most loathsome to read his own utterances; yet, with all the disgust, it is impossible not to feel also that here was a piece of human nature on a gigantic scale. No doubt Hitler personified the ignorance, brutality, and greed of millions of his countrymen. He became more than life-size. The millions made their weight felt in all Hitler's words and acts.

Hitler lived on two planes more than most men. He was a man of action, rising to supreme power in Germany and thereafter almost a world-conqueror. He was also what for want of a better word must be called a 'thinker'. The great problem is to find a link between the two. Hitler, though evil, was great in action. He knew when to wait, when to act; his intuition simplified everything and cut to the heart of the situation. At the end of his career he made gross miscalculations which ruined him; but they were the miscalculations of a gambler who knew that he was playing for the highest stakes. But when he philosophized, he was opaque. His thought moved in a fog of his own making, a mixture of prejudices and misconceptions. The men round him were often playing a part, pretending to believe for the sake of their own advantage. Hitler had unquestioning faith in the rubbish that filled his mind. How could a man so ignorant, so enslaved by stupid dogmas, have achieved such practical success?

A new book gives a picture of Hitler at the height of his power.[1] Martin Bormann, Hitler's most devoted sycophant, was anxious not to lose any of his master's words; and he arranged for a shorthand writer to attend at meal-times in headquarters. Dr Picker performed this duty from 21 March until 2 August 1942; and, as well, he drew on the scantier notes of his predecessor who had begun his task in the previous July. Hitler had overcome the difficulties of the first Russian winter; Stalingrad and the entry of the United States into the war were still before him. He imagined himself within sight of decisive victory and could talk of his plans for making an Aryan world. He had always been given to monologue, and success made him pontificate more than ever. No one interrupted, hardly anyone spoke once Hitler had been launched on some theme; and the massive tedium is made worse by the fact that the shorthand-writer laid down his pencil whenever Hitler ran dry. After all, the poor chap had somehow to eat his dinner with one hand, while scribbling with the other. These interminable meal-time harangues in the bunkers, or in Hitler's special trains, can be paralleled only by Coleridge table-talking, as immortalized by Sir Max Beerbohm. But at least Coleridge's hearers could nod; the participants at Hitler's headquarters had to sit bolt upright and maintain an intelligent interest. It must have been among the graver perils of high office to have to listen to this relentless bore. Yet a leading German historian has edited Dr Picker's notes with scholarly gravity. Each fragment is numbered and given a title; and there is a weighty introduction, combining praise and blame. Certainly Professor Ritter condemns Hitler for thinking himself a superman; but only a great statesman would deserve to have his opinions reproduced so fully, and it is likely that more Germans will read this book for Hitler's inspiration than for Professor Ritter's criticism.

The table-talk is a revelation of Hitler rather as he wished to appear than as he was. He was talking before an audience of some twenty people, half of them professional soldiers, and no doubt his eye never wandered far from the shorthand-writer. Though he spoke little of himself, neither he nor his listeners had any doubt that he was 'one of Germany's greatest sons'. He made

1. *Hitlers Tischgespräche im Führerhauptquartier.* Edited by Dr Henry Picker. 1941–2.

no attempt to hide his origins or to erase them. He was the man from the gutter; and he explained on one occasion that he had become a non-smoker in Vienna because he could not afford both cigarettes and bread. The audience was not suited to the reminiscences of early days in the party, which he favoured when he was with his old comrades. Once he gave a detailed account of his coming to power, emphasizing its legality and placing the responsibility on Hindenburg and Papen. All the same, this seizure of power was never far from his thoughts. It was the time when he had known how to wait and to let his rivals destroy each other. Now he was waiting for a similar miracle, by which the enemy coalition would somehow be dissolved. He hated both Russia and America, and despised them. His dream was that the English governing classes would somehow come to their senses and make peace with him. 'If Hoare comes to power he only needs to release the Fascists.' He had hopes even of Mr Churchill. 'Better a hundred times Churchill than Cripps'; and he blamed the German diplomatists for not managing to arrange a love affair with one of Mr Churchill's daughters – this, he imagined, would have reversed British policy.

These were mere asides. More often Hitler would philosophize in the common German way. There is nothing here to sustain the view that he was a close student of Nietzsche; it would be nearer the truth to say that he translated Wagner into political terms. His hostility to Christianity was vulgar claptrap; it was a religion for women and weaklings. The Gods and the laws of nature, which he often invoked, were merely a cloak for his principle that the stronger were always right; this principle, though he did not know it, was soon to operate against himself. He praised the Oberammergau passion play as a wonderful demonstration of the Jewish danger: 'Pontius Pilate appears as a Roman so superior racially and intellectually that he stands out as a rock in the midst of the Near Eastern scum and swarm.' Hitler was confident that he himself belonged to Olympus, if there was one: 'the most enlightened spirits of all times will be found there'. And with the present period of struggle, 'we are moving towards a sunny, really tolerant outlook: man shall be in the position to develop the faculties given to him by God'.

But only one sort of men shall be in this sunny position:

Germanic men. The striking revelation of these disquisitions' is that Hitler believed implicitly his own racial theory. This was not merely anti-Semitism, though he held, for instance, that a single Jewish ancestor would still reveal effects even though he was as far off as the sixteenth century. But all his judgements were based on blood and breeding. Thus he thought that the population of northern France had been made tougher by the intermixture of German blood during the occupation of the First World War; and he said of the Grand Mufti: 'He gives the impression of a man among whose ancestors there was more than one Aryan and who perhaps springs from the best Roman blood.' For he held, of course, that the ancient Greeks and Romans were of Teutonic stock; hence the true Germans were to be found among the monuments of antiquity, not in the primitive forests. His illusion did not, however, extend to the modern Italians. Mussolini was the only man among them, and even here his approval sprang from the fact that, when they met, they were always in agreement. Only the Scandinavians and the Dutch were to be included in the new German Empire (the Swiss would be used as hotel-keepers); and to make this empire attractive to them Berlin was to change its name to 'Germania'.

This imperial theme was Hitler's favourite; he returned to it again and again. The only human element in it was his intention to develop Linz into a great city and to endow it with the artistic plunder of Europe; this would humble Vienna and punish the Viennese for their early neglect of him. But for the most part his plans were far more grandiose: to turn Europe into a German Valhalla, built of concrete instead of stage-props. Concrete fascinated him; it expressed what he imagined his character to be. Cities of concrete, inhabited by hard Aryan men, and bound together by concrete roads. Such was his vision of the future. He had already attained this ideal. These talks were delivered in a concrete cellar, far in the Russian plains; and his dreams turned always to the empire that he had conquered. Most empire-builders claim to benefit the 'colonial' peoples whom they have subdued; or at the very least intend to exploit them. Hitler was concerned only with 'German soil'. It was not enough to turn the Russians into slaves; they must disappear. He stormed against the idiocy of denying them the means of birth-control; at the same time they should be encouraged in their superstition against inoculation. The German conquerors were to live in their fortified towns, isolated from the Russians and above all never inter-breeding with them. The Russians were to become ignorant, diseased, rotten, and finally to perish. As to the lesser Slav peoples, the process of extermination could already be begun with them. Such was the German cultural mission, the defence of European civilization against the barbarism of the East.

Yet, absurdly enough, Hitler had little confidence in these Germans whose imperial greatness he was creating. He railed against the methods of German bureaucracy and often envied Stalin, 'a man of real genius'. Some of his hearers must have shivered to themselves as Hitler described how he would deal with a 'mutiny' in the Reich: 'Execute all leading men of opposition outlook, and especially those of political Catholicism, at once; shoot all the inmates of the concentration camps within three days; shoot all criminal elements, whether free or in prison, within three days.' This would involve 'some hundred thousands of men' and would make other measures superfluous. This, and not the sunny tolerance of moral outlook, was the reality in Hitler's future. His 'Germania' was imaginary. He feared and hated the actual Germans only a little less than he hated the inferior races. The only Germans he cared for were the men of the S.S., and they were to breed for the future as well as to fight for it. Though he was 'one of Germany's greatest sons', he dared not, as he confessed, drive unguarded through the streets of any German town; it did not even occur to him to regret that he could not walk there. Choosing terror, he had condemned himself to a life of fear. Hitler was beyond good and evil only in the sense that any criminal or gangster is beyond good and evil. He believed that with power he could do anything; and the Germans who supported him shared this belief. Though he was wrong, they were wrong also; and most wrong now, if they suppose they can shoulder all their faults and crimes on to Hitler's shoulders.

29

HITLER'S SEIZURE OF POWER

NATIONAL Socialism was based on fraud; and no fraud was greater than the legend that a seizure of power by Hitler took place on 30 January 1933. Certainly this day, on which Hitler became Chancellor, was the most important moment in his life and a turning-point in German history. But there was no seizure of power. That had been tried by Hitler at Munich in November 1923. It had failed; and he was determined never to repeat the attempt. There was an alternative path to power which he sometimes contemplated: that the Nazi party should actually win a majority of the popular vote and thus install Hitler as Chancellor by strict democratic choice. But this alternative, too, proved beyond him. The Nazis never received more than 37 per cent of votes at a free election for the Reichstag. The third path, and that which Hitler followed, was the way of intrigue; he would become Chancellor as the leader of a minority and would then use the power of the State to establish his dictatorship. The answer to the question how Hitler came to power is therefore to be found more in the actions of those German politicians who were not National Socialists than in those of Hitler himself. He waited; they decided.

The Weimar Republic always suffered from a multiplicity of parties. No single party ever possessed a majority in the Reichstag and every German Government after 1918 rested on a coalition. This would have mattered less if there had been at least a majority in favour of the Republic; but this, too, was lacking after the first elections in 1919. The middle-class Liberal parties faded and disappeared. Only the Social Democrats remained a genuine Weimar party. The Nationalists welcomed anything that weakened the Republic; the Communists welcomed anything that discredited the Social Democrats. The Roman Catholic Centre party certainly took part in republican governments along with the Social Democrats; but it had no republican principles. It was a sectarian party, ready to work with any system that would protect Roman

Catholic interests; and in the last days of the Republic it stretched out its hand to the forces of destruction, just as in the last days of the empire it had turned to the republicans. Every party contributed to the fall of the Weimar Republic – the Social Democrats from timidity, the others with conscious ill-will. But none contributed with such cynicism as the Centre – indifferent to the Republic or even to Germany, so long as the Roman Catholic schools enjoyed their favoured position.

The failure to establish strong stable governments brought unexpected power to the President. The makers of the constitution in 1919 had intended to give him the position of monarch in a parliamentary state: choosing the Chancellor, but without independent authority in himself. The Chancellor was to be the heir of Bismarck, the true wielder of power. But the short-lived Chancellors never held this position. They were little more than parliamentary managers for the President. Even Ebert drew on his reserve of authority. Hindenburg, who became President in 1925, possessed it in greater measure and believed that his duty was to use it. Moreover, as the military leader of the World War, Hindenburg both commanded the allegiance of the army and voiced its demands. The army was the one stable point of order in an unstable society. It is a mistake to suggest, as some have done, that the army chiefs were bent on overthrowing the Republic. They would have attempted this only if the republican politicians had accepted permanently and sincerely the disarmament imposed upon Germany by the Treaty of Versailles; and none did so. The generals were willing to work with the Republic if it provided stable government. But this it failed to do; and the generals were obsessed with anxiety lest Germany's limited army, the Reichswehr, be called upon to intervene in civil strife. They did not make this civil strife, nor even welcome it. They were insistent that a civil solution should be found for it. That solution, they supposed, could only be strong government; and, since this was beyond the Republic, it must come in some other form. They were indifferent whether this form should be a presidial government (i.e., one resting on the authority of the President), monarchy, or dictatorship. Their overriding concern was to keep the army out of politics.

There was another impulse making for strong government between 1929 and 1933. These were the years of the great depression, which – starting in the United States – carried unemployment and financial collapse across the world. Keynesian economics were unknown, at least among public men; and it was universally supposed that, when men lacked the money to buy goods, the answer to the crisis was to deprive them even of the little money that they had. When, in the autumn of 1931, the British National Government unwillingly abandoned the gold standard, and so stumbled on the path to recovery, a former Labour minister exclaimed plaintively: 'No one told us we could do this!' His ignorance was universally shared. The only solution proposed was the reduction of wages and unemployment benefit; and for this a strong government was needed. Moreover, in times of bewilderment and distress men demand authority for its own sake. They have no idea what should be done, but they long for a commanding voice which will resolve their doubts. Here again it is a mistake to suppose that Germany's economic leaders were consciously set on overthrowing the Republic or destroying the trade unions. They would have accepted a republican leader if one had appeared with unquestioned authority and self-confidence, just as Franklin D. Roosevelt was accepted by the business leaders of the U.S.A. But they demanded strong government from somebody; and they were rightly convinced that the Republic could not provide it.

This, then, was the background of Hitler's rise to power. Far from his hammering at a door which was long kept closed against him, he was constantly being invited to enter by those within; and he held back in order to increase his market value. Everyone assumed that he would end up as Chancellor sooner or later. The real problem in German history is why so few of the educated, civilized classes recognized Hitler as the embodiment of evil. University professors; army officers; business-men and bankers – these had a background of culture, and even of respect for law. Yet virtually none of them exclaimed: 'This is anti-Christ.' Later, they were to make out that Hitler had deceived them and that the bestial nature of National Socialism could not have been foreseen. This is not true. The real character of National Socialism was exposed by many foreign, and even by some German, observers long before Hitler came to power. It could be judged from Hitler's writings and his speeches; it was displayed in every street brawl that the Nazi Brown Shirts organized. Hitler did not deceive the responsible classes in Germany: they deceived themselves. Their self-deception had a simple cause: they were engaged in fighting the wrong battle and in saving Germany from the wrong enemy. Hitler's hostility to Communism was his strongest asset. The Bolshevik peril in Germany had once perhaps been real: therefore anyone who was anti-Communist seemed to be on the side of civilization, and the Communists themselves fed this illusion by treating Hitler as their only serious enemy. 'Better Hitler than Communism' was the phrase which opened the way for Hitler first within Germany and then on a wider scale in Europe.

Further, the directors of German policy were obsessed with the struggle against the Treaty of Versailles. They regarded the disarmament clauses as a personal humiliation; and they genuinely believed, though without justification, that reparations were the cause of Germany's economic difficulties. They could not repudiate wholeheartedly a movement which raged against the Versailles system. Rather they welcomed it as an ally. Every advance of National Socialism strengthened the argument that Germany should receive concessions in foreign affairs – otherwise the National Socialists would get stronger still. And the argument was not without force. Can any English or French observer honestly maintain that reparations would have been ended or the Rhineland evacuated without the mounting shadow of Hitler? Even apart from questions of foreign policy, respectable Germans – especially army officers – were bound to look with favour on a movement equipped with uniforms and acting under military discipline. More than one general remarked: 'It would be a shame to have to fire on these splendid young men in their brown shirts.' Experience in other countries has repeatedly shown that the only answer to a Fascist party, with an organized private army, is to suppress it by force of law. The Red peril and the system of Versailles made it impossible to give this answer in Germany.

Even so, the lack of alarm among civilized Germans remains a strange puzzle. The explanation may perhaps be found in the taste which so many of them had for political intrigue. A country with a long constitutional history develops a political class. The politicians look after government. The generals and bankers and professors mind their own business. This has always been true in England; and it was largely true in the third French republic, despite an occasional political general. In Germany men were always coming in from outside; a political class never had a chance to develop. Even Bismarck was a gifted amateur, who knew nothing of politics until he started at the top. Of his successors as Imperial Chancellor, one was a general, one a diplomatist, one a civil servant. In the reign of William II generals like Waldersee and Ludendorff pushed into politics on one side; and business-men like Ballin or Rathenau pushed in on the other. The practice was maintained in the Weimar Republic. There was no true statesman in Germany after the death of Stresemann in 1929. Her fate was in the hands of amateurs, who mistook intrigue for political activity. Hindenburg, the President, was a retired professional soldier, a field-marshal over eighty years old. Bruening, who became Chancellor in 1930, was half scholar, half army captain, but never strictly a party leader. Papen, his successor, was a dashing cavalry-man of great wealth, with no political standing. Schleicher, the most influential of all, lived for intrigue and nothing else: claiming to represent army opinion with the President and the President's authority to the army, but in fact playing off one against the other. All four thought that they were a great deal cleverer than Hitler and that they would take him prisoner in no time. They never feared Hitler or took precautions against him. Indeed, the fact that he was a politician and the leader of a political party made them despise him, as they despised the other politicians. The Austrian generals of the old regime made much the same mistake when they came up against Bonaparte.

Intrigue took the place of politics when Bruening became Chancellor in March 1930. The previous republican governments claimed to rest on a majority of the Reichstag, even though the claim was not always justified. Bruening did not attempt to construct a parliamentary Cabinet. He relied on the authority of the President and ordered the Reichstag to vote for him, much as Bismarck had done in his great days. The Reichstag had not always responded to Bismarck's commands; it was even less likely to be overawed by Bruening. In July 1930 his measures were defeated; and the Reichstag was dissolved. Political theorists in other countries with a multiplicity of parties often lament that the executive cannot threaten parliament with dissolution. The German example shows that the remedy can be worse than the disease. General elections may provide a solution when they are contested by two strong parties. But the voter cannot be expected to solve the riddle that has baffled his leaders. A dissolution could have only one effect in the existing circumstances. The voters were told by Bruening, the Chancellor, that all the parties were equally factious and difficult. Many voters therefore turned to the political leader who said exactly the same. And this leader was Hitler. The National Socialist party had been an insignificant group in the previous Reichstag. It was inflated and artificially fostered by the repeated electoral campaigns of the two years that followed. How otherwise could the voters respond to Bruening's demand and return a Reichstag of a different character? If there had been no 'Bruening experiment', and hence no general election in September 1930; if Germany had struggled on with weak coalition governments throughout the great depression, the National Socialist party would never have won at the polls and Hitler would never have triumphed.

The election of September 1930 brought great gains to the National Socialists, and only slightly smaller gains to the Communists. It lessened Bruening's chance of achieving a parliamentary majority. Even now there was plenty of time for the forces of order and decency to unite against National Socialist barbarism. But Hitler's victory elated the political jugglers, instead of frightening them. They imagined that they could use the threat of National Socialism against the other parties in the Reichstag without ever being endangered themselves; and they even hoped that Hitler would be obliging enough to act as their agent. Bruening depended on the authority of President Hindenburg; but the President's term ran out in 1932. At the beginning of the year Bruening proposed a bargain to Hitler: Hindenburg's term should be prolonged for one or two years; then Bruening would resign, and the way would be clear for Hitler. Bruening's calculation was clear. Hitler was to perform a service now in exchange for a reward that might never have to be paid. Hitler's answer was equally clear: Bruening must be dismissed and a new Reichstag elected (with, no doubt, a larger Nazi representation); then he would support a prolongation of Hindenburg's term. In other words, he must have his price before he would perform his service. The negotiations broke down. A presidential election was held, with Hitler as candidate of the Nazis and the Nationalists, Hindenburg – absurdly enough – as the candidate of the Left, including the Social Democrats. Hindenburg was elected. The voters had rejected National Socialism; but they had not supported anything, except a figurehead of eighty-five. The problem of finding a strong government, based on a Reichstag majority, remained.

Bruening did not recognize this problem. He proposed to remain in office and to continue to govern with the support of the President and the Reichswehr. But this programme was rejected by the generals and, above all, by Schleicher, their political spokesman; they were determined not to be drawn into the conflict of parties. Bruening and Groener, his Minister of Defence, thought that they could now act against Hitler. On 14 April 1932 the Nazi armed forces were dissolved by decree. On 12 May Schleicher told Groener that the Reichswehr had no confidence in him; and the following day he resigned. A fortnight later, on 30 May, Bruening also resigned, on Hindenburg's order. The old man had been persuaded that Bruening was the sole obstacle to a deal with Hitler and so to a government with a democratic majority. The instrument chosen for this deal was Franz von Papen, a wealthy aristocrat of no sense, though much courage. Schleicher said of him: 'People sometimes say that Herr von Papen is frivolous. But that is what we need.' And Papen characterized himself when he asked an economist for a programme: 'I know nothing of economics, but I'll do whatever you suggest. I'm a gentleman-rider; and I'll jump, I'll jump.'

Papen, like Bruening, was a member of the Centre Party, though, unlike Bruening, he carried no weight in it. Schleicher did not understand this. He supposed that the Centre would support Papen and, with Hitler supporting him as well, the 'functioning Reichstag' would be made. This scheme at once broke down. The Centre insisted that Hitler must take real responsibility, not exercise influence behind the scenes; failing this, they opposed Papen's government. Hitler, on his side, demanded power; and he, too, continued in opposition when this was refused. Papen's was perhaps the weakest government that has ever ruled a great country – a Cabinet of elderly 'Barons' and no support at all in the Reichstag. This did not worry Papen. He was content to wait until Hitler came to heel. And Hitler also waited until Papen's difficulties swept him away. Both gambled on Germany's distress – the one a vain intriguer, the other the greatest demagogue of modern times. In June, Papen dissolved the Reichstag, not with any hope of getting support for himself, but solely as a demonstration to Hitler that he could wear him down. The Nazi election funds would not last for ever; and, besides, the voters might turn elsewhere if Hitler failed to achieve anything.

The election of 31 July gave Hitler his greatest success: 37·3 per cent of the votes cast. But he was still far from an independent majority, and the Nazi rate of increase was slowing down. In fact, as the next election showed, the tide had already turned. The bargaining of May was renewed. Hitler demanded full power; himself as Chancellor, other Nazis in all the key posts. It is true that he was prepared to include also some non-Nazis and asked only 'as much power as Mussolini got in 1922'. Papen and Schleicher were not well-grounded in current history. They only knew that Mussolini was dictator of Italy, and forgot the slow process by which he had reached that position. In any case, the analogy was revealing enough: however Hitler began, he, too, would end as dictator, and they were only prepared to employ him as their parliamentary agent. They offered Hitler the post of Vice-Chancellor, safely under Papen's control. On 13 August Hitler was summoned to appear before Hindenburg. The President rated him for the violence and illegality of the Nazi party. 'He was ready to accept Hitler in a coalition government ... but he could not take responsibility for giving exclusive power to Hitler alone.' Hitler tried to repeat that he wanted 'only as much as Mussolini'. The fatal analogy roused Hindenburg's anger.

The interview of 13 August was the sharpest set-back that National Socialism ever received. Until then its prestige and the votes cast for it had been growing steadily. Hitler had spoken openly of the seizure of power and of the 'St Bartholomew's night' that would follow. Now it was clearly established that the so-called national revolution could take place only with the permission of the President. And that permission had been refused. Papen's gamble seemed to be working. Many of the lesser Nazis lost heart. Some worried over their security as deputies; a few over the future of the party. Hitler's great triumph lay in the iron control which he managed to maintain over his party during the next few months. If it had once begun to crumble, he would have been left isolated in a very short time. It is in this sense that Hitler was brought to power by his gifts for leadership. The National Socialist party was never strong enough to force Hitler into power but he never needed to look over his shoulder. The other politicians worried about their followers and their voters; and worry breaks a politician's nerve sooner or later. Hitler always assumed that his control of the party was unshakeable – rather as Napoleon always assumed that he would win a battle, and therefore never wasted men in securing a line of retreat.

But for the moment it was Papen who went over to the offensive. On 12 September the Reichstag was again dissolved; and Germany was involved in yet another general election, in order to wear down the National Socialists. The results, which came in on 6 November, seemed to confirm Papen's calculation. The Nazis lost two million votes; their share of the total fell to 33 per cent and their deputies from 230 to 196. It was less encouraging that most of these votes were transferred to the Communists, who increased their representation to 100. Still, Papen hoped to repeat his manoeuvre of August under more favourable conditions: Hitler should be offered office without power, under strict control, in order to save himself from further decline. On 16 November Hitler again refused. Papen swung over to his alternative line: he would show that no one was capable of producing a parliamentary majority, and would then transform his temporary dictatorship into a permanent one. Instead of again dissolving the Reichstag, he would govern without it. On 17 November Papen resigned, ostensibly to give Hitler his chance. The step was meant as a pretence; for Hitler could obviously not produce a Reichstag majority. He came again to Hindenburg, this time in a rather more friendly atmosphere. But the deadlock remained. Hindenburg would make Hitler Chancellor if he could offer 'a secure workable majority in the Reichstag with a coherent programme'. Hitler demanded to be made Chancellor on the same terms as

Papen – governing, that is, on the President's authority. Hindenburg refused. With Hitler as Chancellor, the Cabinet would not be a presidential government, but a party dictatorship. The future was to prove him right.

Papen seemed to have played his cards correctly. He could now resume office without being open to the reproach of barring the way against a majority cabinet. On 1 December he went to Hindenburg with his plan: he would prorogue the Reichstag, proclaim a state of emergency, and govern by decree. If there was opposition from Nazis or Communists, he would crush it by force. But this was the very proposal for involving the Reichswehr in civil strife which the generals had always rejected. Schleicher opposed Papen's scheme, both as Hindenburg's military adviser and as spokesman of the army. Besides, he claimed he could succeed where Bruening and Papen had failed: he could provide a parliamentary majority. He had been negotiating with Nazi leaders, such as Gregor Strasser, who were dissatisfied with Hitler's rigid line; and he believed, as well, that he could win the support of the trade unions. The Social Democrats, the Centre, and the dissident Nazis would give him a workable coalition. Hindenburg preferred Papen to Schleicher; and he authorized him to form a government.

But Schleicher soon carried the day. On 2 December the new Cabinet met. Schleicher produced a report from Major Ott of the General Staff, which asserted that the Reichswehr could not do what Papen wanted. The Poles might seize the chance of internal disturbance in Germany to attack her eastern frontier; and 'defence of the frontiers and the maintenance of order against both Nazis and Communists was beyond the strength of the forces at the disposal of the Federal and State Governments'. The Reichswehr was, no doubt, a limited force; yet it had managed to maintain internal order in 1920 and 1923, when the chance of Polish intervention had been much greater. There is little doubt that even now the Reichswehr would have been prepared to act if it had been against the Communists alone. But the Nazis, whatever their violence, were a 'national' element. This was the underlying sentiment of Ott's memorandum. Papen was still ready to face the risk, but his colleagues were reluctant, and Hindenburg still more so. He said to Papen: 'I am too old and have been through too much to accept the responsibility for a civil war. Our only hope is to let Schleicher try his luck.' Schleicher became Chancellor the same day.

His luck turned out to be a poor resource. He offered to make Strasser Vice-Chancellor; and Strasser was willing to accept. But he could not carry the Nazi party with him. Hitler forbade any bargaining with Schleicher; and Strasser lost his nerve. On 8 December he went off to Italy for a holiday. Hitler reasserted his domination over the party and determined once more to 'throw the whole party into the struggle'. Strasser's abortive revolt and failure actually strengthened Hitler's appeal to the propertied classes; for he could claim to have shaken off the extreme, socialist wing of his party. Nazi finances were in a bad state. Even Goebbels had a feeling of 'dark hopelessness'. But Hitler's resolution was as strong as ever; and this time he was justified. Schleicher's feeble attempts at coalition had broken down. What is more, Papen – though out of office – continued to live next door to Hindenburg and to busy himself in political intrigue. He would have been more than human if he had not wanted his revenge on Schleicher; and while the latter had failed with Strasser, himself hoped to succeed with Hitler. On a more elevated plane, he could make out to be still pursuing the bargain with Hitler which had been everyone's object for the last two years. Papen and Hitler met, more or less secretly, on 4 January 1933. Papen, according to his own account, merely urged – in the most disinterested way – that Hitler should become Vice-Chancellor in Schleicher's Government. Schroeder, the Cologne banker in whose house the meeting was held, gives a different and more likely story. Hitler insisted on becoming Chancellor, though with Papen and his friends as ministers; in particular he did not ask for control of either the army or foreign affairs. Papen thought that he had performed the miracle: he had taken Hitler prisoner, figurehead of a respectable non-Nazi Cabinet. Wealthy Germans drew the same conclusion. Subscriptions began to flow into the Nazi funds. Goebbels noted: 'The financial situation has improved very suddenly.'

Schleicher did not realize that the position had changed. Once in office he thought, like Bruening and Papen before him, that he had only to issue orders for the crisis to disappear. It soon ceased to worry him that his political combinations collapsed. Gregor Strasser turned out to be a broken reed : he could not carry a single National Socialist with him. The Social Democrats and the trade unions were not won over. Like everyone else, they seem to have come round to the view that office was the best means of taming Hitler; and they still imagined that they could resist him if he attempted anything illegal. On the other hand, the extreme Right, though they distrusted Hitler, were alienated by the steps Schleicher had taken to conciliate the Social Democrats. The Reichstag was due to meet on 31 January. Its first subject for discussion was the *Osthilfe* – the subsidies to landowners in eastern Germany, which had involved many scandals reaching even to Hindenburg himself. On 28 January Schleicher had to confess to Hindenburg that he could not control the Reichstag; and he asked, as his two predecessors had done, for a decree dissolving it. This was the very policy of governing Germany by force which Schleicher had rejected when it had been put forward by Papen in December. Hindenburg liked Papen and by now disliked Schleicher. He refused the decree of dissolution. Schleicher then claimed that he could produce a parliamentary majority by negotiating with the National Socialists. But this was exactly what he had failed to do during the last six weeks. Moreover, Hindenburg knew, as Schleicher did not, that Papen could do it more successfully. Schleicher was dismissed; and Papen was entrusted with the formation of a new government.

A single pattern ran through all the negotiations from the fall of Bruening, or even before, to the accession of Hitler. The President and his confidential advisers worked persistently for a coalition government, in which Hitler would provide the votes and would yet be held in check by his associates. There was never any attempt to build a coalition government which would exclude Hitler or the National Socialist party; and the delay came from Hitler, not from the side of the respectable classes. Now Hitler agreed to come in. It is impossible to say what led him to compromise. Perhaps he recognized that the Nazi tide was ebbing; perhaps he felt that the old order was now sufficiently weakened and would crumble of itself; perhaps the position of Chancellor, even under Papen's control, made the difference. More probably, his decision sprang from his unconscious sense of timing, just as a great general might find it difficult to explain why he flung in his reserves at the critical moment.

On 30 January Hitler became Chancellor. This was far from a seizure of power. Indeed, the forces of the old order imagined that they had seized Hitler. Though he was Chancellor, there were only three Nazis in a Cabinet of eleven; the two key posts of Foreign Minister and Minister of Defence were in the hands of non-political agents of the President; and Hitler could not see Hindenburg except in the presence of Papen, who was Vice-Chancellor. No arrangement could have been neater or more cynical. Yet it broke down within the first few days. What Hitler appreciated and his conservative associates did not was that, while the Nazi party was not strong enough to seize power when the forces of the State were hostile, it was strong enough to do so once these forces were neutral or on its side. Papen remarks regretfully that 'existing institutions and parties gave up without a fight'. What else could they do? They might have resisted the Nazis if the police and the courts were there to maintain order. They could no longer do so when the police were under Nazi control and when, therefore, the defence of democracy took on a revolutionary character. Again, Hitler had been crippled by the fact that he did not possess a majority in the Reichstag; this had driven him to accept Papen's terms. But once in office he could argue that a further general election would give him a majority; and, since this had been the object of all the negotiations, his demand for a dissolution could not be refused. This time Hitler supposed that he could indeed deliver the parliamentary majority which had hitherto evaded everybody. Once the National Socialists dominated the Reichstag, he could shake off Papen and the other elderly gentlemen who controlled him, and establish a Nazi dictatorship by law.

Hitler's calculation did not succeed. The election campaign was conducted with every weapon of Nazi terror; and the burning of the Reichstag building on 27 February enabled Hitler to declare the Communist Party illegal. Nevertheless on 5 March the National Socialists secured only 43·9 per cent of the votes. Even with the co-operation of the right-wing Nationalists they had only a bare majority – enough to control the Reichstag from day to day, but not enough to carry through any fundamental change in the constitution. Hitler, however, was set on an Enabling Law which would give him all the powers of a dictator. If the so-called democratic parties had held together, Hitler would have been driven to illegal action – or would have remained powerless. The Communists had been driven underground. The Social Democrats, though feeble in action, held nobly to their principles and voted against the Enabling Law, despite the threats of terror against them. The decision rested on the Centre, with its 102 votes. The leaders of the Centre were men of personal courage. But their party cared little for democracy; it was concerned only to secure the position of the Roman Catholic schools. It had a long tradition of doing this by intriguing with successive parties and governments; it had long lost the tradition of resistance which had once enabled it to defeat Bismarck. The Centre leaders were fobbed off with promises from Hitler in which they only half-believed; and on 23 March the Centre votes were cast in favour of the Enabling Law. These votes alone gave Hitler's dictatorship its legal character.

One barrier remained: Hindenburg's veto, and Hitler's promise that he would do nothing to override it. But Hitler, who had wooed millions of voters, did not find it difficult to cajole an old man, never mentally acute and now senile. Papen soon found that he was not needed when Hitler had his interviews with the President. He went on dreaming that some day Hindenburg would reassert his independence and that the Nazis would be overthrown – again under Papen's direction. He waited patiently, as he had waited before. And fifteen months later he thought that his chance had come. On 17 June 1934 Papen delivered at Marburg the only public speech against the Nazi dictatorship ever made in Germany after Hitler's seizure of power. Even now his line was equivocal. His appeal was to Hitler to behave better, rather than to Hindenburg and the generals to overthrow him. In any case, Hitler was soon able to outbid Papen's feeble gesture. He, too, had his difficulties with the Nazi extremists – the leaders of the Brown Shirts who wanted to carry through a real social revolution now that their party was in power. He broke them in the bloodbath of 30 June. This seemed a guarantee to the generals that there would be no demagogic interference with the army. Hitler was already promising them rearmament on a great scale. Why, then, should they resist him for the sake of democracy or the constitution? This would be the very interference in politics which they had always rejected.

On 2 August 1934 Hindenburg died. The army leaders were content that Hitler should take his place. Within an hour of Hindenburg's death, the office of President was merged with that of Chancellor; and Hitler became undisputed Head of the State. He kept his bargain with the army. For three and a half years it remained autonomous, standing outside politics and repudiating all responsibility for the Nazi terror. Early in 1938 Hitler overthrew this balance. He was now moving towards an aggressive war in Europe; and he could tolerate no independent authority. The army leaders were discredited by a series of personal scandals, some of them without foundation. Hitler dismissed those who stood out against him; made himself head of the armed forces, the Wehrmacht; and at the same time put his agent, Ribbentrop, in the Foreign Office in place of Neurath. By February 1938 the seizure of power was complete. It had taken Hitler four years to destroy legality in Germany by legal means.

If we look back over this wretched story, we see a man bent on success on the one side, and a group of politicians without ideas or principles on the other. Hitler was resolved to gain power. He did not know how he would do it, and he tried many means which failed; but he had an unbreakable purpose. The others were only concerned to strike a bargain with him. If there had been a strong democratic sentiment in Germany, Hitler would never have come to power – or even to prominence. He would have failed even if the weak democratic parties had held together. He had two great weapons. He could promise the generals a great army, if they let him in; he could threaten civil disturbance, if they kept him out. The promise was more potent than the threat. One can blame all parties in turn. The Communists started the habit of violence and disrupted the working-class front. The Social Democrats had lost all ability to act and faith in their strength. The Centre would bargain with anybody, even with Hitler. But the greatest responsibility lay with those who let Hitler in and established him as Chancellor. Hitler recognized it himself. In 1938 Papen, then German ambassador at Vienna, accompanied Schuschnigg to the fateful interview at Berchtesgaden which ended Austrian independence. In the course of the argument, Hitler turned to Papen and said: 'By making me Chancellor, Herr von Papen, you made possible the National Socialist revolution in Germany. I shall never forget it.' And Papen answered with soldierly pride: 'Certainly, my Führer.'

30

THE SUPERMEN:
HITLER AND MUSSOLINI

A GREAT idea seldom gets a free run. The scientist in his laboratory can concentrate on a single line of research and work it to
fruition – or to death. In the world of real life experiments are
always being interrupted or broken off halfway. Thus, the policy
of treating the Germans resolutely was broken off by the French
in 1923 just when it was succeeding: and the policy of co-operating with the Russians was broken off in 1945 before the rewards
(and difficulties) of this policy became plain. The great question
of the future is whether mankind will turn against the scientists
before they succeed in blowing up the planet – certainly an experiment of great interest. One idea has had a real run for its
money – tried out without restriction and carried to its extreme.
This is the idea of the Hero or Superman, the political saviour for
whom many Europeans have been craving ever since the
time of Napoleon. The myth was launched by Napoleon himself
and took his own nephew prisoner; Carlyle preached it with
religious frenzy; Wagner dressed it up in musical form for the
Germans; and in the early twentieth century practically every
writer offered some form of anti-democratic, superman doctrine.

Twenty years later the superman arrived – or rather two supermen arrived, Mussolini and Hitler, Napoleons of the twentieth
century, the heroes of our time. Both were pure-hero types, without any of the adventitious aids of their predecessors. Frederick
the Great inherited his crown; Napoleon had a background of
military success; Cromwell and Lenin rested on a compact revolutionary class. Hitler and Mussolini made themselves. Except
as heroes, they were nobodies. Before they attained power, they
had achieved nothing; and the supposed class-basis of their rule
(Fascism as the last stage of Capitalism) was arrant nonsense.
Their real supporters were men as classless as themselves, not
great capitalists or even the petty *bourgeoisie*. General Beck said

of Hitler: 'this man has no country', and one could add – no class, no past, no family. Mussolini had a family and even a mistress: this did not prevent his ordering the execution of his son-in-law. Certainly he sometimes repeated 'proletarian' echoes of his past, as Hitler lived on the Greater German rhetoric that he had picked up in Vienna. These were merely incantations, phrases to produce the popular roar; not genuine beliefs, still less the motives of their actions. These heroes believed only in themselves. Like all men in public life, they craved for power. The exceptional thing in them was the addition of intense personal vanity: they wished both to stand in the limelight and to control the switchboard, to be actor, producer and playwright. In short, they wished to be God; and mankind having lost its faith in God, acquiesced in their wish.

Heroes are not of mortal clay; that we know of all supermen from Siegfried to Jack Tanner. We cannot expect them to act according to normal standards or even to notice the human beings around them. But how do they get on with each other? This is the fascinating topic of Miss Wiskemann's book[1]: the relations of the two supermen. According to all authorities, heroes recognize each other instinctively: they keep faith with each other, though they betray all the world besides. Miss Wiskemann attributes to Hitler and Mussolini a common intellectual ancestry: she puts all the blame on Nietzsche. This seems to me too narrow a basis: there is little to it except that Hitler once fell into a trance before the bust of the master. It leaves out of account the long hero-tradition in modern Europe. Mussolini summed up the Latin line of that tradition from Bonaparte to Georges Sorel; Hitler sprang directly from Carlyle and Wagner. More deeply (and this is the sense in the hero-idea) each in his way expressed the 'genius' of his people – a parody, no doubt, as summaries always are, but no more a parody than Churchill, say, is of the British people. One can safely adapt for both Hitler and Mussolini Gardiner's phrase about Cromwell: 'the greatest, because the most typical Englishman of all time'. Of course both men were lunatics, as Miss Wiskemann firmly establishes of Hitler, though doubtfully of Mussolini (such is her soft-heartedness for all Italians). The point is not of moment. All men are mad who devote

1. *The Rome–Berlin Axis*. By Elizabeth Wiskemann.

themselves to the pursuit of power when they could be fishing, painting pictures, or simply sitting in the sun. If men were sane, there would be no history. Though lunatics do not follow the rules of sane behaviour, they have rules of their own. The task of the historian is to discover these rules. No man acts out of character; and, as Machiavelli said, a man has only one character, as he has only one face. Hitler's rules and character ran true to a form that is easily mapped; Mussolini's behaviour was more complicated and therefore Miss Wiskemann inclines to believe him sane – or suffering from a duodenal ulcer, which comes to the same thing. There is a more profound explanation: even the hero cannot escape reality, even he remains rooted in the ground from which he has sprung.

Miss Wiskemann disapproves of such high subjects as Hitler and Mussolini being treated by 'witty Oxford dons' (alas! this is not a reference to the present writer). Wit has its advantages: it puts the hero in his historic setting. The difference between Hitler and Mussolini was the difference between their two countries. In Miss Wiskemann's book Germany and Italy come in too little. They are treated as two sovereign States of comparable importance; there is no analysis of their historic background or (apart from a table of Italy's coal imports) of their economic strength. The coal statistics give the game away. Coal is the most important index of power. Italy has no coal; therefore she is dependent for her power on others, condemned to a jackal diplomacy – or to none at all. The hesitations and manoeuvres of Mussolini were not, as Miss Wiskemann thinks, the results of doubt so much as a hero's resentment against the limitations of real life – truly, Mussolini was a hero of the suburbs. Vain and arrogant as he was, he yet had the sense to see that Italy could simulate greatness only by hunting with Hitler: he never shared the futile misjudgement of those western diplomats who thought that Italy could take the place of Russia in an anti-Hitler coalition (a favourite idea of the British Foreign Office), and he never accepted for a moment the ambition of Italian diplomats, from Ciano downwards, to play fast-and-loose with Germany and yet swagger among the great. Hitler saw the dilemma just as clearly. He wrote to Mussolini on 6 March 1940:

The outcome of this war will also decide the future of Italy. If this future is considered in your country in terms of merely perpetuating the existence of a European state of modest pretensions, then I am wrong. But if this future is considered in terms of a guarantee of the existence of the Italian people from a historical, geopolitical and moral point of view, or according to the rights of your people, those who are fighting Germany today will be your enemies too.

Against this profound analysis, Miss Wiskemann concludes: 'It was not mere rhetoric to say that one Italian alone forced Italy into the war in June 1940.' It is all very well to like Italians better than Germans. Who doesn't? This does not alter the fact that Germany was (and is) the only country on the European continent of Great Power stature; and that Italy could be carried to greatness only on Germany's back. Miss Wiskemann writes as though the Axis was an aberration of Mussolini's; in reality it came at the end of a tradition which includes Charlemagne and Napoleon, Metternich and Bismarck.

This, indeed, is the most curious thing about these heroes. According to the prophets, they were to be men without a past, beyond good and evil, and – what is more important – beyond tradition and habit. Both Hitler and Mussolini tried to follow the teachings of the prophetic books. They invented their uniforms and their methods of address – Duce and Fuehrer, titles never heard before. They wrote each other interminable letters, which were meant to be the correspondence of gods. Miss Wiskemann quotes a description by Shirer of the signing of the Pact with Japan: 'Three loud knocks on the giant door are heard. There is a tense hush in the great hall. The Japanese hold their breath. The door swings slowly open and in strides Hitler.' It is like a scene from *The Great Dictator*, except that no one is allowed to laugh. Yet as soon as it comes to practical affairs, these heroes turn out to be creatures of history like anyone else. Hitler's ideas were the commonplace of Pan-Germans in Vienna; Mussolini's policy is what one would expect from a countryman of Cavour and Crispi. Thus the history of the Axis is a story on two planes. On one level it expressed merely the personality of two lunatics; on the other it was a profoundly important chapter in the diplomacy of Germany and Italy, the two revolutionary nations of 1848. This contradiction baffled the two heroes themselves. As the only gods in

Europe, they ought to have been on terms of peculiar confidence, faithfully united against all others. This was the impression they tried to give to the world and even to themselves: each believed in the other – Mussolini was hypnotized by Hitler, and Hitler was genuinely taken in by Mussolini. All the same, the pull of real life was too strong for them. Hitler despised Mussolini at the very moment of believing in him; Mussolini knew that Hitler was leading him to disaster, even though he followed him with conviction. Each tricked the other and intrigued against the other though each knew that this was a sin against the hero in himself. Thus Mussolini encouraged the Czechs to become Communists in the autumn of 1939 in order to make things difficult between Moscow and Berlin; he protected Polish refugees and even hoped that Yugoslavia would be a barrier against German expansion in the Balkans. Hitler kept German irredentism in Tyrol up his sleeve, cut down Italy's share of Yugoslavia after its conquest, rejected Italy's claims against France. As a final oddity, though both were liars without restraint or scruple, each swallowed the other's lies and then was genuinely hurt at having been deceived. Probably each was happiest in the last phase, securely divorced from reality, Mussolini rattling the bones of the Fascist Republic and dreaming of St Helena, Hitler reading Carlyle and preparing a stupendous *Götterdämmerung*. Both ran true to form to the end. Hitler's last letter reproached Mussolini for having lost the war by invading Greece; Mussolini carried this letter in his pocket to show that he had been the first of the resisters. In these last acts each expressed national character as well as his own – the hard-luck story of the German, the smart intrigue of the Italian. They were a very nasty and ridiculous pair. The worst part of the story is that millions of people believed in them and applauded their every action. No doubt men deserved what they got, when they went around crying for a hero, a human saviour, a superman, instead of making the best of their own virtues and defects. Perhaps the Axis will sicken humanity with heroes for a long time to come. But I doubt it. Despite Miss Wiskemann, despite witty Oxford dons, Hitler and Mussolini seem safe for Valhalla.

31

SPAIN AND THE AXIS

THE third volume of documents[1] from the archives of the German Foreign Ministry is sadly lacking in scandal and sensation. Devoted to the Spanish civil war, it contains little evidence of a Fascist conspiracy and none at all of British or French connivance in it. Either the Western friends of Franco were discreet in their conversation or the German diplomatists were discreet in their reports. There is a solitary sentence to the contrary. On 16 October 1936 the German chargé d'affaires with Franco reported from Alicante:

England is supplying the Whites with ammunition via Gibraltar, and the British cruiser commander here has recently been supplying us with information of Russian arms deliveries to the Red Government, which he certainly would not do without instructions.

The first part of the sentence sounds like gossip; the second may record only the aberration of a single officer. Perhaps the British pro-Fascists let themselves go only in the more congenial company of the Italians. As to France, the one interesting story is of an approach to Franco by Laval in April 1937, with the programme of a Pétain Government which would work for Franco's victory. This certainly blows on the current legend of Laval as a maligned champion of democracy.

These are sidelines. The bulk of this inordinately long volume sticks closely to German policy, or rather the lack of it. For the Spanish civil war took the Germans entirely by surprise and it was a long time before they decided what use to make of it. The material here is, of course, drawn exclusively from the diplomatic archives; there is very little from the military side, and not a single directive from Hitler. No doubt wild ideas were aired at Berchtesgaden and wild projects sketched. But it certainly appears that the professional diplomatists were left to deal with the

1. *Documents on German Foreign Policy, 1918–45.* Series D, volume iii: The Spanish Civil War.

Spanish affair as best they could, gathering a little prestige and improving the international situation for Germany, but without risking a general war.

The German authorities on Spain at first expected Franco to be defeated, and therefore did not commit themselves deeply; they even welcomed the British proposal of non-intervention as a way of escape from an embarrassing situation. It is clear from this record that a firm French stand in the early autumn of 1936 would have settled the civil war to the advantage of the Spanish Government, without any risk of a general conflict; but of course the real French fear was of conflict within their own country. Another curious point is that in the opinion of the German Ambassador in Moscow (and of the French Ambassador also) the Russian Government, too, did not care much about the Spanish question, but was dragged into it in order to please the Communists of Western Europe.

Mussolini was Franco's real patron; and Italian zest outran German policy and patience. In December 1936, Mussolini made an agreement with Franco, securing economic and political advantages for Italy; the Germans were so annoyed that they cut down their aid to Franco and insisted that Italy carry the main burden of intervention. All the Germans secured during the civil war was an innocuous agreement of friendship made on 20 March 1937. The main concern of German policy was not directly with Spain: it was to keep Italy estranged from England and France, a purpose admirably served by the Italian intervention in Spain. Hence the Germans did not trouble themselves much about Franco or about the fortunes of war; they were ready to do anything which could keep Italy securely committed to intervention without unduly risking themselves. It was hopeless for the British to ask the Germans to exercise a moderating influence on Mussolini; this was the last thing that the Germans intended to do. But then the British Government hit on the strangest devices. In May 1938, according to Jordana, the Spanish Foreign Minister, they urged the Spanish rebel Government 'to use its influence with Mussolini to get him to take a stiffer attitude towards France'; then the French frontier would be more rigidly closed and the civil war the sooner over.

German policy only came alive as the civil war drew to a close;

after all, they wanted to have something to show for the activities of the Condor Legion. Throughout the war German adventurers – combining profit and Nazi principles – had been on the hunt for mining concessions; and Franco had held out grandiose prospects to them. But the concessions proved elusive. In November 1937, the Germans threatened 'to re-examine their attitude towards the Spanish Nationalist Government on various questions'. But, as they confessed to themselves, they could not repudiate their political line for the sake of mining concessions; and Franco knew it. When told that he ought not to be surprised at the German claims, he smiled and said in a conciliatory tone: 'Well, when you're surprised, you're just surprised.' Efforts to reach a political agreement were equally fruitless; and Franco ostentatiously announced his neutrality during the Munich crisis – according to one report, he even promised the French to intern the Condor Legion if war broke out.

After the Munich crisis agreement was easier. It was now obvious that France would never be provoked into action; the Germans, on their side, realized that a Spain independent of France, even if not hostile to her, was much to their advantage. Besides, Franco needed German capital equipment for internal reconstruction; and he paid the price in favoured treatment for the German mining interests. It also suited Franco's book to be taken seriously as a Fascist leader. In January 1939, he signed an agreement for cultural co-operation with Germany; this had no serious import and was never ratified, owing to the objections of the Vatican. In March, after a characteristic delay, he adhered to the Anti-Comintern Pact and renewed, in more formal shape, the friendship agreement of March 1937. All along, Franco was quite as concerned to assert his equality and independence as to do anything to please the Germans. The volume ends with the vain endeavours of Göring to meet Franco during his cruise in Spanish waters, just after the end of the civil war; Franco had no intention of showing gratitude or subservience.

In short, there was no Fascist solidarity nor even any deliberate German plan. The Spanish affair came to the Germans by accident. Franco's victory gave the anti-democratic cause a certain prestige everywhere; it did not bring the Germans any solid advantage – and the Italians seem to have done no better.

German intervention was not a success even as a venture in 'economic imperialism'. As soon as Franco had won he cut down the German concessions and began to seek capital aid from the City of London. Those who argue that Franco tricked Hitler are quite right; but this would not make him a reliable member of Western union. If he could trick Hitler, he could certainly trick us.

32

M. FLANDIN AND
FRENCH POLICY

M. FLANDIN, one-time Prime Minister, is the latest French politician to essay a defence of his pre-war policy; in this case defence is literal, for the book[1] was written while M. Flandin was in prison in Algiers after the Allied landing. The defence is disguised as a history of French foreign policy between the wars; this records the errors of others, often with justification. However, one hardly need trouble about M. Flandin as a historian; the useful part of the book is the personal reminiscences. These concern Stresa, when he was Prime Minister, and the reoccupation of the Rhineland, when he was Foreign Minister. M. Flandin became Prime Minister in November 1934. His aim, he explains, was to restore good relations with England and Italy, and, at the same time, to develop the entente with Russia which Barthou had begun; here he claims to have imposed the Franco-Soviet Pact on Laval, his Foreign Minister. His purpose in keeping Laval as Foreign Minister, he adds, was 'to shelter under Laval's policy of Franco-German reconciliation, which secured me against attacks from the Germanophil Anglo-Saxon super-pacifists'. Thus it was really British public opinion which kept Laval in office! M. Flandin claims, too, that he secured a military convention with Italy, but that this was resisted by Laval, in order not to offend German feelings.

On Abyssinia, Flandin claims to have warned Mussolini (through Ciano) not to act without British approval; Ciano answered that there would be no difficulties on the British side. This view was based on the silence of MacDonald and Sir John Simon at the Stresa meeting, when Mussolini had hinted at African questions without provoking a response. Flandin was out of office during the height of the Abyssinian crisis. In April 1936, as Foreign Minister, he proposed to Mr Eden a compromise which would have preserved some part of Abyssinia for the Emperor.

1. *Politique Française, 1919–40.* By Pierre-Etienne Flandin.

Mr Eden is alleged to have replied that rapid Italian success was not likely: 'Not only will they not be in Addis Ababa in a few weeks, but the rainy season will soon begin, which will give the Negus time and possibility to reinforce his army, and, when we meet here in September for the Assembly, believe me, Mussolini's claims will be much lower.' The Italian armies entered Addis Ababa early in May.

The reoccupation of the Rhineland was the turning-point of French policy, as it is of this book. In January 1936 Flandin asked the British Government what it would do in case of a German violation of the neutralization of the Rhineland. Baldwin answered: What has the French Government decided to do? It had decided nothing; and Flandin returned to Paris to attempt to extract a decision from his Government. All he got was a declaration of French readiness 'to place at the disposal of the League of Nations her military, naval and air forces, to oppose by force a violation of the Treaties'. Nothing was, in fact, decided, when the Germans acted on 7 March. In the French Cabinet the Minister of War declared that, in order to intervene in the Rhineland, general mobilization was necessary.

With the elections six weeks off, this was judged impossible; and only four Ministers – Sarraut, the Prime Minister, Mandel, Paul-Boncour, and Flandin – favoured immediate action. Instead, France waited for the meeting of the Locarno Powers; these merely referred the question to the Council of the League and – again according to Flandin – Mr Eden argued that the German entry into the Rhineland was 'simply a symbolic act'. Finally came the meeting of the Council in London, when France was opposed by every member except Mr Litvinov, 'who supported me throughout by speech and vote.' M. Flandin has a special word of bitterness for Beck, who, he alleges, certainly offered to fight side by side with France against Germany, but refused to confirm the breach of Locarno on the ground that it did not concern Poland. Since Flandin was to argue three years later that Poland did not concern France, he had somehow to argue away the indisputable offer of help from Poland in 1936.

Flandin finally abandoned all hope of action after an interview with Baldwin. Flandin explained that France did not want to drag Great Britain into war.

She will bear alone all the costs and risks of the operation, which will be a simple police affair. All that we ask is that you should let us act. But he replied repeatedly: 'Great Britain cannot run the risk of war.' And as I disputed this risk he replied: 'You may be right; but, even if there is only one chance in a hundred of war coming from your police operation, I have not the right to involve England; because' – and his hesitation showed what it cost him to admit this – 'England is not in a condition to make war.'

Action on the Rhine after this, Flandin argues, would have involved a breach with Great Britain; instead he emerged from the crisis with a precise Anglo-French Alliance. This tactic was, of course, repeated in the guarantee given to Czechoslovakia after Munich; in both cases the Powers pledged themselves to action only after action had become impossible.

Flandin left office in 1936 and did not return to it. His comments on later events are therefore those of an outsider. He is at pains to insist that the Anschluss was popular in Austria; that France was not pledged to support Czechoslovakia; and that, in any case, there was never a crisis in 1938, since Czechoslovakia did not appeal to the League of Nations. Similarly he argues that France was not committed to Poland in 1939 and that she should have waited for war until her military position had improved. Flandin adds some interesting details on the French declaration of war. On 27 August 1939, he went to Daladier to urge him not to go to war. Daladier argued that Poland was France's last ally in the East; without Poland there could be no second front. Gamelin, too, was optimistic of Polish chances: 'The soldiers are excellent and the Command up to its job. The Poles will hold and will give us plenty of time to go to their help . . . they will hold at least six months and we shall go to help them through Rumania.' Finally, Flandin claims that on 2 September the Chamber was persuaded into voting credits without debate by the argument that discussion would interfere with the success of Italian mediation; Daladier was allowed to make a resolute speech, with unanimous support, for the sake of a second Munich. British and Polish obstinacy defeated this manoeuvre; and France was tricked into war.

It would be a mistake to take M. Flandin at his own valuation as a statesman, or even as a witness. For instance, his account of the events of 1936 does not square with that given by General Gamelin, who, naturally, is concerned to stress the hesitations of the civilians. Still, Flandin's book confirms what we know from other sources: there was no one in France with the character or courage to give a resolute lead, and the disaster of 1940 condemned an entire generation of politicians and soldiers. Of this generation M. Flandin was one.

33

THE TRADITIONS OF
BRITISH FOREIGN POLICY

THE great thing about foreign policy is that it is a matter of talk, of general principles. In most public affairs, there comes a point when you proceed from talk to action. When you have talked about education, you go on to build schools – though not to paying school-teachers enough : and when you talk about Socialism, you end up by nationalizing steel. But foreign policy is essentially a matter of saying what you are going to do. When you do it, it becomes something else. If you go to war, it becomes a matter for the War Office and the Admiralty; if you co-operate economically, the Treasury or the Board of Trade see to it. The only *action* that a Foreign Secretary ever takes is to sign treaties; and treaties (though people often forget this) are not action – they are only promises to act like this or that in a given set of circumstances. Foreign policy is displayed in discussion – either in Parliament or with foreigners – and therefore it is a good topic for an anthology in a series on the British political tradition. It is much easier to show in this way than, say housing policy, which would have to be shown in a collection of plans and photographs – very boring for those of us who would still rather read books than look at pictures, whether still or moving.

James Joll has put together a collection of extracts – speeches, pamphlets, newspaper-articles – to illustrate the theme Britain and Europe, from Pitt to Churchill.[1] It starts with Pitt explaining in 1793 why England was going to war with revolutionary France; it ends with Winston Churchill in 1940 looking forward to an ever closer cooperation with the United States. In between are some of the best-known episodes in British foreign policy, and some not so well-known; Castlereagh refusing to join the continental Powers in a reactionary policing of Europe; Canning keeping out of intervention in Spain; Palmerston defending his intervention in Greece; and Lord John Russell blessing the

1. *Britain and Europe: Pitt to Churchill, 1793–1940*. Edited by James Joll.

revolutionary unification of Italy. You can guess what it ends up with just before Churchill: Munich and the argument over appeasement, which still supplies superficial parallels and superficial terms of abuse for the present day.

Throughout the nineteenth century – and indeed ever since the wars with Spain in the sixteenth century – British foreign policy rested on the assumption that it had a choice, even if only a choice of evils. You could co-operate with the Holy Alliance to maintain the existing settlement of Europe or you could work with France to revise it; you could help Turkey to resist Russia or you could work with Russia to impose reforms on Turkey, or even to partition her; you could reconcile Germany, even Hitler, by appeasement, or you could build up a system of collective security to resist Hitler. These were not always good choices; but they were respectable choices, honestly advocated by intelligent and well-informed men. There was a choice, because we had, or thought we had, freedom to choose. I do not say it did not matter which policy was chosen; all I say is that it was a balance of advantages. There's a remarkable passage in Sir Edward Grey's speech at the time of the outbreak of war with Germany in 1914. That might seem a matter of life and death. But Grey says, 'if we are engaged in war, we shall suffer but little more than we shall suffer even if we stand aside'. And he goes on to say that, in any case, we shall only suffer by the loss of our trade with the continent.

We have been so used to this freedom of choice over a long period that we perhaps fail to see how unusual it is. Most countries have their foreign policy dictated to them by their situation and by the behaviour of their neighbours. Very often they have only the choice between resisting or being overrun without a fight. For instance, this country chose deliberately to go to war with Germany in September 1939: we declared war and we could have kept out of it if we had wanted to – no doubt only for the time being. Russia had no such choice in June 1941: war was imposed upon her by Hitler and would have been imposed whatever policy Stalin had tried to follow. It is worth while trying to understand why we had this freedom of choice in the past: it casts a good deal of light on our policy, and still more American policy, in the present. Primarily it came from our being a bit further off: the straits which divide us from Europe gave us that extra time for deliberation. But it is a mistake to think that British security rested only on sea-power or ever has. The fiercest and most prolonged debate over British foreign policy has always gone on between those, usually a minority, who regard sea-power as enough in itself; and those, usually in control of policy, who have insisted that sea-power was only the beginning, the foundation of British security. Curiously enough, it has usually been the Left in British history, who have been isolationists, wanting to rely solely on the strength of the British Navy – from Charles James Fox opposing the war against Napoleon to John Bright opposing any active foreign policy at all, and finally to the radicals before 1914 who opposed the ententes with France and Russia. In fact, if you pushed the question a little nearer our times, you would find the opponents of collective security and advocates of a straight deal with Germany at the time of Munich were mostly radicals gone sour from Neville Chamberlain downwards. Nevertheless isolationism, based on sea-power, has been by and large the voice of a minority in British history.

The classical basis of British security – as established at the Glorious Revolution and practised throughout the eighteenth and early nineteenth centuries – was the Balance of Power. In those days English people prized control of the seas simply because it enabled them to play their part in maintaining this Balance. Observe the phrase 'maintaining the Balance of Power'. The old school of English statesmen, from Somers and Montague in William III's reign to Palmerston in Queen Victoria's, did not think that there was an automatic Balance of Power on the continent of Europe, by which the Great Powers cancelled each other out and so left us alone. They thought that the Balance had to be constantly adjusted by changes in British policy; in fact they recognized that it demanded a more active foreign policy, even involved Great Britain more in wars, than if they had done without it. Mr Joll remarks, quite rightly, that the Balance of Power in Europe has broken down. The old-fashioned British statesmen would have answered, 'then put it back again; make it the object of British policy to restore the Balance'. It is worth while considering why this answer does not appeal to us; the answer will tell us a lot about the change in British political thinking.

The first part of the answer is that in the second half of the nineteenth century English people got the Balance of Power theory wrong. They came to think that it worked automatically, like the law of supply and demand or any other of the famous economic 'laws' that the Victorians imagined they had discovered. In international affairs, as in economic affairs, you only had to look after your own interests and everything would be perfect; when this did not happen and the Balance broke down, at the time of the first German war, people thought that the policy of the Balance of Power was no good. People also came to think that it was wicked, cynical. This is a very old radical attitude. But not all radicals were satisfied with isolationism. They wanted to substitute something for the Balance of Power; and they thought – the idea was invented by Gladstone – that they had discovered this substitute in the 'Concert of Europe'. The League of Nations and the United Nations are later versions of the same outlook. Not rivalry, but harmony; not conflict of interests, but co-operation in improvement were to be the determining motives in international affairs. Most of all, disputes between nations were to be settled by judging rights and wrongs, not by weighing the strength of the opposing sides. This theory sounds morally superior to the Balance of Power; and so it is, so long as the same international morality is accepted by all the Great Powers. Gladstone would never have preached the Concert of Europe unless he held – rightly or wrongly – that Russia was 'a great Christian power' – that is, had the same moral outlook as himself. It is a very different matter when you set up institutions based on international harmony, not because this harmony exists, but because you hope that these institutions will create it. This was done both with the League of Nations and with the United Nations. It is as though a man and woman who did not care for each other got married in the hope that they would then fall in love. This sometimes happens between individuals, not, I think, in the world of international relations.

To go back to the point of Great Britain's having freedom of choice; consider the consequence. That consequence is simple: it is a sensation of being morally superior. If you do things because you have to, as most continental nations have done, you cannot waste time thinking about right and wrong: you act. When you have time to weigh advantages, you also weigh moral claims. Ever since Great Britain had an independent foreign policy, this has always had a moral element. First it was the defence of the Protestant religion: then it was the defence of the kings and princes of Europe against the encroachments of the French revolution; and in the nineteenth century it became the encouraging of national liberty, and not merely of the independence of states. It would have been very difficult for English people to conduct either the first or the second war against Germany – or for that matter the present cold war against Russia – unless they had felt, and now feel, morally superior to their opponents. But in the old days British statesmen knew how to keep their moral sentiments within practical bounds. Canning defended Spanish independence against Napoleon; he did not think it worth while defending Spanish liberalism against the intervention of conservative France. Palmerston welcomed the liberation of Italy and helped to promote it; he would do nothing for Poland or for Hungary – the one was beyond his reach, the liberation of the other he supposed would have been against British interests. I do not commend this attitude; I record it. C. P. Scott, a great British liberal, once said, 'Truth like everything else should be economized'. This sensible attitude looks very different when seen through foreign eyes. And those who believe in the moral superiority of British, or now of Anglo-American, foreign policy, should ask themselves why this country has always been known abroad as perfidious Albion. Is it merely the jealousy of rival and less successful Powers? I doubt it. It is rather the price you have to pay for having freedom of choice. Compared to continental countries, England has been a bad ally. She has always assumed, rightly in the past, that her allies needed her more than she needed them – that is what the phrase 'natural allies' really means. This was expressed in Salisbury's proud sentence, 'England does not solicit alliances; she grants them'. And Palmerston meant much the same when he said that alliances were impossible between equals: one Power has to be dependent on the other and to need protection.

It may be that these considerations are now all out-of-date

and that there is very little to be learnt from the study of past foreign policy. I would not easily dismiss that view. Indeed I have long thought that we learn too much from history rather than the reverse. For instance the appeasement of Germany would not have been tried so obstinately in the nineteen-thirties, if it had not been for the recollection or myth or legend that the appeasement of France had worked in the eighteen-thirties. And similarly a conciliatory policy towards Russia would not be rejected so firmly now if it were not for the recollection of the appeasement towards Germany that failed a decade ago. Both historical analogies were profoundly misleading and did nothing but harm. All the same you cannot escape so simply from the factors that have shaped British foreign policy in the past. At the present time we seem committed to the doctrine that we have no longer a freedom of choice and that policy is determined for us by the actions of others – by the actions of either the Russians or the Americans – at any rate not by our initiative. If this were true then indeed every tradition in British policy would have to go overboard. But is it really true? Or do we perversely want it to be true in order to escape our responsibilities? Have the Straits of Dover ceased to exist as a military factor? Has sea-power ceased to count in the world? Even the Balance of Power is not so hopelessly destroyed, if anyone had the courage to juggle the weights round. And even the Concert of Great Powers, or harmony of interests, might occasionally sound a note in unison, if British diplomatists were more concerned to act as piano-tuners. Certainly the theory of British policy nowadays is that we have lost freedom of choice. The practice of British policy – from our attitude towards the Council of Europe to our attempt to follow a more reasonable line towards China – asserts that we are still an independent Power. Here again I do not commend; I record. Almost the last words in James Joll's book are from the speech by Churchill in which he said that the organizations of the British Empire and the United States will have to be somewhat mixed up ... for mutual and general advantage. 'Let it roll on full flood, inexorable, irresistible, benignant.' I wonder whether history will show that Churchill was right.

34

FULL SPEED TO MUNICH

THE unique feature of the Munich crisis is that everyone expected it. Unlike most crises, it was announced months in advance: it would begin on 12 September with the meeting of the Nazi party in Nuremberg. The British Government had been caught out by the crisis over Austria in March; they were determined not to be caught out again. They wanted to get ahead of Hitler and of events. In March they had acquiesced in a German act of violence: this had shaken the peace of Europe. But if they could induce the Czechs to give way voluntarily and could prevent the French from supporting the Czechs, then there would be no humiliation. Hitler would get his way as an act of justice and appeasement, not by conquest; and the peace of Europe would be strengthened. Better to be seduced than raped; better still to appear as the seducer. British public opinion might suppose that the problem was how to resist Hitler; official policy was concerned to offer him concessions before he made demands. Germany was a secondary problem so far as policy went. The overriding problem was to get the Czechs launched on the path of surrender and then to keep a tight rein on the French.

The object of the Runciman mission was to prove that the Czechs were eager to yield. 'It will be less difficult for the Czechoslovak Government to collaborate if it can be represented that initiative in proposal had been theirs – and that his Majesty's Government had acceded to it.'[1] Runciman doubtless acted in good faith, and genuinely believed that the Sudeten Germans desired only a remedy for grievance. Mr Ashton-Gwatkin, his assistant, wrote of Henlein, the Sudeten leader (now known to have been acting throughout under Hitler's orders), 'he is courteous, friendly and (I believe) honest'. Again, 'he is simple and honest .... He is anxious to dissociate his movement from identification with the Reich Nazis and he repudiates absolutely the

1. *Documents on British Foreign Policy, 1919–39*. Third Series, volume ii. Edited by E. L. Woodward, 1938.

spirit of persecution.' British pressure worked. On 5 September the Czechs accepted the full Sudeten programme; instead of averting the crisis, this precipitated it. Lord Runciman had, however, a more pressing care than to reconcile Czechs and Germans; he had to avoid committing Great Britain, however reasonable the Czechs and however violent Hitler might be. He rejected the suggestion made by Lord Halifax that he should appeal directly to Hitler: 'Price of failure in Berlin would be to make solution here impossible and in the event of hostilities morally to commit Great Britain on the side of Czechoslovakia.'

All the same, Berlin was more important than Prague; and for the Foreign Office, Berlin meant Nevile Henderson. Lord Halifax wrote to Henderson on 5 August, 'Write as often as you can or like. It is very helpful.' Two of Henderson's judgements were decisive – Hitler did not want war, and the German claims were morally justified. He wrote on 26 July:

War would doubtless serve the purposes of all the Jews, Communists, and doctrinaires in the world for whom Nazism is anathema, but it would be a terrible risk today for Germany herself. . . . That this is not apparent to Hitler, I cannot believe.

The Czechs are a pig-headed race and Benes not the least pig-headed among them. . . . We shall have at long last to put our foot down very firmly and say to Benes, 'You must'.

On 12 August:

I doubt if Germany would actually go to war this year with Czechoslovakia if she was certain it meant British intervention. It might be a near thing but I think that Hitler's good sense would prevail. . . . I trust that we shall not use the definite menace of British participation in a war, unless our case is morally copper-bottomed. The British Empire cannot set its face against the principle of self-determination. Personally I am sorry to say, I am convinced that we cannot permanently prevent these Sudeten Germans from coming into the Reich if they wish it, and undoubtedly the majority today do so.

On 6 September:

I do wish it might be possible to get at any rate 'The Times', Camrose, Beaverbrook Press, &c. to write up Hitler as the apostle of Peace. It will be terribly short-sighted if this is not done.

Lord Halifax was necessarily influenced by Henderson and accepted his arguments to a certain extent. He acted on the theory that Hitler was a moderate man surrounded by extremists such as Ribbentrop; hence the letter of 11 August, in which Chamberlain and Halifax appealed directly to Hitler 'not to do anything which might sterilise Lord Runciman's mission and prematurely and unnecessarily create a fresh crisis in Europe'. But even if Hitler was an extremist there was little to be done. 'I have always felt that to fight a war for one, two, or three years to protect or recreate something that you knew you could not directly protect, and probably could never recreate, did not make sense.' In conversation with the French Ambassador:

The French Government felt that if this contemplated aggression were allowed to pass unresisted, their turn would come next. I said that this really was an argument in favour of a certain war now, against the possibility of war, perhaps in more favourable conditions, later. With that argument I had never been able to feel any sympathy.

For lack of anything better, Halifax followed traditional British practice. He would not promise support to the Czechs; he would not promise neutrality to the Germans. No attempt was made to draw in the two Great Powers who were outside Europe. On 17 August Mr Maisky expressed disappointment at the undue weakness of the Western democracies. He was fobbed off with a reference to the definition of policy made in Parliament on 24 March and 'regretted that we had not found it possible to be more precise'.

No explanations were given to the United States until 2 September; and these were provoked by a direct inquiry from Mr Kennedy. He asked should the President make another speech. 'The Prime Minister thought not, at any rate at present.' Nothing was made of Mr Kennedy's opinion 'that if France went in and we had to go in too, the United States would follow before long'.

But would France go in? On 31 August Bonnet said, 'France would honour her engagements, but if what His Majesty's Government considered a fair solution was refused by Czechs that was their look out, *tant pis pour eux*'. Daladier was more resolute. On 8 September 'Daladier declares most positively that, if German troops cross the Czechoslovak frontier the French will march to a man'.

When the crisis arrived on 13 September Bonnet 'said that peace must be preserved at any price' and 'seemed genuinely pleased at the negative nature' of Lord Halifax's reply to his query concerning British support. Daladier wavered longer; 'he said, but with evident lack of enthusiasm, that if Germans used force, French would be obliged also'.

Then at 10 p.m., Daladier appealed to Chamberlain : 'Entry of German troops into Czechoslovakia must at all costs be prevented. If not, France will be faced with her obligation.' Daladier proposed 'a meeting of the Three Powers – namely, Germany for Sudetens, France for the Czechs, and Great Britain for Lord Runciman'.

Chamberlain, however, decided to carry out a plan which he had had in mind 'as early as 30 August' – he would visit Hitler alone. When told of Chamberlain's plan 'Daladier did not look very pleased'; Bonnet 'expressed the warm thanks of himself and of his Government for the magnificent gesture of the Prime Minister'.

There is not much to add to the story of Chamberlain's first visit to Hitler on 15 September. After a good deal of ranting from Hitler, Chamberlain said, 'On principle I had nothing to say against the separation of the Sudeten Germans from the rest of Czechoslovakia, provided that the practical difficulties could be overcome'; and he agreed to return home to persuade his colleagues.

Nevile Henderson at once underlined the implications of this policy. He telegraphed on 16 September, 'French Government should definitely notify Czechoslovak Government that the latter cannot count on French support if they decide to go to war rather than accept such a solution'. On the morning of 17 September, 'if we do accept the principle of secession we must be prepared to coerce the Czechoslovak Government or leave her to her fate'. And the same evening, 'If we decline to admit self-determination we must face world war : if we recognize it, we must coerce Czechoslovakia or sit by and watch her coerced by Germany'. The British Ministers (to say nothing of the French) were less honest : they still hoped to persuade the Czechs to commit suicide for their own good.

On 18 September Daladier and Bonnet came to London to meet the British Ministers. Chamberlain gave an account of his interview with Hitler and insisted that the question was whether to accept the partition of Czechoslovakia (or, as he called it, 'the principle of self-determination'). Daladier tried to shift the ground. 'He feared that Germany's real aim was the disintegration of Czechoslovakia and the realization of Pan-German ideals through a march to the East.' He argued that plebiscites could be used to disrupt every State in Eastern Europe.

Lord Halifax now took a hand.

Nothing was further from their thoughts than that the French Government should fail to honour their obligations to the Czechoslovak Government. ... On the other hand we all knew – and he certainly thought their technical advisers would agree with them in this – that whatever action were taken by ourselves, by the French Government, or by the Soviet Government, at any given moment, it would be impossible to give effective protection to the Czechoslovak State. We might fight a war against German aggression, but at the peace conference which followed such a war he did not think that the statesmen concerned would redraft the present boundaries of Czechoslovakia.

Chamberlain seized on the Czech objection to a plebiscite:

The idea of territorial cession would be likely to have a much more favourable reception from the British public if it could be represented as the choice of the Czechoslovak Government themselves and it could be made clear that they had been offered the choice of a plebiscite or of territorial cession and had preferred the latter. That would dispose of any idea that we were ourselves carving up Czechoslovak territory.

Daladier had to give way, but he posed an essential condition – Great Britain must guarantee the Czechoslovakia that remained. This was not for the sake of the Czechs – the British and French Governments had already decided that they could do nothing to help the Czechs either now or hereafter. The British were being asked to underwrite Hitler's statement that this was his last territorial demand in Europe. Daladier said:

If he were certain that Herr Hitler were speaking the truth when he repeated the usual Nazi propaganda to the effect that nothing more was wanted than the Sudeten Germans and that German aims stopped there, then he would not insist upon a British guarantee. But he was convinced in his heart that Germany was aiming at something far greater. ... A British guarantee for Czechoslovakia would therefore help France in the sense that it would help to stop the German march to the East.

The British Ministers withdrew for two hours, and on their return Chamberlain said, 'If the Czechoslovak Government accepted the proposals now being put to them and provided no military coup had taken place meanwhile, his Majesty's Government were prepared to join in the suggested guarantee'. The guarantee, that is, was to operate only after Czechoslovakia had been partitioned. All the same, Daladier had built better than he knew. He had committed Great Britain to oppose Hitler's march to the East; six months later the British public insisted on taking the promise seriously in spite of the wrigglings of Chamberlain and his associates. In fact, Daladier gave Great Britain the decisive, though delayed, push on the path of resistance to Germany.

Chamberlain had asked, What would be the position if Dr Benes said 'No'? Daladier answered, 'If that situation arose, the question would have to be discussed at the Council of Ministers'. Events turned out differently. At 7.45 p.m. on 20 September the Czechs refused the Anglo-French terms and invoked their arbitration treaty with Germany. An hour later Newton, British Minister in Prague, telegraphed:

I have very good reason from an even better source [than the Minister of Foreign Affairs] to believe that ... if I can deliver a kind of ultimatum to President Benes, he and his Government will feel able to bow to 'force majeure'.

Since this even better source can only be Hodza, the Prime Minister, Newton's telegram confirms Bonnet's story that the Anglo-French ultimatum was delivered at Czech request. But telegrams received in the Foreign Office from Paris at 6.20 p.m., 7.45 p.m. and 8.30 p.m. on 20 September show Bonnet was urging the threat of 'washing their hands of Czechoslovakia' long before the message was sent from Prague. Thus even if Hodza asked France to repudiate Czechoslovakia, Bonnet had already decided to do so. At 2 a.m. on 21 September Newton and the French Minister broke the resistance of Benes: 'We told him our démarche had character of an ultimatum.'

On 22 September Chamberlain met Hitler at Godesberg to

announce that he had succeeded. Chamberlain concluded, 'The guarantee would not necessarily mean that the present Czech frontiers would be guaranteed in perpetuity. ['Present' means, of course, the new frontiers.] They could be altered by negotiation, as was being done in the present case.' Hitler rejected Chamberlain's offer, even with its invitation to further plunder. Chamberlain wanted an 'agreed settlement' for the sake of British public opinion and, perhaps, of his self-esteem; Hitler wanted a settlement by conquest to strengthen his position in Germany and perhaps for his self-esteem also. Chamberlain cared nothing for the Czechs; Hitler cared nothing for the Sudeten Germans.

After two days of argument, deadlock was reached. Meanwhile, in London, Lord Halifax had revolted. On 22 September the French urged that the advice given to the Czechs not to mobilize should be withdrawn; Halifax agreed. Sir Horace Wilson, however, telephoned from Godesberg against this message and it was held up during the evening. On 23 September Halifax, prompted by Daladier, again insisted; and Chamberlain gave way. 'In doing so, however, Prime Minister thinks it should be pointed out that such action may very well precipitate action by others.'

On the news of the failure at Godesberg only Nevile Henderson was undismayed, 'Only hope of preventing or at least localising war is for his Majesty's Government to make it absolutely clear at Prague that they must accept German plan or forfeit claim to further support from Western Powers.' Henderson at least had the courage of his convictions. On 23 September Lord Halifax sent a message to Chamberlain at Godesberg which concluded: 'It seems to your colleagues of vital importance that you should not leave without making it plain to Chancellor .... that, after great concessions made by Czechoslovak Government, for him to reject opportunity of peaceful solution in favour of one that must involve war would be an unpardonable crime against humanity.'

Halifax also sent a message to Geneva (where the League of Nations was in session) asking Litvinov 'what action Soviet Government would take in event of Czechoslovakia being thus involved in war with Germany, and at what point they would be prepared to take it'. On 24 September Litvinov answered, 'If

French came to the assistance of the Czechs, Russia would take action'. He added:

He had for long been hoping for conversations between Great Britain, France, and Russia, and he would like to suggest ... that a meeting of the three Powers mentioned, together with Rumania and any other small Power who could be regarded as reliable, should take place away from the atmosphere of Geneva, and preferably in Paris, and so show Germans that we mean business.

It was even more urgent to know French intentions. On 24 September Phipps wired from Paris, 'All that is best in France is against war, almost at any price', and he warned against 'even appearing to encourage small, but noisy and corrupt, war group here'. (In a later telegram he explained that by this he meant 'the Communists who are paid by Moscow'.) Phipps also reported the opposition to war voiced by Caillaux and Flandin. On 25 September he was instructed to make wider inquiries and replied the following day, 'People are resigned but resolute .... The "petit bourgeois" may feel disinclined to risk his life for Czechoslovakia, while most of the workmen are said to be in favour of France complying with her obligations.'

Meanwhile Daladier and Bonnet had come to London on 25 September for another meeting with British Ministers. Daladier was in fighting spirit. Hitler should be asked to return to the Anglo-French proposals of 18 September. If he refused 'each of us would have to do his duty'; and, again, 'each of us would do what was incumbent upon him'. Chamberlain answered, 'One could not go into so great a conflict with one's eyes and ears closed. It was essential to know the conditions before taking any decision. He would, therefore, like further information and would ask Sir John Simon to put certain points to M. Daladier.'

There followed an incredible scene in which the Chancellor of the Exchequer cross-examined the Prime Minister of France as though he were a hostile witness or a criminal. Daladier did his best to prove that war was possible and returned to the question of policy: 'There was one concession he would never make, and that was ... the destruction of a country and Herr Hitler's domination of the world.'

It was finally decided to ask Gamelin to come over and to meet again the following day.

However, on 26 September, instead of producing Gamelin and plans for war, Chamberlain announced that he had sent Horace Wilson to Hitler with a personal message from himself. The French Ministers acquiesced and went home. Lord Halifax 'authorised the issue of a communiqué' to the press: 'If a German attack is made upon Czechoslovakia ... France will be bound to come to her assistance, and Great Britain and Russia will certainly stand by France.'

Wilson saw Hitler on 26 September without effect. Chamberlain then instructed him, 'We do not think it possible for you to leave without delivering special message, in view of what we said to French .... But message should be given more in sorrow than in anger.' This special message was delivered by Wilson shortly after noon on 27 September:

If Germany attacked Czechoslovakia France would feel that she must fulfil her treaty obligations.... If that meant that the forces of France became actively engaged in hostilities against Germany the British Government would feel obliged to support her.

In spite of these firm words both Henderson and Wilson continued to urge that the Czechs be forced to give way. Henderson's final message on 28 September condemned resisting Hitler: 'This course involves far greater losses with regard to prestige to ourselves and results in complete destruction of Czechoslovakia, which will become, like Abyssinia, a further victim to pacifist enthusiasm. The only alternative is to compel Czechoslovakia to yield by informing her at once ... categorically that if she does not do so we shall not support her.' Henderson also telegraphed, 'Is it not essential to ensure that France should take no action without first consulting his Majesty's Government that is not calculated to have effective military result?' A telegram on these lines was sent to Paris forty minutes after receipt of Henderson's prompting.

There followed Mussolini's initiative and the meeting at Munich on 29 September. Before leaving, Chamberlain telegraphed to Prague, 'Please assure Dr Benes that I shall have the interests of Czechoslovakia fully in mind'. Bonnet, when seeing Daladier off, 'begged me to urge you [Halifax] how absolutely vital he felt it was that an arrangement should be reached over Sudeten question at Munich at almost any price. M. Bonnet feels that after that, and in the near future, we must make up our minds to a peaceful modification of many existing frontiers in Europe, as the Treaty of Versailles has collapsed.'

Bonnet grew feebler when Daladier was away; Halifax tougher in the absence of Chamberlain. On 29 September (too late to influence the conference) he telegraphed to Chamberlain: 'Information has reached me from moderate sources in Germany that the firm attitude taken by his Majesty's Government during the last few days ... has had considerable effect on German public opinion.' Halifax also saw Maisky and explained to him that the exclusion of Russia at Munich 'in no way signified any weakening of a desire on our part, any more, no doubt, than on that of the French Government, to preserve our understandings and relations with the Soviet Government'. Halifax also implied that Russia was to become a guarantor of the new Czechoslovakia. Maisky's 'general attitude seemed to me, as, indeed, it was likely to be, one of some suspicion'.

Chamberlain's mind was on different things. After partitioning Czechoslovakia he had a private discussion with Hitler on 30 September. This culminated in the signature of the Anglo-German declaration of friendship to cries of 'Ja! Ja!' from Hitler. The opening of the discussion was still more remarkable. Chamberlain said:

he was obliged to consider the possibility that the Czech Government might be mad enough to refuse the terms and attempt resistance. In such an eventuality he wanted to ask Herr Hitler to make sure that nothing should be done which would diminish the high opinion of him which would be held throughout the world in consequence of yesterday's proceedings. In particular, he trusted that there would be no bombardment of Prague or killing of women and children by attacks from the air.

Hitler replied, 'he hated the thought of little babies being killed by gas bombs'.

35

THE DIPLOMACY OF M. BONNET

M. BONNET, French Foreign Minister in 1938 and 1939, feels himself, perhaps with some reason, the scapegoat for Munich; he was the 'fall guy'. Daladier was vindicated in the French parliament; Neville Chamberlain was eulogized by Churchill after his death; Lord Halifax served the Coalition and Labour governments as ambassador at Washington. Only M. Bonnet is reduced to defending himself. His first volume runs from his appointment as Foreign Minister until the end of the Munich crisis; the second from Munich to the outbreak of war.[1] This book will certainly serve to acquit Bonnet of one charge. Superficial, fatuous, self-satisfied, the author of these memoirs could never have been a cynical, far-sighted plotter, engineering the destruction of Czechoslovakia or organizing a European coalition against the Soviet Union.

The book seems almost to have been written by two different hands. One Bonnet, rambling and diffuse, gives a rehash of the old Munichite stock-in-trade or, as he calls it, 'the philosophy of the crisis'. France was too weak to fight; alternatively she would have fought if she had not been prevented by the unwillingness of her allies, including the Czechs. Munich was a device for buying time; alternatively, it was a just revision of the settlement of 1919, a victory for the principle of self-determination. France was unable to help Czechoslovakia; alternatively, by obtaining a British guarantee for post-Munich Czechoslovakia, France made Czechoslovakia stronger than before. Most of all, war would destroy 'all that gave a value to life'. No more Radical-Socialist party! No more Third Republic! In truth, the French and British ministers were resolved from the beginning to do nothing. Their world was coming to an end, and they had only one aim: to postpone the earthquake for a year, for a month, for a day.

1. Volume I: *Défense de la Paix. De Washington au Quai d'Orsay.* Volume II: *Fin d'une Europe. De Munich à la Guerre.* By Georges Bonnet.

The other Bonnet is a skilled diplomatist or, at any rate, had skilled diplomatists at his service. France, it appears, was attempting to build a grand alliance against Germany; every ally failed her, only France remained true to her obligations. Bonnet's real aim was different. He was convinced that the French system in Europe would collapse at the first touch and was concerned to put the blame on others, to possess written proofs against the allies of France without leaving on paper proofs against himself. With America his task was easy. The United States would do nothing; and when, in September, Bullitt, the American Ambassador, expressed a few harmless phrases about Franco-American friendship, he was at once repudiated by Roosevelt. England comes next. The British Government clung obstinately to the basic contradiction of its Locarno policy: it would defend the independence of France, but it would not defend the international order in eastern Europe on which this independence rested. In April 1938 the British Government agreed to 'bluff' Hitler: it would give the Czechs diplomatic support in order to prod them into concessions, but it would not go to war. Before 1914 the British Government had also tried to draw a dividing line between the security of France and the state of things in eastern Europe; but then there had been a French Government proud enough to follow an independent line which finally brought England and Russia into the war as allies. In 1938 the French Government dared not act independently; the British refusal left it helpless and at a loss.

British policy, unchanged since 1925, was only one element in the French collapse. The system of alliances in eastern Europe collapsed also. The deepest cause of this collapse was Poland, a country without real strength, which aspired to play the part of a Great Power. The Polish Government would do nothing to help Czechoslovakia, still less would they permit the passage of a Russian army across Polish territory. Instead, they intended to join Hitler in dismembering Czechoslovakia. Bonnet says of his allies: 'We heard only one bellicose voice: that of Poland. But she was thinking of making war on Czechoslovakia!' But who had inflated Poland to give her the appearance of a Great Power? Who had encouraged her to act as a rampart of anti-Bolshevism? A succession of French governments. Bonnet failed to see that the position of Poland as a so-called Great Power rested on the alliance with France and that a firm French policy must have immediately brought the Poles to reason. Poland could flirt with Germany so long as she had France as an ally; she could never risk being left alone with Germany.

Once Polish hostility has been satisfactorily proved, Bonnet has got past his most awkward moment: the refusal of the Russian efforts at co-operation. The Russians would support Czechoslovakia provided that France did the same; but they would cross Poland or Rumania only with the consent of the government concerned and, since France was the ally of both, it was for France to obtain their consent. This was the reply given by Litvinov on 12 May and repeated by him on 11 September. Poland put a veto on Russian action; therefore there was nothing more to be done. Besides, Poland was so strong that she could even forbid the passage of Russian troops across Rumania; and, in any case, the Rumanians feared for Bessarabia – they were glad enough to shelter behind the Polish veto. The Rumanians hinted that their anti-aircraft batteries were too weak to interfere with the flight of Russian planes. Bonnet does not appear to have conveyed this information to the Russians. But, then, it is the essence of his case that the Russians (unlike the French) did not mean their declarations of support for Czechoslovakia to be taken seriously. Thus, with Poland hostile and Russia barred from action, France was helpless.

The final blow was delivered by the Czechs themselves, who shrank from resistance. On 21 September, Hodza, the Czech Prime Minister, implored Bonnet to repudiate the Franco-Czech alliance, so that the Czech ministers would be obliged to give way; and Bonnet gave him this 'cover'. Bonnet is not content with this gesture of self-sacrifice; he seeks to prove his own success and makes much of the British guarantee which was given to Czechoslovakia after Munich. Great Britain and France claimed that because of their military weakness and their geographic position they could do nothing to help Czechoslovakia, when she was fully mobilized and entrenched behind her natural frontiers. They deprived her of these frontiers and of her defensive equipment; they broke her national spirit and obliged her to disarm. And at the same moment they declared themselves capable of protecting her against future danger. It was the worst transaction of a shameless era.

Munich was the collapse of a European system, of a system which tried to give Europe security without asking any military or diplomatic effort from the Great Powers. This system rested on a series of pretences. It assumed that France was the strongest Power in Europe and that Germany had been converted to a peaceful policy; that Russia was not a Great Power and could be permanently excluded from Europe; above all, that the States of eastern Europe could maintain their economic and political independence without assistance. This system was bound to collapse. The problem of the overwhelming power of Germany could not be solved within the limits of the European continent. It could be solved only if Germany, who overshadowed Europe, could be eclipsed in her turn by the two great world Powers, who had tried to turn their backs on Europe. It was hopeless for France to try to maintain this European system alone, as she had done in the years after Versailles. And it was hardly less hopeless to try to maintain it solely with British assistance. A wise French policy would have aimed to win the support of Russia and the United States. With America there was nothing to be done. Alliance with Soviet Russia was the more essential. This was the key to the survival of France as a great, or even as an independent, Power. Instead, the policy of Munich destroyed Russian belief (never very strong) in French determination and so opened the way to the Nazi-Soviet pact. A system of politics was in collapse. Twenty years of taking phrases for reality produced their inevitable result, and the statesmen of every country behaved meanly, feebly. The worst fault was to be complacent, to be proud of their work; this fault, too, Bonnet shared with others.

In the second volume the reader will soon detect the familiar sleight of hand. For instance, in reference to Ribbentrop's visit to Paris in December 1938, there occur the innocent sentences: 'He then attended a lunch at which I was not present. Towards the end of the afternoon he was taken to visit the Louvre.' Who would guess from this that Bonnet and Ribbentrop passed the afternoon together at the Louvre alone? On the other hand, those who study in detail the written record will be confirmed in the view that M.

Bonnet was rather more adroit, and not markedly less scrupulous, than most other Foreign Ministers of the Third Republic.

Bonnet has little to tell concerning the Franco-German declaration of 6 December 1938, by which he was accused later of handing over eastern Europe to Germany. His documents show that he reminded Ribbentrop of the Franco-Polish alliance and of the Franco-Soviet pact, and that Ribbentrop accepted these reservations. No doubt this amounted to little at a time when Poland, after seizing Teschen, seemed on better terms with Germany than with France. The Franco-German declaration assumed a German preponderance in eastern Europe and such 'moderate' gains as the recovery of Danzig; but it also assumed that Germany would proceed in a plausible way and would save the faces of French and especially British statesmen. Instead, Hitler seized Prague and made it impossible for Chamberlain and Lord Halifax to continue the line of appeasement, even if they had wished to do so. They needed a symbol of their new resolve; this symbol was the guarantee of Poland.

The guarantee to Poland was a disaster to French policy. Since England had no army, the guarantee was in effect a promise that France would not fail the Poles as she had failed the Czechs. France could not break with England, yet was incapable of helping the Poles. The only solution was to bring in the Soviet Union. Poland had been the decisive obstacle to this at the time of Munich; and the Polish refusal was reaffirmed by Beck on 26 March 1939. M. Bonnet devised a new tactic: he would secure Soviet aid and then threaten to abandon Poland to her fate unless she accepted it – a move which would also perhaps clear France in British eyes. This tactic was explained to the Soviet Ambassador on 10 April. France and the Soviet Union, M. Bonnet said, should settle Soviet aid to Rumania and Poland: 'We should then have to decide the attitude to take in case either Rumania or Poland refused this aid.' But the Soviet rulers were not satisfied with the French alliance which Bonnet offered; the British guarantee to Poland would enable Poland to resist Franco-Soviet pressure and therefore they insisted that Great Britain must be included in the alliance negotiations. Hence the prolonged negotiations from April until July. The Russians demanded an alliance of mutual guarantee and the virtual recognition of the Soviet Union as the preponderant Power in eastern Europe; the British desired a bargain by which the Soviet Union would aid her neighbours only if called upon to do so. The British Government tried to give the impression that England and France were conducting a joint negotiation with the Soviet Union; in reality, as M. Bonnet shows, France was willing from the first to accept the Soviet terms and used every means (including the threat of French impotence) to drag Britain along with her.

French diplomacy succeeded. On 24 July a political agreement was reached which accepted all the Soviet demands – mutual assistance, inclusion of the Baltic countries, freedom to act without a request for assistance from the country attacked, and a wide definition of indirect aggression as 'an act accepted by the State in question under threat of force by another Power and involving the abandonment of its independence or of its neutrality.' All these demands had been backed by the French with extreme urgency. It was a striking achievement on paper. In practice, England and Russia were probably more suspicious of each other than before, and the agreement was to come into force only when a military convention had been made. Poland's refusal remained the core of the matter.

With Russia the problem had been to reach an agreement; with Poland it was to avoid one. Immediately after the British guarantee to Poland, the Poles asked Bonnet to add to the Franco-Polish alliance a similar guarantee. He agreed, since he was already committed by the British action. The Poles attempted to smuggle in a new clause extending the guarantee to Danzig and alleged that a similar clause was being settled in London. Inquiry in London proved (according to Bonnet's evidence) that this was untrue: the British, like the French, were hanging back until they had settled with the Russians. M. Corbin, the French Ambassador in London, reported on 5 June that the Foreign Office 'thought that it could be inconvenient to establish definitively the text of the Anglo-Polish agreement before knowing certainly what form the tripartite treaty with the U.S.S.R. will take'. Bonnet hints also that he, at any rate, was still keeping Danzig up his sleeve as a bargaining counter with Germany. The discussions with Poland had, however, an outcome highly inconvenient to Bonnet's policy. To divert the Poles from revising the political terms, Bonnet (and Daladier) proposed staff conversations, and on 19 May Gamelin concluded a military convention embracing Danzig. Gamelin, according to Bonnet, was taken in by the Polish story that a political agreement had already been signed – a version much removed from Gamelin's story, which puts the blame on Bonnet. At all events, the Poles, instead of being told that France could do nothing for them except strive for Russian aid, secured a French promise to launch a major offensive on the fifteenth day of mobilization. Thus, when the crisis arrived in August 1939, France had a military convention with Poland which vitiated her diplomacy and still lacked the military convention with the Soviet Union without which she could do nothing.

Bonnet claims always to have expected the crisis to arrive in August 1939. For him it remained a crisis of diplomacy; he aimed to stop Hitler by the show of a 'peace front' in eastern Europe, and for this he had to reconcile two conflicting wills – the Soviet demand for military collaboration with Poland before war started and the Polish determination to accept Soviet aid only after the war had begun. On 15 July, Noël, French Ambassador in Warsaw, reported: 'M. Beck gave me to understand that the day war broke out Poland, the preservation of which the U.S.S.R. desires in its own interest, would be better placed than anyone else to obtain from Moscow collaboration in a common action.' Thus French diplomacy had to sail as near the wind as possible – to postpone the question of Soviet-Polish co-operation to a moment which should still seem like peace to the Russians but like war to the Poles.

·The question was exploded by Voroshilov on 14 August. Bonnet launched his diplomatic offensive against the Poles on 16 August. He placed on Poland 'the responsibility for a failure of the military conversations with Moscow and for all the consequences which would follow'. And again, on 19 August, when the Poles repeated their refusal: 'The Polish Government must measure the full extent of its responsibilities if its attitude should lead to the breaking off of negotiations with the U.S.S.R.' The tone of this is not far removed from the message of 21 September 1938, in which M. Bonnet had declared French inability to help the Czechs. A concession was finally extracted from Beck. On

23 August he told Noël that the French could use the following language to the Russians: 'We have acquired the certainty that in the event of common action against a German aggression collaboration between Poland and the U.S.S.R., in technical conditions to be determined, is not excluded (or: is possible).' No wonder Molotov on 25 August 'put all the responsibility on the Government of Warsaw. A great country like the U.S.S.R. could not, he said, go so far as to beg Poland to accept a Russian assistance which she did not wish at any price.' In any case the Polish reply was fraudulent: it was given only after the news of Ribbentrop's visit to Moscow was already known and when therefore all chance of Soviet collaboration had been lost. But then the Soviet demand was fraudulent also, for the decision to receive Ribbentrop on 23 August was communicated to the Germans on 21 August, before Voroshilov heard from the French of their failure to extract any concessions from the Poles. In fact, as is usual in diplomacy, all sides behaved in a discreditable fashion and put themselves almost equally in the wrong.

The great manoeuvre had failed. Thereafter Bonnet's aim was to find an escape from the approaching war. After all, he suggests, the Russians had insisted that they could not fight Germany without a common frontier; the German conquest of Poland would provide one, and the Franco-Soviet pact could then be revived. On 23 August Bonnet asked Daladier to call the Committee of National Defence (actually the meeting was a less formal 'Council of War') and there hinted, not obscurely, at this line: 'Must we apply blindly our alliance with Poland? Would it be better, on the contrary, to push Warsaw into a compromise? We could thus gain time to perfect our material, to increase our military power, to improve our diplomatic situation in a manner to resist Germany more effectively in case she should turn against France later.' Gamelin refused to play Bonnet's game: he would not confess France's military weakness and insisted on the value of the Polish alliance. Thus Bonnet successfully loaded on to Gamelin the decision in favour of war – as Gamelin implicitly admits by his later unconvincing attempts to question the validity of the record of the council meeting. In fact Bonnet could blame the generals for the failure of his diplomacy, as later the generals blamed the politicians for their military defeat.

Bonnet's last card was the attempted mediation of Mussolini. This, too, had to be delayed to the last minute; for the Poles,
it was supposed, could be coerced into surrendering Danzig only
at the very moment of the explosion of war. Bonnet continued to
advocate accepting Mussolini's offer even after the German attack on Poland on 1 September. Hence his anxiety to postpone the
ultimatum to Germany until noon on Sunday, 3 September. The
British Government insisted on the preceding midnight, hostilities
to begin at 6 a.m.; finally they compromised so far as to deliver
the ultimatum at 9 a.m. (one hour before the meeting of
Parliament), hostilities to begin at 11 a.m. At 5 a.m. on Sunday
morning Bonnet heard of Ciano's final 'Impossible!' to a further
approach through De Monzie. Committed now to war, he became, by a last absurdity, the advocate of advancing the French
time-table in order to keep up diplomatic appearances with the
British.

The French ultimatum, presented at noon on Sunday, was to
expire only at 5 a.m. the following morning: the General Staff
insisted on this delay. Complaints followed from London. At
11.30 on Sunday morning Daladier agreed to advance the opening
of hostilities to 5 p.m. that afternoon. At 11.45 a.m. Bonnet
telephoned to Coulondre, the Ambassador in Berlin, who was
already leaving for the German Foreign Office, and informed him
of the change. Coulondre had no doubt experienced Bonnet's
telephone messages before. 'With much presence of mind he
asked that such news should be confirmed to him by one or two
of my collaborators whose voice he would also recognize. I
passed the telephone successively to M. Léger and to M. Bressy,
who were by me.' Bonnet spent the last few hours of peace
drafting a Note for Warsaw which repudiated the Polish charges
of delay and complained that Beck had failed to visit him in
January: 'Whatever the capital mistakes of the Polish Government have been in the past, history will record that no breach
of honour or of the pledged word can be levelled against the
French Government.' On 4 September Bonnet signed the protocol
to the Franco-Polish alliance which he had refused in May; this
brought the military convention of 19 May automatically into
operation and Bonnet was given a last chance to score off Gamelin, who failed to carry it out. On 15 September Bonnet left the

Foreign Office. He received the following letter from Lord Halifax (retranslated from the French):

> When I received the news that you were leaving your crushing duties at the Quai d'Orsay I wished to write to you at once in order to say how much I have appreciated our collaboration and the friendly, personal relations which have sprung from it.
>
> We have together passed through the most difficult and the most depressing times that a Minister of Foreign Affairs has had to face: they have left us many bitter memories. But it is a great comfort for us to recall the loyal collaboration of our two Governments in mutual confidence and to have the conviction that it was impossible to follow any other policy.

The testimonial was somewhat flattering.

36

THE ALLIANCE THAT FAILED

THE failure to make an alliance with the Soviet Union in 1939 was the greatest setback for British diplomacy in the twentieth century. All our troubles from that day to this stem from it. What caused the failure? Were the Russians cheating all along, pushing up the British offers in order to reach an agreement with Hitler? Or were they driven into Hitler's arms by the belief, based on experience, that the British did not take the talk of alliance seriously? We shall not know the answer until some future generation sees the archives of the Kremlin; and perhaps not even then. But we are getting nearer. Hitherto we have relied on contemporary newspaper reports, to which have been added the German documents and Bonnet's somewhat selective memoirs. Now at last we have the record from the British Foreign Office;[1] only the discussions in the Cabinet are still lacking on the British side. These documents came out at a bad time. It had become established doctrine that the Nazi–Soviet pact caused the Second World War; and no one wanted to raise awkward questions that might shake this legend or disturb the moral unity of the western world. It was a symbol of 'the cold war' that the lesson of these Foreign Office documents was ignored and the documents themselves soon forgotten. The man in the street, so far as he reflected at all, continued to believe that the Russians had been offered an alliance by the West and that they had deliberately preferred to make a robbers' pact with Hitler.

Here is the story from the British papers, summarized in detachment. Like many stories, it begins at the point where it was also to end. The British Government had given guarantees at a moment's notice to Poland and Rumania. It occurred to them belatedly that there was no means by which these could be fulfilled. The Soviet Union would have to supply the aid if it came to fighting: but the British Government knew well that neither

1. *Documents on British Foreign Policy, 1919–1939. Third Series, volumes* v-vii.

Poland nor Rumania would accept Soviet assistance. Unable to find any escape from this pit of their own digging, the British Government invited the Russians to do it for them. The Soviet proposal for a Four-Power declaration had been vetoed by the Poles; hence the British tried to commit the Soviet Union to a one-sided bargain. On 14 April they proposed that if any neighbour of the Soviet Union was attacked, 'the assistance of the Soviet Government would be available, if desired, and would be afforded in such manner as would be found most convenient'. On 18 April the Soviet Government replied by demanding a full-scale alliance with England and France for mutual assistance against aggression. This would not do at all. 'His Majesty's Government might be drawn into a war not for the preservation of the independence of a minor European state but for the support of the Soviet Union against Germany. On this issue opinion in this country might be seriously divided.' This was indeed exactly what the Russians feared.

The British beat around for a fortnight. They inquired of Poland and Rumania what arrangements these two countries would allow them to make with Russia. They also tried to invoke French diplomatic ingenuity. But the French let them down. On 3 May Bonnet revealed to the Soviet ambassador 'in the heat of conversation' that France favoured a pact of mutual assistance. On 9 May the British at last tried again: in view of the British guarantees to Poland and Rumania, 'the Soviet Government would undertake that in the event of Great Britain and France being involved in hostilities in fulfilment of these obligations the assistance of the Soviet Government would be immediately available, if desired, and would be afforded in such manner and on such terms as might be agreed'. Molotov had now become Commissar for Foreign Affairs (on 3 May). On 14 May he rejected the British proposal and demanded 'reciprocity': a pact of mutual assistance, a guarantee of all eastern European countries, and 'the conclusion of a concrete agreement as to forms and extent of assistance'. Once more there were discussions with France, Poland, and Rumania, and now with the Baltic States as well. On 27 May the British Government accepted the principle of mutual assistance, though dressed up – for the sake of public opinion – with references to 'the principles of the Covenant of the League of Nations'. The three governments 'would concert together as to the methods by which such mutual support and assistance could, in case of need, be made most effective', but 'this rendering of support and assistance' was to be 'without prejudice to the rights and position of other Powers'.

Molotov at once rejected this proposal. It was 'cumbrous', 'no serious contribution', 'vaguely worded and referred to some distant future and unending conversations'; 'the Soviet Government wanted immediate and effective action'. On 2 June he again proposed a pact of mutual assistance, with guarantees to a number of named countries. This pact was to come into force as soon as the three States had made an agreement 'as to methods, forms, and extent of assistance' – in other words, a military convention. The British jibbed only at the Russian demand that any threat to one of the Baltic States should bring the alliance into action; and the Russians were to decide whether a State was threatened. This, the Foreign Office complained, would make the Russians 'the sole judge of what was a *casus belli* in the Eastern Baltic'. The British wished to keep this decision in their own hands; they would even put it into the hands of the Baltic States – anything to keep it from Russia. On 15 June they submitted a compromise. There should be immediate action by the three Allies if one of them went to the assistance of another State 'which had, by its own consent, received an undertaking of assistance'. There should be consultation only if one of the three 'should consider its security menaced by a threat to the independence or neutrality of any other European Power'.

Molotov rejected this on 16 June. Russia, he said, had been asked to join in guaranteeing Poland, Rumania, Greece, and Turkey. It would be 'a position of inequality, humiliating for Soviet Union', if Great Britain and France refused to join in guaranteeing the Baltic States. He therefore proposed to return to a simple defensive pact if one of the Allies were directly attacked. The British at once objected: 'Soviet Government would obtain the benefit of the guarantees we have given to Rumania and Poland without Great Britain and France receiving any reciprocal benefit on their side.' But this of course was already true. The British tried again. The alliance should operate in case of aggression 'which, being directed against another European

State, thereby constituted a menace to the security of one of the three Allies'. On 21 June Molotov asked: 'Who would decide whether the menace constituted aggression?' Sir William Seeds, Ambassador at Moscow, answered: 'Nothing was said in our draft on this point.' Molotov therefore rejected the proposal.

On 1 July the British gave way. They agreed that the alliance should operate in case of aggression against 'another European State whose independence or neutrality the contracting country concerned felt obliged to defend against such aggression'. Molotov demanded that the States should be mentioned individually in a secret list. The British agreed, but on condition that, if the Baltic States were named, Holland and Switzerland should be named also. Molotov refused: these two States did not recognize the Soviet Union. Further, he wanted to include 'indirect aggression', by which he meant 'an internal *coup d'état* or a reversal of policy in the interests of the aggressor'. The British found this 'completely unacceptable'. They suggested, however, that aggression 'is to be understood as covering action accepted by the State in question under threat of force by another Power and involving the abandonment by it of its independence or neutrality'. This was submitted to Molotov on 8 July and rejected by him on 9 July. He defined indirect aggression as 'action accepted by any of the above-mentioned States under threat of force by another Power or, without any such threat, involving the use of territory and forces of the State in question for purposes of aggression ... and consequently the loss of, by that State, its independence or violation of its neutrality'. He further refused to include Luxembourg, which the French had tried to slip in, and would include Holland and Switzerland only 'if, and when, Poland and Turkey conclude pacts of mutual assistance with the U.S.S.R.'

There were again 'serious difficulties'. It would 'undermine our whole moral position in Europe generally'. The British stuck to their guns, or lack of them. On 17 July they again submitted their formula of 8 July and Molotov again rejected it, referring to the example of President Hacha of Czechoslovakia. The British agreed to drop Holland and Switzerland and proposed only that there should be consultation 'in the event of aggression or threat of aggression by a European Power against a European State not named in the list'. Molotov did not object to this, but he raised a new point. There must be a military agreement, and 'the political part would have no existence without it'. The French jumped at this proposal. They were ready to meet the Russians over 'indirect aggression' if they could get a military pact in exchange. The British still wanted to get their definition of 'indirect aggression' accepted before they would agree to military talks. This idea was put to Molotov on 23 July. He rejected it. Further political discussions without military talks would be 'a waste of time'. 'During military conversations outstanding political points could easily be settled.'

On 27 July the British agreed to military talks before the political agreement was settled. But they did not mean to give way over 'indirect aggression' – despite Bonnet's statement that the political agreement was initialled. On the contrary, with military talks in progress, 'we feel that we can afford to take a somewhat stiffer line in regard to the one point to which we have always attached capital importance'. It also occurred to them, apparently for the first time, that the draft treaty did not cover Danzig; moreover, unless they were careful, it might land them in guaranteeing the Soviet Union against Poland – which they certainly did not intend to do. A discussion with Molotov on 3 August showed that the conflict was still unresolved. The British would include indirect aggression only if the victim gave way 'under threat of force'; Molotov insisted on adding 'or without any such threat'. On 17 August the British sent to Moscow a mixed bag of alternatives, each designed to give the impression that they met Molotov's demand without actually doing so. There was to be 'threat of force, overt or covert', or 'pressure', instead of a reference to 'the action against Czechoslovakia in March 1939' – which came to the same thing. But as none of these proposals was put to Molotov, it is hardly worth dissecting them.

Meanwhile the military missions were proceeding slowly to Moscow by sea. They did not imply the decisive concession which the Russians perhaps imagined. Molotov had said that a military agreement must be made before the political agreement was concluded; the British were still determined to have a political agreement before taking the military talks seriously. The British mission was told: 'Unless such time as the political agreement is concluded, the Delegation should go very slowly with the conversations', and 'until the political agreement is reached the Delegation must treat the Russians with reserve'. Out of the nineteen points of 'general policy' eleven specified subjects which the delegation should not discuss with the Russians or information which it should not give them. The military mission was, in fact, designed to keep Russia 'in play' during the critical weeks at Danzig which were now seen to be approaching. In this light, Annex IV of the instructions to the military mission is not without humour. It is entitled 'The Russian Character' and begins: 'The Russian is suspicious by nature and a hard bargainer.' This wisdom was as profound as the rest of the negotiations.

The British military mission started with the cheerful assumption that 'agreement on the many points discussed may take months to achieve'. They were soon hustled out of their lethargy by the Russian insistence. Admiral Drax, the leader, had to confess that he had no proper credentials. He got them, though only on 21 August. The reservations were abandoned one after another; soon the Russians were being told everything of British and French plans – plans which indeed were far from reality as the events of May 1940 were to show. All this was a mere preliminary. On 14 August Voroshilov, leader of the Soviet delegation, asked the decisive question: 'Can the Red Army move across North Poland and across Galicia in order to make contact with the enemy? Will Soviet troops be allowed to cross Rumania?' The British and French were unable to answer. The talks were adjourned, never to be resumed seriously. No effective inquiry was ever made of Rumania; but the French did their best with the Poles, the British trailing along complainingly behind. The Poles, however, held out. Beck said: 'This is a new partition that we are asked to sign.' On 22 August the French tried a last trick. They offered to agree to the passage of Russian troops through Poland and Rumania without reference to the governments of these countries. With this offer the British were not associated. In any case it was of no use. Voroshilov wanted an assurance from Poland and Rumania, not from France. 'We do not want Poland to boast that she has refused our aid – which we have no intention of forcing her to accept. . . . Surely we cannot be obliged to beg for the right to fight the common enemy?' On the following day, 23 August, the Russians made their decision: they concluded the

Nazi-Soviet pact. The British had remained firm to the end. They would leave the decision on peace or war to the Poles; they would not leave it to the Russians. Yet it was perhaps the Russians who won: for the Nazi-Soviet pact helped the decision towards war, even though it did not produce it.

The preceding summary contains one surprise, though by no means an unusual one. The documents reveal practically nothing that we did not know before. The account given by Sir Lewis Namier in *Diplomatic Prelude* was based almost entirely on contemporary newspaper reports – there was in 1946 little else for him to base it on. Nearly everything in his account is precisely accurate – not only in dates but even in the very phrases. Who made these elaborate 'leaks' to the press? No one has asked the question, let alone answered it; yet it must surely point to at least part of the explanation. The source can hardly have been the British Government. They were constantly embarrassed by these 'leaks' and driven by them from one concession to another. It must then have been the Soviet Government. For what purpose? Not to inform or influence their own people; Soviet public opinion could be manoeuvred at a nod as its reception of the Nazi-Soviet pact showed. The revelations were aimed at British opinion, or at western opinion generally. Again, for what purpose? The simplest explanation would be that the Russians genuinely wanted an alliance and believed, rightly, that they could get it only if public opinion forced the British Government on. They may have been playing a more elaborate political game. Convinced that they could never get sincere friendship from the existing right-wing governments, they may have been hoping for a political upheaval in both England and France which would bring the Left to power. Whether they would then have concluded an effective alliance with such governments or whether they would have sat back, more or less securely, as they did in the Spanish civil war, is a speculation too remote to answer. But it seems more likely that the Russians carried on these negotiations for the sake of their effect, whatever that might be, on British opinion than that they built up a façade merely to frighten Hitler. Of course there may be a much simpler explanation. The Russians always like to show that they are entirely in the right; and the 'leaks' may have been made solely for this reason. But it is almost inconceivable that they were resolved on the Nazi-Soviet pact all along.

The same point can be made in another way. If the Russians were merely concerned to alarm Hitler and to drag out negotiations until the critical last week in August, then the delays should have come from their side. But the opposite is the case. Here is the rhythm, British proposals on the one side, Soviet on the other:

British	Soviet	British	Soviet
14 April	18 April	1 July	3 July
9 May	14 May	8 July	9 July
27 May	2 June	17 July	17 July
15 June	16 June	23 July	23 July
21 June	22 June	17 August	

The contrast is startling. The Russians replied within three days, five days, six days; thereafter at breakneck speed, usually on the same day. The British took three weeks, twelve days, thirteen days, and then a week or more on each occasion. If dates mean anything, then the British were spinning things out, the Russians were anxious to conclude. There is other evidence of British reluctance. On 12 June Maisky invited Lord Halifax to Moscow, though admittedly 'when things were quieter'. On 21 June Chamberlain, questioned in Parliament whether 'the Russian Government had ever asked for the visit of a British Minister to Moscow', replied with a flat denial. The story of the military mission points the same moral. The British agreed to military talks on 23 July. Yet the mission did not reach Moscow until 11 August, only to reveal that it had no credentials. It would be plausible to deduce that the British, not the Russians, negotiated throughout with one eye on Hitler.

Yet this is probably not the explanation. Both sides wanted agreement, but they did not want the same agreement. The pattern of negotiations did not change despite the fog of phrases and trivialities. The Russians wanted a precise alliance for mutual assistance. The British wanted a promise of Russian aid 'if desired'. Each step by one side increased the suspicion of the other. The Russians had behind them the emptiness of the Franco-Soviet pact. After all, if Daladier and Bonnet had really been as keen on Soviet co-operation as they later claimed, they could have added a military convention to this pact without waiting for the British. The French aim seems rather to have been to put the odium of failure on the British; and the British certainly obliged them. The Russians remembered, too, the desertion of Czechoslovakia by Great Britain and France, and their own exclusion from the conference at Munich. Now they feared not for Poland, but for themselves. A German invasion of Russia, not any mere shifting of the European balance in Germany's favour, was their nightmare. All they were offered was the loss of such freedom of action as they still possessed.

The British did not share these Russian fears, and therefore could not understand them. It never crossed their minds that within twelve months the British Isles themselves would be threatened with invasion. The military mission were told that, if Germany attacked in the west, 'sooner or later, this front would be stabilized'. Hence the Russian demand for a direct alliance seemed to be irrelevant, and the Russian fear of attack through the Baltic States an excuse for aggression. The British wished to keep the Russians dangling at the end of a string which only the British (or perhaps the Poles) could pull. Halifax defined British policy with his usual felicity: 'It was desirable not to estrange Russia but always to keep her in play.' Sir Edward Grey would have appreciated the fishing metaphor. But in 1914 Grey landed his fish. In 1939 the fish broke away, to the moral indignation of the angler. The British Government conceived alliance with Russia as a diplomatic manoeuvre, not as a prelude to action. The Red Army was assumed to have no fighting value. Halifax held that 'the Red Army might be efficient for purposes of defence, but not for purposes of offensive operations'. There would be 'no point' in getting Soviet assistance if Poland and Rumania, who were ranked higher as military powers, then broke away. Moreover a mutual assistance pact 'would further infuriate Herr Hitler'. 'It would be said that – abandoning any further attempt to remain impartial – we were deliberately aligning for war between rival groups of Powers.' Italy, Spain, Japan would be offended; 'nor must it be forgotten that the Vatican regard Moscow even to a greater extent than Berlin as Anti-Christ'.

With many arguments for delay and few for decision, men who had long hesitated about everything now hesitated again. Mr

Strang, a member of the Foreign Office who was sent to Moscow for some obscure purpose (certainly not to conclude an alliance), wrote cheerfully on 21 June: 'I dare say we shall arrive at something in the end. When I say "in the end" I recall a remark of Naggiar's [the French ambassador] this afternoon that he will probably have reached the age limit and gone into retirement before I get away from Moscow.' The only argument for the alliance which the Foreign Office could think of was that foreign material could then be imported into Poland through Russia. But this could be done without an alliance; and in fact the Russians would have allowed it in September if the Poles had held out longer. There was a more general ground. 'It was essential, if there must be a war, to try to involve the Soviet Union in it, otherwise at the end of the war the Soviet Union, with her army intact and England and Germany in ruins, would dominate Europe.' Yet it never occurred to the Foreign Office that the Russians might make this calculation for themselves. On 8 May rumours of a Nazi-Soviet pact were dismissed as 'inherently improbable'. On 30 May Mr Kirkpatrick said: 'It would be a mistake to imagine that a Russo-German agreement could be so easily concluded as some people in Germany thought.' Lord Halifax telegraphed to Moscow on 28 July: 'There is no danger now of an imminent breakdown in the next critical weeks.' Ignorance reinforced complacency. Sir Orme Sargent, a high official of the Foreign Office, referred to Molotov in one letter as 'M. Momtchiloff.' A footnote adds: 'M. Momtchiloff was Bulgarian Minister in London.' A revealing slip of the pen. Momtchiloff or Molotov – what did it matter? They were both ministers of Slav countries, distant and unimportant.

Men project the dangers of the present into the future; they do not foresee the dangers that actually occur. Then, looking back, they imagine that they have been guarding against these all the time. In 1942 Stalin told Churchill that the Russians would have had to provide three hundred divisions, while the French provided one hundred and the British 'two now and two later'. This reflected the situation at the time of the battle of Stalingrad. It was not the decisive point for the Russians in 1939. The question of relative strengths was raised only casually and late in the day during the military talks; and then the Russians produced an absurd plan by which they would put into the field only as many divisions as the western Powers. The disagreement in 1939 was over policy, not over practical contributions. The Russians then did not fear a war in which they would bear an unequal burden; they feared a war which they would have to fight alone. Were their fears all that unreasonable? We know now that Hitler would not have been deterred from war by the conclusion of a Triple Alliance. He would have swept through Poland just the same; and would probably have inflicted great defeats on the Red Army. Would the British have stood by Russia to the death without the experience of Dunkirk and the blitz? Even now some, including Professor Butterfield, regret that Russia and Germany were not left to fight it out. That feeling was certainly much stronger in 1939. The Russian fears were exaggerated, but not groundless. They may have done the wrong sum, but at least they got its answer right. It was Soviet policy in 1939 which largely ensured that, when Soviet Russia was attacked, the western Powers were her ally.

British policy not only did the wrong sum; it failed even within its own terms of reference. The British were more anxious to keep Soviet Russia out of Poland and the Baltic States than to secure her aid against Hitler. They did not secure her aid; they also did not keep her out of Poland and the Baltic States. The only thing saved from the wreck was their reputation; to this Englishmen attach much importance. The Soviet leaders have never recovered in the eyes of their western admirers the moral superiority which they forfeited by making the Nazi–Soviet pact. The members of the British Foreign Office concerned with the Anglo-Soviet negotiations all rose to the highest positions. Respect for their abilities has survived even the revelation of the most incompetent transactions in British history since the loss of the American colonies. The minister responsible has done best of all. Many Foreign Secretaries have remained subjects of controversy. No one has been found to question the wisdom of Lord Halifax, K.G., O.M., G.C.S.I., G.C.I.E., D.C.L.

37

THE SPRINGS OF
SOVIET DIPLOMACY

SCHOLARS once combed the Scriptures for polemical texts; now the Powers fling at each other fragments from the German archives, a more long-winded and less elegant substitute. The Americans launched the campaign with 'Nazi-Soviet Relations, 1939–1941' (even the title is polemical); the Russians have retaliated with documents on Munich. Since the Americans had no foreign policy before the war, it is impossible to discredit them (or the reverse); therefore, the Russian counter-blow, so far as it hits anyone (which is not much), misses them and lands on the British – a symbol of present international relations. We get the knocks intended for the Americans. When Bismarck started this type of appeal with French documents captured during the Franco-German war, there was perhaps a 'world-opinion' affected by it; and the Germans were even more successful with the documents which they published between the wars. Hitler's success would hardly have been possible without the guilty conscience in England and America which the fifty-four volumes of German documents did much to create.

This world opinion no longer exists, and each side publishes documents merely in order to bolster its own convictions. British opinion is not likely to be shaken by the discovery that when Chamberlain and Halifax negotiated with Hitler, they did so in the hope of reaching an agreement with him. The same charity is not extended to the Russians. The *Economist* headed its account of the Nazi-Soviet documents, 'When Stalin toasted Hitler'. What else was he expected to do? After all, Stalin has toasted other notorious anti-Bolsheviks. Even Professor Namier, previously reticent in his judgements on Soviet policy, after reading 'Nazi-Soviet Relations', spoke of 'Stalin's war-guilt'. These condemnations are based on the view that the Soviet effort at collaboration with the Germans was sincere. Other commentators have taken a smarter line and have accused the Soviet Government of cheating the Germans. The moral is clear: since they cheated in their deals with the Germans, they will cheat us, too, and therefore, I suppose (thought this is not said so openly), we had better apply Hitler's remedy. Pseudo-historical speculation by journalists is not really very profitable, except to the writers; and the historical conclusions which can be drawn from 'Nazi-Soviet Relations, 1939–1941' are of a more humdrum character.

Still, conclusions can be drawn. Since the Franco-Soviet pact was still-born, the Nazi-Soviet pact of 23 August 1939, marked the first appearance of Russia as a European Great Power since the revolution. Like traditional Russian foreign policy (including the original Franco-Russian alliance), Soviet policy in 1939 aimed to keep out of Europe, not to return to it; or, more strictly, to keep Europe out of Russia. Between August 1939 and June 1941 Soviet policy worked for a *cordon sanitaire* in reverse. The Baltic States and the Western (Polish) Ukraine were the first stage; Finland and Bulgaria the second; the straits leading from the Baltic and Black Seas a more remote third. These latter steps were represented to the Germans as a defence against England, to the British as a defence against Germany; in reality they were both – the *cordon sanitaire* does not discriminate in the germ-carriers that it bars. Soviet statesmen claim to be far-sighted; in fact, their programme of 1939 was mostly improvised. Since 1917 they had only the experience of warding off dangers, never of making demands. In 1939 they were courted by both sides and brushed up the diplomacy of twenty years before; after all, States, like individuals, can only start again where they left off. The alliance negotiations with England and France make sense only on the assumption that the Soviet statesmen genuinely desired an alliance and discovered its impossibility (for them as much as for others) only as they came to formulate precise conditions. Similarly, the Soviet rulers had not thought out what gains they were to demand from the Nazi-Soviet pact; their full schedule was not ready until Molotov's visit to Berlin in November 1940, and then it was too late – the Soviet insistence on control of Finland, Bulgaria and the Straits led Hitler to resolve on war. In fact, Constantinople was the stake in the war of 1941 just as much as it had been in the war of 1812. For Hitler, as for Napoleon, Constantinople was the symbol for the mastery of the world. For

Molotov, as for Alexander I, the Straits were the one chink in Russia's defensive armour; in Molotov's words, 'England's historic gateway for attack on the Soviet Union'. The demand for Soviet garrisons at the Straits was an old-fashioned way of closing this gateway; nevertheless, it is difficult to think of any other.

Beyond the *cordon sanitaire*, Soviet statesmen thought in terms of the Balance of Power. There was sincerity in Stalin's words: 'A strong Germany is the absolute requisite for peace in Europe, whence it follows that the Soviet Union is interested in the existence of a strong Germany.' This is the exact counterpart of the attitude of the Western Powers, who had welcomed a strong Germany as a barrier against Bolshevism. Both sides burnt their fingers (and most of their bodies) with this policy and now hesitate to renew it; hence the present confusion of policy with regard to Germany. Still, the bidding for German friendship must start soon; the only slender hope of preventing it lies in a possible German weariness with their warrior role. In 1939 Stalin counted on the French to keep Germany occupied; he told Ribbentrop 'that France had an army worthy of consideration'. Hence the indignation with France which Stalin still showed in 1945: he complained at Yalta that 'France opened the gates to the enemy'. The French defended their own gates, though inadequately; the gates which they opened to the enemy were the gates of Russia. Soviet statesmen are not likely to fall victims again to the illusion that France is a Great Power; and this lack of a Balance of Power probably accounts for their apprehensions ever since the end of the war. Those who could sit unmoved through the endless harangues of Hitler, with his visions of a new world order, will not easily be affected by American good intentions; and, short of faith in these, it is difficult to devise security except by means of the Balance of Power. Maybe a more independent British policy since the war would have lessened Soviet anxieties; on the admittedly inadequate evidence of the German documents, however, Soviet opinion wrote off British power almost as much as French.

The German documents give a reminder of one factor often overlooked: Soviet policy is as intimately concerned with the Far East as with Europe. Here, too, the Soviet aim was a Balance of Power: Japan was to keep China in order and act as a buffer against America, yet not to conquer China nor be conquered by America. This Balance, too, has collapsed, though not so disastrously as the Balance in Europe; but, unless Communist China can be transformed into an adequate buffer, the Soviet Union will, one day, have to enter the competition for Japanese favour.

It may be objected that these considerations were valid only in the period of German and Japanese aggression; but the Soviet leaders do not distinguish between one capitalist State and another. Indeed, they found it easier to understand the Germans than the British and French or, subsequently, the Americans; and their anger at having been taken in by Hitler has made them resolve never to be taken in again. The Marxism which underlies their long-term policy reinforces these suspicions; their day-to-day policy would be much the same whether they were Marxists or not. After all, the Soviet Minister of Transport, also a Marxist, is concerned in day-to-day practice with the specifically 'Russian' problems which spring from broad-gauge railways and a great land mass; the same is true of Soviet diplomacy. It is therefore a fair general deduction that the object of Soviet policy is security, based on a ring of buffer States and a Balance of Power beyond this ring.

There is, however, one economic factor, not specifically Marxist, since it was also characteristic of Tsarist policy in the days of the Franco-Russian alliance. The deepest force in Nazi-Soviet friendship was the exchange of raw materials and foodstuffs for machine-tools. This economic bargain was the essential preliminary to a political agreement on which Molotov insisted, and the Soviet outlook is not likely to have changed. Machine-tools would buy Soviet friendship on favourable economic and political terms for a long time to come. The peace and future of the world probably depends on whether anyone has machine-tools to offer and cares to offer them.

38

FROM MUNICH TO PRAGUE:

(1) BRITISH VERSION

IN the months after Munich, British policy proceeded in a daze – confusedly aware that 'the Munich spirit' had evaporated, but at a loss for something to take its place. The third volume of Foreign Office documents[1] rambles over a variety of subjects – the execution of the Munich agreement, the revived German hostility, relations with Italy, and the beginnings of the Danzig question.

The working-out of the Munich agreement is a squalid story. The International Commission at Berlin was supposed to see fair play between Germany and Czechoslovakia. But as one British diplomatist wrote: 'Once the principle of negotiation under the threat of violence has been accepted it is difficult to find a position at which a stand is possible.' Even Sir Nevile Henderson complained. 'I never want to work with the Germans again.' Still, he stuck to his logical point – the Czechs must come within the political and economic orbit of Germany, 'there will never be any peace for Czechs or Europe till they accept the harsh fact'. Hence he supported the German case on every disputed detail.

Worse, and far more discreditable, is the affair of the guarantee to Czechoslovakia, which the British Government had promised at the height of the crisis in order to persuade the French to yield. To guarantee a helpless State when it had been impossible to defend a fully armed one was an obvious absurdity; and the British Government now tried to escape the consequences of its rash act. At the meeting with Daladier and Bonnet on 24 November Chamberlain tried to make out that the British had only intended to promise a collective guarantee of the four Munich Powers; and he was seconded by Lord Halifax 'from a practical

---

1. *Documents on British Foreign Policy, 1919–39*. Edited by E. L. Woodward and Rohan Butler. Assisted by Margaret Lambert. Third series, volume iii. 1938–9.

point of view'. 'This did not seem to be out of conformity with the letter of the Anglo-French declaration.' The French Ministers had been swindled and they knew it.

The solution was more discreditable still: it was to ask the Czechs themselves to get the British out of the difficulty. If Czechoslovakia professed herself satisfied with a collective guarantee the British conscience would be satisfied too. When the Czechs failed to respond, Lord Halifax lost patience:

His Majesty's Government cannot undertake a guarantee which would oblige them to go to the assistance of Czechoslovakia in circumstances in which effective help could not be rendered.

The search for new allies was pursued with less zest than the desertion of an old one. Russia, promised a share in the Czech guarantee by Lord Halifax in September, was cold-shouldered thereafter; and Chamberlain inquired anxiously whether the Franco-Soviet pact would operate 'if Russia were to ask France for assistance on the grounds that a separatist movement in Ukraine was provoked by Germany'. Lord Halifax, on the other hand, recognized the danger of renouncing Eastern Europe altogether: 'It is one thing to allow German expansion in Central Europe, which to my mind is a normal and natural thing, but we must be able to resist German expansion in Western Europe or else our whole position is undermined.' Therefore a balance against Germany was still needed: 'Subject only to the consideration that I should hope France would protect herself – and us – from being entangled by Russia in war with Germany I should hesitate to advise the French Government to denounce the Franco-Soviet pact as the future is still far too uncertain.' In plain English: Russia should fight for our interests, but we should not fight for hers.

The same difficulty appeared in regard to Poland. The British Government was rightly shocked at the Polish behaviour during the Munich crisis; it had been as bad as their own. But malicious pleasure at the mounting difficulties in Danzig was not a policy; and by the end of the year the British were well on the way to being entangled in the Danzig affair. One of the permanent officials, Sir Orme Sargent, explained the dilemma after Ribbentrop's visit to Paris. If Germany were free to pursue her aims in

Eastern Europe without French interference, she might become so strong that the security of France would be 'under imminent menace'. If, on the other hand, the French Government decided not to leave Germany with freedom of action in Eastern Europe, Great Britain might be drawn into war in order to support France.

The solution seemed to be Italy. In Lord Halifax's words: 'Although we do not expect to detach Italy from the Axis, we believe the [Anglo-Italian] Agreement will increase Mussolini's power of manoeuvre and so make him less dependent on Hitler and therefore freer to resume the classic Italian role of balancing between Germany and the Western Powers.' In other words, by paying Mussolini blackmail we will encourage him to demand more. Hence the Anglo-Italian Agreement was 'brought into force', although the Italians had not fulfilled the condition of withdrawing from Spain; hence Chamberlain and Lord Halifax travelled to Rome in January 1939. Mussolini probably expected them to try to buy him with concessions at the expense of France; instead, he got a high-minded plea from Chamberlain for some assurances that Hitler was not going to war. Not surprisingly, Mussolini 'thrust out his chin' and retaliated with an attack on the British press. The visit to Rome, which should have been the triumph of Chamberlain's policy, was really the end of the Italian illusion; the price for this mistaken bet was paid by the Spanish Republic.

The British were left with France – acutely aware of French weakness yet inescapably tied to her. The only way out would have been for France to rearm on such a scale that she would need neither Great Britain nor her eastern allies – an impossibility. When Chamberlain tried to urge on French rearmament Daladier was provoked into replying with the grotesque claim that France would be producing four hundred planes a month by the spring of 1939; his more effective reply was that the British should speed up their own rearmament and not concentrate so much on the anti-aircraft defence of London. The Foreign Office and Lord Halifax, perhaps even Chamberlain, knew that the policy of Munich had failed; their hopelessness and helplessness was preparing the equally exaggerated swing the other way, which produced the wild guarantees of March 1939.

As often happens, appeasement was the prelude to bellicosity.

At the beginning of 1939 British foreign policy was still pursuing its traditional course, avoiding precise commitments and seeking to balance between the Great Powers of the Continent. Three months later Britain was distributing guarantees to the States of Eastern Europe and preaching collective security against the aggressor. It was the greatest revolution in the history of our foreign policy; and the volume of Foreign Office documents, which exactly covers this decisive period, surpasses any of its predecessors in interest and importance.[1] It opens with the return of Halifax and Chamberlain from their visit to Rome – the last kick of appeasement; it closes with the announcement of the British guarantee to Poland. This great change was not the result of foresight or calculation; it sprang in an improvised way from bewilderment and anxiety. In fact, the right policy was adopted for the wrong reasons and applied by wrong methods.

In January 1939, the British Government were puzzling their heads as to Hitler's next move. They feared a German invasion of Holland and resolved to treat it as a *casus belli*. But while they passed this on as an encouragement to their friends (France, Belgium, and the United States) they did not deliver it as a warning to their potential enemy. They were still hoping, in fact, that he would not be their enemy. Lord Halifax said to the French Ambassador on 10 February:

The strategical importance of the Netherlands is so great that a German attack on them must be regarded as a direct threat to the security of the Western Powers ... a German attack on Switzerland would also be clear evidence of an attempt to dominate Europe by force.

Thus Hitler would be seeking to dominate Europe only if he threatened British interests; expansion in Eastern Europe was harmless so long as it was done by respectable methods. From Berlin Nevile Henderson renewed his belief in Hitler's good intentions. Thus on 18 February:

My definite impression is that Herr Hitler does not contemplate any adventures at the moment.

1. *Documents on British Foreign Policy, 1919-1939.* Edited by E. L. Woodward and Rohan Butler. Assisted by Margaret Lambert. Third series, volume iv. 1938–9.

On 22 February:

> I would feel confident if it were not for the British press, or at any rate that section of it which is inspired by an intelligentsia, which hates Hitler and the Nazis so much that it sees red whatever the facts are, or by alarmists by profession and Jews.

Finally, on 9 March, he argued at length that British policy should aim at switching German energies against Russia:

> The best approach to good relations with Germany is therefore along the lines of the avoidance of constant and vexatious interference in matters in which British interests are not directly or vitally involved and the prospect of British neutrality in the event of Germany being engaged in the East.

On 15 March when Hitler seized Prague, Henderson at first contented himself with sending a message to Weizsäcker 'that if this is his conception of "decency" it is not mine'. He wrote to Lord Halifax: 'What distresses me more than anything else is the handle which it will give to the critics of Munich. Not that I did not always realize that the complete subservience of the Czechs to Germany was inevitable.' As to the future: 'We cannot make war on Germany, but we can reduce relations to a minimum: at heart I am in favour of that.' Henderson at least stuck to his line: his last proposal meant in practice that the British should turn their backs while Hitler conquered Eastern Europe.

But Henderson's day was over. The Prague coup destroyed Chamberlain's faith in him, at any rate for the time being, and opened the way for Henderson's critics at the Foreign Office. It is difficult to say when Lord Halifax shook off the Munich line. On 15 March he spoke strongly to the German Ambassador:

> The immediate result was that nobody felt the assurances of the German Government to be worth very much. . . . I could well understand Herr Hitler's taste for bloodless victories, but one of these days he would find himself up against something that would not be bloodless.

But on the same day he said to the French Ambassador: 'The one compensating advantage that I saw was that it had brought to a natural end the somewhat embarrassing commitment of a guarantee, in which we and the French had both been involved.'

This was a surprising prelude to a policy which ended by guaranteeing practically every State in Europe. No doubt public opinion was the main force in bringing about this great change; but there were also purely diplomatic factors. The British Government were now ready to swallow any story, however alarmist (including that of an immediate attack by Hitler on the British fleet). Hence, they at once believed the Rumanian Minister when he appealed for assistance on 16 March. Though Mr Tilea was disavowed by his own Government the British – and Chamberlain in particular – were convinced that a peace front must be created overnight. On 20 March Chamberlain himself drafted a declaration of collective security, which the French, Soviet, and Polish Governments were invited to sign. The French agreed at once; the Soviet Government would sign as soon as France and Poland accepted it; the Poles, however, held out – they would sign a declaration with Great Britain but not with the Soviet Union. By simple impudence, Colonel Beck and the Polish Government played themselves into the position of dictating policy to the British Government.

Men think in terms of immediate questions and of their own interests, even when they imagine that they are conducting a policy of abstract principle. The crisis had started because of Rumania; and the British continued to judge the situation from the Rumanian angle even when this proved a false alarm. Therefore aid from Poland seemed more urgent than from anyone else. Moreover, the British were conscious of their own military weakness; they needed a second front in Europe and, as a glance at the map showed, only Poland could provide it. Anxious for Rumania and ultimately for the Middle East, it never occurred to them to ask whether Poland could remain neutral in the coming war. Beck had kept them almost completely in the dark concerning German demands on Danzig; and in any case they imagined that Danzig could be somehow jettisoned without endangering Poland. The key to British policy in the decisive days between 22 March and 30 March, when Chamberlain himself drafted the guarantee to Poland, is to be found here: the British regarded Poland as the essential country and believed that her co-operation must be bought, however high the price.

Relations with the Soviet Union had to be subordinated to

Polish needs and wishes. As Bonnet said, to the entire agreement of Lord Halifax, on 21 March:

> It was absolutely essential to get Poland in. Russian help would only be effective if Poland were collaborating. If Poland collaborated, Russia could give very great assistance; if not, Russia could give much less.

No doubt the British Government were influenced by reports that Hungary, Spain, and Italy would be offended by a British alliance with the Soviet Union (and Chamberlain was still whining to Mussolini for sympathy on 20 March); but Poland was undoubtedly the decisive factor. Lord Halifax remarked to Chamberlain and Bonnet on 22 March: 'It would be unfortunate if we were now so to act as to give the Soviet Government the idea that we were pushing her to one side.' The Ambassador in Moscow had given repeated warning that Soviet policy was now isolationist, recognizing no distinction between the two sides in 'the second Imperialist war'. This did not shake Chamberlain and Halifax: they assumed that Moscow would respond to any casual British gesture. And if it did not, they were not perturbed: Soviet neutrality would be almost as useful as their participation in war – in some ways better, since it would not alarm Poland and Rumania. This is clearly implied in a dispatch written by Lord Halifax on 27 March. The Nazi-Soviet pact was the logical outcome of the new British policy as Munich had been the logical outcome of the old one.

(2) GERMAN VERSION

The six months between the Munich conference and the German occupation of Prague were the brief heyday of appeasement, when Hitler and his associates believed that they had won the mastery of Europe without a struggle. What led Hitler to abandon this position of vantage and to take the steps which forced England and France into war? Though the German Foreign Ministry was almost as much in the dark as to Hitler's motives as we are, the new set of documents from its archives does something to resolve the problem.[1] The answer seems to be twofold.

1. *Documents on German Foreign Policy, 1918–45.* Series D (1937–45), volume iv: The Aftermath of Munich. October 1938–March 1939.

On the one hand the disintegration of Central Europe was so great that Hitler could not resist the temptation to go farther. On the other British and French policy seemed to imply that he could advance eastwards without serious protest from the Western Powers.

The story of Hitler's final aggression against truncated Czechoslovakia was revealed in the Nuremberg documents and told in a masterly essay by Sir Lewis Namier on 'The Ides of March'. There is little to be added. At the time of the original Czech crisis Hitler did not think beyond annexing the German areas. He seems to have assumed that Czechoslovakia would continue to exist, though after some loss of territory to Hungary. He became impatient when the Czechs hesitated to abandon every scrap of democracy and increasingly impatient when they continued to show interest in an international guarantee. But his final move seems to have been directed not so much against the Czechs as against Hungary. In September 1938, he had encouraged the Hungarians to arm and to invade Czechoslovakia. He was angry that they had tried to keep in with both sides and told them that they had 'missed the bus'. Moreover, the German General Staff warned against allowing a common frontier between Poland and Hungary: this would bar the way against future German expansion.

When the Slovak autonomists grew turbulent Hitler was threatened with two outcomes, either of which was unwelcome to him. Either the Slovaks would be subdued from Prague and the Czechs would recover some prestige, or Slovakia would be incorporated in Hungary, which would then become more independent than ever. The only solution for Hitler was to back an independent Slovakia. The occupation of Prague was little more than a by-product; the decisive event was the defeat of Hungarian ambitions. It would be an exaggeration to say that Hitler lost the mastery of the world for the sake of Hungary and Slovakia; but it is a fair judgement that he, like so many European politicians, attached an inflated importance to these 'Balkan' trivialities. The Allied statesmen made the same mistake during the war – and perhaps do so now.

In September 1938, the British Government had been the pacemaker in appeasement and the French an unwilling second.

Afterwards the position was reversed. The Germans early learnt that appeasement had been purely Chamberlain's policy and that the Foreign Office 'had striven to sabotage his plans and commit Great Britain to warlike action against Germany'. Certainly they were told by the Prime Minister's press officer that his attitude:

had never been dictated by a consciousness of military weakness but exclusively by the religious idea that Germany must have justice, and that the injustice of Versailles must be made good;

and Sir Samuel Hoare talked of a guarantee by the four European Great Powers against Soviet Russia. But the British Government pressed for some concrete gesture of friendship – a further agreement on naval armaments or co-operation in the Far East.

Hitler, however, aimed to 'split' British opinion – no doubt an idea of Ribbentrop's; and he calculated that if the Chamberlain Government was driven to rearmament this would stir up increasing opposition among the pro-Germans. Moreover the directors of British economic policy, led by Sir Frederick Leith-Ross, were constantly urging measures of economic co-operation; and this also helped to convince the Germans that the British were coming to them as suppliants. In fact the only serious Anglo-German negotiations during this period were on the coal cartel, sharing out the European export market; and this was supposed to provide a pattern for other agreements. The British protagonists of this policy no doubt hoped that prosperity would make Hitler more moderate in political methods; but the only effect was to convince him of British weakness. Finally, the British approach to Italy in January 1939 made him suspicious that an attempt was being made to revive 'the Stresa front'. It was little consolation to know that Lord Halifax had had discussions with 'the notorious Low' to prevent excesses in the press.

With France the situation was reversed. On Hitler's orders the Germans ignored Bonnet's efforts at appeasement, which culminated in the Franco-German declaration of 6 December. These documents do not settle the controversy whether Bonnet washed his hands of Eastern Europe during his conversations with Ribbentrop. Clearly Bonnet did not intend to protect Czechoslovakia; but neither of the two men mentioned Poland –

the subject did not at that time occur to them. Bonnet was not the only advocate of appeasement. On 22 October M. Reynaud defended himself to Abetz, Ribbentrop's representative, 'against the charge of being an enemy of Franco-German understanding'.

He hinted that France needed the spectre of the German danger in order to remain strong internally, because otherwise the willingness of the people to defend themselves and make sacrifices would disappear completely. He held the view that an agreement could not be made with *mous* (by which he obviously meant Flandin), but that it could be made with *durs* (with a plain hint at himself).

In the New Year, when the British were seeking to appease Italy, the French took the opposite course. They talked of a war for Tunis and asked the Germans to 'exercise a conciliatory influence on Italy'. Though the Germans did not respond to this invitation, they counted on the disunity of the Western Powers and even took it out of the Italians by not revealing to them their military plans against France nor even for the occupation of Prague.

The Germans thought only of the three European Powers, still supposedly 'the Great'. They assumed that Russia was safely excluded from Europe and limited their dealings with her to trading agreements. In fact the Nazi-Soviet pact was already implicitly in operation. The United States they ignored still more confidently and rather welcomed estrangement as increasing the gulf between them.

Though the Munich conference founded Hitler's empire, it also caused his ruin. He supposed that the Munich Powers were all that mattered: if he could dictate to them, he could dictate to everybody. As well, he attributed to British policy a greater logic than it possessed: surely the British knew that when they surrendered the Sudeten areas they surrendered all east-central Europe. The occupation of Prague was a triviality in comparison. Hitler took the decisive step in his career without realizing that it was decisive or indeed noticing that he had made it.

39

MUNICH TEN YEARS AFTER

THE crisis of Munich has few mysteries for the historian. We know as much about it as about, say, Agadir or the affair of the Hohenzollern candidate which preceded the Franco-German war of 1870. We know, for instance, that Hitler intended all along to destroy Czechoslovakia and that the Sudeten grievances were humbug; we know that Chamberlain's policy of appeasement was sincerely held and deliberately conducted, and that the argument of British weakness was an excuse invented after the event; we know why the French did not fight, even though the French military advisers thought themselves in a better position to fight in 1938 than in 1939; we even know why the Czechs did not fight; we know what the Russians offered (though not their fighting quality). In short, we know – as much as a historian ever knows – the record of facts; and doubt is cast on this record only by those who want to cover something shameful in their own past. There we arrive at what we do not know – why Munich should have such psychological symbolism; why it should still rouse such passion and lead honourable men to lie and cheat about it; why, indeed, it touched off in the House of Commons a scene of 'mass-hysteria' without parallel in history. Incidentally here is one of the few points of detail we do not know – who among the Members of Parliament remained silent when all the rest were screaming and sobbing. One observer says Eden and Harold Nicolson; another speaks of Churchill, Eden, and Amery. Both, revealingly, omit Gallacher.

At Munich, for the last time, Europe seemed the centre of the world. As in the fifth act of a Shakespearean tragedy, the characters made a final proud appearance, unwitting that the hand of death was already upon them. The Munich Conference was the last version of the Concert of Europe and, thus, the heir of the Congress of Vienna. It was a meeting of empires. The British Empire, *l'Empire français*, *Deutsches Reich* – these had been names of confident power. Even Mussolini brandished Imperial phrases and echoed the great claims of Rome. The Munich figures genuinely supposed that they were the 'Big Four' on whom depended the peace and security of the world. Yet at the back of their minds all, even Hitler, were haunted by the fear that greatness was passing them by. These rulers of empires buried themselves in the details of Czech frontier adjustments so as not to lift their eyes and see the writing on the wall. Still, the most gloomy or clear-sighted observer could not have foretold that within ten years only one of the four Munich Powers would be numbered, though with some doubt, among the Great; and even this one is a pensioner of an extra-European Power.

Both the United States and the Soviet Union were absent from Munich, deliberately excluded by the self-confident spokesmen of 'Europe'. Though Roosevelt was no doubt restrained by the immaturity of American public opinion, Chamberlain, as we now know, had set his face against American participation in the interests of appeasement. Munich rested on the assumption that America was not a Great Power and would never become one. Still more, Munich rounded off twenty years of pretending that Russia did not exist. The Anglo-French wars of intervention between 1917 and 1920, undertaken against a former ally, were the worst international crimes of the century; for they fed the Bolshevik belief that there was inescapable hostility between capitalism and Communism. In the nineteen-thirties this belief weakened a little, and the Russians – lacking other means of defence against Germany – perhaps took seriously the principles which the Western Powers professed. If ever there was a chance of bringing Russia back into the European order on a basis of international morality, that chance was lost at Munich – probably for ever. Russia alone had remained faithful to the idea of .collective security; and was made to look foolish for her pains. Later it became fashionable to argue that Russia, too, had been cheating like all the rest. At the time the 'men of Munich' were more honest; they did not want Russia in Europe and prided themselves on having kept her out. Anti-Bolshevism, no doubt, strengthened this attitude and gave the relief its hysterical note; still, it was not the main motive – after all, they were just as pleased to have excluded America.

Insistence on Europe to the exclusion of the rest of the world led England and France to inevitable defeat. Munich was the penalty exacted for a misreading of history – the illusion that France and even England were the victors in the first German war. Yet France would have been defeated in 1914 without Russia; England could not have carried the war to final victory without America. But though Munich became a term of reproach in both France and England, it signified different things in the two countries. To the French it meant a conscious retreat from greatness; France gave up the fruits of the victory of 1918 and abandoned her allies in eastern Europe. The French 'men of Munich' were traitors to French greatness and, from Daladier downwards, themselves admitted it. They justified their betrayal by arguing that the price of greatness was too high in blood and social upheaval. The French path ran straight from Munich to Vichy; and, after Munich, collaboration alone made sense. Frenchmen who turned against Munich were demanding revolution. This was obvious in the Communists; but Jacobinism – the course of Clemenceau or of de Gaulle – was an equal threat to the Third, as it is to the Fourth Republic. In 1938 the Radicals accepted Munich to preserve the Republic; and today, for the same reason, they acquiesce unwillingly in European plans which will again put France in the shadow of German economic power.

In 1938 some Englishmen, too, used the arguments of declining greatness and of the Balance of Power. These arguments still had a harsh, alien ring. Significantly, Duff Cooper, the only Minister to resign, was spiritually at home in France, and had written a distinguished book on the greatest of French diplomats. For most Englishmen Munich was a moral issue, not a question of power. One must be just even to the English 'men of Munich': they genuinely believed that what they had done was appeasement, not capitulation. Fear of war – for the whole world, not merely for themselves – was, no doubt, the prime motive; and, besides, they could argue that they could not aid the Czechs effectively. The same argument, even better founded, seemed irrelevant a year later, and the English people would have given ineffective aid to the Czechs, as they did to the Poles, if they had been morally prepared against Germany. As it was, they felt the moral strength of the German case. For twenty years, English writers, particularly on the Left, had denounced the injustice of the Versailles settlement and the narrow Nationalism of the Succession States. English and American historians, of irreproachable liberalism, had declared that Germany was no more responsible than any other Power for the war of 1914. Who among us can claim innocence? I, for one, look back with shame to the university lectures on the origins of the war of 1914 which I gave before the German occupation of the Rhineland brought me to my senses.

Liberal opinion had accepted the national principle ever since the creation of national Italy in 1860; and the partition of Czechoslovakia seemed the last victory of nationalism. Moreover, the Czechs were, in some sort, the victims of the propaganda in favour of collective security. Englishmen had had it dinned into them for years that peace was indivisible and that they ought to resist aggression anywhere and everywhere. This appeal for a universal crusade asked too much of ordinary Englishmen; what is more, it led them to regard all resistance to aggression as abstract 'idealism'. They felt that, except as vindication of a theoretical principle, it did not matter whether the Italians ruled in Addis Ababa – or, for that matter, the Abyssinians in Rome. From this sound conclusion they proceeded to the unsound conclusion that equally it did not matter whether Hitler or Benes ruled in Prague. On the other hand, the teachings of collective security, though ineffective for action, made them ashamed to fight for 'selfish' national interests and for the Balance of Power. Englishmen lacked a clear moral cause; and we, the clerks in Julien Benda's phrase, were the real 'guilty men' of Munich in that we failed to provide it.

The Czechs, too, were hampered by their moral position. The Czech leaders, Benes most of all, were liberals by historical background and social origin – men of bargaining and discussion. They could manoeuvre and evade; they could not defy and perish. Without the long series of Czech concessions and offers to the Germans Munich would not have been possible; and the Munich Conference was the last display of liberal civilization. Reason and negotiation were ineffective against German power; the only answer was cannon, the *ultima ratio regum*. Benes could not bring himself to make this answer; it was given by Colonel Beck, a man of infinitely lower moral calibre, but all the same the man who gave the signal for Hitler's fall.

As it was, Munich seemed to bring Hitler triumph; and he deserved it. The other 'men of Munich' were all, in their way, playing old parts and trying to dodge reality; they dreamt of a pacific Europe without conflicts of power. Hitler took Munich seriously and supposed that the others did so too. If Europe was to stand alone without either Russia or America, then Germany, as the only Great Power in Europe, must dominate it. The Europe of equal and independent states was finished, blighted by the chimneys of the Ruhr. If Munich did not mean this, then it had no sense.

The former 'men of Munich' in this country now parade their conversion: the greater the readiness to conciliate Hitler ten years ago, the more determined the resolve to resist the Russians now. The argument from experience is trivial and was indeed proved wrong by Munich itself. 'Appeasement' of France over the Belgian question proved successful in the eighteen-thirties; therefore it was supposed that it would prove successful with Germany over the Czech question in the nineteen-thirties. What will prove successful with the Russians has to be decided by serious political analysis, not by such twaddling scraps of history. In any case appeasement or resistance was not the fundamental issue of Munich. The fundamental issue of Munich was whether England (or more generally the Western Powers) could work with Russia in order to give all Europe – including Germany – a settled existence. Thus, at bottom, the 'men of Munich' are being true to themselves when they lick their lips over the prospect of a conflict which will expel Russia from Europe and so restore the European circumstances of October 1938.

40

GENERAL GAMELIN:
OR HOW TO LOSE

GAMELIN, a generalissimo now forgotten, began his memoirs, it is said, on 19 May 1940, the day of his dismissal.[1] Even after the events of 1940 it was possible to discuss his military gifts; after his book, controversy is ended. There are limits to absurdity even in a soldier. Gamelin's wisest course would have been to remain silent, or at the very least to insert the events of 1940 in the general course of his memoirs, presenting his failure as the inevitable result of the failures of the preceding twenty years. Instead he repeats the mistake of the advance into Belgium: recognizing his weak points, he seeks to hide them by an impetuous advance – perhaps the enemy (in this case posterity), seeing him charge, will be taken in and will imagine him stronger than he is. His heaviest arm, used therefore in the first chapter, is an order to counter-attack, which he claims to have given at the moment of his dismissal on 19 May – an order which, judged by its timid phrases and the circumstances of the moment, it is difficult to take serious-ly. His most vulnerable spot, tackled therefore in Chapter II, is the declaration which he is alleged to have made on 23 August 1939: 'The army is ready.' By this, it seems, he meant only: 'The army is ready for the order for mobilization and concentra-tion.' Later he admits that even this was not true. As to the ad-vance into Belgium, he falls back on political arguments: 'Could France and England abandon Belgium, which they had always guaranteed? This would admit their helplessness.' In any case, he adds, it was only by advancing into Belgium that a decis-ive battle could be provoked. This he certainly obtained.

The bulk of his first volume is devoted to proving that the French armies of 1940 were well equipped; this only serves to underline Gamelin's failure. He could plead, it is true, that his failure was not unique: the Russians made disastrous blunders in

1. *Servir*. I. Les Armées françaises de 1940. II. Le Prologue du drame. III. La Guerre. By General Gamelin.

the summer of 1941 and the Anglo-American armies were surprised in the Ardennes as late as 1944. Their commanders learnt from their mistakes; Gamelin did not. He still talks in terms of a continuous line of defence and knows no method of resisting an attack other than fighting 'without retreat', a sure recipe for disaster.

The second volume, which runs from his appointment as second-in-command to Weygand in 1930 until the outbreak of war in 1939, is of more value to the historian. Gamelin owed his position to his gifts as a conciliator. He was loyal to the civilian Ministers, never intrigued against them, always tried to make their paths easy. As he complacently remarks on more than one occasion, his motto was '*Servir*'. The motto was hardly the most suitable for the commander-in-chief of a great army, but it made him a good politician and diplomatist. Naturally he never obtained all the credits that he asked; but his book contains no evidence that he would have known how to use them, even if he had obtained them. Since French economic resources were limited, how could they be best employed? Gamelin never envisaged this question; he followed the military principles of an earlier age, when men and not machines decided the lot of war. Besides, even if French resources were used more wisely, could France still hope to undertake a great offensive war? If not, could her international policy be changed from top to bottom? The politicians asked Gamelin the first question; neither they nor he dared ask the second.

Faced with the question of an offensive war, Gamelin was placed in an inescapable dilemma. If he admitted that the French armies could not invade Germany, the politicians would demand what had happened to their money and perhaps refuse further supplies. Gamelin had therefore to answer that the French army could perform its task, if only a little more money was spent on it. But he had to cover himself against the time when the additional money had been spent and the question was asked again. He therefore always added: the French army could act only if France was supported by her allies. Thus France built up a system of alliances in eastern Europe which rested on the assumption that France could attack Germany without British assistance; yet Gamelin would promise an offensive only if England was in alliance with France and if her eastern allies would cooperate against Germany. In short, to make the offensive possible, Gamelin insisted on alliances which would make it unnecessary. But as his sole diplomatic argument was the offensive capacity of the French armies, this landed Gamelin in new contradictions.

His dilemma was clearly shown when the Germans reoccupied the Rhineland on 7 March, 1936. German rearmament had only begun; France had been able to maintain her army without restrictions. French territory was fortified; the Rhineland was open. Yet the only assurance that Gamelin could give was that French soil would not be invaded; he could take a 'pledge' of German territory only on condition of complete mobilization, and he could expel the German forces from the Rhineland only after a long war, in which Belgian and British support would be necessary. Thus, once again, when the politicians asked a military question, Gamelin returned a diplomatist's answer.

So, too, during the Spanish civil war and the crisis of Munich, Gamelin, on paper, was always in favour of resistance; but he always attached conditions – a total war-effort in France and effective British assistance – which the politicians were unable to fulfil. The French army can take the offensive against Germany (therefore the money spent on it has not been wasted); it cannot finish off the job alone (therefore more money must be spent on it and allies must be found). Still, Gamelin regarded war in 1938 as practical and even believed that the Czechs could hold out in Moravia; perhaps he gave this judgement the more confidently because he knew all along that the politicians had decided against war, and he was glad to embarrass them. Gamelin had a much poorer opinion of the Poles than of the Czechs, and disapproved of the guarantee given to Poland in March 1939; it should have been conditional, he says, on the Poles agreeing to the passage of a Russian army across their territory. Yet on 18 May 1939, Gamelin signed a military convention with the Poles, by which he promised that 'France would launch an offensive action with the bulk [*les gros*] of her forces on the fifteenth day after the first day of French mobilization.' His defence of this discreditable transaction is remarkable. It was not, he says, a promise to use the bulk (*le gros*) of the French army against Germany, but only to use the forces (*les gros*) mobilized in the front line. Besides, he says, the military convention was signed by mistake and was never valid. It was meant to be the sequel to a political agreement with the Poles, defining more closely the obligations of the Franco-Polish alliance. Once the military convention was drafted the Poles were satisfied. Bonnet, French Foreign Minister, was also satisfied; for the Poles were now committed to launching an offensive if Germany attacked France, yet he could always plead that France was not committed without the political agreement. Therefore the political agreement was dropped. Even this argument does not excuse Gamelin. The political agreement was, in fact, signed on 1 September 1939, after the outbreak of war; and the impossible obligation of 18 May then came into operation. These are specious excuses. In 1939 the traditional policy of France had collapsed and France behaved like the chicken which continues to run round the farmyard after its head has been cut off.

With his third volume Gamelin at last arrives at the period of the war. Even now he is most concerned to show the correctness of his behaviour. He was never guilty of an intrigue, of a harsh word, of an act of betrayal; alas, he was also never guilty of a victory. Gamelin's personal contribution to the war was 'the offensive for Poland'. The offensive satisfied Gamelin's honour; it did not help the Poles. It was launched on condition that it involved no risk to the French; it therefore involved no risk also to the Germans. Gamelin called off this timorous offensive even before the collapse of Poland and boasts of the skilful withdrawal without casualties – as though the Germans minded whether the French withdrew or not. Gamelin dared not stay in the Saar even when the German armies were still in Poland; yet the following May he flung his armies into Belgium when all the German armies were in the west.

When Poland was conquered, the 'phoney' war began. 'What next?' was the baffling question facing the Allies in the winter of 1939–40, discussed again and again without result. The Allies hoped that Hitler would make his first move in the Balkans; this, they calculated, would give them 'a hundred divisions' (without equipment and untrained for modern war!) Since Hitler failed to 'solve' their problem for them, the Allies looked north and south – to the iron mines of Sweden and the oil wells of Baku. Darlan wished to bomb Baku and to send submarines into the Black Sea. When it was pointed out that this would need Turkish permission and would involve war with Russia, he replied that these were problems which the politicians must solve. But, Gamelin adds, in any case there were no aeroplanes in the Middle East capable of bombing Baku; Darlan was proposing an impossible scheme merely for the pleasure of blaming the politicians. Gamelin himself favoured an expedition to Narvik in order to 'draw out' the Germans. The Allies hoped that if they threatened the Germans at points of less importance, the Germans would overlook the fact that they could threaten the Allies at the point of decisive importance – on the western front.

Yet, far from diverting the Germans, the Allies could not even take precautions against them. The Belgian problem baffled both soldiers and politicians. The Allies knew that they could not defend Belgium effectively unless they entered before the Germans; yet they dared not force an entry by threatening to leave Belgium to her fate. Fearful of German preponderance, they exaggerated the value of swelling their forces with the Belgian divisions, and for the sake of the Belgian army lost their own. Besides, as Gamelin points out, the frontier between Belgium and France was unfortified, so that once the Germans had conquered Belgium they could invade France at their leisure. The French army, equipped for defensive warfare, had no line of defence on which to meet a German attack. Gamelin's 'solution' was to prophesy a war of movement. This was more intelligent than those who relied confidently on a continuous defence; only his intelligence led to no useful conclusion. Gamelin would have made a more effective excuse if he had confessed the mistake that he shared with everyone else – with every French general, with the British, with the Russians, and with every German except Hitler: though he expected that the Germans might overrun Belgium and perhaps part of northern France, he also expected that they would be stopped somewhere. The Belgian campaign had to be faced, like having a tooth out; after it the front would be stabilized, and the Allies could begin to build up their strength for a counter-offensive in 1941 and 1942. Gamelin shared, too, the universal error that the only answer to the Blitzkrieg was to meet it head on. Later, the British in North Africa and then the

Russians stumbled on the true answer much against their will: the only solution was to run very far and very fast.

Gamelin has little to say about the decisive days between 10 May and 19 May, the only days of his life which will give him a place in the history books – or at least a footnote. 10 May ended the period of political manoeuvre, began the conflict of real forces; and there was no place for Gamelin, the political soldier. His book tails off as though he had become a ghost, all life evaporating from him as the guns began to fire. Even now Gamelin is mainly concerned to prove his correct behaviour: he left General Georges freedom of action and so responsibility before posterity. It would have been better to be less correct and more successful; rudeness to General Georges could have been overlooked if it had also defeated the Germans. Can one imagine Foch or Joffre, Gamelin's master, standing by in philosophical detachment while a subordinate general led the French armies to hopeless defeat? Gamelin cannot escape the position of having been in supreme command of the army which suffered the greatest disaster in history since the battle of Jena. Joffre said of the battle of the Marne: 'I do not know if I won it, but I know who would have been responsible if it had been lost.'

41

FRANCE IN DEFEAT

A SPECIAL chair of Vichy history will soon have to be created; nothing short of this will keep up with the flow of books on the defeat of France and the first year of Pétain's Government. Some of the participants have had to defend themselves before French tribunals; others write to satisfy their own consciences; others again – and these the most part – to display their cleverness both then and now. There are two new contributors. Weygand has published his memoirs;[1] these start with his appointment to the Near East on the outbreak of war, and end with his dismissal from the post of Delegate General in North Africa in November 1941. M. Bouthillier, appointed Minister of Finance by Reynaud in June 1940, defends the armistice and then gives his recollections of Vichy until Darlan's arrival in power in January 1941.[2]

So far as Weygand's book deals with the campaign of 1940 this is not new. Two years ago he published an account of his part in this campaign entitled *Conversations with his Son*. It now appears that Weygand has limited conversational powers: all he did was to read to his son selected passages from his memoirs and add anti-British comments. These have now disappeared. Hardly anything remains of his earlier version that Gort ruined the plan for a counter-offensive on 24 May by failing to attack at Arras; and even Churchill's refusal to throw in all the British fighter strength has now become a modest grievance.

Instead Reynaud is blamed for his obstinacy in wishing to withdraw the Government overseas. If he had asked for an armistice sooner, this would have been less severe; moreover a frank discussion with the British would have cleared away the misunderstandings about the French Fleet. There is something in this last point. It seems clear that Reynaud, in his anxiety to avoid the policy of armistice, never explained to his colleagues

1. *Mémoires: Rappelé au Service*. By General Weygand.

2. *Le Drame de Vichy*. I – *Face à l'Ennemi, face à l'Allié*. By Yves Bouthillier.

the British insistence on the fleet being put out of reach of the Germans. This could have been done early in June. On 16 June it was too late; besides, the French were beyond caring. Both Weygand and Bouthillier make out that the British anxiety over the fleet was never communicated adequately to the French Government; they would do better to admit that in June 1940 a continued British resistance never crossed their minds, and that they were satisfied with a theoretical security for French honour. Both, too, now make out that they were taking the courageous line by staying in France. Mandel thought differently. At the decisive Cabinet meeting on 16 June he said, 'The Cabinet is divided. The brave men on one side, the cowards on the other!'

The evidence of what followed the armistice is more novel. The armistice, according to all its advocates, was 'attentism' – a manoeuvre of waiting. But waiting for what? Weygand claims to have been waiting for a chance to renew the war against Germany. First in his short period as Minister of National Defence, then for rather over a year as supreme authority in North Africa, he tried to build up French military strength on the Prussian model of Stein and Scharnhorst after 1807. In December 1940 Churchill, de Gaulle, and Catroux all appealed to Weygand to bring North Africa back into the war. He insists that he rejected their appeals as premature, not because he was opposed to them; in fact, Weygand claims that the Allied landings in November 1942 should be put to his credit.

In practice, waiting to re-enter the war worked out very much like waiting for others to win it – the policy of the true men of Vichy. M. Bouthillier is their representative. It suits him now to say nothing of his dreams for a 'national revolution', which other accounts attribute to him in 1940; he was, he claims, simply concerned to give France time to breathe, and meanwhile to see what would happen. More honest than Weygand, he writes of Pétain, 'At bottom his attitude to the Germans was the same as towards the English'; in other words, he waited for them to wear each other out, and imagined an impossible outcome, when a neutral France would hold the balance between the exhausted combatants.

Hence French policy after the armistice swung pendulum-like, hoping never to tip over. The armistice was a swing towards Germany. Then came Hitler's demand of 15 July for the use of the French bases in North Africa; this was refused – a swing towards England. Pétain and his associates had the illusion that they were recovering their independence; the height of this illusion was the defence of Dakar against de Gaulle and the British in September. But once again the pendulum threatened to swing too much in Germany's favour. Laval, though also an 'attentiste', waited for a German victory; and in October 1940 grew tired of waiting. He wished to commit France to the side of Germany before it was too late.

Thus, according to M. Bouthillier, there were two policies of 'Montoire' – Laval's policy of usurping Italy's place as the principal ally of Germany and Pétain's policy of continuing to balance. M. Bouthillier does not exaggerate Pétain's achievement; he admits that Franco's refusal to enter the war was the more decisive act. On the other hand, he exaggerates, as Weygand does too, the extent of Pétain's reconciliation with England in the London mission of Professor Rougier – an affair always absurdly inflated in Vichy writings. Throughout November 1940 Laval pushed ever harder on Germany's side. He made repeated concessions in return for fine words. Early in December Bouthillier revolted, won over his colleagues, and then persuaded Pétain to break with Laval. The details of this intrigue are the most important part of his book. Laval was dismissed on 13 December, and Pétain withstood the German storm. Flandin was called in – a swing towards England – and the Germans seemed to acquiesce in his nomination. But in January 1941, Pétain characteristically swung again. He had an interview with Laval; and Flandin, in his effort to discredit Laval, published a communiqué against him which instead brought about his own fall. Once more policy swung to Germany, though under Darlan's direction. The peak of this swing was Darlan's proposal of June 1941 (described by Weygand) to allow the Axis Powers to use Dakar and Bizerta. This proposal was defeated by Weygand – the last swing towards England. In November 1941 Weygand was dismissed on German orders; in March 1942 Laval returned to power. Instead of gaining freedom of manoeuvre, France was losing it, and lost it altogether in November 1942. The 'men of Vichy' were not as clever

as they thought; still, in the first year after defeat France had no
resource except cleverness. The great blunder of Vichy was to fail
to understand when it had outlived its usefulness.

42

DE GAULLE:
TRIUMPH OF A LEGEND

THE career of General de Gaulle is without parallel in modern times. When he left France in 1940 he had had no political experience and only a few weeks' military experience in a minor command. Four years later this general who had never conducted a battle and politician who had never presented himself at an election returned as the undisputed master of France, ranking with Clemenceau and almost with Napoleon himself. Instead of starting as a hero and becoming a legend, General de Gaulle started as a legend and became a hero on the way. His qualities were neither tested in battle nor challenged in debate. Posterity may perhaps ponder whether any reality lay behind the legend or whether General de Gaulle was simply a creature of air, created by the only medium in which he could have contact with the people of France. Yet there is an answer to these doubts. Other Frenchmen repudiated the surrender of 1940; only de Gaulle rose to the level of the historic moment, and only de Gaulle maintained without failing a clairvoyant grasp of French feeling.

The doubts spring in part from lack of evidence or, worse, from evidence of the wrong kind. Apart from de Gaulle's own speeches, the only Gaullist testimony has been from Colonel Passy; and this was primarily concerned to tell the story of the secret service which Passy organized. On the other side, almost every supporter of Vichy, great or small, has by now told his story; and every trivial incident among Pétain's entourage has been analyzed in as great detail as one of Napoleon's campaigns. The opponents of Pétain who have spoken have also been for the most part opponents of de Gaulle; indeed they have usually been keener to make a case against de Gaulle than against Vichy. General Catroux's memoirs, as one would expect, are perfectly loyal to de Gaulle; but, as one would also expect from that man of supreme tact, they are skilfully designed so as not to serve the legend. Now at last we have a full expression of the legend in historical form. M. Jacques

Soustelle was for long General de Gaulle's Commissar of Information during the war; and he is now secretary-general of the
Gaullist movement. For such an experienced propagandist his
two volumes betray a curious uncertainty of aim.[1] Personal re-
miniscence is mixed with general narrative; yet these episodes are
too selective to provide a full history of the Free French movement throughout the war. Again, it is difficult to suppose that
these volumes have not been written with one eye on political
effect in the present; yet equally difficult to grasp what this political effect was intended to be.

If the two volumes had sub-titles, the first would be called 'The
making of a Legend', and the second 'Its Victory'. When de
Gaulle appealed for the continuance of the war on 18 June 1940,
he established himself for good and all as the first of the resisters;
this was his great historic act. But he had expected a very different
response – the rallying, in fact, of all the French Empire overseas.
Instead he was followed only by Equatorial Africa. This changed
at once the character of the movement. If the French pro-consuls
had all proclaimed their independence of Vichy, de Gaulle could
never have achieved predominance. As it was, he became undisputed leader in a movement composed of junior officers and
junior administrators. The successes of Fighting France in 1940
came from the personal initiative of a few adventurous men; this
was the spirit of individual daring which had created the French
colonial empire in the later nineteenth century. These adventurers
could succeed where individual character and the single voice
could still be effective. Their efforts failed where, as in Dakar,
North Africa, or Syria, they ran against a solid structure of
government and a hierarchy of authority. Though de Gaulle's
movement in London tried to create an impression of formality,
it could not rank truly as an exiled Government; it was an association of individuals, displaying to the full the individual spirit of
the French revolution.

Apart from the winning of Equatorial Africa, Gaullism in its
early days had one concrete achievement – the creation of a system of information from occupied France. It is this success which

1. *Envers et Contre Tous.* Souvenirs et documents de la France Libre
(1940–44). I. *De Londres à Alger, 1940–42*: II. *D'Alger à Paris, 1942–44.*
By Jacques Soustelle.

Colonel Passy has described at length; and it is therefore passed
over in summary by M. Soustelle. In his account, the war against
the Germans takes second place; the real struggle appears rather
against the supporters of Vichy and almost as much against the
allies of Free France. M. Soustelle's harshest words are reserved
for the Attentistes, those who tried to keep France above the
battle, rather than for the collaborators, who could be safely left
to discredit themselves. This is indeed an essential part of the
story. Though de Gaulle often insisted on the contribution of his
movement to the war against Germany, his real preoccupation
was with the revival of French spirit. As he said to Mr Churchill
on 10 June 1942, in the course of a dispute over Madagascar:
'The only problem is to encourage the will to resistance of the
French people and to revive their will to wage war. This aim
will not be achieved by snubbing those French who are fighting.'
For de Gaulle and his followers the greatest evil was to admit
the patriotism of those who were trying to keep France neutral
or to leave a way open by which they might return to the allied
side.

This could not be the outlook of the great Powers who were
engaged in the actual war. They had to think of the present; de
Gaulle was relieved of the present by Pétain, and could concentrate on the future. De Gaulle was accepted by the British Government as the sole representative of France only until the failure at
Dakar; thereafter he had to justify his claims by solid achievement and was often unable to do so. The attitude of the American
Government was even more critical. In view of its own neutrality
it could not condemn Vichy whole-heartedly; and besides, there
was in Roosevelt's scepticism an element of almost personal
jealousy not yet fully explained. As M. Soustelle admits, Mr
Churchill was the most sympathetic of allied statesmen; yet, to
moderate American doubts, he had to press doubts of his own. In
September 1942 he said to de Gaulle: 'After all, are you France?
There may be other parties in France who may be summoned, in
the course of events, to occupy a more important place than today.' De Gaulle replied 'If I do not represent France, why discuss
with me?' This interchange summarized the essential question.
De Gaulle was not a party leader; he was not a general in command of great armies; apart from a handful of colonies without

industrial resources he had no material basis. Either he represented France or he was nothing.

In November 1942, when M. Soustelle's first volume ends, de Gaulle seemed to be nothing. French North Africa was liberated without his assistance, even without his being informed; in fact, one might almost say that it was liberated against him. De Gaulle's only contribution, described by M. Soustelle in moving terms, was to address a crowded meeting at the Albert Hall. M. Soustelle's second volume is less inspiring, but more revealing. It is the story of how the man of mythical reputation took on flesh, grasped at real power, and prepared the way for his triumph in France. The title of the volume, as of the first, is misleading. In November 1942, de Gaulle was still in London, not in Algiers; and the core of the second volume is concerned with how he got to Algiers, not with how he left Algiers for Paris. Once de Gaulle became chairman of a governing committee in Algiers, the legend was officially recognized; and even those who had been most opposed to him would seek its shelter. Yet the North African campaign, far from being designed to benefit de Gaulle, was expected by Roosevelt to ruin him; and Mr Churchill said to de Gaulle: 'I do not want to abandon you. But if I have to choose between Roosevelt and you, I shall choose Roosevelt.' M. Soustelle does not grasp the deep implications of that remark. He seriously argues that Mr Churchill wanted to draw the Americans into North Africa in order to rescue the British army in Egypt from certain defeat at the hands of Rommel – an argument unworthy of a man of his intelligence. His explanation of Roosevelt is even more trivial: he was a 'patrician', excited by his unexpected elevation to the position of ruler of the greatest empire that the world had ever known; he was set on world-supremacy for himself and could brook no rival, only those who were subservient. Hence he could tolerate Mr Churchill, but not General de Gaulle. These wild guesses reveal the central weakness of all Gaullists: themselves the expression of an idea, they exaggerated the importance of intellectual concepts in others and failed to understand the material considerations which are usually decisive, especially in war.

M. Soustelle can explain de Gaulle's success in Algiers only as the victory of a superior idea. And in a sense he is right. De

Gaulle triumphed not so much from his own strength as from the insufficiency of his rivals. He had an idea without material resources; they had not even an idea. Darlan and Giraud represented nothing in themselves; they were merely negation – they were not de Gaulle. Yet most of M. Soustelle's second volume is concerned with them, rather than with his own hero. De Gaulle simply waited in London, first for Darlan to be assassinated, then for Giraud to discredit himself by his political clumsiness; neither de Gaulle nor his supporters contributed anything to either event. Of course M. Soustelle has to make out that there was a strong Gaullist movement in North Africa, only waiting to be roused into enthusiasm. This is to fly in the face of the evidence. North Africa would have been administered for the allies, and French forces would have contributed to the Tunisian and Italian campaigns just as effectively if de Gaulle had never existed. The truth lies elsewhere. De Gaulle succeeded because, in politics as in other things, nature abhors a vacuum. Both Darlan and Giraud, in their different ways, acquiesced in Roosevelt's judgement. De Gaulle alone denied it; and since even the Americans could not treat French territory as ownerless desert, they had ultimately to accept the only man who had the self-confidence to speak for France.

There is another aspect of events which M. Soustelle keeps in the background. De Gaulle was certainly carried to Algiers by his superiority as a man with an idea over the men who had none. But once he and Giraud became uneasy partners the experienced talent for political manoeuvre and even for intrigue which the Gaullists had developed in London was turned to good account. Giraud was undoubtedly stupid; but he would probably not have behaved quite so stupidly if there had not been a body of clever men eager to exploit his stupidity. Indeed, this part – and it is a long part – of M. Soustelle's book suggests nothing so much as the narration by a spider of the extraordinary and unexpected accidents by which a fly fell into its web. Yet even in Algiers the political struggle was artificial. M. Soustelle refers constantly to French public opinion, as expressed in the feeling in Algiers; but the connexion was remote. Here indeed one can discover the basic flaw which was to lead to de Gaulle's failure after the war. M. Soustelle argues that all the pre-war parties had been discredited; and he complains that British and American doubts compelled de Gaulle to justify his position by accepting support from the political parties and thus resurrected what should have remained dead. The English reader is bewildered by this train of thought. He is ready to acquit de Gaulle of being a Fascist or even of having predominantly Fascist supporters; M. Soustelle himself is the proof of the contrary. De Gaulle was overwhelmingly sincere when he promised to restore French democracy and the liberties of the French people. But how can you have democracies without political parties? The contemporary answer stares us in the face: democracies without parties become 'people's democracies', and their character is now well known.

This point goes far to explain a theme which M. Soustelle constantly approaches without fully grasping: de Gaulle's relations with the French Communists. In his latter-day anxiety to present de Gaulle as the principal barrier against Communism M. Soustelle tries to claim that the Communists supported Giraud. And so, with their usual unscrupulous manoeuvres for power, they did. But they also supported de Gaulle. Indeed, they might almost claim to have created him as the personification of the French resistance. It is true that, meaning to create an instrument, they created a rival. If de Gaulle had not existed, the Communists might have seized power in France in the autumn of 1944. This does not alter the fact that de Gaulle succeeded against the Communists by being like them, not by being different. He had the same readiness to dictate in the name of France; the same hostility to political parties and even to political scruples; the same fallacious promise of something untarnished with the corruptions and failures of the past. Like the Communists, he tried to make politics heroic and dramatic; as with the Communists, this often meant deliberately ignoring the material factors on which he relied. The essential difference between de Gaulle and the Communists does not appear in this book. Both talked of a temporary dictatorship; he kept his word.

De Gaulle's aim was to restore France to the position of an independent great Power. Though anti-German in the circumstances of 1940, he was equally anti-American, anti-Russian and even anti-British. He thought of France as still the greatest Power in the world, materially as well as intellectually. This flew in the face of facts. Not merely the material facts of the dwindling French resources compared with those of others; it defied still more the spiritual fact that the French people had wearied of greatness. The despised parties, with their corruption and sectarian manoeuvres, offered the French people what they desired. De Gaulle believed that the French people could be again illuminated into grandeur; he created his legend for their sake, not for his own. He was indeed narrow, unyielding, impatient of human weakness; yet with all this, more understanding than his supporters made him out. In spite of the failures and even blunders which followed the liberation of France, it is impossible to review the record of de Gaulle's achievement during the war without admitting that he earned his fame; indeed he deserved well of the Republic.

43

STUMBLING INTO WAR

BRITISH policy reached its moment of decision in September 1939. Hence our interest is in the road which led from Munich to Danzig. But for the Americans these were still far-off events which concerned them little. Even 'the phoney war' might almost have been fought on another planet. Messrs Langer and Gleason called their previous volume on American foreign policy *The Challenge to Isolation*; and though the destroyers-for-bases deal, with which the volume ended, implied that isolation was over, America's entry into the Second World War was still more than a year away. Their new volume[1] covers this period, when the United States stumbled into war, and so into world power.

They have used all the most secret papers, including the private notes of Mr Morgenthau, Mr Stimson, and President Roosevelt himself; and they repeat the claim that their book 'is in no sense a work of official or even semi-official history'. Certainly they often pass harsh verdicts on the muddle of American policy. But their independence is a little formal. Both writers, according to the preface, returned to government service in 1950; and it must have involved complicated feats of personal adjustment to decide when they were acting as independent historians and when as government servants. Even with its reserve their book establishes itself at once as the leading authority for the period.

In September 1940 President Roosevelt and his advisers still doubted whether Great Britain would hold out. Mr Hull remarked: 'This whole darn thing is hanging in the balance.' They anticipated having to fight alone against both Germany and Japan, and were concerned only to buy time. The result was words without action. Messrs Langer and Gleason write scathingly at one point: 'When it came to a showdown the Government invariably fell back

1. *The Undeclared War, 1940–41.* By William L. Langer and S. Everett Gleason.

on words and demonstrations.' Again, 'The Greeks derived no material benefit from the sympathy and generous impulse of the President and the American people'. And they quote the Chinese saying, 'There is much noise on the stairs, but no one enters the room.'

The worst moment came in the autumn during the Presidential election campaign, when Roosevelt was driven to pander to the voters' belief that it was easy 'simultaneously to advocate increased aid to Britain and avoidance of war'. Yet this was not conscious deception on Roosevelt's part. It seems clear that even he thought the two could be reconciled. Later, in May 1941, Hopkins surmised: 'The President is loath to get into this war.' There was, of course, the complication that while Roosevelt wished to defeat Hitler and was reluctant to fight Japan, Hitler refused to be provoked and the Japanese pushed relentlessly forward.

Hitler held the initiative even when he had failed to invade Great Britain. The decisive check came perhaps in the late autumn, when he failed to attack Gibraltar. Or perhaps our authors (one of them an old advocate of America's Vichy policy) exaggerated the importance of this. British and American policy remained curiously out of step. The Americans wished to conciliate Pétain and were contemptuous of Franco. The British had no faith in Vichy and much in Franco's obstinacy.

Similarly the two governments had difficulty in co-ordinating their policy towards Soviet Russia. In October 1940 the British offered Stalin fulsome terms in exchange for a genuine neutrality; the State Department bargained more ruthlessly. But in the spring of 1941 the Americans tried to buy Stalin with machine-tools, and the Foreign Office complained of their softness. Even when Hitler invaded Russia there was no clear agreement. The State Department regretted Winston Churchill's eagerness for a Russian alliance until its reserves were swept aside by Roosevelt, who always had more faith in Russia than his advisers. The present authors destroy the legend that Great Britain and the United States missed the chance of imposing rigorous terms on Soviet Russia – such as the freeing of the Baltic States – in exchange for their alliance. On the contrary, they had the greatest difficulty in evading Stalin's demand that they should recognize the Curzon (or Molotov-Ribbentrop) Line and all his conquests of 1940 before he would condescend to make an alliance with them. With the German armies at the gates of Moscow this toughness had a certain grandeur.

Lend-Lease was, as our authors show, the decisive commitment. Decisive not only for the United States but also for Great Britain, who therewith surrendered her sovereign independence. The authors complain that the American people were ready at this point to go faster than Roosevelt; but they would not actually go to war. Even the Atlantic Charter did not move them. The Charter was incidentally a by-product of the Atlantic meeting. The real purpose of the meeting was to co-ordinate supplies and naval strategy. But the Americans had been alarmed by Keynes's prophecy that 'the post-war world economic structure could only be one of closed economics'. They wished to tie Great Britain down to a liberal economic system, not to make a declaration of principles against Hitler. Roosevelt had a solution of his own for the post-war world. Everyone should be disarmed except the United States and, grudgingly enough, Great Britain; then plebiscites should be held almost everywhere – even in Allied countries – under Anglo-American supervision. It is difficult to see how the Soviet Union fitted into this picture. Presumably it was to be exhausted by the war against Hitler.

Roosevelt and his advisers wished to avoid war against Japan but not at the price of surrender. Their aim was peace in the Far East, but on America's terms – an impossible contradiction. Our authors destroy the claim that there was any lost opportunity for peace with Japan in the summer of 1941. The Japanese would not have settled for anything less than permanent domination of China. Yet the American Government did not consciously man-oeuvre Japan into war. The Americans believed almost till the last moment that Japan would give way. And they feared that a Japanese attack, if it came, would be directed solely against Singapore and the Dutch East Indies. Then what would be the reaction of American public opinion? An attack on American territory 'seemed senseless'. Roosevelt and his advisers forgot Pearl Harbor. 'This tragic oversight may be a classic instance of human frailty, but it provides no evidence whatsoever to support

the thesis that the President or any other responsible American
official courted a Japanese attack on the Pearl Harbor base in
order to enable them to lead the country into the European war
by the Pacific back door.'

44

MAN OF AN IDEA

ONE of Frank Horrabin's illustrations for Wells's *Outline of History* is called Tribal Gods of the Nineteenth Century, Symbols for which men would die. There they stand in a row: John Bull in masculine isolation and four females classically draped – Britannia, la France, Germania, Kathleen na Houlihan. Every statesman invokes them; some take them seriously. But after the ringing phrases and the emotional dedication, statesmen have to turn to practical affairs. Bismarck has to manufacture his majority in the Reichstag; Churchill must consider the figures of aircraft production; Clemenceau reckons how long it will take for the American transports to cross the Atlantic. Logistics determined the hard battering of two world wars. The Tribal Gods were pushed into the wings. Yet they, too, represented a reality. Without them the conflicts would have been senseless, indeed could never have been kept going. The Tribal Gods will reward a worshipper if he is single-minded enough. General de Gaulle is the proof of it. That mystical symbol, France, made him a world figure; and in return he brought abstract France to life, if only for a brief period.

His book[1] is called *War Memoirs*; but the Second World War in the ordinary sense takes a small place in it. The pressing question for de Gaulle was how to restore France to greatness, not how to defeat the Germans. One can understand the impatience of the British, and the contempt of the American Government. Pressed for men, harassed by shipping losses, they had no time to conduct the war according to the protocol of an imaginary French sovereignty. Roosevelt could have borrowed Stalin's phrase about the Pope and have asked it of de Gaulle with more devastating effect: 'how many divisions has he?' The men of Vichy had the same standards. Weygand has recently put the case

1. *War Memoirs*. By Charles de Gaulle. Vol. I. *The Call to Honour, 1940–42.*

for them in a plaintive little book.[1] They were trying to maintain French administration and to rebuild the fragments of an army. De Gaulle's heroics, they thought, would only bring new disasters on France. Weygand, Churchill and Roosevelt sent up a common chorus: let de Gaulle help against the Germans with his few followers and neglect political claims. This refrain did not shake de Gaulle. The defeat of Germany would be meaningless for him unless France was present on the day of victory in all her greatness. And he achieved the miracle. France was restored as a Great Power in 1945 thanks to de Gaulle alone, though whether to her advantage or anyone else's is still an open question.

The note is struck firmly in the first paragraph: 'France cannot be France without greatness.' This sets the tone of the book as effectively as Proust's announcement that he used to go to bed early. Most memoirs serve one of two purposes. Either they give a picture of the man, or they record the events in which he took part. Not so the memoirs of General de Gaulle. The human being behind the stern, unbending front never emerges for a moment either in the text or in the photographs. In one of these, indeed, the general is smiling. But it is a political smile: he is shaking hands with a member of the Home Guard. The human being in de Gaulle was of no account, least of all to himself. Napoleon and Trotsky wrote of themselves in the third person in order to assert their individualities more dramatically. The 'I' of de Gaulle is an equally effective disguise, but in the opposite sense. Apart from France he did not exist, and would not wish to exist. He said so himself in argument with Churchill: 'If I do not represent France, why speak to me?' This was the secret of his success, as of his later failure. He could be reduced to nothing; therefore he was relentless in demanding all. Other political leaders could be cajoled or threatened; they might see practical advantages or recognize practical dangers. De Gaulle knew only one rule of conduct: 'limited and alone though I was, and precisely because I was so, I had to climb to the heights and then never come down'.

He withdrew not only from humanity but from events. His

1. *En lisant les mémoires de guerre du Général de Gaulle.* By General Weygand.

book does little to illuminate the course of the war; and even when the lights are turned on, they produce unusual effects. Not that de Gaulle's memoirs are untrue or misleading. But they are not about the Second World War, as it was experienced by millions of men, high and low, in every belligerent country. They are not even about de Gaulle, as others experienced him. Consider the first two chapters which cover the period until the appointment of Pétain as Prime Minister on 16 June 1940. They show de Gaulle seeking to inspire resolution in Reynaud, proposing offensive manoeuvres to Weygand, weighing up Huntziger as a possible commander-in-chief, and finally leaving Bordeaux in calm resolution. 'There was nothing romantic or difficult about the departure.' Others failed to notice the hero in the making. There are innumerable French memoirs on the period before the armistice; de Gaulle's are the only ones to suggest that he played a serious part. Weygand has remarked, probably truly, that he himself was too preoccupied to listen to strategical rhapsodies from a junior general. Sir Edward Spears has drawn a very different picture of the departure: de Gaulle sheltering in the dark behind a pillar, making bogus appointments to conceal his plans for departure, and finally being pulled into the aeroplane as it left the ground. No doubt things happened much like that, though later estrangement may have sharpened a line or two. Yet the historical truth is here a matter of feeling, not of events. Once de Gaulle had become France, he had to hold his head high from the beginning. He became France as he crossed the Channel; and he has never cast himself since for any other part.

Like most legends, the legend of de Gaulle presents itself as all of a piece. The leader arrives in London; he assembles a few devoted followers; and this force continues to grow until, at the climax of this volume, the Fighting French cover themselves with glory at the battle of Bir Hakeim. The real story seems to have been more varied, though equally heroic. When de Gaulle first came to London, he did not realize that he would be alone. He supposed that the colonial governors would continue their resistance; and his own task was to be the representative of France in London only in the sense of being her ambassador. The governors obeyed the orders of Vichy with one outstanding exception. Even then de Gaulle thought that his isolation would be temporary. He anticipated that all Africa would turn against Vichy, despite the governors. Instead the expedition to Dakar ended in failure. This was the real turning-point of de Gaulle's career. Not only was he alone. His warmest adherents, Churchill and Spears, doubted his effectiveness. Spears showed reports from London that 'de Gaulle, in despair, abandoned by his partisans, dropped by the British into the bargain, would renounce all activity'. De Gaulle adds:

I, in my narrow cabin, in a harbour crushed by the heat, was completing my education in what the reactions of fear could be, both among adversaries taking revenge for having felt it and among allies suddenly alarmed by a set-back.

He did not weaken. From this moment he set out to embody 'the image of a France indomitable in the midst of her trials'. This was 'to dictate my bearing and to impose upon my personality an attitude I could never again change'.

Until Dakar, de Gaulle and the British Government both assumed that his movement would soon bring large concrete advantage to the allied cause. After Dakar, de Gaulle had few assets, and these were more or less stable. Equatorial Africa sent colonial troops which performed miracles of valour at Bir Hakeim; France itself provided some centres of intelligence, though hardly a resistance. De Gaulle was left willy-nilly to fight a different war, the war against the allies; and there is nothing to suggest that he fought it with any reluctance. Roughly half the present volume deals with this absorbing struggle. No doubt something real and important was at stake, if only for de Gaulle. Yet in retrospect it provides material for comedy. There was first the struggle for followers. The British Intelligence Services were eager to kidnap every fresh arrival from France, and would assert cheerfully that de Gaulle and the British were the same thing. In the dark winter blitz of 1940–41 British and French agents dodged and manoeuvred for 'bodies' as mercantilist powers used to dispute over skilled craftsmen. Then, on a higher level of farce, comes the war over Admiral Muselier. He was accused of treachery on the basis of forgeries so crude that only M.I.5 could have been taken in by them; released after a crisis of international magnitude; then became a rebel against de

Gaulle; and was finally confined by the British on de Gaulle's request. It must have been puzzling for Churchill to decide whether de Gaulle was asking to have a Free Frenchman released or imprisoned.

This was small beer compared to the conflict over Syria. There must be something in the Near East which deprives men of their common sense. How otherwise explain the long-standing British craze for the Arabs, even at their Egyptian stage of decay? Why should England and France have quarrelled over Syria even as allies, ever since the Crusades? Everyone behaved badly in the Syrian affair. Dentz, the Vichy general, outdid his government in collaborating with the Germans; the British authorities first neglected Syria and then blamed de Gaulle for the consequences of their own mistakes; and de Gaulle claimed to liberate Syria, though it turned out to be impossible for him to do so. The story has all the futility which makes men dismiss diplomatic history as trivial. It had important personal consequences, however. De Gaulle and Spears were permanently estranged; as were many British and French officials in the Middle East. But, of course, it amounted to little in the long run. Both Great Britain and France have been pushed out of the Arab countries; and the events in Syria merely determined the order of their going.

There was a similar dispute when the British acted in Madagascar without de Gaulle's approval; and a tremendous row with Washington when he ordered Muselier to liberate the islands of St Pierre and Miquelon solely because the American Government had forbidden the operation. De Gaulle was indeed relentless in asserting himself. Did the British commander in the Middle East plead that he had no transport with which to move French troops from Syria to the North African battlefield? Within twenty-four hours de Gaulle had approached the Soviet Ambassador in London and offered to send a French army to Russia. The same superb assurance served de Gaulle well with the Communists. He makes out now that he welcomed them in order that France should be for once united. Did he not also welcome their assistance against the British and American Governments? The Communists no doubt thought that they had captured him. They were wrong: he had captured them and will go down in history as the only man who has ever outwitted Communists on their own ground.

The whole makes a strange story, a triumph of the human will over material circumstances. Was there any sense, any use in it? So far as winning the war goes, not much; nor can it be said that present-day France has profited from the Gaullist epic. De Gaulle was the servant of an idea, not a statesman, still less a politician. He appealed to others of the same kind – novelists, anthropologists, perhaps most of all to foreigners who loved France from afar. The France he worshipped meant little to the Frenchmen who lived there. Still, an individual defying the world and succeeding in his defiance, however briefly, will always inspire admiration until the rule of the masses submerges us. The story of de Gaulle has, maybe, little to do with the Second World War, but it is magnificent all the same.

45

AMERICA'S WAR

To judge by the memoirs, every American in high place was fighting a different war. Cordell Hull was concerned to restore a vanished world of Free Trade; Harry Hopkins tried to make the New Deal universal; Stimson wanted to renew the victory of the First World War. Admiral Leahy was representative of those Americans who distrusted their allies as much as they disliked the Germans. In his own words:[1]

> Our problem in Washington would not have been difficult if we had not been required to distribute our men, ships, and supplies to support allies who, with the exception of Russia, seemed incapable of surviving without assistance.

His speciality was denigration, and perhaps Roosevelt employed him as personal Chief of Staff so that his ungenerous scepticism should balance the enthusiasm of others. He certainly fulfilled expectations. Thus, of the French Army: 'To me, the "magnificent French Army" was only pretty fast on its feet. It almost got away – by running.' Another example: when Admiral Cunningham left Washington to assume command in the Mediterranean in October 1942: 'Lady Cunningham did not seem to be very happy at the prospect of her husband's going back to such a dangerous spot.' He draws repeated attention to de Gaulle's not being 'anywhere near the battlefield' (the Admiral himself did not hear many shots fired in anger) and describes him as suffering 'from a severe over-supply of national pride'.

Leahy extended his scepticism to the atomic bomb. Four days before Hiroshima Leahy said to King George VI: 'I do not think it will be as effective as is expected. It sounds like a professor's dream to me!' The King did not agree.

As Chief of Staff to the President, Leahy presided over the American Joint Chiefs of Staff and also took a leading part in the Combined Chiefs of Staff with the British. No doubt Leahy's

1. Admiral Leahy, *I Was There.*

real function was to act as connecting link with Roosevelt; still, his drops of acid must have affected the flavour of Allied co-operation. For Leahy, in spite of his pose as a professional sailor, was a political officer, advising the most important politician in the world. His book is a selection from the notes he made at the time for his conversations with Roosevelt; though most of them are tedious when not unreadable, they give a striking impression of the confused years when America was first growing up to her responsibilities as a Great Power.

To judge by Leahy's account, American strategy was decided by picking out objectives with the butt-end of a cigar. So rival generals and admirals would prod at maps of the Pacific; so too France presented itself as the obvious theatre for an invasion of Europe. The Mediterranean and Balkan alternatives seem never to have been weighed strategically; the American rejection of it was political – that the British were trying to exploit American forces 'to acquire for the Empire post-war advantages in the Balkan States'.

Distrust of Great Britain is a constant theme. In 1942 Leahy wrote: 'A large segment of the British Government regarded the Mediterranean as a vital and legitimate British preserve and were most unhappy to see the United States taking the leading role in that area.' Later Leahy thought America had been outsmarted by the British by being drawn into the Mediterranean at all. It is not surprising that Leahy was the most fervent advocate of ending Lend-Lease immediately hostilities ceased. After a conversation with Winant Leahy noted:

The Britons were using all of their energies to safeguard those things considered necessary for the preservation of the British Empire. We Americans were devoting our efforts exclusively to destroying the Germans, with not too much thought about the future.

Almost his final word on Churchill was: 'He was basically more concerned over preserving England's position in Europe than in preserving peace.' Though Roosevelt's attitude was less grudging, he, too, disliked the British Empire. At Yalta he intended to propose that Hong-Kong be returned to China and was only deterred by the Russian demand for Dairen. Leahy leant over to Roosevelt and said: 'Mr President, you are going to lose out on

Hong-Kong if you agree to give the Russians half of Dairen.' Roosevelt shook his head in resignation and said: 'Well, Bill, I can't help it.'

The policy of the Russians during and immediately after the war becomes much clearer when it is borne in mind that they received two constant impressions from the Americans – that America was incurably opposed to the continuance of the British Empire and that American forces would be withdrawn from Europe at latest within two years of the ending of hostilities. A partition of the world between 'the only two major Powers remaining in the world', as Leahy called them, seemed the logical conclusion, especially when the Americans were pressing urgently for Russian help in the Far East. The Russian blunder was to suppose that the Americans were as logical as themselves. But American policy rested on the assumption that Russia, like America, was fundamentally isolationist and non-aggressive. Roosevelt wrote to Leahy on 26 June 1941: 'I do not think we need worry about any possibility of Russian domination', and this remained his unshakeable conviction until after Yalta.

The Russians, on their side, regarded Roosevelt's insistence on free elections in Poland as an interference in their 'sphere' and could explain it only as an attempt to revive the *cordon sanitaire*, Neither side understood the other. If the Americans would not divide the world with the Russians, the only alternative would have been to impose a free Eastern Europe on the Russians in 1945 by superior force. This was also too logical for the Americans. They hoped vaguely for a Russian change of heart and so, as Leahy shows, drifted into the 'cold war'. This was not an issue of power. It was a clash between two fundamental conceptions of the world – the one logical and ruthless, the other benevolent and muddled and undefined.

Three anecdotes from Leahy illustrate the character of the heads of 'the only two major Powers'. At Teheran Churchill objected to Stalin's list of 50,000 German officers who should be brought to trial and spoke eloquently 'for maintenance of the traditional concept of justice'. 'Roosevelt suggested that if 50,000 German officers were too many to be tried, why not compromise on a smaller number, such as 49,000?' At Potsdam Churchill defended the rights of the Catholics in Poland. 'Stalin reflected a moment, stroking his moustache, and then asked the Prime Minister in a hard, even tone, "How many divisions has the Pope?" ' On the way back from Potsdam news came of the atomic bomb at Hiroshima. 'Truman was excited over the news and said, "This is the greatest thing in history".' On such men depend the destinies of mankind.

46

THE TWILIGHT OF THE GOD

THE writing of contemporary history is often dismissed as an impossibility. We stand too near the events that we seek to record and are too deeply involved in them to make a detached judgement. Moreover, men in public affairs know how to conceal their springs of action and appear to the world made up like any film star. Yet the trained historian should be able to break through this crust to the reality beneath. Many of the actors are still living; and the historian has some chance of discovering the answers, if only he can devise the right questions – more chance, it would seem, than if he ransacks a casual heap of documents. Given the historical temperament, the contemporary world can yield results as good as any other. Time does not always bring detachment; and a historian might well feel himself more engaged in the controversies of Luther than in those of Hitler. Dislike and contempt may be dangerous if they dominate the historian's mind. Yet the example of Gibbon is there to show that they need be no barrier to a work of genius.

All the same, the British intelligence officer who was given the task in September 1945 of discovering the circumstances of Hitler's death could not have been expected to produce a masterpiece. The inquiry might well have been barren. The witnesses, even if found, might have had little to tell. Moreover, intelligence reports, however dramatic their evidence, do not usually produce a dramatic story, as other attempts to describe Hitler's death bear witness. Our times are packed with tremendous themes which have never been exploited. The great Renaissance tragedy of Mussolini's end, for instance, remains unwritten. Hitler's fate, too, might never have got beyond the intelligence files. But the intelligence officer happened to be Mr Trevor-Roper, an Oxford historian who had already proved his merit in a biography of Archbishop Laud; and what was more important, a man of confident judgement, anxious – as every great historian must be – to reach a wide audience and capable of giving events their true historical setting. The British Intelligence Service got more than they bargained for. Mr Trevor-Roper certainly accounted for every detail in Hitler's last days; but he also produced, almost by accident, the wisest and most profound analysis of the third Reich and so implicitly of German civilization.

His book is a model judged simply as a work of detection. In fact it eclipses the fictional efforts in this vein which are said to be the favourite reading of intellectuals. Every statement is grounded on fact; and a long introduction to the second edition showed how these facts had been arrived at. The dank gloom of Hitler's bunker might have been expected to remain for ever obscure; the last political writhings of the Nazi leaders hopelessly entangled. Thanks to Mr Trevor-Roper, the opposite is the case. Few stories in history are known more accurately or more fully. We can follow Hitler's every act until the 180 litres of petrol consumed him; and we understand the manoeuvres of Himmler, Goering and Bormann more clearly than those of most democratic leaders. There is one flaw to prove that Mr Trevor-Roper is human. He has not accounted for Hitler's ashes or bones. He guessed that they had passed into the possession of Artur Axmann, the Nazi youth-leader. But his guess came too late. Axmann was in American hands; and their intelligence officers, tardily jealous of Mr Trevor-Roper's success, would not allow further questioning. Axmann vanished – perhaps with the bones, perhaps without them. For, as Mr Trevor-Roper suggests, Hitler's remains may have disappeared in the general ruin of the Chancellery garden. Apart from this, no mystery remains. Even if the participants who fell into Russian hands are still alive, they would have nothing new to tell. We shall never know for certain whether Bormann died during his attempt to escape. Only his reappearance could disprove it.

The original object of the inquiry was to prove beyond all doubt that Hitler was dead. This object was successfully accomplished. No false Hitler will ever make a plausible claim to survival. But the political calculation behind the inquiry miscarried. The British authorities sought to kill National Socialism by proving that Hitler was dead. Instead they provided the Germans with a scapegoat for all their crimes and failures. There seemed no disloyalty in loading on to a dead Hitler the full responsibility that he had claimed when still alive. German generals blamed him for the defeat. German politicians blamed him for the policy of aggression and racial extermination. Far from being an act of desertion, suicide turned out to be Hitler's greatest service to the German people. He was guilty. Therefore they could be acquitted. This was far from Mr Trevor-Roper's verdict. With artistic skill and perhaps some artistic exaggeration, he built up Speer as the one man of supreme ability among Hitler's supporters and showed how his detachment from political responsibility made him 'the real criminal of Nazi Germany'. Speer was the symbol of all those other devoted Germans who did their duty while Hitler drove to triumph through fraud and blood.

Speer could at least claim that he considered the Germany that would follow Hitler's defeat and sought to preserve it. The other Nazi leaders never thought of Germany's future, but much of their own. This was the most extraordinary of Mr Trevor-Roper's extraordinary discoveries. Germany was falling to pieces; the allied armies were on the point of joining hands; the Russians were in the suburbs of Berlin. Yet every Nazi leader was obsessed with the ambition of seizing the succession as soon as Hitler would commit suicide. None of them except Speer dared to criticize or oppose him; but all longed to step into his shoes. Goering was the first to claim his place as the constitutional heir. Himmler was not far behind. Bormann discredited them both with Hitler and ensured their excommunication. Yet he, too, imagined that he could continue to wield power from behind the throne even when Hitler was dead. Only Goebbels, with what Mr Trevor-Roper rather fancifully calls his Latin clarity, recognized that they were nothing without Hitler and clung to the dead leader's chariot-wheels by committing suicide in more modest form. Mr Trevor-Roper calls this atmosphere of rivalry and intrigue 'Byzantine'; but the parallel is not exact. The story of the Byzantine empire was punctuated by an endless series of rebellious generals and successful challengers for the imperial throne. A Byzantine emperor could expect to be murdered or dethroned; few went to a voluntary suicide. Nothing like this happened at Hitler's court. He would have reigned for ever if it had not been for the victory of the allied armies.

This is the central problem of Mr Trevor-Roper's book, as it must be in any book devoted to Nazi Germany. Why should Hitler have been for so long the undisputed master of a great nation? He had no originality of thought or of expression. His oratory to the masses was no more remarkable than that of any other demagogue. His eyes were glazed and dull, his grasp soft, his voice toneless. He looked well preserved and even youthful until the middle of the war. Then time caught up on him. His whole left side trembled; his senile face twitched. He moved like an automaton. His mental powers had crumbled to vanishing-point. Often he could not follow a discussion or even articulate clearly. Yet even now he remained the sole master. Generals obeyed the directions of his lunatic strategy. The most ruthless and ambitious politicians were helpless before him. Indeed one has the feeling that Hitler could have pulled Germany into an abyss of utter destruction, if he had not at the end lost interest and destroyed himself. There indeed may be found the answer to the mystery. The Germans have always lacked certainty and self-confidence. Hitler possessed these qualities and gave them to others. He never doubted even in 1923, or in the dark days at the end of 1932. The Germans wanted orders. No one has ever known so well as Hitler how to give them.

The Germans were never devoted to Hitler. Mr Trevor-Roper's account makes this clear. The clerks and orderlies in the bunker put a dance-tune on the gramophone when they heard that Hitler was going to commit suicide; and everyone up to the highest ranks smoked in a relaxed way as soon as the suicide had actually taken place. Hitler was Germany's voice of conscience. The Germans were sometimes impatient at this voice or regretted its existence; but they had to obey it. And Hitler on his side had equally little devotion to the German people. He often doubted whether they deserved him; and when their failures of 1945 confirmed his doubts he withdrew proudly from the stage. Goebbels may have meant the last scenes in the bunker to found a legend and to prepare for a Nazi resurrection. Hitler had no such projects. He did not believe in a future life either in this world or the next. He had walked the earth as a god; and now he wanted the destruction of Valhalla. The only delight of his last days was to topple others from their pedestals before crashing down himself.

It would be an exaggeration to say that this was the end that he had always expected; but it was no surprise to him.

Mr Trevor-Roper has written in this book and elsewhere of 'the mind of Adolf Hitler'. This is better than to treat him as an illiterate vulgarian or even as an adventurer pursuing personal power. Hitler's ideas can be reduced to a system with a pedigree and rational consequences. But it is a risky business. Even Mr Trevor-Roper has had to plump for a system and lays down that for Hitler the attack on Russia was more important than anything else. But could Hitler have exercised his superhuman sway if he been merely a mouthpiece of Professor Haushofer's geopolitics? Of course the Germans succumb easily to this or any other rubbishy generalization about the course of history. But they succumb only enough to add the system to their stock of platitudes and grievances. Hitler had more than mind. He had vision. It was no doubt a detestable vision – ranging from total destruction to an earthly paradise where every German ate cream buns – but vision all the same. The sons of petty officials often have fantasies; Hitler differed in turning these fantasies into reality. This gave him supreme power. Perhaps gods can only destroy themselves. But if the voice of reason can contribute anything to weaken them it has spoken through Mr Trevor-Roper.

No one cares now about Germany's bid to conquer Europe. Few care about the fate of Adolf Hitler. In the present situation of international politics both are better forgotten. Mr Trevor-Roper's book would be forgotten along with them if it merely solved the riddle which he was originally set. But it transcended its subject. Though it treated of evil men and degraded themes, it vindicated human reason. In a world where emotion has taken the place of judgement and where hysteria has become meritorious, Mr Trevor-Roper has remained as cool and detached as any philosopher of the Enlightenment. Fools and lunatics may overrun the world; but later on, in some future century, a rational man will rediscover *The Last Days of Hitler* and realize that there were men of his own sort still alive. He will wish, as every rational man must, that he had written Mr Trevor-Roper's book. There are not many books in our age of which that could be said.

47

THE AUSTRIAN ILLUSION

THE 'state of war' with Austria has come to an end; and the British Government has been at pains to stress its friendship with 'Independent Austria'. An Austria, truly independent of Germany, offers great attractions. It bars the way against German aggression in Central Europe; it provides a centre for economic and political co-operation between the neighbouring countries; merely by existing, it reduces the total of Germans in Europe by six or seven million. The Austrian republic in the nineteen-twenties had added advantages. Its enlightened social services and constructive Labour movement captured the affections of the British Labour party, as did no other country in Europe; at the same time, the musty charm of its decayed aristocracy and its ski-instructors, disguised as Tyrolese peasants, appealed to the British upper classes. Politically, culturally and socially, no country was so popular in England. It would be dangerous if this affection, so skilfully built up by the Austrians, was used as the foundation for political illusions. It is one thing to say, as Palacky did: 'If Austria did not exist, it would be necessary to invent it'; for Palacky referred to the great Habsburg monarchy, a going concern. It is quite another thing to say: 'Though Austria does not exist, it will be quite easy to invent it – and indeed we will pretend that we have already done so.' Yet this is, in different forms, the policy of all the Great Powers.

The fragment of German territory called Austria has no roots in history, no support in the feeling of its people, no record even of resistance to Nazi rule. It was part of the old German Reich (the Holy Roman Empire of the German Nation) from beginning to end; and for many centuries the ruler of Austria was also German Emperor. When the Austrians were excluded from Germany in 1866, this was not their doing; it was the result of Austria's defeat at the hands of Bismarck. The Austrians remained Germans – German in speech, German in culture, German in political allegiance. To describe them as 'Austrians' gives them a false historical background. Every subject of the Habsburg Monarchy was an 'Austrian' – Czechs, Poles and Slovenes as much as Germans. Historically, the only other sense which could be attached to the word 'Austrian' would be an inhabitant of Lower or Upper Austria, a provincial definition of no real weight. The present use of the word 'Austrian', repudiating the historical definition, means: 'an inhabitant of one of the six German provinces of the Habsburg monarchy which were left over when the rest of the monarchy broke away to form national states'.

This definition distinguishes in two ways. The Austrians are different from other subjects of the Habsburgs in being Germans; they are different from other Germans in having been subjects of the Habsburgs. Of these two differences the first is essential. It remains true with the passage of time. Since there are now no dynasties in Germany, nor have been since 1918, the second difference is trivial. This was accepted by the founders of 'Austria' in 1918. What they intended to create was not an independent state, but 'German-Austria', member of a democratic German republic. They demanded self-determination, not for the 'Austrians', but for the Germans of Austria and they included in this the German inhabitants of Bohemia and Moravia. Thus Hitler, who got his anti-Semitism and German nationalism from the German nationalists in the Habsburg Empire, got the programme of dismembering Czechoslovakia from the Social Democrats of Vienna in 1918. 'German-Austria' remained separate from the German Reich, not from the will of her people, but from the order of the victorious allies; and this severance was regarded by Germans, both in Austria and in the Reich, as the gravest injustice of the peace settlement of 1919. As indeed it was, if self-determination had been truly its guiding principle.

Independent Austria never repudiated its German character or allegiance. Parties in Austria often opposed various political trends in Germany, but not more so than many Germans of the Reich did themselves. In the 'twenties the Austrian Clericals disliked German Social Democracy; in the 'thirties the Austrian Socialists disliked German National Socialism. This did not make them the less German. Austria is often described as having been 'occupied' or 'conquered' by Hitler. When Hitler entered

Vienna in 1938, he was welcomed by wilder and more enthusiastic crowds than Vienna had ever known. Was Hitler welcomed by cheering crowds in Prague? in Warsaw? in Rotterdam? in Paris? in Belgrade? in Stalingrad? And among those who welcomed the completion of national unity was Karl Renner, now President of independent Austria. The Austrian republic was 'German' also in deeds: it continued the campaign against the Slovenes in Carinthia which had been begun by the German Nationalists before 1918. In fact, Austrian rule, in this way, surpassed Hitler's. The Austrian census, taken in 1934, allowed the existence of only 26,122 Slovenes. The Nazi census, taken in 1939, acknowledged 45,000. It is not surprising that in 1945 the Nazi Gauleiter handed over Carinthia voluntarily to a Social Democrat. This new government announced: 'It considers its first task to be the preservation of a free and indivisible Carinthia.'

No one disputes that many Austrians are democratically minded; so are many Germans. In fact, the Reich Germans have a much more creditable record of resistance to Hitler. But, democratic or not, the Austrians remain German in national loyalty. The only pure Austrians were the Jews of Vienna; and they have been exterminated. The Communists claim to be pure Austrians; hence their unpopularity in Austria. The solution of the Austrian problem lies in Germany; and not the other way round. When (if ever) there is a peaceful, democratic Germany, Austria will be a contented part of it. But Austria will never be an effective barrier against German nationalism.

48

UP FROM UTOPIA:
HOW TWO GENERATIONS SURVIVED
THEIR WARS

IN 1923 everyone was conscious of being 'post-war'; this war was the Great War, the World War. Once it had been the War to End War; and even after five years no one supposed that it would have a rival. In 1950 men were conscious of being more pre-war than post-war. The war they lived through had not even been dignified with a name of its own; it was merely World War II, a repeat performance, and interest was already focused on World War III. After the first war, memorials to the dead were put up in every town and village – in England, in France, in Germany, in the United States, though not, I suppose, in Russia. Millions of names were inscribed on these memorials: for King and Country, for God and the Fatherland, for Peace and Freedom. After the second war there were no new memorials. The names of the dead were added to any blank space that could be found on the existing memorials. The dead, if commemorated at all, were honoured in some practical way – a village playing-field, a new heater for the local library. King and Country, Peace and Freedom – these made no fresh appearance. After World War I men went on celebrating Armistice Day for twenty years – and it was abandoned in 1939 only because the sirens would cause confusion. After World War II there was no armistice; and by 1950 men had forgotten which day they ought to celebrate. The Declaration of Independence, the fall of the Bastille, Shakespeare's birthday, are more alive in our memories.

World War I seemed unique, a cosmic catastrophe. England had not been involved in a Continental war for a hundred years, the United States never. Even France and Germany, Italy and Austria-Hungary had been at peace for more than a generation. Only Russia had had recent experience of war – hence perhaps the different path which Russia followed at the end. Before 1914 there had been a universal conviction that war was at last impossible, a

confident assumption that human affairs would improve indefinitely. When it came again, war seemed incredible, unnatural,
and men therefore tried to saddle individual statesmen with 'war
guilt'. The Allies blaimed Kaiser Wilhelm; the Germans blamed
'the Entente criminals', Poincaré and Izvolski. By 1923 the more
enlightened had changed their tune and were blaming their own
statesmen. English liberals turned on Sir Edward Grey; American
on President Wilson; only the Germans continued to find themselves guiltless. But before long, the search for individual criminals began to flag. Instead, men sought the 'causes of war' as
though war were the most unusual, instead of the most regular, of
human activities. Not every civilization has Christianity; not
every civilization has machinery; not every civilization has mono-
gamy: they all have war.

World War II startled men less. They were dejected at having
to go through it again; but they were not surprised. Everyone
over thirty could remember World War I. So far as men sought
for causes, they sought them for this particular war, not for war
in general. And the causes this time were easy to find – almost too
easy. Hitler and Mussolini had planned war as Wilhelm II, or
Poincaré and Izvolski, had not. Even the Germans acquiesced in
this conclusion – they showed themselves eager to repudiate
Hitler in a way that a previous generation had not been prepared
to repudiate, say, Bethmann Hollweg. Indeed the conclusion is so
obvious as to be tame; besides, it does not lead to any 'constructive' outcome. With Hitler and Mussolini dead, the causes of
World War II were certainly removed; but how could war be prevented in future? By 1950, minds had moved forward – had discovered, instead of war criminals, those who really should be
blamed for World War II. They were not Hitler and Mussolini,
or even their supporters, but those who failed to oppose them.

The statesmen of the pre-1914 era had been condemned for not
negotiating with Germany enough; the statesmen of the pre-1939
era were condemned for negotiating with Germany at all.
'Appeasement' – that is, the attempt at conciliation and agreement – was discovered to have caused World War II; and so, in a
sense, it had. From this it was easy to jump to the general conclusion: 'Appeasement' was the cause not only of World War II,
but of all wars. Certainly American policy by 1950 was designed

to show that American statesmen had learned from the mistakes of the first 'post-war'. Whether standing on your head is the reverse of falling down may, however, be debated.

To consider the cause of a single war instead of the cause of war in general shows, at any rate, a practical spirit; and the second 'post-war' seems more practical, more realistic than the first. Being incredible, World War I could not be justified merely as a war, a struggle for survival or even for conquest. Therefore it had to be justified by reference to high ideals – the War to End War, the War to Make the World Safe for Democracy. Wilson's Fourteen Points dominated the last two years of World War I, and no man in modern history so focused the ideal hopes of mankind as Wilson did for a few brief months at the opening of 1919. The contrast between these hopes and the reality of the following years produced the disillusionment characteristic of the first 'post-war'. Indeed, 'post-war' became a synonym for embitterment, a political hangover on a gigantic scale. Men had died in millions, endured the mud and filth of the trenches – for what? To return to a world very like the old one. Those who had remained at home writing tracts on wartime ideals were even more disillusioned than those who had fought. 'War achieves nothing' became the common remark. In reality, World War I achieved a great deal: it would have been worth waging simply to turn the Germans out of the countries which they had invaded. But in addition, it liberated from alien rule peoples who had had no expectation of liberation when the war began. All this was brushed aside by the dogma, 'war achieves nothing'. Therefore the things the war had achieved – national freedom for hitherto unknown peoples, even the liberation of Belgium – were nothing; by definition worthless. The men of 1923 reached disillusionment as much by what had been done as by what had not.

The peoples who fought World War II were determined not to be deceived a second time. They fought for survival, not for ideals. And quite rightly: apart from the United States, survival as independent states was the immediate issue. In 1923 men were still lamenting that the Fourteen Points had not been applied; in 1950 few recollected the existence, and none the terms, of the Atlantic Charter. After World War II men's aspirations were lower and their achievements higher than after World War I. The Germans were denounced more fiercely in World War II and treated better afterwards. Economic recovery in every country was more rapid and yet accompanied by fewer promises. In 1950 no one was surprised that Utopia had not been reached. Their error was perhaps the opposite: they were content with too little, not ashamed to find that things were turning out much as they had expected. In 1923 men everywhere felt that they had been deceived, merely because Utopia was not in sight. If they had been asked to fight a new war there would have been a universal explosion – indeed, danger of a very minor war drove Lloyd George out of power for life in 1922. Now men go off obediently to what may be the opening of World War III, and no one complains that Western statesmen have thrown away their victory, as men complained against Wilson and Clemenceau. Men in the West were not asked a second time to fight the War to End War; they were asked to fight the Germans and they did so successfully.

There is another side to this acquiescence in the hardships of the present and the future. Though there was more talk of ideals in World War I, more serious ideals were at stake in World War II and were taken more seriously. The Kaiser's Germany was branded a military despotism, a tyranny; as a matter of fact it was a constitutional monarchy and could have qualified as a founding member of the United Nations. The Tommy, *poilu* or doughboy of World War I thought that he was being exploited; believed, rightly, that there was little difference between himself and the German soldier in the opposite trench. Hitler's Germany really was a bestial tyranny; the concentration camps, the extermination of the Jews, the Gestapo, were all real. No Allied soldier who saw Buchenwald or Dachau could doubt that the war had been worth while. And not only Allied countries were liberated. Italy was genuinely liberated from Mussolini; and, whereas the Germans had not thanked the Allies for ridding them of Wilhelm II, this time they at least had to pretend gratitude for being relieved of Hitler. After World War II the peoples of the Western world were a good deal more doubtful that their ideals could be universally exported; on the other hand, they were much more confident that those ideals were genuine and worth defending.

The difference of spirit in the times had another cause. World War I was, on the whole, a bourgeois war: the masses fought for their masters, not for their own convictions. The Right fought enthusiastically, without reserve; the Left fought regretfully or not at all. The fifth column, a phrase in World War II, had been a reality in World War I. Every nation had a pacifist or anti-war group, led by men of noble character – MacDonald, Debs, Liebknecht, Adler, Lenin. By 1923 MacDonald was on the point of becoming Prime Minister; Lenin had ruled Russia for six years; even the French pacifists around Caillaux had been restored to favour and Clemenceau discredited. In World War II it was the Left that fought with conviction, the Right with regret. Winston Churchill has described how, in his first months as Prime Minister, he was received with cheers from the Labour, and silence from the Conservative, benches; many of those who cheered him (including even Herbert Morrison, the Home Secretary) had been imprisoned as war-resisters in World War I. Similarly in the United States, World War I had been backed by the richer and more educated classes, by the legendary figures of Wall Street; and Wilson had won the votes of the masses in 1916 by keeping out of war. The opposition to Roosevelt, on the other hand, came from conservative Republicans; and support from the men of the New Deal. The labour movement in England and America supported World War II without reserve; it was the capitalists who found themselves involved in a struggle against collective bargaining, social security, and equal opportunity between rich and poor. Bourgeois ideals are abstract, fine phrases for a peroration. Working-class ideals are concrete, drab in a speech, but more telling when it comes to vital statistics. After 1918 young English people were promised Homes Fit for Heroes; after 1945 English children got orange juice and free milk. Years ago an American writer deprecated political democracy with the phrase: 'The rich want liberty; the poor want ham and eggs.' In 1950 the 'poor' of the Anglo-Saxon world wanted both and were in a fair way to get them.

The year 1923 was 'post-war' in feeling as well as in time. 'Post-war' excused every evil. Unemployment was 'post-war'; sexual immorality was 'post-war'; discontent in Asia was 'post-war'. For, though the age imagined itself to be progressive, Utopian, looking to the future, in reality the 'normalcy' that it demanded was a romantic version of the days before 1914, when capitalist economics and Christian morals had supposedly worked without a flaw. Harding, Bonar Law, Poincaré, Stresemann – the representative statesmen of 1923 – were all concerned to restore a vanished past. For that matter even Wilson's ideal of self-determination was a dying echo of Gladstonian doctrine, not a vision of the future. The statesmen of 1950 – Truman or Attlee – looked forward. Maybe their vision did not extend very far; but at least they had escaped from the illusion that it was possible to retrace their steps. In this they were representative. No Englishman imagined that it was possible to restore the British Empire as it was in the nineteenth century; no American imagined that the United States could ever again lead a life of irresponsible isolation. Or rather, though a few imagined these things, public opinion rejected their dreams.

It is a temptation to make this the conclusion. The English-speaking world of the second 'post-war' was more mature, more level-headed, more adult, than that of 1923; incredible, indeed, that it should have improved so much in less than a generation. In 1923 a conclusion based on the English-speaking world and that of Western Europe could have passed a verdict on the world as a whole. Western capitalism was still master. The statesmen who met at Paris in 1919 had called themselves the Supreme Council; and they truly supposed that they were supreme in the world. Even when the United States withdrew, the destinies of the world seemed to depend on the decisions of England, France, and Italy. Add a reconciled Germany, rank the Japanese as honorary Europeans, and the world would be complete. Much of the disappointment of that post-war world sprang from the illusion that the Big Three, squeezed away in the western extremity of Eurasia, controlled events. Here lies the greatest contrast with 1950. Once upon a time, Western Europe issued orders to all the world; now it could not even defend itself. Though there were endless meetings of Western European statesmen, no one supposed that these could dictate events elsewhere; hitherto they have produced only paper projects for co-ordinating European defence before it is too late. Even the United States, despite its preponderance of material resources, stood on the defensive; it allowed things to happen, instead of determining the agenda of history. The Western world of 1950 improved socially and

politically on the world of 1923; but now it existed on suffer-
ance, not of its own right.

The Atlantic community ceased to be the centre of the world
culturally as well as politically. In 1923 it seemed certain that
Western values and beliefs would soon encircle the globe. All
other civilizations – Mohammedan, Chinese, Hindu – were dead
or dying. Soon everyone would wear a collar and tie; keep office
hours; exercise vote by ballot; practise birth control; drive an
automobile; pay an income tax; enjoy freedom from arbitrary
arrest. By 1950 it had become clear that Western man exported
his mechanical powers without exporting his ideas. His economic,
military, cultural weapons were being turned against him by
those who lacked his virtues – though perhaps they had virtues
of their own. The first post-war knew Communism; but it seemed
then a disease of Western civilization, not a challenge to it. The
first Bolshevik leaders were men of European mind, concerned
to draw Russia more into Europe; their isolation was imposed
upon them by the blunders of Western statesmen. The Communist
movements of Germany, France, and Italy grew out of earlier
Socialist movements; they were not created or, at first, directed
from without. Communist Russia was certainly idealized by millions of workers in Western Europe; but it was an ideal because it
was supposed to be accomplishing the Western principles of
Socialist democracy, not because it repudiated Western values.
Moreover, Communism was still regarded as a European problem. No one noticed the Congress of Eastern Peoples which met
in Turkestan in 1921.

By 1950 liberal civilization, supreme and universal after World
War I, had lost much of Asia and now seemed in danger of losing
the continent of Europe as well. European statesmen talked
more sensibly, perhaps even acted more sensibly, than after
World War I; but their spur was a new fear, not a new wisdom.
In 1923 men's minds were taken up with the French occupation
of the Ruhr; if only German reparations could be settled, the
world – it was believed – would be secure and at peace. In 1950
who cared about reparations? Not even the Russians, now that
they had carried home their loot. Who cared about 'the German
problem'? The only German problem was when and how to arm
the Germans against the Russians; it seemed beyond the bounds

of credibility that the Germans themselves might again menace the world. Thus it was not only better sense that made the men of 1950 resist the excuse of labelling everything evil 'post-war'; they had found a larger label, one that could stretch even farther. Both labels served the same purpose: they enabled men to evade their problems or to give out that they were insoluble. When men said unemployment was 'post-war', they meant that nothing could be done about it except to lament that World War I had taken place. And when men say that Communism is sweeping Asia, they are halfway to implying that nothing can be done about *it*.

As a matter of fact, many 'post-war' problems of the twenties found a solution in the thirties; but these solutions did not depend on merely waiting until the effects of World War I should wear off. Thus Keynesian economics (a very different matter from Keynes's ill-founded attack on reparations) broke the problem of mass unemployment. In the same way, 'Communism' would lose its hypnotic, paralysing sound if there were a serious attempt to answer the question: 'What causes men to become Communists?' The mortal error of the Western world is to imagine that Communism is caused by terror – by the secret police and the concentration camp. These are part of Communism, not its cause. Communism is caused by the sense of economic and social injustice; by unquestioning belief; by the longing for Utopia. The Western world will get Communism only if it is false to its own standards and tries to fight Communism in kind. The answer to intolerance is tolerance; the answer to intransigence is compromise; the answer to unquestioning enthusiasm is scepticism; the answer to grievances is to redress them. The men of 1923 erred when they looked back regretfully to the past and lamented that the Great War had taken place, instead of facing their problems as they came. The men of 1950 made the same mistake when they regretted the growth of Communism and lamented the days when Russia was not a Great Power. The appeal of Communism was real; and so was the strength of Soviet Russia. To suppose that either of them could be made to disappear was the last of the Utopian illusions which the men of 1950 had inherited from a previous generation.

In 1923 men thought that the only alternative to Utopia was to be disillusioned and embittered. But men will not live for ever in cynicism and despair. Fascism and Communism, new Utopias, were called in to take the place of the liberal Utopia that had failed. But the men of 1923 were wrong: there is a third way between Utopianism and despair. That is to take the world as it is and to improve it; to have faith without a creed, hope without illusions, love without God. The Western world is committed to the proposition that rational man will in the end prove stronger and more successful than irrational man. If the Western world abandons this proposition, it may conquer Communism but it will destroy itself.

49

IS STALIN A STATESMAN?

THE Duke of Wellington said that the great task for a general was to divine what was happening 'on the other side of the hill'. Our great task is to divine what is happening, and what is likely to happen, on the other side of the Iron Curtain. A historian is tempted to believe that if we can be clear about the past, this will help us to foresee the pattern of the future. Men do not learn new tricks when they are over seventy: and a study of Stalin's successes and failures in the twenty-five years he has ruled Russia should give us some idea at any rate of what we can expect from Russian policy now.

A preliminary word of warning is necessary. If we ask 'Is Stalin a statesman?' we cannot use the word 'statesman' in its Western meaning. The great statesmen whom we admire – a Gladstone or a Lincoln – were animated by a moral sense. Though they sought power, it was to serve noble ends; they were concerned to build a free humanity, to appease warring factions; to promote the peace of the world. Stalin is not affected by the moral principles in which we believe.

His object is power pure and simple: to keep his position of supreme power in Russia; to make Russia more powerful in the world; and, perhaps, though this is more doubtful, to bring Communists into power elsewhere. I say this last is more doubtful, for it is clear that Stalin is interested in the victory of Communists only so far as they are subservient to him. Thus we are really asking: 'Is Stalin clever? Is he adroit in manoeuvre and far-sighted from his own point of view?' We have to examine his record as we would that of a champion chess player without worrying whether the chess master pays his taxes or beats his wife.

If we were discussing the career of a statesman in a democratic country, we should not hesitate as to the answer. A politician who had been continuously in high office since 1917 and supreme ruler of his country since 1926 would be a very great statesman indeed.

In a totalitarian country this proves little or nothing. It needed very great skill for Stalin to become dictator in Russia; but much less skill to remain so.

Stalin has 'reigned' in Russia for twenty-four years. Plenty of tsars and emperors reigned for far longer in the past; yet many of them were notoriously incompetent. With all the resources of tyranny and the secret police, it is not very easy for a dictator to be overthrown by anything short of a catastrophic defeat in war. Mussolini would still be ruling Italy if he had not gone to war; and General Franco, who is certainly not much good at his job, is still secure in Spain. We should therefore not give Stalin too much credit merely for the achievement of keeping power. There is a further difficulty in examining Stalin's record. We have ample stories from rivals, from detached observers and supporters, of the ten years between 1917 and 1927 when Stalin was advancing to supreme power. The moment he attained it, darkness descended; and we have to judge Stalin from the outside. We see only the effects of his actions; we have to guess at his policy. As a personality he disappeared. The curtain was lifted for the Americans and Englishmen who saw him at Teheran, at Yalta, and – to a lesser extent – at Potsdam. Then he vanished again into the Russian mists; and we were left guessing once more. We have to build up a picture of his personality from this fragmentary material, then to judge the qualities which Stalin has shown, first as ruler of Russia, and second, in his dealings with the rest of the world.

All the evidence that we have from the period between 1917 and 1927, or again from Teheran and Yalta, goes to show that Stalin is a political tactician of the highest order. He knows how to play men off against each other and how to keep himself in the background. In the first years of the revolution Stalin was the only one who never differed from Lenin or challenged his leadership; yet all the time Stalin was building up for himself a control of the party machinery which even Lenin could not dispute.

Similarly, in the struggle which followed Lenin's death, Stalin appeared to leave the struggle to others. He let Zinoviev and Bucharin oust Trotsky, then used Bucharin to destroy Zinoviev, and himself slipped into the dictatorship imperceptibly. Trotsky tells that at the decisive meeting where he was to be drummed out of the party, Stalin was the only one who greeted him with a handshake and a friendly word.

At the Allied meetings during the war Stalin likewise impressed the greatest figures of the Western world and made them feel that he was anxious to co-operate with them; when difficulties arose, they always seemed to come from his advisers. In fact, a myth grew up in Anglo-American circles that Stalin was a friendly and conciliatory old gentleman, who was kept on a tight rein by the remote Politburo; Trotsky fell into the same error twenty years before. Stalin certainly seems to have the political gift of translating great issues into personal terms and of getting his way by playing on the reactions of individuals. This is the essential qualification for a party manager, the job in which Stalin started his career; it is not necessarily a sign of statesmanship or even political cleverness. Stanley Baldwin had it in England to a supreme degree; yet he had no ideas, and his influence on British foreign policy was disastrous.

It may seem curious that with his great gift for handling men, even of the highest standing, Stalin should keep himself so much in the background. But that has always been his method. He prefers to let other people make the mistakes. Just as he sat quiet during the party wrangles at the time of Trotsky's struggle, so he used Teheran and Yalta in order to play off President Roosevelt against Winston Churchill; and rejected further Allied meetings when it became clear that Great Britain and the United States could not be pushed into conflict with each other.

The present situation by which Soviet diplomatists are tied to instructions from Moscow and can be disavowed if they take initiative suits him very well. The mistakes are theirs; the successes are his. This is not a system that makes for daring strokes of policy. What Stalin wants from his men is rigid obedience to orders, not criticism nor even facts that go against his policy.

It was the same during the war. Russian officers, from top to bottom, had to follow a preconceived plan without any freedom of manoeuvre. It was of the Russians that Tennyson's lines ought to have been written:

> Theirs not to reason why,
> Theirs but to do and die.

Strategy of this kind leads to great obstinacy in defence and to ponderousness in victory; we shall look in vain for ability to deal with unexpected difficulties or to seize the initiative quickly if some sudden chance turns up.

This is exactly what we find when we come to examine the record of Stalin's policy. After Lenin's death there was prolonged discussion of a very high order among the Bolshevik leaders as to what line of economic development they should follow. Stalin hated these clever arguments, hated – above all – the workings of Trotsky's quick mind, endlessly throwing out new ideas. For long Stalin sat silent; finally he grasped at a single idea – the industrial-ization of Russia by means of the Five Year Plan and, especially, the collectivization of agriculture. For this he will be remembered in history, for good or ill.

It was an attractive idea on paper, the only way indeed in which the productivity of agriculture could be so increased as to carry the weight of a great heavy industry. But it ran against the im-placable resistance of the Russian peasantry. Stalin forced it through with an obstinacy as great as theirs, forced it over mil-lions of dead bodies. Other Bolshevik leaders lost their nerve and wanted to call a halt. Stalin never wavered. He had committed himself to collectivization, and he was determined to achieve it at whatever cost in human suffering.

At the same time he always had his ear to the ground; he knew what the Russian people were thinking. He managed to give the impression that the worst hardships of collectivization were due to the blunders of subordinate officials and that he, Stalin, was trying to keep them on a more moderate line. He rebuked the Communists for being 'dizzy with success'. He himself has been often successful, but never dizzy. He gauged with calculated accuracy what the Russian people would stand; and he knew that they could stand a great deal.

He is a man of steel, ruling a people of stone, and trying to shape them; it is a painful process for both sides. Stalin is very sensitive to feeling among the officials of the Communist party; affected, though to a lesser degree, by feeling among the factory workers; and caring least for the feeling of the Russian peasants. He cares nothing at all for the feelings of foreigners, even if the foreigners are Communists.

Thus, when we come to foreign policy during the long period of Stalin's power, we see that it has a single aim: Russian security. He wants to keep Russia remote from the rest of the world and to prevent any kind of foreign influence or interference. Foreign Communists are exploited to serve the needs of this policy.

This was shown from the beginning. In 1923, when Stalin was only mounting to power, the German Communists were ordered into rebellion in Hamburg, not in order to win a victory in Germany but solely to make things easier for Russia. Similarly, the Chinese Communists were ordered to work with Chiang Kaishek so as to make Russia more secure in the Far East; and this brought them almost to destruction in 1927. Both these were great blunders; since Stalin was not yet supreme, one cannot ascribe them to Stalin alone.

His first undoubted initiative was in 1933 when he switched international Communism over to the Popular Front and Russian policy over to collective security. Here his purpose was clear. He feared the strength of Germany and wanted to ensure that Hitler should not lead a crusade of united Europe against the Soviet Union. His aim was to keep Germany divided from the Western Powers; and since the split was already there, he had an easy time of it.

It is sometimes said that he welcomed the Spanish civil war in the hope of setting up a Communist state in Spain. This is to exaggerate his enthusiasm for Communism. Rather, he hoped that the civil war would increase the tension between England and France on the one side, and Germany and Italy on the other, and that thus Russia would be left in peace at the other end of Europe.

As to the crisis of Czechoslovakia in 1938, historians are still debating whether Stalin ever had any serious intention of going to the help of the Czechs. He certainly never revealed his intentions to the Western Powers; but then he was never given any encouragement to do so. Perhaps we can detect here an example of Stalin's usual method: hanging back himself, shifting the responsibility on to others.

There can, however, be no doubt of his initiative in the next crisis, the conflict over Poland which started World War II. The Nazi-Soviet pact was as much Stalin's decision as Hitler's – in fact, more so, in that Stalin had an alternative and Hitler had none. It is easy in retrospect to see what led Stalin to his decision. Alliance with the Western Powers would have involved Russia in difficult events: she might even have had to bear the brunt of the war from the outset. The Nazi-Soviet pact enabled her to stand aside and to watch the troubles of others; it was a choice for neutrality and for isolation.

All the same it was the most gigantic blunder in Stalin's career. It allowed Hitler to conquer all Europe and then to turn with tremendous force against an isolated Soviet Union. Two things led Stalin to this mistake.

First, he was out of date in his information. He thought that England and France were stronger than they were and that therefore he had achieved a balance in Europe; and he thought this simply because England and France had been strong years before.

Secondly, and more decisively, he did not understand the difference between democracies and dictatorships; he lumped them all together as states pursuing solely a cynical policy of power (as he was); he never allowed for the influence of public opinion in democratic countries, or realized that there are many strokes of Machiavellian policy which are impossible for them.

We can go even further. Though he regarded all foreign governments with suspicion, he believed that it would be easier to get on with a totalitarian country than with a democratic one. If there has ever been a period in which Stalin was sincere in his attempts at collaboration, it was between August 1939 and June 1941, when he was working in friendly neutrality with Nazi Germany. It might even be said that, so far as Stalin got on with Churchill and President Roosevelt, it was because he saw them as 'war dictators', not as the freely elected leaders of democratic communities.

The Grand Alliance of World War II was not the outcome of Stalin's policy; it was forced on him by Hitler, and he would never have entered it except for the German attack. During the war Stalin showed great qualities as a military leader. He had the capacity to hold out against staggering blows; to wait patiently for his opportunity, and then to pursue his victory relentlessly.

In his dealings with his allies the same qualities appeared as faults. Certainly he made great gains for Russia; but he could have made them by conciliation and friendship instead of by disputing with his allies and finally estranging them. Allied policy also made mistakes: sometimes they gave concessions where they should have been firm; sometimes they resisted where they might have been generous. Still, it seems very unlikely that genuine co-operation in peacetime with the Soviet Union was ever possible.

Stalin suspected others of having the same motives as himself, and therefore distrusted them. At the same time, he underrated the courage and capacity of democratic statesmen. He thought that he had only to stand aside for the Western world to dissolve in political and economic anarchy.

In 1947 the Marshall Plan forced him to a decision; he made the wrong one, even from his own point of view. If America had the evil design of dominating all the world that he attributed to her, the effective way of opposing this would have been inside the Marshall Plan organization; instead he thought he could halt it by threats. Ever since, he has been making tactical gains at the expense of strategical losses.

The Communist seizure of Czechoslovakia in 1948 is a striking illustration. It made Czechoslovakia perhaps a more secure outpost of Soviet power; but only at the price of stirring up alarm and resistance in the whole free world.

More recently the war in Korea has reinforced the same lesson. It started because Stalin thought that America and the United Nations would retreat before a show of force. When they did not, his only course was to keep doggedly on; though he could have built up a capital of goodwill in the West by settling the Korean war on terms of reasonable compromise. There is his greatest weakness. He knows how to wait, but not how to conciliate; and since he does not understand compromise, his policy always leads in the long run to a head-on collision.

Looking back over the whole record, we can agree that Stalin has some high qualities of statesmanship. He has infinite patience and obstinacy. No difficulties will ever wear him down or make him relax. He is a master of defence, whether in politics or war. On the other hand, he is barren of constructive ideas; fear is the only argument he uses and perhaps understands.

He lacks the greatest quality of the statesman: he does not know how to co-operate with other men of equal political stature and to trust them. When dealing with others, his only tactic is to divide them; if this fails, he has no resource except to wait. Whenever he overcomes his natural reluctance and takes an initiative, he does this rigidly and with the same dogmatic obstinacy as in defence. Once committed to a policy, he clings to it despite all difficulties and failures.

The great mistake we make in the West is to suppose that Russian policy is 'clever'. Quite the reverse: it is without flexibility or imagination, incapable of a sudden initiative.

It may be objected that this estimate of Stalin is based principally on an already distant past and that the picture of him lumbering cautiously along does not correspond with the vast gains which the Soviet Union has made in 1945 and the following years.

Though these gains were made, they showed little subtlety or cleverness in their making. Eastern Europe fell into Stalin's hands at the end of World War II simply because of the vacuum which followed the collapse of German armed strength: the Russians moved on until they ran against the lines of the Western allies. As to China – certainly the biggest Soviet success since 1917 – no one was more surprised than Stalin when it went Communist.

We know that at the end of the war he was expecting to do business with Chiang Kai-shek, and the harsh bargain that he drove with respect to Manchuria was evidence of this. Of course, the defeat of Germany and Japan changed the picture of the world for everyone – including the Russians. But they took longer to adapt themselves to these changes than did anyone else; and to some extent have not made the adaptation even yet.

No doubt their attacks on rearming Germany and Japan are in part a political manoeuvre to weaken the forces of the West; but partly, too, they are simply old tunes in which the Russians, Stalin included, still believe. Any interpretation of Russian policy is bound to be highly speculative, but it is at any rate an arguable proposition that its greatest defect is to be out of date.

Stalin has continued to see Russia as weak when she has shown herself as strong; he sees her as still encircled and isolated when in fact she is secure and with all great powers willing to be her friends. Far from being clever, Soviet policy since 1945 has been heavy-handed.

With more skill and understanding the Soviet Union could have made practically all its present gains and yet possessed a real security in co-operating with the other great Powers. Like all men, Stalin judges the present in terms of the past, and it is a handicap that his memory is longer than that of others. He is always thinking of the wars of intervention which ended in 1921, of the way in which he was cold-shouldered by the Western Powers at Munich in 1938 or betrayed by his close associate Hitler in 1941, instead of judging the situation in terms adapted to the second half of the twentieth century.

His outlook and policy are so old-fashioned as to be almost prehistoric, and it is difficult to analyse his career without thinking of those ponderous, slow-moving monsters from a dim antiquity.

What should be our line of policy in answer to a man with Stalin's past? Pretty clearly, it is no good appealing to him on grounds simply of goodwill; no good even suggesting what is best for the Russian people. Stalin will leave others alone only as long as they are stronger than he is. Moreover he will always be trying to divide his opponents, and if he does more against them, it will be through others, his satellites, not by risking himself.

The last thing to expect – if history is any guide – is direct Russian aggression. Stalin will not fight a world war unless it is forced upon him. What is more, once he recognizes that the democratic front against him will not crumble, he will be ready to strike a bargain and – so long as the balance of forces remains the same – he will keep his bargain as he did with Hitler between 1939 and 1941.

Western policy cannot hope that Russia will change her course. Changes can only come among the satellites, as they have already come with Yugoslavia. Our great object should be to make the satellites feel that if they move away from Russia they will not be changing one master for another, but will gain real independence. More broadly, the answer to Stalin can be summed up in three maxims: Be strong; be united, and then be friendly.

50

CAN WE AGREE WITH
THE RUSSIANS?

IF a question can be given a simple answer, it is not worth asking.
If one could say either 'yes' or 'no' to the question: Can we
agree with the Russians? the matter would not be worrying the
world so much. The answer is not simple; therefore the question
persists. Of course, if the Western world went Communist, it
could agree with the Russians – at any rate for a short time. And
if the Communist system fell to pieces in Russia, its successor
could probably agree with us. But when we ask this question we
really mean, Can a Western world, which retains its free institutions and its independence, agree with a Soviet Russia dominated
by the Communist party?

But we must go a stage farther in deciding what we mean. If by
'agree' we mean Can the two systems settle down side by side,
each disarmed, each trusting each other as much as, say, France
and Italy trust each other, neither interfering in the other's
affairs? – then, any responsible writer on international affairs
must at once say, No, this is impossible and will be impossible
so long as the two systems exist.

On the other hand, the alternative to this state of idyllic agreement is not necessarily World War III. It may be anything from
mutual non-recognition to agreements on all kinds of limited
issues, despite the suspicion on more general points. Hardly anyone in the West, except the Communists, would claim that full-
scale agreement is possible with the Russians here and now or
even in the future. But the great majority of people in Western
Europe and, I think, a majority in the United States, have still not
made up their minds that a complete breach with the Soviet
Union is inevitable as, say, the majority of people in England
thought it was a waste of time to bargain with Hitler after the
occupation of Prague in March 1939. It is the purpose of this
article to examine the no-man's-land between full agreement,

which we think impossible, and war, which we still think can be avoided.

In discussing any subject connected with Soviet Russia there is a preliminary warning which should be compulsory on all writers on international affairs. We know nothing about it; everything we write is guesswork, though we hope intelligent guesswork. Take the parallel case of Hitler. Though there was a good deal of secrecy connected with the Nazis, these secrets could be broken. We knew which men around Hitler had influence; we knew the general line of his ideas; we knew broadly his resources and his intentions. After all, plenty of foreigners met Hitler at close quarters, and he spoke frankly to them.

None of this is true in regard to the Soviet Union. We do not know who are the really important men in the Politburo; we do not know which of them has influence with Stalin; we do not even know whether Stalin has influence; we know little of Russian economic development since the war and nothing reliable about her military strength. No independent foreign observer has had any real meeting with Stalin since he was at Potsdam in 1945, and even then he may have been playing an elaborate part. We do not know, though we can guess, whether the rulers of Russia are Marxists or nationalists; whether they are frightened or aggressive. All our judgements have to be made from outside; none can be based on knowledge, only on information.

On a technical point, for instance, we have no means of knowing whether Soviet diplomatists abroad write honest and well-informed reports of public opinion in the countries where they are posted; just as little do we know whether Stalin reads their reports or takes any notice of them. During World War II many competent judges, from President Roosevelt and Mr Eden downward, were confident that Russia would settle down and become a peaceful, non-aggressive state; now judges, equally competent, hold that the Soviet Union will remain a permanently disturbing element in the world. Both judgements are based on guesswork, on observation from outside; neither is based on knowledge of how the Soviet Union is governed or of how its rulers feel.

My guess, for what it is worth (and it is worth as much as anyone else's), is that the Soviet rulers are not as black as they have been painted – and not as white either. They like to think that, because they are Marxists, they are quite different from anyone else, much cleverer and much more successful. In practice, they are very like the rulers of any other country, pushed along by events, making a good many blunders, and delighted to keep the show going at all. They have long got rid of any organized opposition inside their own country, and therefore they are at a loss when they run into it elsewhere. The abuse which they then turn on is the political method which they learned in the days when they had opposition inside Russia; it is simply habit like any other, though a very unpleasant one. Of course, it would be more convenient for them if they could 'liquidate' opposition in the outer world as they once got rid of it inside the Soviet Union; but then it would also be more convenient for us if the Soviet Union did not exist – so we must not count that too much against them.

The Soviet rulers are Marxists. They genuinely think that their system is the best in the world and that it is bound to triumph. On the other hand, absurdly enough, they live in an atmosphere of ceaseless fear, expecting conspiracies and wars of intervention at any moment. In fact they are very like a gambler who believes that he has invented an infallible 'system', yet is terrified of being robbed or even assassinated on the way to the casino.

The Russian rulers are, in theory, revolutionary; but that was a long time ago. A friend of mine was with the Soviet general who was 'dropped' to Tito during the last war. The old warrior had once been a leading guerrilla; by 1943 he expected to move around in a staff car and then be served with a four-course dinner every evening. In the same way the revolutionary joints of the Soviet leaders would creak a good deal if it ever came to action. In practice, they are much like politicians in other countries, though more ruthless in their methods; they want to keep in office and to enjoy the very considerable rewards which office brings. In short, though they would like to promote world revolution, they are not going to do it at the risk of any real catastrophe to Russia, or, more especially, to themselves.

This is a very important point. Soviet Russia is a despotism, the most complete of modern times. But this does not mean that the rulers of Russia are not affected by the feelings of the Russian people. On the contrary, they are in a state of continual anxiety about the development of public opinion and constantly trim their policy in order to satisfy it. All our evidence, such as it is, suggests that, while the Russian people are extremely ill-informed about the outer world, they have retained a critical intelligence. Far from being made docile by ceaseless propaganda, they are more and more conditioned against it. They could not be carried into a general war unless they were convinced that Russia was the attacked and innocent party; and they would grow restless if the war was badly conducted.

There is not much purpose in trying to compete with the propaganda of the Kremlin; the competition has to come from the facts and from the good sense of the Russian people themselves. But this factor does give Western policy one tangible asset; a general war is virtually excluded from the calculations of the Russian rulers.

How then are we to try for agreement with these men, despotic, ruthless, suspicious? The answer can be found only in the world of facts, not in the world of ideals. Communist Russia and Western democracy are as separated as were Islam and Christianity in the early Middle Ages. It would have been useless to appeal to Mohammed on the grounds of common humanity and it is equally useless to appeal to Stalin.

Indeed, every appeal to ideals reminds the Russians that they are Marxists and therefore deepens the cleavage between the two communities. There is no sense in asking the Russians to cease to be Communists; and therefore no sense in demanding that they should stop Communist propaganda. For one thing, it is a mistake to suppose that Communism is caused solely by Russian propaganda. Communism is caused by resentment against economic or racial inferiority; by the appeal of a dogmatic creed to men who have lost their traditional faith; by a whole host of psychological factors which have nothing to do with Russia. In fact, Communist movements would probably be stronger and more dangerous to the democratic world than they are now if they were not under Russian influence.

But there is another and even more decisive argument. The price to be paid if the Russians ceased Communist propaganda would be too high. For it is that democratic propaganda should cease, too. But what is democratic propaganda? It is simply the truth arrived at after free discussion. If the Russians agreed to stop Communist propaganda, the Western countries would have to agree in return to silence all criticism of the way in which Russia was governed. They would have to introduce a censorship of the Press and to forbid their statesmen to make critical speeches. This was the demand which Hitler made to the British Government in the autumn of 1938 and which was contemptuously refused.

After all it is hypocritical to pretend that it is only the Russians who believe in the superiority of their system and who expect the collapse of ours. We believe just as strongly that ours is superior; we believe that, by our preaching and demonstrating the superiority of free institutions, Russian despotism will one day collapse. When men demand the silencing of Communist propaganda, they implicitly admit that Communism will be victorious in the field of open argument; no believer in democracy should make this admission.

Thus any bargaining with the Russians must be confined to the world of concrete interests. The first and greatest of these interests is economic; and it is here, I have always believed, that practical agreement could most easily be reached. Communism flourishes on hardship; and it is therefore a Western interest that Soviet Russia should become increasingly prosperous. Every rise in the Russian standard of life lessens the punch of Communism as a fighting creed. It is argued against this that increasing Russia's economic strength merely increases her strength for war. This is a false conclusion. Russia's strength for war does not lie in her economic resources, which are and will long remain inferior to those of the Western world; it lies in her resources in men and in the incredible toughness of these men. Economic development will both use up the manpower and soften the men.

Moreover, though this is often forgotten, economic agreements have two sides. The Russians will pay for whatever they receive from the industrial West; and they will pay with goods, which, if Western traders are wise, will benefit the West as much as Western goods benefit Russia. Richard Cobden believed that trade between two countries always lessened the tension between them; this is a belief that has not lost its force.

Still, we must also face the question of political agreements.

The Western world has rightly taken the line that there is nothing to be gained by succumbing to threats and that, in bargaining with the Russians, it must be able to show itself strong, ready even to face a general war, if this is necessary. But we must not fall over on the other side and make the Russian mistake of trying, in our turn, to get our way by threats. To guess once more about Russian policy, I would say that the overriding Russian motive is still fear and not aggression or desire to dominate the world.

This has always been true of Russian policy. Alexander I feared the great Napoleon. The Crimean War was caused by the Russian fear that England and France meant to control Constantinople and to force their way into the Black Sea; World War I was caused, on the Russian side, by the same fear that Germany was going to control Constantinople as part of her project for an empire from Berlin to Baghdad; and in World War II the Russians provoked Hitler's attack by refusing to allow him to advance on Constantinople and the Near East.

It is often forgotten in the West that Russia has been repeatedly invaded from the West, but has herself never started an aggressive war into Europe. Russian troops have once occupied Paris (1814) and once occupied Berlin and Vienna (1945); but both times after a long defensive war. On the other hand, Russia has been invaded time after time in modern history; by Napoleon in 1812; by the English and French in the Crimea in 1854; by the Germans in 1917; by the Entente powers during the wars of intervention in 1919 and 1920; and by Hitler in 1941.

These things seem remote from us and particularly from the Americans. But the Russians do not distinguish between the Germans and the French, the British and the Americans. For them we are all simply the men of Western civilization, with our higher standard of life, with our superior machines and weapons, and with our refusal to treat the Russians as equals. We are certainly not going to give up our standard of life or our superior equipment to please the Russians; all the more reason to treat them as equals in every question of diplomacy.

Thus, while doing nothing to weaken Western strength, our diplomacy should always be on the watch to lessen Russian fears and Russian suspicions. It is a great nuisance that Russia should exist at all; but since she does, it is up to us who are not driven mad by fear and suspicion to treat her sensibly. Many of the Russian fears are groundless; we can do nothing to meet them. Some, however, have a basis in history and even a crazy rationality.

This is particularly true of Germany. There can be no doubt that the Russians fear a revived and united Germany more than anything else in the world; and so should we, if we had had the German invasion of 1941, the endless destruction and twenty million Russian dead. Unless we regard World War III as certain, it is worth paying almost any price in order to keep Germany disarmed; and the Russians will pay a price too.

We have to accept the fact that the Russians will go on being Communists, just as we shall go on being democratic; and we have to accept the fact that the Russians no more believe our expressions of peacefulness and goodwill than we believe theirs. Yet even on this basis of mutual distrust, it might be possible to agree on the neutralization of Germany, and on the withdrawal of our forces to the frontiers. If this worked, it would enormously lessen Russian suspicions and perhaps even prepare the way for a general lessening of tension; if it did not work, the resources of the free world are still enough to defeat Russia in a general war.

To put the argument on a more general plane, the way to reach agreement with the Russians is to have confidence in ourselves – confidence that we can conduct our political affairs with wisdom; confidence that human beings will not fall victims indefinitely to the fallacies of Communism; confidence that the democratic cause can always afford to be tolerant and patient. Western diplomacy in recent years has given the impression of running away from negotiating with the Russians, as though afraid that they would wear us down. Nothing is lost by argument even if it goes on for ever; after all argument is itself a form of agreement.

The one certain way not to reach agreement with the Russians is the way of all or nothing: either the Russians abandon all their fears, disarm at once, drop their support of Communism, or else there is no alternative but World War III. This is not the way in which any business deal is concluded. The great aim of Western policy should be to estimate what the Russians would like us to do and then to do the opposite. What the Russians would like us to do is to decide that Communism is irresistible by political methods; to spend all our resources on armaments; to tell the peoples of the world that there was no escape from World War III. The alternative is to take the political initiative from the Russians and to keep it; always to be ready to discuss with them; always to be ready to conciliate; to answer intolerance with tolerance and despotism with freedom.

The real problem about agreeing with the Russians is within ourselves. In private life an adult knows that there are lots of ways of living besides his own; and the secret of happiness is not to interfere with the way in which other people conduct their lives. It is much more difficult to be adult in political affairs; but it is also the essential condition for a successful democracy. We shall never get an agreement with the Russians if we insist that they must look at things in the way in which we do; and we are certainly not going to start looking at things their way.

What we aim at is not so much agreement as a truce, confident that everything which lessens the tension and postpones the crisis helps our cause. This is what happened between Christendom and Islam. Neither side had any confidence in the other or accepted its point of view. But in the long periods of truce, when active warfare flagged, Christendom found ever new resources within itself and Islam did not. This will happen in every period of truce between the Western World and Soviet Russia. Democracy will show itself ever more fertile and constructive; and Communism will be shown for the barren thing it is.

51

DEMOCRACY AND DIPLOMACY

EVERY diplomatist dreams of independence. In an ideal world, he imagines, he would be pitted against the representative of a rival power as in a game of chess. He would be free to make his moves without anyone at his shoulder suggesting other moves or even forbidding the moves that he would like to make. Then, he supposes (quite wrongly), he would always win. But this ideal situation has never existed. Not only do spectators comment and interfere. In the diplomatic game of chess the very pieces have a will of their own and rush over the board in unexpected directions. Kings and queens have always insisted that the player of the game is their servant, not the other way round. Bishops announce that they take their orders, not from the player, but from someone who is not in the room at all. Knights develop absurd points of honour. Nowadays, worst of all, the pawns assert the rights of 'the common man', and insist on having the moves explained to them before they will move at all, and then often move in quite a different direction. The diplomatic player abuses his pieces, declares that foreign policy is impossible in a democracy, and refuses to accept responsibility for the outcome. He expects to lose; and he remains disgruntled even when he wins.

This is not a new problem. At most, the problem is presented in new terms. No diplomatist has ever enjoyed a completely free hand. Perhaps Richelieu could really do what he liked; but that was in days so far off as to be by now legendary. No other foreign minister could rattle along according to his own inclination. Every royal master had whims of his own – antiquated prejudices, family ties, fragments of knowledge to which he attached exaggerated importance. Which of the old masters could count on getting his own way? Certainly not Talleyrand, whose ideas were constantly overruled by Napoleon. Nor Metternich, who had the greatest difficulty in drawing his emperor Francis into action of any sort. And least of all Bismarck, who admitted that William I caused him more trouble than any foreign power. These great men sometimes cheated their employers: but for most of their careers they were absolutely dependent on decisions of slow-witted, suspicious monarchs they had to cajole. And yet they succeeded, though not as completely as they liked. If our present-day diplomatists say that foreign policy is impossible in a democracy, that is their fault, not the fault of the people. Diplomatists are the servants of the state. In a democracy they exist to serve the needs of the people; the people do not exist to serve theirs.

Those who conduct foreign policy always resent this. They like to make out that foreign affairs are a mystery; and they really believe it. Diplomatists live in a world apart. They spend much of their time in foreign countries; and even at home they move in artificial surroundings. Few of them have experience of ordinary life. Indeed, diplomatists of different countries – even, say, of the United States and Soviet Russia at the present day – have more in common with each other than with other citizens of their own countries. They worry over details of procedure; run after fragments of gossip; and are bewildered by many things which are obvious to the plain citizen. For instance, the ordinary Englishman realized that Hitler was a nasty man when many of our great diplomatists were still trying to appeal to his better nature. The diplomatist wants to deal with foreign affairs as an abstraction, free from principles, emotions, or ideals. This is called 'realism', concentrating on 'the national interest', and so forth. It is nothing of the sort. The hydrogen-bomb, let us say, is real. But the dislike of the British or American citizen for political intolerance is equally real. Writing off general principles is not realism. It is merely idealism standing on its head. And this, contrary to the diplomatists' belief, is not a position of strength – especially when their heads are not particularly good.

Diplomatists know more about foreign affairs, and therefore claim to judge them better. Even their superior knowledge is doubtful – they are often surprisingly ill-informed. In any case it is a great mistake to suppose that knowledge of itself brings understanding, still less wisdom. The men who succeed in this world are not those whose heads are stuffed with facts, but those with a native shrewdness and an ability to make the right decision by instinct. The gardener with 'green fingers' does better than the man whose shelves are crammed with horticultural books. This is true in business; it is true of the great inventors; it is equally true in the world of states. The people may seem ignorant and narrow-minded when taken as individuals. But they possess a collective wisdom which nearly always judges right. If I ever had to direct British foreign policy I would sooner do it after listening to conversations in a public house than on the advice of the experts in our Foreign Office. Democratic assemblies are not all that far removed from the saloon bars. That is their strength. They fail when they try to set themselves up as experts and to deliver a more informed verdict.

The advocates of professional diplomacy will answer that the collective wisdom of the people is a piece of mysticism – like the Holy Alliance, 'sound and fury, signifying nothing'. I don't think so. After all, the people have a vital stake in the right conduct of foreign affairs. They pay the bills; they fight the wars. If a diplomatist makes a mess of a job he is merely moved to another capital. If the people let things go wrong they get killed, and the taxes go up. They certainly have to bear the responsibility. It is only right that they should make the decisions. In old Europe the budding statesman studied the personal characteristics of the monarch whom he was going to serve. Nowadays the diplomatist is encouraged to despise the people and seeks for tricks by which he can dodge their control. He would do better to find out what sort of foreign policy a democracy wants and then try to translate this into practical terms. The people in their collective wisdom tend to be either much better or much worse than they would be as individuals – usually much better. Democracies have been swept into wars of unprincipled aggression, such as the Spanish-American War of 1898 or the Boer War in 1899. But even then they demanded a moral motive and had to be convinced that they were discharging a civilizing mission. The people can succumb to panic, though not worse than the neurotic panic of William II or Ludendorff in 1918. But they are also capable of a sustained idealism quite beyond any individual ruler; and a foreign policy which refuses to appeal to this idealism will fail.

The great majority of mankind are not dominated by self-interest. Of course they want a decent living for themselves and their families; they want reasonable security and a quiet life. But they are not driven on by an insatiable appetite for power or even for great wealth. The men who have these appetites come to the top as political leaders or as captains of industry. They would find very few willing to change places with them; or rather few willing to pay the price which changing places with them would involve. Therefore, when the people are called upon to sacrifice their quiet life for an active foreign policy or, still more, in war, it is useless appealing to them on grounds of self-interest. This is the very cause which they have rejected unconsciously as the motive for their private lives; they will reject it equally when it is put forward as the basis for foreign policy. When George Kennan writes that 'our national interest is all that we are really capable of knowing and understanding', or when Hans Morgenthau calls his book *In Defense of the National Interest*, he strikes the one note which alienates democratic opinion. Let the people get it into their heads that a policy is selfish and they will not follow it. There was perhaps a case in terms of profit-and-loss for holding the Persian oilfields and the refinery at Abadan by force in 1950. But no British Government dared make that case to the British people. Even those who wanted to use force had to assert that we were discharging a great civilizing mission which was much to the benefit of the Persians themselves. Now a Conservative Government has won universal approval by making an agreement which the Persians find satisfactory.

A democratic foreign policy has got to be idealistic; or at the very least it has to be justified in terms of great general principles. If the people are to exert themselves they must be convinced that what they are doing is for the good of mankind and that a better world will come out of it. The 'realists' smiled at 'the war to end war' (First World War) and at the hopes for a lasting peace in the Second World War; but these wars could not have been kept going without these appeals. Once tell people that they are fighting only for their properties or their lives and they will discover that there is an easier way to do it – to surrender. France had more 'realist' diplomatists than any other country and this realism went deeper. This is the basic reason why France surrendered in 1940, and why most Frenchmen accepted the policy of the Vichy Government. A realist foreign policy must always end at Vichy – cautious collaboration with the aggressor. When the people go wrong it is not from selfishness or materialism, but because they have got their moral values wrong. For instance, American 'isolationism' in the 1930's did not rest on selfishness. It sprang from the conviction that the First World War had been a crooked conspiracy of armament manufacturers and that it served no moral purpose. Once the American people discarded this belief isolationism was dead; and the few isolationists who still survive are not the most selfish Americans, but the most obstinately idealist – though perhaps the most mistaken.

In exactly the same way, the British failure to resist Hitler before 1939 sprang from moral confusion, not from cowardice. It is now becoming the fashion in England to argue that the long series of retreats from 1935 to 1938 was caused by our military weakness; and Chamberlain is praised for buying time at Munich. My recollection is different. The British people were told over and over again by their most idealistic advisers that Germany had been hardly used. Reparations, one-sided disarmament, the peace settlement of 1919 were condemned by liberals and the Comintern alike. I can remember when I first visited Prague, in 1928, thinking how backward it was and how Dresden and Vienna were more civilized and democratic. For the vast majority of British people Hitler's demands seemed justified, however evil Hitler was in himself – otherwise they would have opposed him despite the risk. The military experts may have held that we were too weak to go to war when Hitler reoccupied the Rhineland in 1936. That was not how the question presented itself to public opinion: English people felt that the Germans had the right to reoccupy their own territory, and that was all there was to it. The debate over supporting Czechoslovakia in 1938 was conducted entirely in moral terms; and in fairness to Neville Chamberlain it should be said that he stuck to these terms – he never used the argument of military weakness by which he is now defended. The Sudeten Germans were supposed to have a justified grievance; the Czechs were supposed to be in the wrong. Those of us who wanted to stand by Czechoslovakia lost not because the country was short of fighter aircraft or radar defence. We lost because we could not undo in six months twenty years of moral propaganda in favour of Germany. But the moment that Hitler destroyed his moral prestige by occupying Prague in March 1939 the British people were determined to oppose him; and nothing could have stopped them.

It is one thing to say that democratic opinion is usually right; quite another to say the same of democratic statesmen. The almost universal pattern of democratic countries is the lack of faith in the people shown by those who are supposed to be leading them. The prototype of democratic statesmen is the revolutionary of 1848 who was seen trailing after a crowd and who said: 'I am their leader; I must follow them.' Democratic statesmen have excused their failures again and again by asserting that the people would not have stomached a stronger policy, though in fact the experiment of offering the stronger policy was never tried. How are the people to appreciate the hard truth when their leaders go on assuring them that all is well? The failure of Great Britain and France to rearm against Hitler is always held up as the warning example. But the people were never given the chance to judge this issue. Stanley Baldwin, who determined British policy, believed that he would lose a general election if he advocated great armaments. The British people were therefore told that Great Britain was stronger than Germany and that, in any case, Hitler was not dangerous. Baldwin won the general election of 1935; but even then he did not rearm. At every stage the British Government was driven forward by public opinion, not held back. When I woke up to the German danger in 1936 (rather late in the day) I wanted the Labour party to come out for great armaments and uncompromising resistance to Hitler. I was told that this would lose the next general election. Instead the war came. There was no general election; and Winston Churchill, the only man who had advocated resistance to Hitler, was swept into supreme power.

Recent American history teaches the same lesson. Franklin D. Roosevelt may have been ahead of public opinion in 1937; but those detached historians, William L. Langer and S. Everett Gleason, insist that he was a long way behind it in 1940. During his campaign for re-election he inserted – against the advice of his closest colleagues – the sentence 'Your boys are not going to be sent into foreign wars.' His subsequent difficulties were not forced on him by public opinion; they sprang from his own desire to have it both ways. Messrs Langer and Gleason refer to 'the mental confusion which had made it so easy for the American people simultaneously to advocate increased aid to Britain and avoidance of war'; and they add: 'The only conclusion which voters were logically entitled to draw from the campaign of 1940 was their right, on the very highest authority, to persist in incompatible courses of action.' The behaviour of Baldwin and Roosevelt may be reduced to a general proposition. When a democratic leader is faced with the choice between remaining in power and telling the truth to the people he will follow the course which he thinks will keep him in power. We may add a further proposition: the choice is wrong, even for him, in the long run. Baldwin became so unpopular that in 1940 he dared not visit London – 'they hate me so'. Roosevelt's historical reputation was redeemed only when he was forced into war against his previous pledges, in 1941.

The people judge soundly on great issues. They cannot be expected to determine tactics. In diplomacy they are impatient with formality and delay; in war they expect fleets and armies to be in two places at once. The experts – whether generals or diplomats – are doing their right job when they translate the will of the people into practical terms. They err when they try to substitute a will of their own. The people lose faith in the cynical exponents of the practical; and they turn in disillusionment to those false prophets – the whole-hogging idealists. It is tempting to argue, that since it pursues idealistic aims, foreign policy should be uncompromisingly idealistic all the time. We went to war to free Poland; therefore every country in the world should receive a democratic constitution straight away. We dislike methods of violence and hate war; therefore all wars must be immediately forbidden. The common man knows that there is a difference between right and wrong, between black and white. That is his strength and his virtue. His weakness is to suppose that there is only black and white with nothing in between. He is impatient with the suggestion that they shade into each other or that there is something to be said on both sides. Such arguments seem to him 'expediency'. They savour of the 'realism' which he has rightly rejected. The idealists play into his hands. They too know little of the practical difficulties; they too want a ready-made answer; they too are exasperated when an ideal, once formulated, is not immediately achieved – and even more exasperated if its moral superiority is challenged. And in their impatience they advocate the victory of idealism by the most violent methods.

The League of Nations and the United Nations roused the idealists in this way. Both organizations rested on the dogma that war between nations must cease. This moral purpose was their sole justification. As an ultimate goal, it represents the only foreign policy which a democratic public opinion can applaud. But how can we move towards this ultimate goal? By seeking to limit and to end such wars as occur? Or by blowing up every little war into a big one? The idealists gave the second answer. The man in the street has too much common sense to follow them. Though he needs an abstract principle for which to fight, he also needs to be convinced that some practical issue is at stake. The Abyssinian crisis of 1935 was the outcome of this contradiction. The idealists wanted to assert the prestige of the League of Nations. The man in the street had a shrewd idea that it did not matter whether Italy conquered Abyssinia – or Abyssinia conquered Italy. The worst of all possible outcomes followed. The League of Nations was ruined; and Abyssinia was ruined also. Indeed, Abyssinia would have preserved some of its independence if there had been no League of Nations. There was something wrong with an international organization against war which could protect its members only by making war universal.

The United Nations was supposed to have more modest aims. Hence the veto which its creators deliberately put into the hands of the founding Great Powers. No action could be taken without their unanimous permission; therefore, it was thought, no great war would be possible. Russia's temporary absence from the Security Council in 1950 gave the idealists their chance. They set out to do in Korea what they had failed to do in Abyssinia. They would make war on war; and they cheerfully faced the risk of world war for an issue that was not in itself worth war at all. Had not the American chiefs of staff themselves proposed withdrawal from Korea before the invasion started? We got the war, but not the reward. Korea was not liberated; it was devastated and, in the end, partitioned, just as it could have been at the beginning. There were many practical reasons why the forces of the United Nations failed to achieve complete victory in Korea. But the basic reason was that this victory could be won only at the risk of general war; and the people would not run this risk for a question that did not matter in itself.

The people temper their idealism with common sense. They will make sacrifices for an ideal cause; but they have to be convinced that the ideals are genuine and that the sacrifices will bring commensurate rewards – for others, if not for themselves. The British and, later, the American people were so convinced in regard to Hitler. They believed that he was wholly evil and that liberation was a real boon to the peoples of Europe – as anyone who saw them in the first days after 1945 must have recognized that it was. They do not hold these beliefs so clearly about Soviet Communism. They detest the political tyranny of Communism; but they also think that it has brought great social gains. They may be wrong in this belief, but it is widespread. It can be found not only in the speeches of Labour politicians, but in a recent book by the correspondent of a Conservative newspaper, the *Daily Telegraph*. Liberation from Hitler seemed a worthy cause, even though it meant restoring the systems of government and of society which had existed before Hitler's conquest of Europe. Liberation from the Communists does not seem a worthy cause, if it means putting back the systems (now no doubt exaggeratedly blamed) which the Communists overthrew. Popular opinion has a confused hope that the Communists will become less tyrannical if they are left alone. It believes that prosperity ruins dictatorship; and therefore, perhaps absurdly, pins its faith to the economic success of Communism.

The confusions and hesitations of the West spring from the attempt of the idealists to drive the people too fast and too far. The people will ride out on a Crusade. They have done it before; and they will do it again. But they cannot go crusading all the time, particularly when they are not convinced that good will follow. It is not enough to prove that Communism is evil; we have also to show a better alternative. Every anti-Communist is an asset for Communism; for he implies that Communism is the only positive value. Faith, not resistance, made the Crusades. Lacking this faith the people relapse into cynicism and indifference. But it is not the cynicism of the 'realist' diplomat. The people are as sceptical of realism as of everything else. It is a cynicism of negation, of indifference, if not of despair. Railing against democracy will not remove this cynicism. Constitutional changes will not alter the character of democratic foreign policy. Everyone in private life strikes a balance between self-interest and high principle. The people want the same in public affairs. They will never support a policy which thinks of 'the national interest' alone; nor will they sacrifice themselves, and others, for an idealism which does not count the cost. It is for the leaders, not for the people, to find a solution. The professional diplomats must have ideals; and the idealists must have some common sense.

52

OLD DIPLOMACY – AND NEW

DIPLOMACY is the method by which sovereign states reach agreement with each other. The methods change; but so long as there are sovereign states and so long as they wish to agree, there will always be diplomacy – and even diplomats. What makes international affairs so bewildering at present is that the methods are changing and that the basic assumptions are being challenged at the same time. The change in methods can be exaggerated. It is true that things move faster nowadays. Diplomats telephone and send telegrams where they used to write dispatches; they listen for the ring of the telephone-bell where they used to wait for the arrival of the messenger. But what they say on the telephone is very much what they used to write in their dispatches; maybe the style is a little less elegant. In any case, the essential job of the diplomat is personal contact with the rulers of other countries; and this job has changed very little. It is still important to have an able British ambassador in Washington and an able American ambassador in London. A good diplomat cannot make two countries agree if they do not want to agree, but he can make their agreement easier if they want to agree.

A great change is often found in the way in which the man at the top – President, Prime Minister, or dictator – cuts across the work of the diplomats and does the job himself. But this is not new at all. In the nineteenth century, Tsars, Emperors, and Kings did a great deal of their own diplomacy, often to the annoyance of the professional diplomats. Napoleon and Alexander I met on a raft in the river Niemen and divided up the world even more casually than the 'Big Three' did at Yalta. A few years later Alexander I conducted his own diplomacy at the Congress of Vienna just as President Wilson did at Paris in 1919. Napoleon III conspired with Cavour, behind the back of his own Foreign Minister, to launch a war against Austria; just as Hitler conspired with Henlein against Czechoslovakia in 1938, without informing the German Foreign Office. Even in England, Lord Salisbury said that Queen Victoria gave him as much trouble as parliament and foreign Powers put together when he was trying to conduct foreign policy. There is a difference all the same. The ruler, though a nuisance, was a tolerable nuisance, so long as he was a single man, an Emperor or a King. Now, in democratic countries, the people rule; and diplomacy has to keep in touch with public opinion. Sometimes public opinion causes unnecessary wars; and sometimes it prevents necessary ones. The British Government, for instance, got itself involved in the Crimean War against Russia, mainly in order to show British public opinion that it was a resolute government, despite being a coalition. On the other hand, most people who knew England and France in 1938 will agree that it would have been impossible for the then governments to take an intransigent line with Germany even if they had wished to do so; their public opinion would not have supported them. It is useless for the diplomat to complain about the public demand to be kept informed. If the people are going to pay taxes and perhaps even to fight a war as the result of diplomatic action, they will want to know what it is about.

No one will pretend that this makes the task of the diplomat easier. It is difficult to negotiate with a foreign government if, at every step, you have to explain in public the limit of your concessions and why you are prepared to make them. In the old days Great Britain and the United States would have kept quiet about the fact that they cannot agree whether to recognize Communist China; now they have to draw the attention of the Soviet Union to this cause of possible difference between them – though no doubt the Soviet Union had noticed the point already. One of the most curious legends of the twentieth century is that 'secret diplomacy' caused World War I. As a matter of fact, it would be more reasonable to argue that World War I was caused by the absence of secret diplomacy: that is, the Great Powers did not negotiate enough between the murder of Archduke Ferdinand on 28 June and the Austrian declaration of war against Serbia a month later. But there was nothing secret about the diplomatic background of World War I. Everyone knew that France had an alliance with Russia and that Germany had an alliance with Austria-Hungary; therefore, if Austria-Hungary and Russia went to war, France and Germany would come in. Everyone knew that Great Britain had guaranteed the neutrality of Belgium; even the German general staff assumed that the British Government would declare war – their mistake was to suppose that British military intervention would be ineffective. Men blamed 'secret diplomacy' for World War I because they shrank from the true explanation. After thirty years and more of European peace that had followed the Congress of Berlin (1878), men had come to regard peace as 'normal'; they could not bring themselves to believe that there were tensions between states which could not be settled by agreement, and therefore fell back on the theory that World War I was a 'blunder' caused by the incompetence of diplomats. Yet the causes of World War I were there for all to see: the rivalry of Slav and German in the Balkans, the naval rivalry between Germany and Great Britain, fundamentally in fact the German determination to dominate the continent of Europe and, ultimately, the world. If proof were needed that World War I was not caused by secret diplomacy, this was provided by World War II. There was virtually no secret diplomacy before World War II: Hitler stated his demands in public and received replies in kind. The only secret diplomacy was with Russia; and this resulted not in war, but in the Nazi-Soviet pact – an agreement for neutrality, though no doubt on a somewhat cynical basis.

This suggests indeed one of the strongest grounds for the popular objection to secret diplomacy: the suspicion that every deal will be a dirty deal. And so in a sense it will. Agreement by diplomacy implies compromise; and compromise implies that you will get less than you want, probably indeed less than you think right. The alternative, however, is not to reach agreement, that is, to get nothing at all. The Hoare-Laval plan, for instance, was a reasonable, though discreditable, bargain by the standards of diplomacy, old or new. It would have saved part of Abyssinia for the Emperor, and perhaps even brought Mussolini back on to the Anglo-French side against Hitler. The British public rejected it as wicked; they would not have been so high-minded if they had understood the danger they were in from Germany. Similarly, in 1939, the French, being in mortal terror of Hitler, would have handed over the Baltic states to Stalin in exchange for a Soviet alliance; the British, still confident of their strength, would not. By 1942 it was the British who were ready to make territorial concessions in Poland to please Stalin; and the Americans who held out. But at Yalta, President Roosevelt outdid the British in concessions because he believed that he needed Russian help against Japan. Yet even these deals were not merely dirty deals. The British Government, for instance, was willing to make concessions to Russia partly because they wanted to keep her in the war; but partly too because there were good ethnic, or even moral, arguments in favour of her demands. The British were ready to agree to Russia's claims up to the Curzon line, their own proposal of 1919; they would not have conceded Polish territory beyond that line even at the crisis of the war. Of course, the British would not have felt the weight of these ethnic and moral arguments in favour of the Curzon line if they had not been in desperate need of the Russian alliance. All this is merely to say of diplomacy what Bismarck said of politics in general: it is the art of the possible.

It would be tempting to add that those who dislike diplomacy want the impossible; it is less controversial to say that they want something different. To go back to the definition in the first sentence of this article, those who dislike diplomacy either want sovereign states to cease to exist or they want them not to agree. So far the only alternatives discovered to diplomacy are isolation or war. Isolation is a reputable alternative to diplomacy of long-standing. The old Chinese Empire before 1840 refused to acknowledge the existence of any other states than itself and therefore, logically enough, excluded all foreigners from its territory. Once it let them in, diplomacy was bound to follow; and very unpleasant diplomacy it turned out to be for the Chinese. Isolationism, whether British, American, or Chinese, is a form of idealism: it rests on the belief that you alone possess standards of right and civilization. In nineteenth-century England, for instance, Bright and Cobden argued that, once British steam-engines spread over the world, everyone would be interested in getting rich and that therefore there would be no need for diplomacy; in fact they thought diplomacy merely an excuse for giving well-paid jobs to members of the upper classes. In Bright's words: 'the Balance of Power is a gigantic system of out-relief for the British aristocracy'. But even the idealism of Bright and Cobden stopped short at the British navy: they held, as American isolationists did later, that isolation was possible only so long as it was based on sea-power. This was a reasonable view so long as sea-power and land-power did not overlap; once they did, the world was back at diplomacy – or war.

The idealism of isolation easily turns into its opposite: the desire that sovereign states should cease to exist. This idealism has come to dominate the policy of the Anglo-Saxon countries in recent times. President Wilson, for instance, believed at bottom that France and Germany were equally responsible for World War I; he wanted to put them, and all other states, under the rule of law. The essence of the League of Nations was that it should be something other than a meeting-place for the representatives of sovereign states; it was to create a conscience of humanity to which all states would become obedient. This is the way the rule of law has grown up in the Anglo-Saxon world: legislation by consent springing from the conscience of the community. But it is not the way in which the rule of law has been established elsewhere in the world: there, in Europe or in the great Oriental empires, it has been imposed from above by authority. President Roosevelt took himself to be a more practical man than Wilson; therefore he accepted what Wilson had not, a world authority based on force. In his original conception of the United Nations, he proposed that every state in the world except the three Great Powers who had fought the war – Great Britain, the Soviet Union, and the United States – should be kept compulsorily disarmed for good. Moreover he assumed – and this was essential to the conception of the United Nations – that, as the three Great Powers were temporarily in agreement, they would remain agreed for ever. In other words, the United Nations was not a new method of diplomacy; it sprang from the belief that diplomacy was no longer necessary. As the assumption has not worked out, the nations are back at diplomacy with the added embarrassment of the United Nations on their hands. The delegates at the Security Council have to make fierce speeches against each other in public and then meet secretly in hotel bedrooms in order to get on with diplomacy, that is, with the task of reaching agreement. The only difference between the old diplomacy and the new is that nowadays the diplomats are ashamed of diplomacy and have to pretend that it is not happening. And of course it may not happen; in which case there is always the alternative of war.

It would be foolish to blame Anglo-Saxon idealism as the sole cause for the breakdown of diplomacy. As a matter of fact, the Russians have exactly the same belief as western idealists that the day of the sovereign state is over and that there should be a single world community; only they expect this community to be Communist and to be run from Moscow, not from Lake Success. There is a three-volume *History of Diplomacy* in Russian, edited by Potemkin, a one-time Vice-Commissar of Foreign Affairs, and very scholarly in its way. This argues that there are two sorts of diplomacy: old-style *bourgeois* diplomacy, which does such wicked things as sharing out the colonial areas of the world or making alliances against the Soviet Union; and new-style Soviet diplomacy, which is engaged in bringing more and more of the world under the beneficial influence of 'the workers' state'. The object of this diplomacy is not to reach agreement, but to man-oeuvre yourself into a more favourable position for the ultimate and inevitable conflict. It is the diplomacy of 'the cold war'. Even this is not as new as Potemkin and his colleagues make out, or as is supposed by people in the western world who find the cold war intolerable. There have been plenty of occasions in history when two civilizations thought that they could not live side by side and believed that a fight to a finish was the only solution. In the sixteenth century, Protestants and Roman Catholics thought that there was no room for both religions in Europe and conducted 'cold war' even when Spain and England were not actually fighting. Yet in the end the two had to put up with each other not only in Europe, but even within Germany, after they had torn central Europe to pieces by a generation of war. The Chinese refused to admit the existence of any civilized Power except themselves; and they described all white men as 'foreign devils' – a phrase quite as offensive as anything coined by Mr Vishinsky. The Ottoman Turks, in the days of their glory, knew only one method of diplomacy: they imprisoned the foreign ambassador in the Castle of the Seven Towers, often for years at a time. Even the western ambassadors in Moscow are still little better treated than that.

The closest parallel to the present deadlock of outlooks is, however, to be found in the French Revolution. The French Jacobins, like the Bolsheviks, thought that they had discovered a 'new diplomacy'; by this they meant that revolutionary France should overrun Europe. The European states of the old order, on the other hand, regarded the Jacobins as criminals, apostles of universal destruction, with whom it was impossible to negotiate: when in 1797 delegates of revolutionary France first attended an international conference they were assassinated on the way home. All the amenities of modern international relations can be found in the dealings between old Europe and revolutionary France. Napoleon called the British ambassador a liar in public; the French ran a Jacobin 'fifth column' in England (complete with peace propaganda and a Convention, or front, of distinguished names) and the British Government subsidized monarchist risings in France. In the end the two rival systems, which had intended to fight each other to the death, had to settle down together. Kings survived in Europe, and the ideas of the French Revolution survived along with them. A hundred and fifty years ago an Englishman could have been sent to prison for speaking in favour of 'liberty, equality, fraternity'; now the phrase could safely be used by a Conservative Member of Parliament or by a Republican Senator.

Thus when men say at the present time that diplomacy has broken down or that new diplomacy is less successful than old diplomacy, they really mean that the basis for diplomacy is lacking. Diplomacy is merely a fine name for doing business; and you cannot do business except with mutual tolerance and a certain confidence that the other man will keep his bargain. This is a very different thing from saying that you want the other man to have things all his own way. When two business-men get together, each wants to make the bigger profit for himself; but he also wants to reach agreement, though a profitable one, with the other fellow. Or put it another way. Diplomacy is a game with elaborate rules, which is played for high stakes. The game has got more difficult in recent years because the spectators now look over the shoulders of the players and shout out the best, or more usually the weakest, cards in their hands. You can win or lose quite a lot in this game even if you stick to the rules. But the game

becomes really too difficult if the two principal players each suspect the other of cheating and are resolved to kick over the table
rather than be beaten; add to this that many of the spectators and
even some of the players think that the game is wicked and ought
not to be played at all, and it will be clear why the new diplomacy is not so successful as the old one. For diplomacy can work
only when there are certain common aims and certain common
interests. At the Congress of Vienna, Russia and Austria had
many conflicts; in fact they almost went to war over the division
of Poland. But when Metternich, the Austrian Chancellor, went
to call on his mistress, he found the carriage of Tsar Alexander
drawn up outside the door; and the two men had a very profitable
discussion in the passage outside the lady's bedroom. It is difficult
to think of common ground where Mr Acheson and Mr Vishinsky could meet in this chance way.

53

THE TURN OF THE HALF-CENTURY

THE nineteenth century has been called the age of Hope; the twentieth century has been the age of Hope Fulfilled. In the first half of the century Western man has achieved every ambition which he set before himself since the time of the Renaissance. He has conquered space, disease, poverty. The scientific method which he has perfected guarantees that he can do anything that he wishes. Atomic energy will give him infinite power; and, if he survives long enough, he will conquer death itself. He has mastered all nature, including his own; for it is only in the last fifty years that families and therewith populations have become 'planned'.

In the social world, too, Western man has shaken himself free from the chains of ignorance and tradition which Rousseau denounced. In 1901 Habsburg, Hohenzollern, and Romanov still towered in Europe; now, every royal dynasty, great or small, has gone, except for the few that have long had only decorative uses. Hereditary right, whether of monarch or noble, now counts for nothing anywhere in the Western world; the House of Lords is too trivial to be an exception. Every Government throughout the world claims to represent the majority of inhabitants in its country; and nearly all make at any rate a show of universal suffrage. Most of all, mankind has been prised up from its roots of custom and traditional belief. Apart from a few surviving sentiments of humanistic morality, reason and self-interest have become the sole motives of man's conduct; the exception is his readiness to sacrifice himself for the nation-State – and even this seems to be dying in most of the Western world.

Every dream of the eighteenth-century philosopher, every theory of the nineteenth-century radical has been fulfilled. If an Englishman could have learnt on the last day of 1850 what his descendants would accomplish in the next hundred years he would have been incredulous with admiration and delight; but it would have amazed him still more to learn that at the end of these hundred years we look forward to the next half-century with harsh anxiety, if not with despair. The first half of the twentieth century has had its share of bitter experiences for the West: two world wars, two Russian famines, the planned slaughter of millions in the Nazi gas-chambers. Yet after all these the most optimistic of us would only dare to say, 'If the next half-century is no worse than the last we shan't do so badly!' A gloom hangs over the future such as the Western world has not known since the first renascence in the twelfth century. It is perhaps a mitigation to bear in mind that this gloom is confined to the world of Renaissance Europe which has now grown into the Atlantic community. Most of mankind outside Europe has still achieved little or nothing; and is therefore still in the age of Hope. From this point of view Asiatic Communism is the last version of nineteenth-century rationalism; like its precursor, it holds out the illusion of infinite possibilities.

Europe has ceased to be the centre of the world. Though it is always unsafe to guess how the present will appear to the eyes of the future, this is a generalization which is likely to stand the test of time; it is the greatest shift in the world balance since the upheavals of the fifteenth century. From the time of Columbus until the time of Gandhi, Stalin, and Mao Tse-tung, European man – and especially the educated classes of Europe – lived on the plunder of the rest of the world. The process has been running down in the last half-century; and its end is now in sight. If that were all, if our gloom was merely the gloom of a French aristocrat on the fall of the Bastille, knowing that his privileges were ending, we could find some consolation: loss of privilege for a few means greater freedom for many. No doubt the game is up for the inhabitants of this island; in the long perspective of history this would be a small price to pay if the inhabitants of Asia were to achieve in the next half-century something like the freedom from want that we have known.

But is this all? Is our gloom confined to a small area which is losing its geographical and historical privileges? Is it merely, as the Communists maintain, a symptom of the decline of capitalism? Or is it not more fundamental – a realization that the values of Western civilization, and not merely the privileges of Western

Europe, are perishing before our eyes? The Russians and the Chinese can master our machines; will they ever have our respect for individual lives, our recognition of the human spirit in every man? The Western world called in America to save it in two world wars; and is now looking to it for salvation in a third. Yet the Americans show none of the confidence that goes with success. On the contrary, the United States is racked far more savagely than we are in Europe by anxiety for the future. This anxiety is disguised as a hysteria against Communism; it springs more deeply from the consciousness of infinite power which man has gained and dare not use. After all, the American ideal is the refrigerator in every home; this is the Russian ideal too. The only difference is that in America the refrigerator has arrived.

Yet there is something else which should be placed on record for the benefit of the future. Although apprehensive and perhaps despairing, we are not decadent. Claudian, writing in the fourth century A.D., was sharply aware that he was an inferior poet to Virgil. The philosophers and scientists of Western Europe are not inferior to their predecessors; even the politicians of the last half-century make a creditable showing. Nowhere in Western Europe can you point to the signs which show that a civilization is in decline. Hitlerism was the nearest thing to it; and this was a disease which Western Europe seems successfully to have overcome. Gibbon said of his history: 'I have depicted the triumph of barbarism and religion.' Western man can still hold his own against both. In fact, he is more sensible, more critical, more tolerant, more intelligent than he has ever been; he has even survived the shock of discovering that when Utopian dreams are translated into real life the perfect world is still far away.

On the whole Western man has justified the hopes of eighteenth-century democrats: the people, it has turned out, can be trusted. It may well be that, just as Greece ceased to be the centre of the ancient world, Western Europe – or even the white nations generally – have ceased to dominate the world of modern times. In that case, the greatest historic success of the Greeks is still before us: to take our conquerors prisoner. The world outside Europe has learnt to handle our machines; it has still to be won for our ideas. At the very least, this task will provide some interest and occupation for the next fifty years. Better that than

emulate medieval man, waiting for the end of the world in
A.D. 1000, and sit in helpless contemplation of the universal
catastrophe that may well have come before A.D. 2001.

BOOK LIST

1   (1) *Napoleon's Memoirs*. Edited by Somerset de Chair. 1948.
1   (2) *Napoleon: For and Against*. By Pieter Geyl. 1949.
4   *Recollections*. By Alexis de Tocqueville. Edited by J. P. Mayer. 1948.
5   This originally appeared as the Introduction to *The Opening of an Era. 1848*. An Historical Symposium, edited by Francois Fejtö. 1948.
9   *Cavour and Garibaldi, 1860*. By D. Mack Smith. 1954.
11 *Bismarck and the German Empire*. By Erich Eyck. 1950. An abridged translation of *Bismarck*, 3 volumes, by Erich Eyck. 1941-4.
15 *The Multinational Empire*, 2 volumes. By R. A. Kann. 1950.
16 *German Marxism and Russian Communism*. By John Plamenatz. 1954.
17 *A History of Socialist Thought*. Volume III: *The Second International*, 2 volumes. By G. D. H. Cole. 1954.
19 *Mes Mémoires*, 3 volumes. By Joseph Caillaux. 1942-7.
20 *Holstein Papers*. Volume I: *Memoirs*. Edited by Norman Rich and M. H. Fisher. 1955.
21 *Das persönliche Regiment Wilhelms II*. By Erich Eyck. 1948.
23 *The Prophet Armed. Trotsky: 1879-1921*. By Isaac Deutscher. 1954.
26 *The Politics of the Prussian Army, 1640-1945*. By Gordon Craig. 1955.
27 *Nietzsche: Philosopher, Psychologist, Antichrist*. By Walter A. Kaufmann. 1951.
28 *Hitler's Table Talk, 1941-4*. 1953.
30 *The Rome-Berlin Axis*. By Elizabeth Wiskemann. 1949.
31 *Documents on German Foreign Policy, 1918-45*. Series D, volume iii. 1951.
32 *Politique française, 1919-40*. By P. É. Flandin. 1947.
33 *Britain and Europe. Pitt to Churchill, 1793-1940*. Edited by James Joll. 1950.
34 *Documents on British Foreign Policy, 1919-39*. Third series, volume ii. 1949.

35 *Défense de la Paix*. Volume I: *De Washington au Quai d'Orsay*.
    1946. Volume II: *Fin d'une Europe*. 1948. By Georges Bonnet.
36 *Documents on British Foreign Policy, 1919–39*. Third series,
    volumes v–vii. 1952–4.
37 *Nazi-Soviet Relations*, 1947.
38 (i) *Documents on British Foreign Policy, 1919–39*. Third series,
    volumes iii–iv. 1950–1.
38 (ii) *Documents on German Foreign Policy, 1919–45*. Series D,
    volume iv. 1951.
40 *Servir*, 3 volumes. By General Gamelin. 1946–7.
41 *Mémoires: Rappelé au Service*. By General Weygand. 1950. *Le
    Drame de Vichy*. Volume I: *Face à l'Ennemi, face à l'Allié*. By
    Yves Bouthillier. 1950.
42 *Envers et Contre Tous*, 2 volumes. By Jacques Soustelle. 1947.
43 *The Undeclared War, 1940–1*. By W. L. Langer and S. Everett
    Gleason. 1953.
44 *War Memoirs*. Volume I: *The Call to Honour 1940–2*. By General
    de Gaulle. 1954.
45 *I Was There*. By W. D. Leahy. 1950.
46 *The Last Days of Hitler*. By H. R. Trevor-Roper. 1955.

MORE ABOUT PENGUINS, PELICANS
AND PUFFINS

For further information about books available from Penguins please write to Dept EP, Penguin Books Ltd, Harmondsworth, Middlesex UB7 0DA.

In the U.S.A.: For a complete list of books available from Penguins in the United States write to Dept DG, Penguin Books, 299 Murray Hill Parkway, East Rutherford, New Jersey 07073.

In Canada: For a complete list of books available from Penguins in Canada write to Penguin Books Canada Ltd, 2801 John Street, Markham, Ontario L3R 1B4.

In Australia: For a complete list of books available from Penguins in Australia write to the Marketing Department, Penguin Books Australia Ltd, P.O. Box 257, Ringwood, Victoria 3134.

In New Zealand: For a complete list of books available from Penguins in New Zealand write to the Marketing Department, Penguin Books (N.Z.) Ltd, Private Bag, Takapuna, Auckland 9.

In India: For a complete list of books available from Penguins in India write to Penguin Overseas Ltd, 706 Eros Apartments, 56 Nehru Place, New Delhi 110019.

A J P Taylor

ESSAYS IN ENGLISH HISTORY

A J P Taylor admits to writing, more often than not, to satisfy his own historical curiosity. However unorthodox or surprising his views, the results are invariably enterprising and unambiguous. In *Essays in English History*, he is mostly concerned with the character of English history seen through the eyes of its great personalities. His choice of subjects is wide-ranging – from Cromwell to Roger Casement, from Queen Victoria to the City of Manchester, his final and most personal essay.

ENGLISH HISTORY 1914–1945

Among several fine historians who have attempted a history of England in this century A J P Taylor is the first to succeed in moulding a continuously readable story out of continuously sound scholarship in this excellent summary of the closing years of the British Empire.

'In his best book so far, Mr Taylor has risen to the challenge. He has written a history in which the various themes, political, military, economic and social, are combined into a single narrative which leaves the reader genuinely wanting to know what is going to happen next . . . A vivid, sophisticated, and persuasive book' – *Listener*

'An impressive achievement. It can be read with profit and enjoyment from cover to cover' – *The Times Educational Supplement*

'This is a book no intelligent person will miss . . . A book to read, and read again' – Geoffrey Barraclough in the *Guardian*

'Disconcertingly profound and provocative . . . Mr Taylor's work must be viewed as a whole. It constitutes an outstanding achievement . . . It is, above all, an exciting and enjoyable book, for historian and layman alike . . . A supremely honest work' – Robert Rhodes James in the *Spectator*

A J P Taylor

THE FIRST WORLD WAR

For four years, while statesmen and generals blundered, the massed armies of Europe writhed in a festival of mud and blood. All the madness, massacres, and mutinies of the foulest war in history are brought home here by action pictures of the day and the text of an uncompromising historian.

THE WAR LORDS

The Second World War, unlike the 1914–18 war, was remarkable in that it produced five great war leaders who dominated their countries' political and military affairs. Most modern wars have been run by committees and rival authorities: the Second World War was uniquely different. Once the British and French governments had declared war on Germany, virtually every decision of the war was made by one of these five men, except when Japan's chaotic anarchy intervened.

Five of the lectures reproduced in this book are biographical studies of the men who exercised supreme power during the war; the sixth explains why there was no such man in Japan. Each was unmistakably a War Lord, determining the fate of mankind – five astonishing assertions of the individual in what is often known as the age of the masses.

'Anything Mr Taylor writes is worth reading . . . he is our greatest popular historian since Macaulay' – Geoffrey Wheatcroft in the *Spectator*

'His informal, pithy style makes the book compelling – even exciting reading' – Charles Davidson in the *Irish Times*

A J P Taylor

THE ORIGINS OF THE SECOND WORLD WAR

'No one who has digested this enthralling work will ever be able to look at the period again in quite the same way' – Max Beloff in the *Sunday Telegraph*

A J P Taylor has not allowed himself to be swayed by popular myths in this narrative of the years and months preceding Hitler's invasion of Poland on 1 September 1939. The integrity of his account upsets many accepted views.

Those who have glibly blamed Hitler for everything accuse Taylor of whitewashing the German dictator whilst those who have conspired to make 'Munich' a dirty word profess to be scandalized by his objective treatment – if not defence – of that settlement.

'The most readable, sceptical and original of modern historians . . . The whole book convinces as much as it startles' – Michael Foot in *Tribune*

THE SECOND WORLD WAR
AN ILLUSTRATED HISTORY

'The Second World War was fought in three seas or oceans (the Mediterranean, the Atlantic and the Pacific) and in four major land campaigns (Russia, North Africa and the Mediterranean, western Europe, and the Far East). Each of these wars had a different character, and historians have often treated them in independent narratives. I have tried to bind them together: to remember that when Pearl Harbor was attacked, the Germans had been halted in front of Moscow; that when Stalingrad was besieged, the British were winning the Battle of El Alamein; and that when the Anglo-Americans landed in Sicily, the Russians were winning the Battle of Kursk. The victory of 1945 was an Allied victory, to which all three great Allies contributed to the best of their ability and resources' – A J P Taylor